Preface

It is often said, not without good reason, that the designers of earlier generation microprocessors more or less cobbled together as many processor actions as the availing technology would allow. Current technology, however, is so far in advance of our ideas about what home and business computers should be doing that the design team of the 68000 family of microprocessors have been able to structure the processors' operation around a complete programming concept. Much of the system control previously carried out by system sofware can now be left to the 'self-consciousness' of the hardware.

The structuring takes another form also: each newer member of the family stands on the shoulders of the last, and practically all programs that will run on early implementations will also run, without change, on later models. All hardware features, instruction types and addressing forms of the earlier models are incorporated in the improved and expanded capacity of each new implementation.

The programming concept behind the 68000-series design does cause a few complications, however. It means, for example, that machine code programming on these machines cannot be introduced without initially describing and explaining aspects of system control. These would ordinarily be regarded as quite advanced and left until later, or even not considered. It also means, when dealing with more than one processor, that much of the book will be taken up with comparison between the different processors or with delineating the extent of their individual capacities.

The 68020 is, to put it bluntly, massive: no book of this size could describe more than a fraction of what it can do. So, rather than attempt to cover every aspect of its operation I have concentrated on the major differences between it and the other three processors, the 68000, 68008 and 68010, which are all very similar. My principal concern has been to offer sufficient information about the 68020 for programmers of the earlier processors to aim their software towards it – by writing emulatory routines that can be replaced by instructions on upgrade to a 68020 machine, by designing programs which allow for the later possibility of greater system control, and so on.

The book is loosely structured in four parts. The first, comprising Chapters 1 to 4, deals with factual information about the 68000 family – the internal architecture, how data is stored and accessed, what the inbuilt hardware self-consciousness is capable of. The ordering of these four chapters is quite important, as indeed is that of the whole book, and I recommend anyone not familiar with the 68000 to follow it closely.

The next part is a single chapter: Chapter 5 is rather large but deals with most aspects of assembly language programming that apply to any processor – hints on the use of assemblers, how to make machine code programming much easier, faster and far less of a tangle than it could be (and often is) and how to write clear and complete documentation for library subroutines.

Chapters 6 and 7 form the third part, and provide some examples of 68000-series instructions and addressing modes in action. Routines to access data held in various data structures are given in Chapter 6 – this sort of routine forms the backbone of programs dealing with large amounts of data and is generally useful in many situations. Chapter 7 contains routines which emulate some of the powerful new instructions of the 68020 on the earlier 68000, 68008 and 68010, and these too will be useful in many applications. Most importantly, the routines are documented to standards set by my series Sub Set in *Personal Computer World* magazine to describe fully the complete actions caused by instructions grouped in structured program constructs.

The last part of the book comprises the appendices, and these contain the most important software programming information set out in quick reference form. Much of the information given in Appendix D (68000, 68008 and 68010 Instructions) is repeated in Appendix E (68020 Instructions). I struggled hard to combine the two but the vast increase in instructions and address forms peculiar to the 68020 virtually smothered the forms common to all processors when the tables were combined. In the end I opted for clarity and wrote two sets of tables.

Writing this book has been a great challenge, far greater than that posed by any of my previous books which have each dealt only with a single processor. In spite of the difficulties, I think it has been worthwhile and rewarding to consider all the processors in one family: the necessary comparison of the different capabilities gives a far better insight into the operations of any one of them than would an individual treatment.

The people who have helped are many and I give them all my thanks, particularly to my patient publishers but mostly to my mother, Irene – without her great labours this book would probably not have been written (no wonder she thinks microchips are smallfry).

David Barrow

Chapter One
Architecture

The architecture of a microprocessor that is of most concern to the applications software programmer is the set of cpu registers that he must use. The registers of the 68000 family are introduced in section A of this chapter.

One other aspect of cpu architecture that is of interest is the method used to fetch instruction code. The 68000-series processors are designed in such a way that fetch of the next instruction can take place during execution of the current instruction. This 'prefetch' mechanism has an effect on the timing of programs – speeding up execution at the expense of exact instruction timing – which introduces difficulties for the programmer writing code that may be time-critical. The prefetch mechanism and its 68020 'pipeline' development and cache memory offshoot are briefly described in section B.

A. THE REGISTER SET

Appendix B summarises, for quick reference, the basic functions and different classifications of the 68000-series registers. This section contains more detailed descriptions of the registers and discusses aspects of their use and the concepts behind the design of the register set.

Privilege modes

Until the advent of the concepts implemented in the 68000-series processors, the programmer was given free rein to use any register he wanted or access any part of the system he desired. The designers of the 68000-series, however, planned a more structured processor operation based on the systems/applications dimorphism obtaining in normal computer use.

The methods of allocating control and task resources have undergone continual development since the inception of microprocessors. System software is generally in overall control, dealing at the very least with screen updates, disk access, printer control and other external communication. To this end, the system software must provide functions available to the user through an internal interrupt system. More importantly, the system must supervise the program and data space allotted to user tasks and ensure that no unwarranted attempts to control the system directly take place.

The system software, or supervisor program, must have access to the complete system and operate at a higher level of privilege than the user applications programs. All user programs must operate at a lower level of privilege, which is subject to the requirements of the controlling system software. They have no right to access system space, nor the space allocated to other user programs. If the user is not restricted in access to the sytem, the system can be overriden, intentionally or accidentally, with ensuing catastrophic and expensive results. This is often the case with more primitive micropro-cessors.

In the 68000-series computers, these two levels or modes of privilege – Supervisor and User – are enforced as operating modes, with one bit in the Status Register (see below) acting as switch. (The 68020 further differentiates between an interrupt processing Supervisor mode which deals with events unconnected with internal tasks and a Master Supervisor mode to control the correct functioning of user multi-tasking.) Consequently, the model for the applications programmer is a restricted sub set of the complete model that is available to the systems programmer.

The User mode programmer's model

The User mode programmer's model is a sub set of the full cpu register set. It is available in both User and Supervisor mode. Furthermore, with one very important exception, this model is identical in all the 68000-series microprocessors, hence any reference to a User model register is fully portable across the 68000-series range.

The one exception is the practical size of the Program Counter and all Address Registers (including the User Stack Pointer, A7). Although nominally 32-bit registers, their size realistically depends on the available width of the address bus, which differs considerably between implementations. In the 68000 and 68010 the address bus is 24 bits wide; in the 68008 it is only 20 bits wide. The 68020, however, supports full 32-bit addressing.

Figure 1.1 is a conceptual diagram of the User mode programmer's model and illustrates the three divisions to which the registers may be considered to belong: Data, Address and Control.

(a) Data
This section comprises the eight identical general purpose data storage registers or accumulators, named D0 through D7. Unlike other microprocessors which differentiate between available multiple general purpose registers and accumulators, assigning particular uses to them, the 68000-series microprocessors make no distinction between any of the eight registers of this type.

Each Data Register may be addressed as a full 32-bit register (long word data) and in this case bits 31 through 0 are affected by or used in the operation, bit 31 being the high order bit of the contained value, as in Figure 1.2(a). Alternatively, word or byte operation may be specified by an instruction, and in both these cases it is only the lowest order bits of the specified Data Register which are affected. Word length operations use

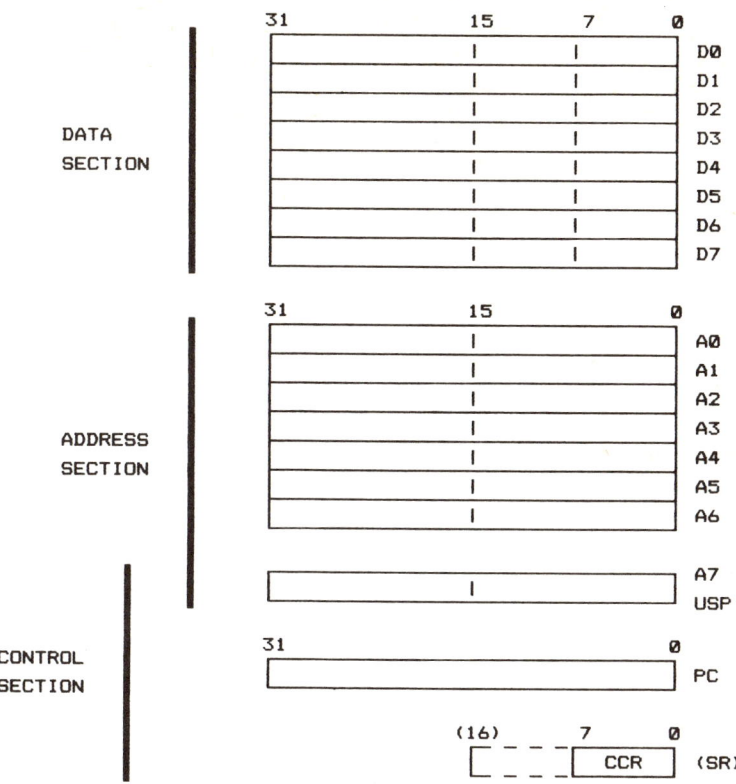

Figure 1.1. User mode programmer's model.

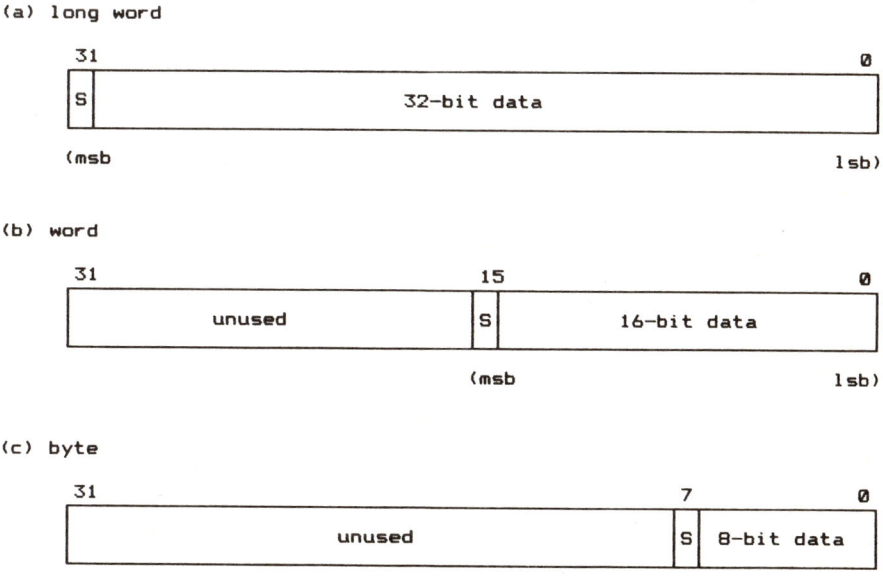

Figure 1.2. Data Register operand lengths.

only bits 15 through Ø, with bit 15 the most significant bit, shown in Figure 1.2(b). Byte length operations use only bits 7 through Ø, with bit 7 the most significant bit, Figure 1.2(c).

In two's complement notation the most significant bit (msb) is used as the sign bit (shown as S in Figure 1.2) and the 68000 has instructions which propagate the msb of byte or word data through the higher order bits to convert byte to word or word to long word data (see Figure 1.3). The 68020 can also sign extend byte data to long word data and, in bit field addressing, access any string of bits inside a Data Register. All processors in the series can also exchange data between the high order word (bits 31 through 16) and the low order word (bits 15 through Ø) in any Data Register. Apart from these few instructions, there is no other provision for addressing the high order word or any of the higher order bytes of Data Registers.

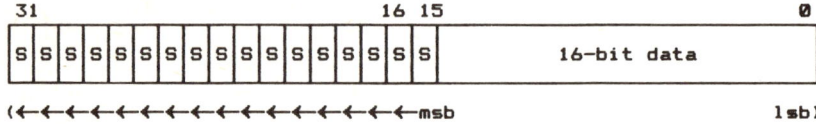

Figure 1.3. Sign extend 16-bit (word) data to 32-bit (long word) data.

(b) Address

This section comprises the seven identical addressing registers, AØ through A6, and one specialised addressing register, A7. Unlike other microprocessors which tend not to differentiate between available multiple general purpose registers used for data and those used for addresses, the 68000-series microprocessors make a conceptual distinction between these register types.

Although Address Registers may be used to hold data, use of them is limited in several ways:

1. The type of operation allowed on data held in Address Registers is restricted to that necessary for address manipulation.
2. No byte length operations are allowed on Address Register contents (as either source or destination) but only word or long word.
3. Word length operands are generally sign extended to full 32-bit long word values (Figure 1.3) before the operation is performed when the destination is an Address Register.
4. The condition codes (result flags) are not affected by most arithmetic operations on Address Registers.

For their primary function, as registers used to address memory indirectly, the operations allowed on the eight Address Registers are extensive, as are the addressing modes in which they are used.

Two of the available addressing modes affect the contents of the specified Address Register; these are the predecrement, −(An), and post-increment, (An)+, modes. These respectively subtract 1, 2 or 4 from the Address Register contents before use, or add 1, 2 or 4 to the contents after use, depending on the operations's data size – byte, word or long word. If the specified Address Register is the Stack Pointer, A7, the amount predecremented or postincremented in byte length operations is not 1 but 2 to keep the Stack Pointer on a word boundary.

As the designation A7 refers to the register used as Stack Pointer, it is generally better to regard it not as an Address Register in the same sense that A∅ to A6 are, but simply as the Stack Pointer, recognising that any operation allowed on or using an Address Register is available for use. In Supervisor mode, the alternate Stack Pointer A7' (or even A7" in the 68020) is used for all references to A7, or SP. These two (or three) Stack Pointers are not accessible concurrently.

Further information on A7 as a control register is given in the following discussion on the control section of the User mode register set.

(c) Control

This section of the register set comprises A7 as User Stack Pointer, the Program Counter, and the low order byte of the Status Register, known as the Condition Codes Register.

Stack Pointer (SP or USP)

The Stack Pointer addresses the last datum placed in a general storage area known as stack – a data storage structure best described as 'last in first out', or LIFO. The stack addressed by A7 is the hardware stack – so called because the Stack Pointer is automatically adjusted to address the new stack top after storage or retrieval of data. Software can be written to set up other stack areas known as user, software or soft stacks: these and other data structures are described later in this book. Each successive word datum is stored in the memory word at a 2-byte sequentially lower address than the last; stack grows downwards in memory. The Stack Pointer should be initialised to address memory one byte higher than the highest address to be included in stack memory. The initial address must be an even number.

The principal purpose of the stack is as a store of return addresses from subroutine calls. From the programmer's point of view, the following actions occur when a subroutine is called:

1. The contents of the Stack Pointer are decremented by 2.
2. The low order word of the Program Counter is written to memory at (SP) and (SP+1), with the high order byte of that word going to lower addressed memory.
3. The contents of the Stack Pointer are decremented by 2.
4. The high order word of the Program Counter is written to memory at (SP) and (SP+1), with the high order byte of that word going to lower addressed memory.
5. The Program Counter is loaded with the subroutine address.

On return (exit) from a subroutine, the current contents of the Program Counter are discarded and the inverse sequence of actions 1 to 4 takes place. The 68000-series also supports a form of subroutine return – the instruction 'RTR' – which loads the Condition Codes Register (CCR) from the word located in memory at (SP) and (SP+1) before restoring the Program Counter. This is shown in Figure 1.4.

A secondary use of stack is for temporary storage of data. Most processor instruction sets support PUSH and PULL (or POP) which respectively save to and restore from stack the contents of specified registers. In the 68000-series, any Address Register may

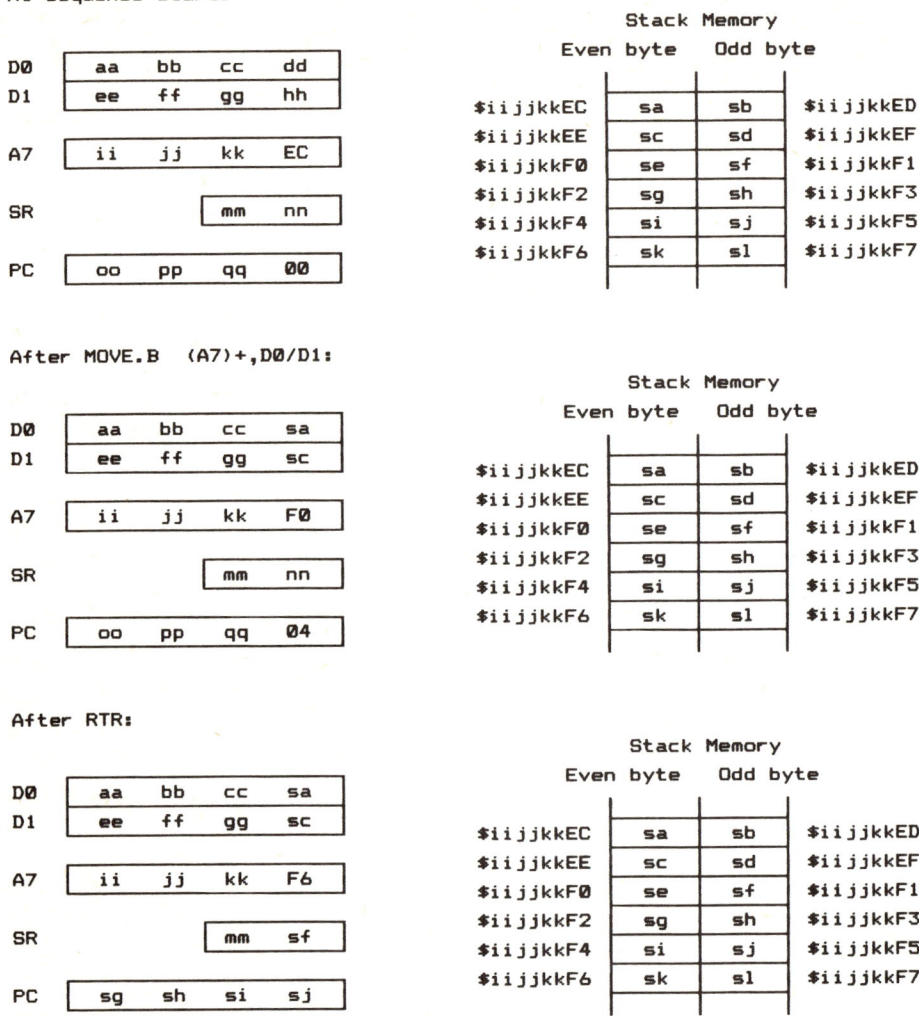

Figure 1.4. Restore (byte) D0, D1 and CCR and return from subroutine.

be used to set up a user stack for this purpose, with PUSH and PULL effected by the instructions:

    MOVEM regs,−(An)

as the equivalent of **PUSH**, and

    MOVEM (An)+,regs

as the equivalent of **PULL**. Since SP, or A7, represents different registers in User and Supervisor modes (see below), setting up a soft stack may be preferable to saving data on the hardware stack.

    All hardware stack saving or restoring (i.e. using A7 as opposed to soft user stack structures addressed by A0 to A6) should take place on word (even number byte) boundaries. Since the Stack Pointer is also classified as an Address Register (see the discussion in the last section), any even byte or odd byte of memory may be addressed for single byte operations. Figure 1.4 shows the effect of the subroutine terminating instruction sequence:

    MOVE.B (A7)+,D∅/D1
    RTS

on the currently operative hardware stack, i.e. A7, A7' or A7" (see below).

68000-series processors support two modes of privilege – User and Supervisor. The 68020 further splits Supervisor mode into Master and Interrupt modes. In order to keep mode references separate, mode-specific Stack Pointers, USP, SSP, ISP and MSP, are implemented; these are not concurrently available to the programmer.

Program Counter (PC)

The Program Counter is used as a pointer to program memory by the cpu for instruction fetches. Since it is incremented when an instruction has been fetched, it generally addresses either the extension words appended to the current instruction or the next instruction in sequence when the operation caused by the current instruction is being enacted. As an example, in 16-bit displacement branches, the Program Counter addresses the displacement word when the branch instruction takes effect. If the branch is made, the displacement from memory at (PC) and (PC+1), already fetched (see section B of this chapter), is added to the value in the Program Counter, resulting in the next instruction being fetched from the displaced address. If, however, the branch is not made, the PC is incremented by 2, past the 2-byte displacement, to address the high order byte of the first word of the next instruction.

The effect of subroutine calls on the Program Counter is given in the discussion on the Stack Pointer, above. Loading of the Program Counter from the hardware stack at the end of a subroutine is shown in Figure 1.4.

Condition Codes Register (CCR)

The Condition Codes Register is the low order byte of the the 16-bit Status Register. Only five of the eight bits available are used to show the condition pertaining to the result of an operation. Figure 1.5 shows the position, single letter abbreviation and name given to each condition bit in the CCR.

Details of the various conditions that may be represented by the utilised bits of the CCR are given in Appendices D and E in Tables D5.1 and E5 and against individual instruction forms in Tables D7.1 to D7.22 and E7.1 to E7.22.

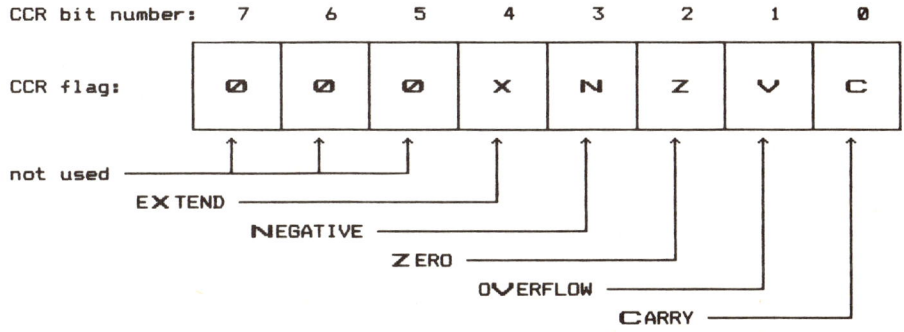

Figure 1.5. The Condition Codes Register.

The 68000 and 68008 programmer operating in User mode is also allowed to read the contents of the high order byte of the Status Register (see the Supervisor mode programmer's model) but not to write to it, since this would infringe privilege. 68010 and 68020 programmers, on the other hand, are not even allowed to read the Status Register high order byte in User mode, since both these processors support virtual machine operation which requires that a program operating in User mode be unaware of that fact. This has resulted in an anomalous situation where two instruction forms are used to access the CCR. On non-virtual machines (68000 and 68008) the instruction **MOVE SR,EA** is not privileged and must be used for any read of the CCR, whilst on virtual machines (68010 and 68020) **MOVE SR,EA** is a privileged operation, and the instruction **MOVE CCR,EA**, not implemented on the 68000 or 68008, has to be used for CCR access. There is no single instruction affording CCR read in User mode which is fully portable across all 68000-series machines, or even upward compatible from the earliest to the more advanced processors. However, it is possible for the Supervisor system to transfer a modified copy of the Status Register to the specified destination register or memory location during the exception processing initiated by an occurrence of **MOVE SR,EA** in User mode. If the destination is the User mode stack, the system will have to step down into a User operation mode by changing the state of the S bit in order to use the User Stack Pointer rather than the Supervisor Stack Pointer.

In allowed transfers of data from stack, to the CCR, word data is pulled from the stack but only the low order byte is written to the Status Register low order byte (CCR); the data high order byte is discarded and the SR high order byte unaffected. This is different from byte length stacking operations where, although the Stack Pointer is adjusted by two bytes, only the high order byte of the stack word is affected (read from or written to) and the low order byte remains unaltered (see Figure 1.4).

The Supervisor mode programmer's model

The Supervisor mode programmer's model comprises the complete cpu register set – except for the User Stack Pointer, which is replaced in this model by the Supervisor Stack Pointer (in the 68020, the Interrupt and Master Stack Pointers). The additional sub set of the full cpu register set that is available only to the programmer operating in Supervisor mode is shown in Figures 1.6 (68000 and 68008), 1.7 (68010) and 1.8 (68020). All registers in these three models have a Control classification, although the Supervisor (Interrupt, Master) Stack Pointer, A7' (A7', A7") may also take the Address classification. With the exception noted above concerning the validity of register contents used to address memory, this model is identical in the 68000 and 68008 but contains additional registers in both the 68010 and the 68020. Reference to a Supervisor model register may not be portable across any two processors in the 68000-series range.

Stack Pointer (SP, SSP, ISP, or MSP)

68000, 68008 and 68010 references to A7 or SP in Supervisor mode access the Supervisor mode alternate Stack Pointer, and all stack memory references use the contents of this alternate register to access memory in Supervisor data space. The SSP is used for all stack references in exception processing.

In the 68020, SSP is either of ISP or MSP, depending on the state of bit M in the Status Register. ISP (A7') corresponds to the single available Supervisor mode Stack

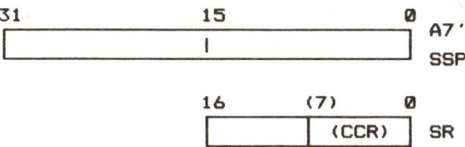

Figure 1.6. Supervisor mode programmer's model additional registers – 68000 and 68008.

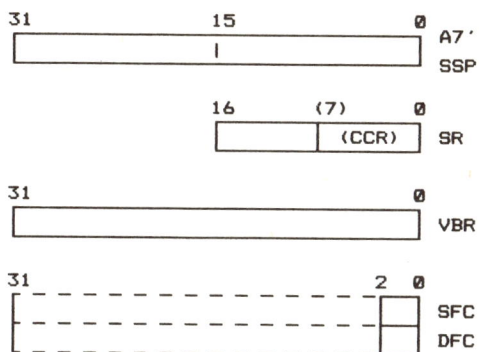

Figure 1.7. Supervisor mode programmer's model additional registers – 68010.

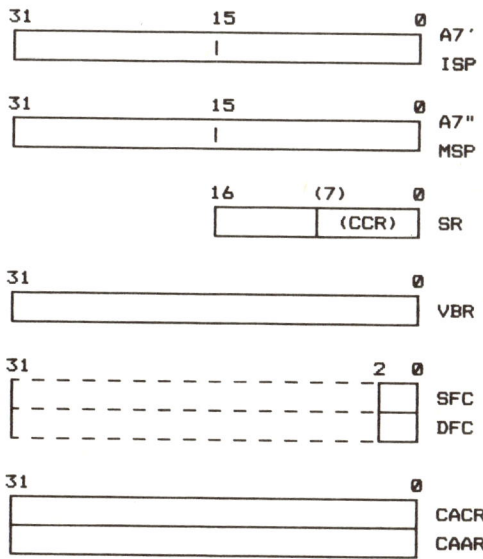

Figure 1.8. Supervisor mode programmer's model additional registers – 68020.

Pointer in the 68000, 68008 and 68010 processors and is available for interrupt processing. MSP (A7") is designed for a multi-tasking environment, allowing Supervisor control of the User mode multi-tasking with a stack space separate from that used for external and unrelated interrupts. If the M bit is set (Master state in effect), it is cleared by an asynchronous (external) interrupt, thus switching Stack Pointers to enable a valid interrupt stack which will not affect (overwrite) the current task stack. At the end of interrupt processing, the interrupted machine state is restored, including the state of the M bit.

For general information about the Stack Pointer, see the above discussion in the User mode programmer's model section.

Status Register (SR)

The programmer operating in Supervisor mode has unrestricted access to the high order byte of the Status Register (system byte) and, of course, to the low order byte, the CCR.

In the 68000, 68008 and 68010, only five of the Status Register high order byte's eight available bits are used. In the 68020, however, seven bits are in use. Unlike the CCR, which bits show the condition pertaining to the result of an operation and may thus be described as a *program control* register, the SR high order byte describes the current system state and is hence a *system control* register. (This is not strictly accurate, since changing the state of any utilised bit in the SR system byte automatically affects system operation, but a CCR bit change will affect program operation only in as much as program control instructions allow.) Figures 1.9 and 1.10 show the position, abbreviation and name given to each control bit in the SR system bytes of the 68000/68008/68010 and the 68020.

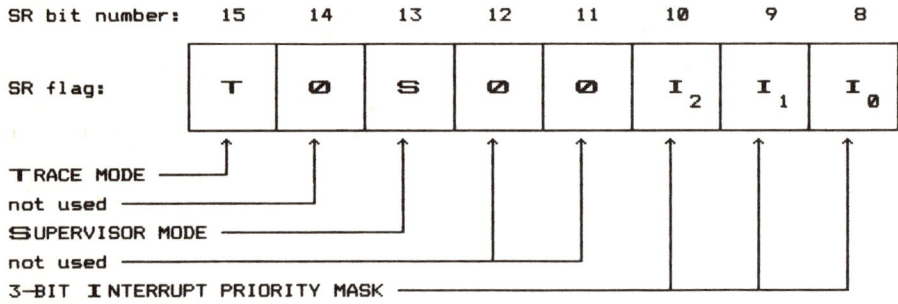

Figure 1.9. The 68000, 68008 and 68010 Status Register high order byte.

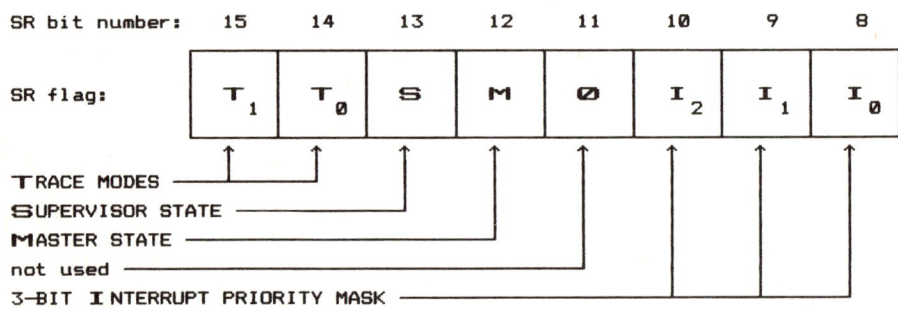

Figure 1.10. The 68020 Status Register high order byte.

Details of the system configuration caused by the utilised bits of the SR system byte are given in Appendices D and E in Tables D5.2. and E5.

Vector Base Register (VBR)

The Vector Base Register is not implemented on the 68000 or 68008 and consequently the Exception Vector Table must be located at addresses $000 through $3FF on these machines. On the 68010 and 68020, the contents of the VBR are used as the 32-bit absolute address of the Exception Vector Table first word. The VBR is programmable by means of the MOVEC instruction (Move to or from a Control Register).

Details of the Exception Vector Table and vector calculation are given in Chapter 4.

Source and Destination Function Code Registers (SFC and DFC)

The Source Function Code (SFC) and Destination Function Code (DFC) Registers are not implemented on the 68000 or 68008. On the 68010 and 68020, use of these two registers allows the systems programmer to access the various address space classifications supported by all the 68000-series processors.

SFC and DFC are 3-bit registers, corresponding to the three function code output lines of the processor, which signal to external logic the current processor state (Supervisor or User) and whether program or data address space is accessed in the current bus cycle; see Table 1.1.

ADDRESS SPACE	OUTPUT LINES			
	FC2	FC1	FC0	SFC/DFC
Reserved for Motorola expansion	0	0	0	0
User Data Space	0	0	1	1
User Program Space	0	1	0	2
Reserved for User definition	0	1	1	3
Reserved for Motorola expansion	1	0	0	4
Supervisor Data Space	1	0	1	5
Supervisor Program Space	1	1	0	6
CPU Space (Interrupt, etc.)	1	1	1	7

Table 1.1. 68000-series function code address space reference.

All writes to, or reads from, SFC or DFC are made using the MOVEC instruction (Move to or from Control Register). MOVEC is classified as a 32-bit operation, so in writing to a Function Code Register the high order bits of the transferred data are disregarded. They are reset to zeros in reading from SFC or DFC.

The MOVES instruction (Move to or from alternate address space) causes the 3-bit value from the SFC to be output on lines FC2-$\emptyset$ for memory reads and the value from DFC to be output on lines FC2-$\emptyset$ for memory writes. This overrides the signal that would normally be sent, making it possible for the programmer to access all implemented address space.

Cache Control and Address Registers (CACR and CAAR)

These two registers are implemented only on the 68020 and are used to control the use of on-chip cache memory. Cache is briefly described in section B below. Like VBR, the Cache Registers are programmed by the MOVEC instruction.

Figure 1.11 shows the assignment of both registers. Only four bits are utilised in the CACR and these enable or disable total cache operation, enable or disable the updating of cache entries from memory instruction fetches, clear single cache entries or clear the entire cache. The CAAR is used in the 68020 only to invalidate a cache entry indexed by the 6-bit value in CAAR bits 7 to 2. The cache function address, bits 31 to 8, corresponds to the tags applied to each cache entry; it has no use within the 68020.

The registers are cleared on reset and must be programmed to enable cache operation.

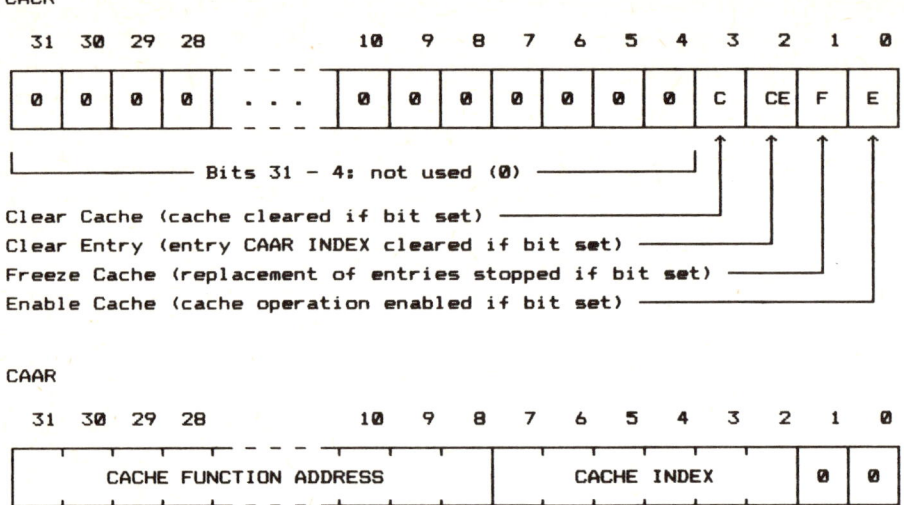

Figure 1.11. The 68020 Cache Registers.

B. PREFETCH, PIPELINE AND CACHE MEMORY

Earlier generation microprocessors, powerful as they may have appeared at the time, were severely limited in their capacity to deal efficiently with the discernible separate aspects of bus operation, instruction decode and data manipulation. The cpu control could deal only with a sequence of single events, consequently the processing of each instruction assumed the following form:

1. Fetch instruction byte [bus operation].
2. Decode instruction byte [instruction decode].
3. If required, repeat from 1.
4. Fetch (read) any specified operand [bus operation].
5. If required, repeat from 4.
6. Perform instructed action [data manipulation].
7. If required, write result [bus operation].
8. Repeat from 1.

The problem with this sequencing of actions is that each cpu component unit is inactive (idle) for a significant part of the instruction's execution time. As external memory reference is far slower than internal cpu activity, the primary target for timing improvement must be the separation of bus control from other cpu actions.

The prefetch queue

One effect of divorcing bus control from the other actions performed by the cpu is to increase its importance with respect to instruction timing. Where all fetch, decode and execute actions are performed consecutively, bus operation is necessarily idle during the other processor activities and becomes active only when an instruction fetch or operand read or write is requested by the sequencer. The total execution time of an instruction in this case is the sum of bus activity time and other processor activity time (bus idle time); improvements to the timing of any process will speed up execution. However, where different processor functions operate concurrently, instruction time depends almost solely on the time taken by the slowest activity, with the quickest actions being, more or less, time-transparent. The slowest activity is, in most cases, external memory reference, and optimisation of bus activity becomes paramount in the reduction of instruction execution time. This is shown in Figure 1.12, which charts the processing of an idealised repetitive sequence of instructions where fetch and write bus cycles take three clock periods and the execution takes two.

Sequential bus activity		Instruction time allocation (clock periods)		Concurrent bus activity	
Bus	Other CPU	instr.	clock	instr.	Bus	Other CPU
FETCH CODE 1	IDLE	instr. 1	1	instr. -1	PREFETCH CODE 1	IDLE
			2			
			3			
IDLE	EXECUTE CODE 1		4	instr. 1	PREFETCH CODE 2	EXECUTE CODE 1
			5			
WRITE CODE 1 RESULT	IDLE		6			IDLE
			7		WRITE CODE 1 RESULT	
			8			
FETCH CODE 2		instr. 2	9			
			10	instr. 2	PREFETCH CODE 3	EXECUTE CODE 2
			11			
IDLE	EXECUTE CODE 2		12			IDLE
			13		WRITE CODE 2 RESULT	
WRITE CODE 2 RESULT	IDLE		14			
			15			
			16	instr. 3	PREFETCH CODE 4	EXECUTE CODE 3
FETCH CODE 3		instr. 3	17			
			18			IDLE
			19		WRITE CODE 3 RESULT	
IDLE	EXECUTE CODE 3		20			
			21			
WRITE CODE 3 RESULT	IDLE		22	instr. 4	PREFETCH CODE 5	EXECUTE CODE 4
			23			
			24			IDLE
FETCH CODE 4		instr. 4	25		WRITE CODE 4 RESULT	
			26			
			27			
IDLE	EXECUTE CODE 3		28	instr. 5	PREFETCH CODE 6	EXECUTE CODE 5
			29			

Figure 1.12. Sequential and concurrent bus activity.

The left side of Figure 1.12. shows sequential bus activity; the processing of each instruction begins with a fetch of its instruction code word and ends with a write of the operation result to external memory: each instruction is processed as a discrete unit.

Execution can only begin when the instruction has been fetched, the result cannot be written until it has been computed, and the next instruction code cannot be fetched until the write bus cycle has terminated. The time taken to complete the processing of each instruction is eight clock periods.

The right side of Figure 1.12 shows the more dynamic approach of concurrent bus and other cpu activity. The initial 'prefetch' of the first instruction code properly belongs to the preceding instruction. The timing for each instruction begins with its execution in the cpu. At the same time, since no bus request has been issued by the sequencer, bus control logic initiates a prefetch of the next instruction code. Execution takes two clock

Instruction time allocation (clock periods)			Bus activity	Other CPU activity
1	instruction		PREFETCH	EXECUTION
2	-1		CODE	OF PREVIOUS
3			1 AND 2	INSTRUCTION
4	instruction		IDLE	EXECUTE
5	1			CODE 1
6			WRITE	CALCULATE
7			CODE 1	SOURCE
8			RESULT	ADDRESS 2
9	instruction		PREFETCH	
10	2		CODE	CALCULATE
11			3 AND 4	DESTINATION
12			READ	ADDRESS 2
13			SOURCE	EXECUTE
14			OPERAND 2	CODE 2
15		instruction	WRITE	EXECUTE
16		3	DESTINATION	CODE 3
17			RESULT 2	CALCULATE
18	instruction		PREFETCH	DESTINATION
19	4		CODE	ADDRESS 4
20			5 AND 6	EXECUTE
21			IDLE	CODE 4
22			WRITE	CALCULATE
23			DESTINATION	SOURCE
24			RESULT 4	ADDRESS 5
25	instruction		READ	CALCULATE
26	5		SOURCE	DESTINATION
27			OPERAND 5	ADDRESS 5
28			READ	EXECUTE
29			DESTINATION	CODE 5
30			OPERAND 5	CALCULATE
31			WRITE	SOURCE
32			DESTINATION	ADDRESS 6
33			RESULT 5	CALCULATE
34	instruction		READ	DESTINATION
35	6		SOURCE	ADDRESS 6

Figure 1.13. Instruction overlap with concurrent bus activity.

periods, at which point the sequencer requests a write bus cycle, but this cannot be honoured until the prefetch is complete. The write cycle completes the instruction processing which has taken only six clock periods; all bus inactivity has been eliminated with the fetch time of each instruction moved backwards into the processing time of the previous instruction. Note that in this example, which corresponds to the sequencing methods of the 68000, each instruction must terminate before the next can start and the timing of any particular instruction never varies.

The 68000-series processors allow two words to be prefetched from the stream of instruction code. These may be extension words to the instruction currently being executed or, in the case of single word instructions, the next two physically sequential instructions. Where the program logic breaks sequence, as in branches, jumps and subroutine calls, the prefetch queue is cleared and reloaded with the first two words from the jump destination before processing resumes after the jump. The time taken to replace the contents of the prefetch queue is included in the execution time of the jump instruction.

Figure 1.13 shows a yet more dynamic approach that corresponds to the instruction overlap sequencing found in the 68020. This model includes the more realistic attributes of source and destination address calculation and operand reads. Bus activity is again concurrent with other cpu activity but the interdependence of these two aspects has decreased. Decoding of the next instruction in the prefetch queue is not delayed until cessation of bus activity associated with the last instruction, as is the case in the 68000, but begins immediately all other cpu operations on the last instruction are complete; trailing write operations from one instruction overlap with execution of the next.

Because instructions are not processed as discrete time units, allocating execution time to any particular instruction is awkward, to say the least. It is usually reckoned as the number of clock periods consumed between completion of the last instruction (i.e. the end of all cpu activity, including the 'last writes') and completion of the instruction being timed. This method of allocation produces the miraculous event known as zero-time execution. Instructions that execute in a very quick time – say, register to register operations – can be processed within the execution time allotted to the immediately preceding instruction; this phenomenon occurs with instruction 3 in Figure 1.13.

Bus control automatically initiates a two-word instruction prefetch cycle at the start of any clock period in which no sequencer bus request is pending and the two-word prefetch queue is empty.

68010 loop mode operation

The 68010 takes advantage of the two-word prefetch queue to speed up execution of a relatively restricted type of looping operation. The looping instruction must be the two-word DBcc (see Table D7.15 in Appendix D) and the looped instruction must be a single word instruction from the list given in Table D8, Appendix D.

The DBcc instruction branches conditionally on the state of allowed combinations of CCR bits and on the result of decrementing a specified count register, as follows: the two-word DBcc instruction (code word and displacement) is in the prefetch queue. The instruction immediately prior to the DBcc instruction (currently in the decode register) is processed normally and discarded. Processing continues with the DBcc instruction, with the next physically sequential instruction word being prefetched. If the DBcc condition is true, or the specified count register decrements to −1, processing continues with the prefetched instruction. If the condition is false or the count register does not decrement to −1 then the prefetched instruction is discarded from the queue and the instruction word at the displaced address is prefetched for next processing.

Loop mode operation is begun at the stage where the DBcc displacement is processed. If the displacement is not −4 (to a single word instruction immediately preceeding the DBcc instruction word) then loop mode cannot start and the normal processing mode is continued, as described above. If the displacement is −4 then the looped instruction is fetched, moved to the decode register and checked for loop mode validity. If the instruction is not one of the allowed forms, loop mode is not entered but normal processing ensues. If it is valid, then loop mode is initiated; the looped instruction is retained in the decode register and the DBcc instruction is fetched to the two-word prefetch queue. Since all instruction words essential for processing this tight little loop are now contained in the cpu, instruction fetch is suppressed and only operand read or write external reference takes place. Loop mode continues until either the specified condition is met, or the count register decrements to −1, when loop mode terminates and normal processing is resumed.

Although three fetch cycles are suppressed, the loop time is not reduced by the full 12 clock periods; some time is added to perform the loop mode logic. However, execution is speeded up quite considerably as can be seen by comparing the loop mode timings, Table D8, with those of normal operation, tables D7.1 to D7.22.

Loop mode is also terminated by interrupt or exceptions but may be re-entered, if the correct conditions apply, on return from the interrupting process. Interrupts are honoured only after the DBcc instruction. Trace exceptions (SR bit 15, 'T', is set) will occur after both the looped instruction and DBcc: this effectively prevents loop mode starting.

Pipelined decoding

The two-word prefetch queue and single word decode register of the 68000, 68008 and 68010 are combined in the 68020 into a three-stage fetch and decode pipeline, Figure 1.14.

Instruction code, taken off the data bus, or from cache, is channelled in to stage one. Decoding is staged so that by the end of third stage, the instruction is validated and fully decoded ready for transfer through the sequencer control to the execution unit. Subsidiary data paths also exist between the second stage and the sequencer and between the first and second stages and the execution unit. Immediate data, absolute addresses and other extension words can thus be taken directly from the pipeline without having to undergo the final, unnecessary instruction word decoding process in stage three.

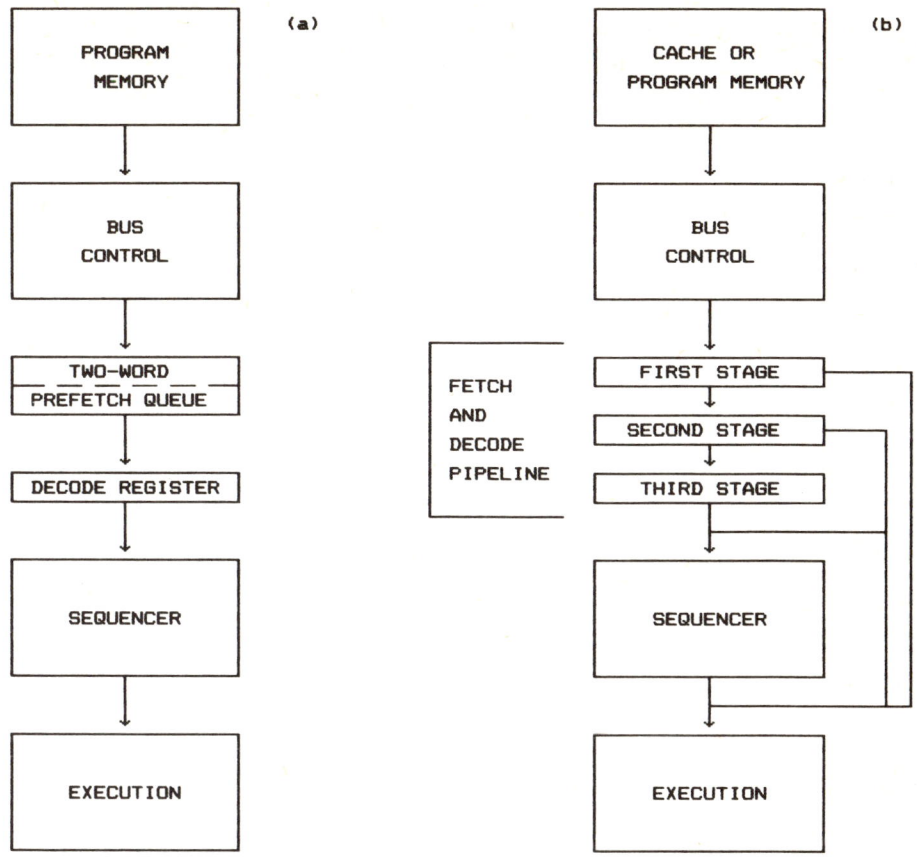

Figure 1.14. Instruction code paths: (a) 68000, (b) 68020.

Cache memory

Cache memory provides a highly efficient method of dealing with iterative programming and may be seen as an extension of the loop mode concept of the 68010, though in a far more refined form. Complete 256-byte instruction blocks can be stored in on-chip memory with each long word tagged for recognition using a combination of partial address and FC2 (see Table 1.1). With cache operative, all two-word instruction fetches are first checked against cache memory and only if the instruction is not held on chip will an external (slower) memory fetch occur. Operand data are not written to cache and so must be fetched from external memory each time they are required.

With cache enabled and unfrozen (see CACR and CAAR in section A of this chapter), new instructions fetched from memory are tagged and stored in cache. Cache then provides a post-fetch, post-execution storehouse rather than a prefetch queue, not particularly useful for long linear sequences but offering useful time savings on any code that loops back within the 256-byte range – as is most common in modular structured programming.

With cache enabled but frozen, cache read can occur but the entries cannot be updated. Cache may then be used as a high speed access device for emulation of unimplemented processes or physical devices.

The tagging of cache entries for rapid verification, shown in Figure 1.15, is of particular interest. The main features of the method may be used for rapid data storage and retrieval in many applications.

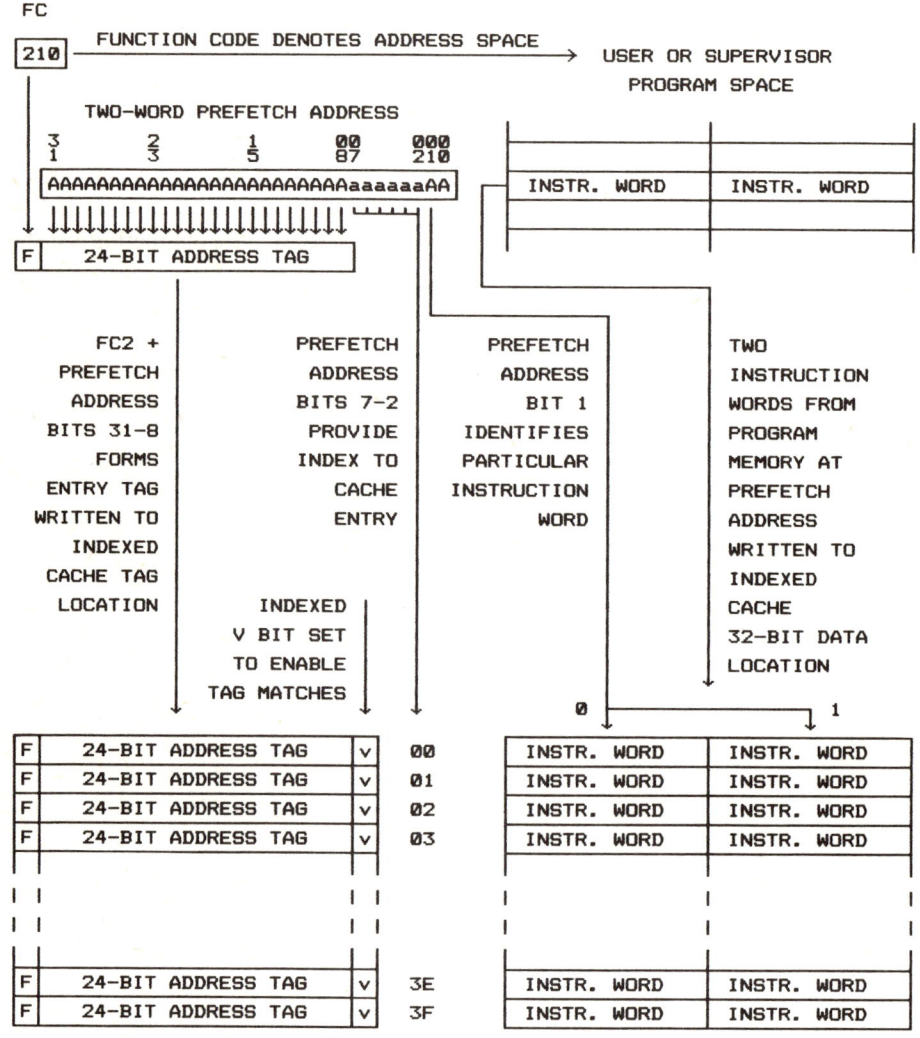

Figure 1.15. Cache reference.

Retrieval of a cache entry must occur only if it is the instruction required and so must be uniquely identified by an appended tag. Since the instruction may originally have been fetched from a location in User space or from a location in Supervisor space with the same address, the function code bit identifying that space, FC2, must be included in the tag. (The S bit from the Status Register could be used, but for the MOVES instruction see the discussion on the SFC and DFC registers in section A of this chapter.) The full 32-bit address is not required to complete the identification, since (a) each entry is a long word, thus removing the need to use address bits 0 and 1 which serve only to identify each byte in the long word, and (b) each entry is written to a cache location corresponding to the position of the two instruction words within a 256-byte block of memory. Thus the cache location index has the same value as address bits 7 to 2 and these too may be left out of the tag. Address bits 31 to 8 are needed to identify the particular 256-byte block from which the two instruction words were originally fetched and these form the major portion of the tag. One other bit is included in the tag and this serves to validate the entry if set, thus any entry may be cleared merely by resetting (clearing) the validation bit.

The cache tagging system removes the need to check every entry when an instruction fetch is initiated with cache enabled. Bits 7 to 2 of the prefetch address are used to index the one specific cache entry where the instruction can be – the tags of all other entries may be identical but it is the cache index which uniquely identifies the two instruction words sought. Bits 31 to 8 of the prefetch address, the current state of function code bit, FC2, and a set validity bit are compared with the entry tag. If the compared values match (a tag hit) then the cache entry is returned, otherwise the two words at the prefetch address in external memory are fetched.

Half of all branches, jumps and subroutine calls will be made to destinations not on a long word boundary. In these cases, instruction prefetch will need to access the low order word in a cache entry but not the high order (preceding) word in the same cache entry. Bit 1 of the prefetch address indicates which of the two words of the indexed entry is needed.

Chapter Two
Memory Organisation

The address bus – memory limitations

Theoretically there is no limit to the amount of memory that may be implemented in any computer system. The method used to obtain this cornucopia of bits and bytes is a technique known as bank switching, which involves outputting a memory bank number to a memory control device. This is the system used when processors can directly address only a small amount of memory – 64K is usually the limit for 8-bit processors such as the 6809, Z80 and 6502. The problem with such a system is that each bank of memory must reside at the same address and large programs must be written so as to avoid the need to access two such banks simultaneously (e.g. one for program space and the other for data space). Such a situation is known as the 'weatherhouse effect' – an allusion to the picturesque rain indicator which separates a man and (presumably) his wife more effectively than computer addiction.

Ideally, each discrete chunk of all implemented memory (whether as bit, nibble, byte, word, or larger identifiable unit) should have a unique address, randomly accessible, for reading from or writing to. This ideal necessitates a wider address bus than the 16-bit width of address buses common in the 8-bit computer generation. So, how do the 68000-series processors fare and what amount of memory will they support? As stated in Chapter 1, the 32-bit width of the Program Counter and Address Registers implies but does not mean that all processors have a 32-bit wide addressing capability.

The massively geared 68020 does support full 32-bit addressing (i.e. there are 32 output lines from the cpu which may be used to select any of 2^{32} memory bytes) and consequently 4 Gigabytes (4 294 967 296 bytes) of random access memory may be addressed directly by any 68020 system. However, since at current (1985) prices the cost of a full 68020 memory complement would approximate to the cost of five, full-blown 8086 business systems, it is unlikely that many systems built around the 68020 will implement maximum memory. Nor is that amount of memory essential, except for specialised applications, since the 68020 is designed as a 'virtual machine': all references to non-existent memory can be diverted by memory management logic to access a smaller portion of memory constantly updated from high speed access, high density external storage beyond the programmer's awareness. To all intents and purposes of the end user, the full 4 Gigabytes of memory is installed in every 68020 'virtual' system.

The 68010, similarly designed as a virtual machine and hence capable of emulating a greater total address space than is actually present, has only a 24-bit address bus. This is equalled by the 68000 (not a virtual machine) and thus both may directly address 16 megabytes (16 777 216 bytes) of memory.

The humble 68008, with its 2∅-bit address bus, is capable of directly accessing only 1 megabyte (1 ∅48 576 bytes) of memory.

24-bit (68000 and 68010)
20-bit (68008)   (68020) 32-bit
16-bit (e.g. 6809, Z80, 6502)

Figure 2.1. Comparative 68000-series memory size.

The comparative size of directly addressed memory that may be implemented in systems built around any of the 68000-series processors is illustrated in Figure 2.1. The 64 Kilobyte maximum memory that has until recently been the norm in both home and business microcomputers is represented by the barely perceptible black square at the bottom left corner. The 68008 has an increased capacity over such processors as the 6809 and Z80 by a factor of 16. The 68000 has an increase over the 68008 again by a factor of 16 and the memory of the 68020 represents an increase by a factor of 256 over that of the 68000.

Memory mapping

With full memory attached, the 68000 programmer cannot specify an address greater than $ØØFFFFFF, and the maximum for the 68008 programmer is $ØØØFFFFF. Furthermore, any real system is unlikely to support even this volume of memory; it will probably have only sections of memory implemented. These will be dedicated to the several address space requirements (see Table 1.1, Chapter 1) and exist as a mixture of RAMs and ROMs.

Two blocks of memory that are almost certain to be present (though not necessarily available to the user) are those addressed by sign-extending a word length short absolute address. These are shown in Table 2.1.

Processor	Addressable by Positive Word	Requiring Long Word address	Addressable by Negative Word
68008	$[000]00000 to $[000]07FFF	$[000]08000 to $[000]F7FFF	$[000]F8000 to $[000]FFFFF
68000/68010	$[00]000000 to $[00]007FFF	$[00]008000 to $[00]FF7FFF	$[00]FF8000 to $[00]FFFFFF
68020	$00000000 to $00007FFF	$00008000 to $FFFF7FFF	$FFFF8000 to $FFFFFFFF

Notes.
1. [...] 8-bit or 12-bit high order part of address is not used.
2. Wraparound addressing means that the two sections, $...F8000 to $...FFFFF and $00000000 to $00007FFF, form one 64K block.

Table 2.1. Sign-extended short address memory.

It is common practice for the manufacturers of computer systems to provide a map of the memory utilisation in their system. Typically, it will delineate those areas available to the user and those off limits to him or her. It will also show which sections are implemented as RAM and as ROM, and the areas that are available for expansion as well as those which are not. Any RAM mapped to a video display will also be shown. Since it is possible for the Supervisor system to call on parallel memory banks, the map may also show an area of 'sideways' memory dedicated to exception processing or other Supervisor requirements. (The reason for using parallel memory when unused addresses are still available is one of safety – the bank can be switched only in Supervisor mode and is totally secure from User interference.) All these possibilities are illustrated in Figure 2.2.

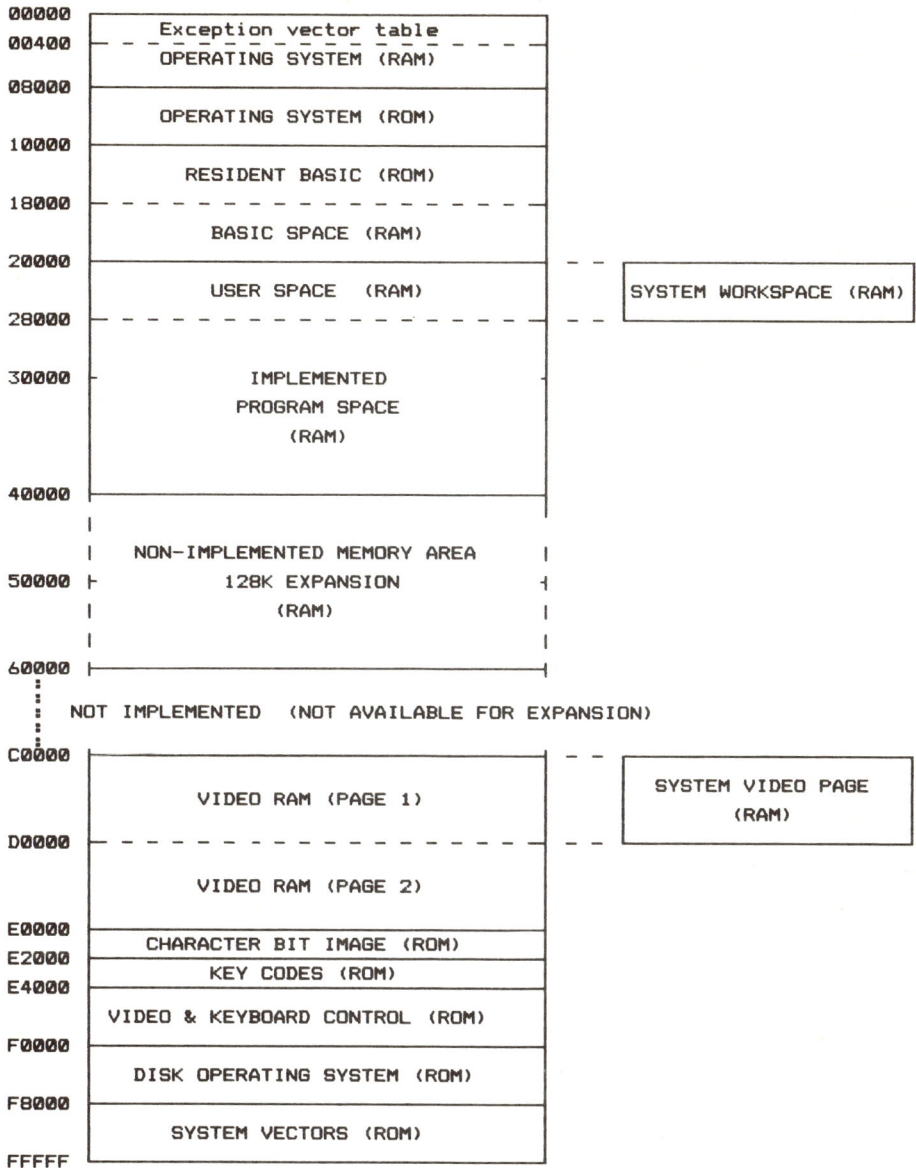

Figure 2.2. A typical small system memory map.

The data bus - speed limitation

Although the size of the address bus in each implementation determines the maximum amount of physical memory that may be addressed directly, the implemented data bus size (i.e. the number of input/output lines between cpu and external memory each available for the simultaneous transfer of one bit of data) does not determine the operand size that may be used. To the software programmer or end user, the only difference between an 8-bit data bus and a 32-bit data bus is that the former operates much more slowly.

The 68000 and 68010 each have a 16-bit data bus. Byte and word data may be transferred in a single bus cycle but long word data requires two bus cycles. One consequence of this is that byte and word size operations are effected at the same speed by these two processors, while long word operations take longer.

The 68008 has an 8-bit data bus. Byte data movement takes 1 bus cycle, word data takes 2 bus cycles and long word data takes 4 bus cycles. This applies both to instruction and operand fetches, and to operand writes.

The 68020 has dynamic bus sizing which allows the transfer of data between it and external devices (memory is external to the cpu) along an 8-bit, 16-bit or 32-bit bus. The optimal bus size for data transfer to and from memory is, of course, 32-bits, allowing all byte, word and long word instruction fetches, operand fetches and operand writes in just one bus cycle. Consequently, with a 32-bit data bus, there is generally no timing difference between the different operation sizes performed on the 68020.

The inclusion of dynamic bus sizing in the design of the 68020 affords the possibility of building relatively cheap 68020 systems based on the plentiful supply of inexpensive memory and support devices for 8-bit data paths. Such systems will operate more slowly than the 32-bit data path equivalents because of the extra fetch, read and write bus cycles, – each taking a minimum of 3 clock cycles – more if slow memory necessitates 'wait' states.

Binary data organisation

The organisation of binary integer data in the memory of all 68000-series processors is based on the 8-bit byte (Figure 2.3). The bit place value within a byte is recognised by describing bit 7, the most significantly placed bit, as the leftmost bit.

bit number:	7	6	5	4	3	2	1	0
BYTE bit states:	0 / 1	0 / 1	0 / 1	0 / 1	0 / 1	0 / 1	0 / 1	0 / 1

Set bit (1) place value:

		7	6	5	4	3	2	1	0
(a) absolute:		+128	+64	+32	+16	+8	+4	+2	+1
as 2^n:		$+2^7$	$+2^6$	$+2^5$	$+2^4$	$+2^3$	$+2^2$	$+2^1$	$+2^0$
(b) signed:		−128	+64	+32	+16	+8	+4	+2	+1
as 2^n:		$-(2^7)$	$+2^6$	$+2^5$	$+2^4$	$+2^3$	$+2^2$	$+2^1$	$+2^0$

Figure 2.3. Byte, with byte data set bit place value.

One byte is the minimum bit-block size that may normally be referenced. Indeed, each unique value in a 32-bit Address Register or the Program Counter refers to a single byte of memory. The single bit reference instructions, **BCHG, BSET,** and so on, must state explicitly the bit position within a memory byte and the 68020's bit field

Memory Address	Byte number (with 8-bit Nos.)	Word number (with 16-bit Nos.)	Long Word number (with 32-bit Nos.)
$00000	(7 00000 0)	(15 00000 8)	(31 00000 24)
$00001	(7 00001 0)	(7 0)	(23 _ _ _ _ 16)
$00002	(7 00002 0)	(15 00001 8)	(15 _ _ _ _ 8)
$00003	(7 00003 0)	(7 0)	(7 0)
$00004	(7 00004 0)	(15 00002 8)	(31 00001 24)
$00005	(7 00005 0)	(7 0)	(23 _ _ _ _ 16)
$00006	(7 00006 0)	(15 00003 8)	(15 _ _ _ _ 8)
$00007	(7 00007 0)	(7 0)	(7 0)
$00008	(7 00008 0)	(15 00004 8)	(31 00002 24)
$00009	(7 00009 0)	(7 0)	(23 _ _ _ _ 16)
$0000A	(7 0000A 0)	(15 00005 8)	(15 _ _ _ _ 8)
$0000B	(7 0000B 0)	(7 0)	(7 0)
.			
.			
.			
.			
$FFFFC	(7 FFFFC 0)	(15 7FFFE 8)	(31 3FFFF 24)
$FFFFD	(7 FFFFD 0)	(7 0)	(23 _ _ _ _ 16)
$FFFFE	(7 FFFFE 0)	(15 7FFFF 8)	(15 _ _ _ _ 8)
$FFFFF	(7 FFFFF 0)	(7 0)	(7 0)

Figure 2.4. 68008 byte, word and long word organisation in memory.

instructions compute the field location as an offset from a byte boundary (with bit 7 of the addressed byte taken as the base bit, offset Ø).

Most 68000-series memory references, however, are to word or long word divisions on even byte boundaries. The 68020 does allow word and long word data to lie on odd byte boundaries but fetch time is increased, as it is when a specified bit field crosses a long word boundary. Exception processing in the other 68000-series processors can deal with the address error caused by odd byte word access – again at the cost of increased execution time.

The general organisation of binary data, from the standpoint of the programmer manipulating an Address Register, takes five forms.

1. A sequence of individually addressed bytes, corresponding to all possible values in the Address Register.
2. A sequence of 8-bit groups, corresponding to bytes with each bit identifiable by specifying a bit number, Ø to 7.
3. A sequence of 16-bit words corresponding to all Address Register values when its lowest order bit remains reset (Ø).
4. A sequence of 32-bit long words corresponding to all Address Register values when its two lowest order bits remain reset.
5. 68020 only; any sequence of up to 32 bits defined by specifying a bit-offset from any Address Register value and the width of the bit sequence.

As stated in the discussion on data buses, fetch, read and write timing depends on the bit width of the data path. Consequently, if execution time is an important

```
Even Byte              Long Word, Word and Byte numbers              Odd Byte
Address        (       with 32-bit, 16-bit and 8-bit numbers     )   Address

$000000        (31          1st half Long Word 000000          16)   $000001
               (15               Word 000000                    0)
               (7      Byte 000000    0) (7      Byte 000001    0)

$000002        (15          2nd half Long Word 000000           0)   $000003
               (15               Word 000001                    0)
               (7      Byte 000002    0) (7      Byte 000003    0)

$000004        (31          1st half Long Word 000001          16)   $000005
               (15               Word 000002                    0)
               (7      Byte 000004    0) (7      Byte 000005    0)

$000006        (15          2nd half Long Word 000001           0)   $000007
               (15               Word 000003                    0)
               (7      Byte 000006    0) (7      Byte 000007    0)

                                       .
                                       .
                                       .
                                       .

$FFFFFC        (31          1st half Long Word 3FFFFF         16)    $FFFFFD
               (15               Word 7FFFFE                    0)
               (7      Byte FFFFFC    0) (7      Byte FFFFFD    0)

$FFFFFE        (15          2nd half Long Word 3FFFFF           0)    $FFFFFF
               (15               Word 7FFFFF                    0)
               (7      Byte FFFFFE    0) (7      Byte FFFFFF    0)
```

Figure 2.5. 68000 and 68010 byte, word and long word organisation in memory.

consideration, as it often is when communicating with external devices, some account must be taken of memory organisation with regard to the data bus rather than simply to effective address. In this respect, the memory of the 68008 is organised primarily in bytes, with two bytes taken jointly to make one word, and four to create a long word, as in Figure 2.4. The primary unit of 68000 and 68010 memory is the word, which may be used as two bytes, or two consecutive words read as one long word, as in Figure 2.5. Since the 68020's data bus width is dynamic, its memory, in particular implementations, may have to be viewed as being organised along the lines of Figure 2.4 or 2.5. With a full 32-bit data bus, however, the long word is the basic memory data unit with the availability of using it as either two 16-bit words or four bytes, as in Figure 2.6.

Decimal data organisation

There are two standard methods of representing decimal data in byte (word or long word) organised memory. The first is as a sequence of ASCII decimal digits (3Ø to $39),

```
  (Address $00000000)
(31                            Long Word 00000000                          0)
(15            Word 00000000            0) (15           Word 00000001          0)
       Byte                 Byte                 Byte                 Byte
(7   00000000    0) (7   00000001    0) (7   00000002    0) (7   00000003    0)

  (Address $00000004)·
(31                            Long Word 00000001                          0)
(15            Word 00000002            0) (15           Word 00000003          0)
       Byte                 Byte                 Byte                 Byte
(7   00000004    0) (7   00000005    0) (7   00000006    0) (7   00000007    0)


  (Address $FFFFFFFC)
(31                            Long Word 3FFFFFFF                          0)
(15            Word 7FFFFFFE            0) (15           Word 7FFFFFFF          0)
       Byte                 Byte                 Byte                 Byte
(7   FFFFFFFC    0) (7   FFFFFFFD    0) (7   FFFFFFFE    0) (7   FFFFFFFF    0)
```

Figure 2.6. 68020 byte, word and long word organisation in memory.

	(a)	7654 3210		(b)	7654 3210		(c)	7654 3210
most significant digit(s)	(45)	0100 0101	(4)		0000 0100	"4"		0011 0100
in low	(25)	0010 0101	(5)		0000 0101	"5"		0011 0101
addressed memory	(19)	0001 1001	(2)		0000 0010	"2"		0011 0010
	(33)	0011 0011	(5)		0000 0101	"5"		0011 0101
	(67)	0110 0111	(1)		0000 0001	"1"		0011 0001
			(9)		0000 1001	"9"		0011 1001
			(3)		0000 0011	"3"		0011 0011
least significant digit(s)			(3)		0000 0011	"3"		0011 0011
in high			(6)		0000 0110	"6"		0011 0110
addressed memory			(7)		0000 0111	"7"		0011 0111

Figure 2.7. Decimal data in byte organised memory – the number 4 525 193 367 stored as (a) packed BCD, (b) unpacked BCD and (c) ASCII.

each taking up one byte of memory, and the second is as binary coded decimal (BCD). This utilises the binary values %0000 to %1010 as the decimal digits 0 to 9 (the remaining six binary values, %1011 to %1111, have no representation in BCD processing and if present would cause errors). Unlike binary representation, where the state of the most significant bit may be used to denote sign (positive if 0, negative if 1), BCD values are always positive or, since some sort of sign code may be appended, always denote the absolute value. The advantage of BCD over the use of ASCII digits is that two BCD digits can be packed in to every byte – known as packed BCD (Figure 2.7(a)). Sometimes it is an advantage to use unpacked BCD, where each digit occupies only the low order four bits of a byte and the high order 'nibble' is either not used (Figure 2.7(b)) or contains some code constant. ASCII decimal digits are a special case of unpacked BCD, Figure 2.7(c)

The special BCD instructions of the 68000-series processors, ABCD, SBCD and NBCD, act on a single byte of packed BCD in memory. Since both ABCD and SBCD may use only the predecrement indirect addressing mode (NBCD is given more latitude) and numbers are added or subtracted from low order digit to high order digit, BCD values are always stored with the high order digit in lower addressed memory.

The 68020 has special instructions, PACK and UNPK, to convert between packed BCD and unpacked BCD with an added constant. These instructions can be used to convert between the decimal forms shown in Figures 2.7(a) and 2.7(c). The code to perform these conversions on the 68000, 68008 and 68010 is given later in this book.

Chapter Three
Forms of Address

The registers of the 68000-series processors and the organisation of memory in 68000-series computer systems, described in Chapters 1 and 2, are brought together in this chapter, which considers how to specify the location of operand data in registers or memory.

The location of an operand may be specified by individual use of a number of methods: the address contents of registers, immediate (i.e. programmed) addresses, or displacement of the data from the instruction acting on it. The 68000 also allows combined use of these methods to produce a unique final value that is used to address the operand. The method of specifying an operand location is known as the Effective Address, or EA.

The Effective Address is a concept found in programming other computers, such as the 6809 and 8086, but not in one of the most successful 8-bit computer families, the 8080 and Z80. Since many of the 68000's EA forms involve intermediate arithmetic processes that build up an address from as many as five separate parts, or addends, they may appear unnecessarily complex to anyone not familiar with the concept. In fact, the Effective Address does tend to simplify programming: with only simple address forms available, complex data structures can be addressed only by programming a lengthy sequence of instructions that will add constituent parts of the address into an 'address' register. A moderately complex data structure would typically require the combination of base address, displacement and index to address any single element. Figure 3.1 shows a transfer of one byte between two such data structures. Access of each structure requires a sequence of address component additions and the data has to be transferred through, and temporarily stored in, an accumulator. Figure 3.2 shows that the equivalent action may be programmed in only half the number of instructions, with no necessity for temporary accumulator or Data Register storage, by using Effective Address operands.

One very important point must be made about the calculation of the Effective Address. With the exception of the Program Counter (incremented normally past the instruction) and two simple EA forms which increment or decrement Address Registers, all registers and memory locations used as EA addends remain unchanged, both during and after the calculation. The EA constituent parts are fetched (read) from registers, data memory or program memory (i.e. immediate data) and added together in the cpu address unit to form the value eventually put on the address bus. Only the location

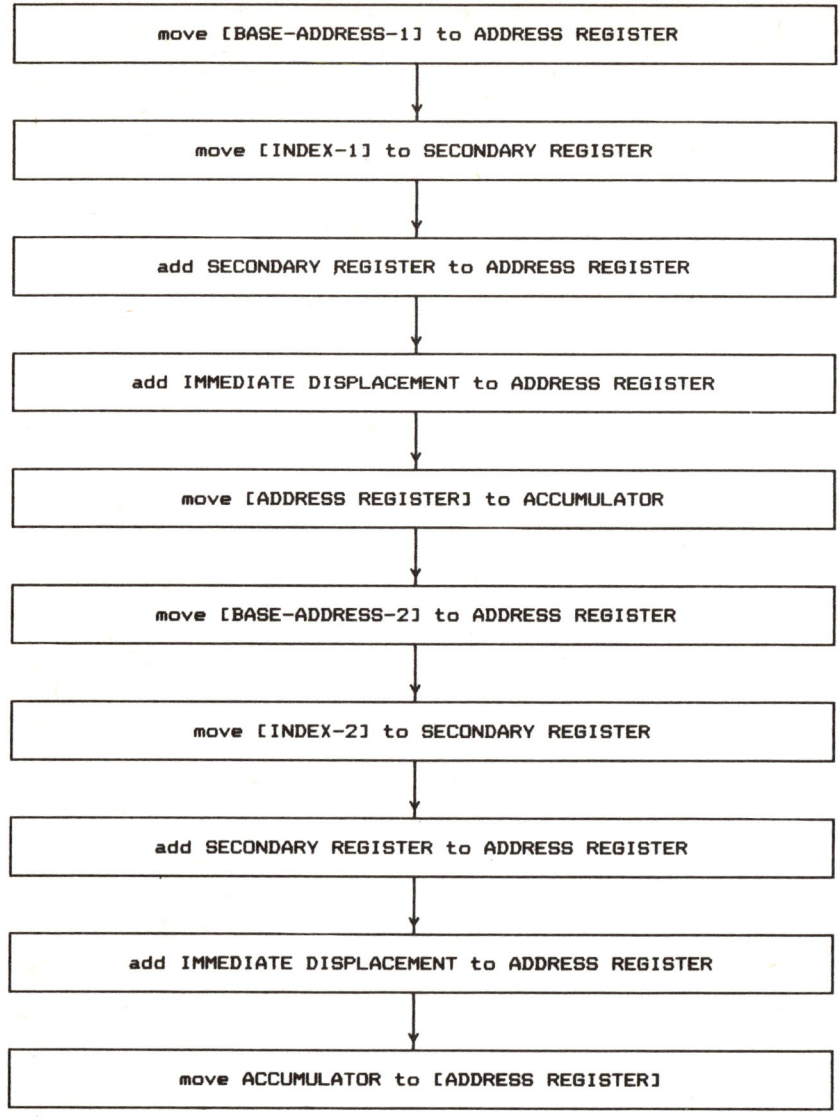

Figure 3.1. Data transfer involving simple register additions.

identified by the Effective Address may be written to (if destination operand; it is only read from if a source operand).

Effective Address form specification

Table D2 (Appendix D, 68000, 68008 and 68010) and Table E2 (Appendix E, 68020) list the standard assembler forms of Effective Address, showing also the various categories which are allowed for particular instruction types. Tables D4.1 and E4.1 give the number and type of extension words required for each form – these extension words are mainly the immediate data addends but also include special index format words.

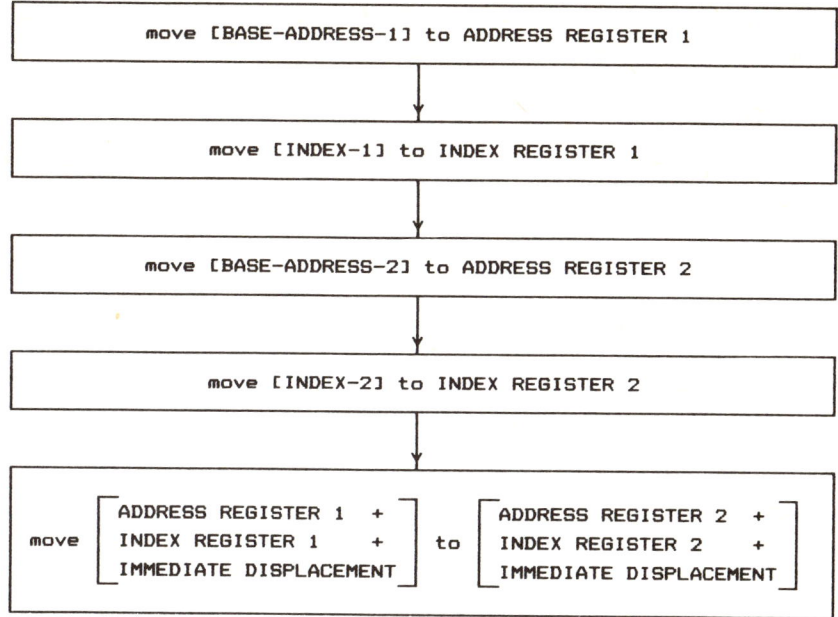

Figure 3.2. Data transfer involving Effective Address operands.

Several of the address forms require no extension words: in these forms the EA addends are registers specified in the instruction word.

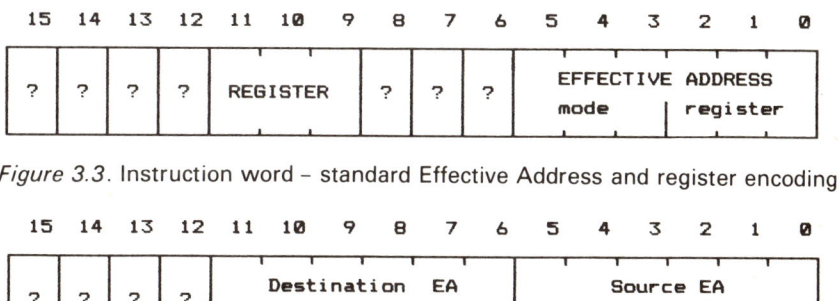

Figure 3.3. Instruction word – standard Effective Address and register encoding.

15	14	13	12	11	10	9	8	7	6	5	4	3	2	1	0

| ? | ? | ? | ? | Destination EA register | | | mode | | | Source EA mode | | | register | | |

Figure 3.4. 'MOVE' instruction Effective Address encoding.

Most instructions allow the programmer to specify an EA form, for either source or destination operand, from any one of the eight EA categories. The EA specification is encoded as a 6-bit field (as two 3-bit sub-fields) in the instruction word, whilst the other of the (usually) two operands is specified as only a 3-bit register number (either D∅ to D7, or A∅ to A7) (see Figure 3.3). The MOVE instruction allows EA specification for both source and destination; it is the only instruction containing two 6-bit EA fields, see Figure 3.4. Some instructions, however, may act only on Data Registers, some only on Address Registers and some only on memory addressed in a particular way. The instruction word of this latter type does not include the full 6-bit EA field but only a 3-bit register number field for source, destination or both. Nevertheless, the operand form is no less an Effective Address than the equivalent form in instructions allowing full choice

– it is merely that the 3 bits of the EA mode field can be put to other uses. The same applies when a Data or Address Register is the other operand in instructions allowing full EA specification.

```
EA Fields
mode     register    Assembler format    Effective Address Mode
```

Non-displaced, non-indexed forms

```
000 (0)  DDD (D)    Dn                  Data Register Direct
001 (1)  AAA (A)    An                  Address Register Direct
010 (2)  AAA (A)    (An)                Address Register Indirect
011 (3)  AAA (A)    (An)+               Post-incremented Address Register
                                            Indirect
100 (4)  AAA (A)    -(An)               Pre-decremented Address Register
                                            Indirect
111 (7)  000 (0)    addr.W              Absolute Short Memory Direct
111 (7)  001 (1)    addr.L              Absolute Long Memory Direct
111 (7)  100 (4)    #data               Immediate Data
```

68000, 68008 and 68010 displaced and indexed forms

```
101 (5)  AAA (A)    sdw(An)             Displaced Address Register
                                            Indirect
110 (6)  AAA (A)    sdb(An,Xx)          Displaced Indexed Address
                                            Register Indirect
111 (7)  010 (2)    sdw(PC)             Program Relative
111 (7)  011 (3)    sdb(PC,Xx)          Indexed Program Relative
```

68020 displaced and indexed forms

```
101 (5)  AAA (A)    (sdw,An)            Displaced Address Register
                                            Indirect
110 (6)  AAA (A)    (sdb,An,Xx)         Displaced Indexed Address
                                            Register Indirect
110 (6)  AAA (A)    (bsd,An,Xx)         Displaced Indexed Base Address
                                            Register Indirect
110 (6)  AAA (A)    ([bsd,An],Xx,osd)   Post-indexed Memory Indirect
110 (6)  AAA (A)    ([bsd,An,Xx],osd)   Pre-indexed Memory Indirect

111 (7)  010 (2)    (sdw,PC)            Program Relative
111 (7)  011 (3)    (sdb,PC,Xx)         Indexed Program Relative
111 (7)  011 (3)    (bsd,PC,Xx)         Base Indexed Program Relative
111 (7)  011 (3)    ([bsd,PC],Xx,osd)   Post-indexed Program Indirect
111 (7)  011 (3)    ([bsd,PC,Xx],osd)   Pre-indexed Program Indirect
```

```
Notes. 1. DDD (D): the Data register number is used.
       2. AAA (A): the Address register number is used.
       3. Xx: Index register is any of D0 to D7 or A0 to A7.
       4. sdb, sdw: signed displacement of byte or word length.
       5. bsd: word or long word signed displacement added to the base
             register An or PC.
       6. osd: word or long word signed displacement added to complete
             the effective address.
       7. The four forms corresponding to each of 110 (6) AAA (A)  and
             111 (7) 011 (3) are distinguished by the index extension word.
       8. A label may replace sdb, sdw, etc. for the Program Relative
             forms – the assembler will calculate the displacement.
```

Table 3.1. Effective Address modes.

Table 3.1 lists the names normally given to the 68000-series Effective Address modes against the instruction EA mode and register number fields, given in both binary and decimal, and the standard assembler notation. Note that for forms not using a Data or Address Register, the Register number is used as an extension to the mode field. A diagrammatic explanation of each EA form is given in Appendix F.

Index form specification – 68000, 68008 and 68010

The indexed Effective Address forms of the 68000, 68008 and 68010 require one extension word. The high order byte of this word specifies which of registers DØ to D7 or AØ to A7 is to be used as Index Register and whether the entire long word held by that register is to be used, or the low order word sign extended to a 32-bit value. The index word low order byte contains an 8-bit displacement sign, extended to a 32-bit value before use. The format is shown in Figure 3.5.

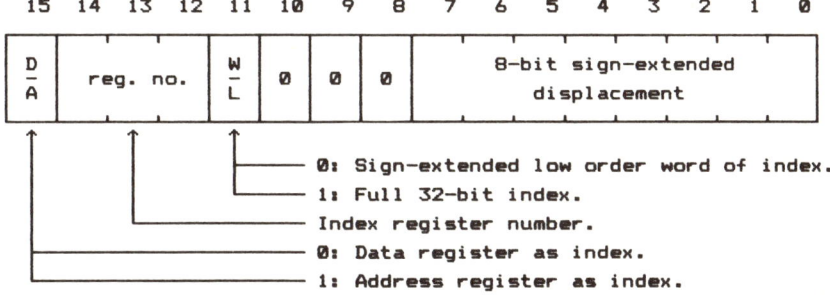

Figure 3.5. 68000, 68008 and 68010 index word.

68020 brief index format specification

The brief index format of the 68020 corresponds to the index format of earlier 68000-series computers but with the sophisticated enhancement of index-scaling. Bits 1Ø and 9

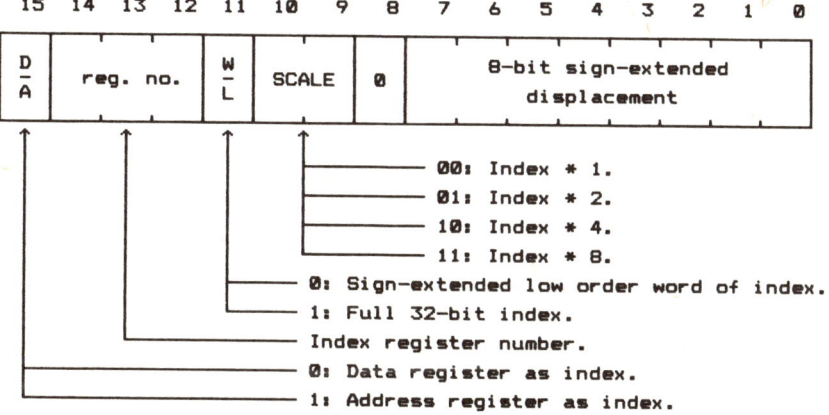

Figure 3.6. 68020 brief format index word.

of the index word may be programmed to scale the Index Register by factors of 1, 2, 4 or 8 before use (i.e. the Index Register content, after any necessary sign extension, is shifted left by 0, 1, 2 or 3 bits before it is added to the Base Register, An or PC). The format is shown in Figure 3.6.

The single index form of the earlier 68000 is upward compatible with the 68020 since the necessarily reset bits 10 and 9 equate to a scale factor of 1 (i.e. no scaling). 68020 brief index formats with scale factors other than 1 (either or both bits 10 and 9 are set) are not downward compatible with the earlier processors. Although the 68000, etc. will not perform a check on the validity of the scale field (thus not incurring exception processing on account of instruction coding error), neither will they perform the scaling necessary to address the intended location. Exception processing may result from the erroneous attempt to address non-existent memory.

68020 full index format specification

The 68020 has a second index form, the full or long format, which allows several variations of memory indirect addressing. The high order byte of the full format index word is similar to the brief format index word but with bit 8 set (i.e. the state of bit 8 distinguishes the two forms). The low order byte does not contain a displacement but four fields that determine:

(a) Base Register inclusion or suppression
(b) Index Register inclusion or suppression
(c) size of the displacement added to the Base Register
(d) size of the displacement added to the address obtained from memory in memory indirection

The length of the complete form is anything from one word (null base and outer displacements) to five words (long word base and outer displacements). With both source and destination operands specified as full index forms, each with two long word displacements, the complete instruction is 11 words (22 bytes) long. The full index format is shown in Figure 3.7.

The full index format is not downward compatible with earlier 68000-series processors. If executed on a 68000, the low order byte of the index word will be read as an 8-bit signed displacement and the wrong memory location will be addressed. Chaos may very well ensue when the base displacement following the index word is read as the first word of a new instruction.

68020 full index format addends

Base Register This is any of A0 to A7 or the Program Counter, specified in the instruction word Effective Address field. It may be suppressed (i.e. the value 0 used in its place) or included. If included, the full 32-bit value is used (all other addends may be specified as null, word or long word; the Base Register may be specified only as null or

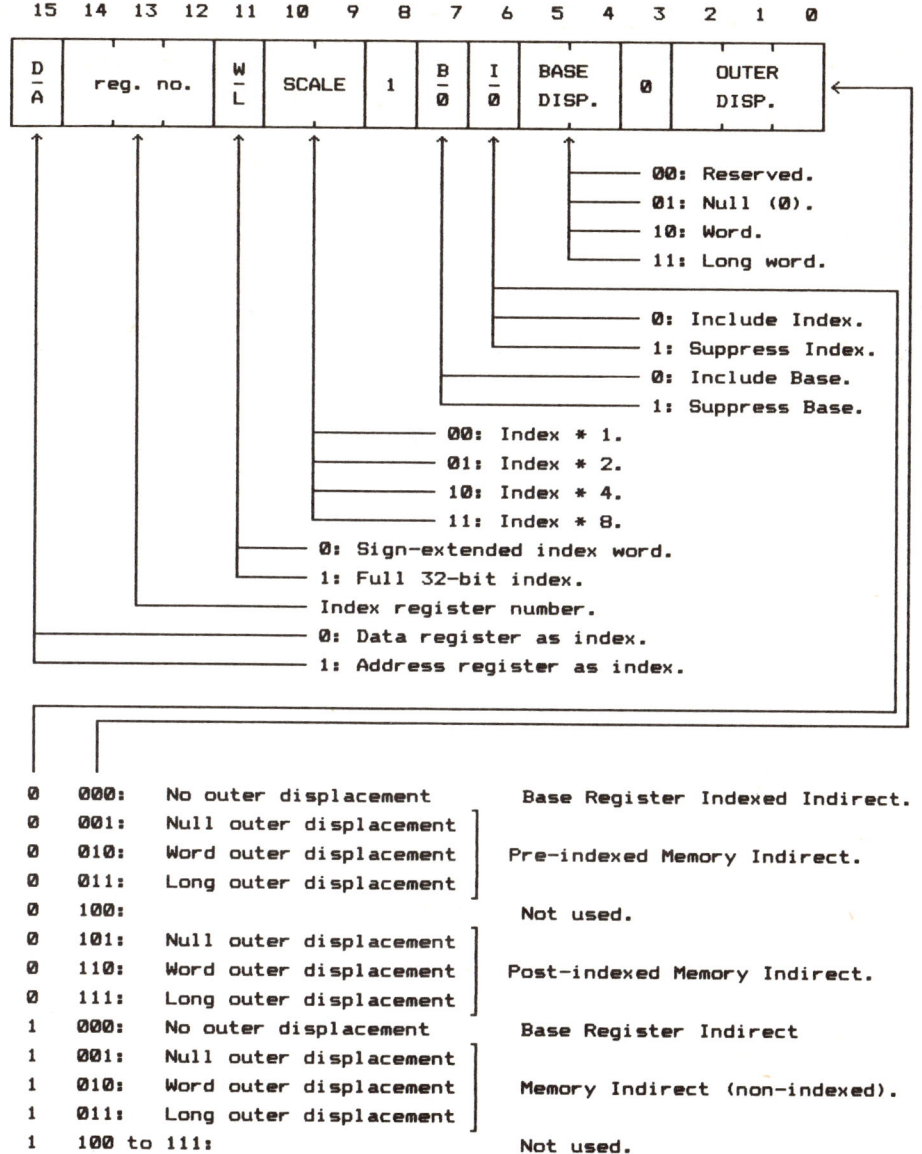

15	14 13	12	11	10 9	8	7	6	5 4	3	2 1 0
D/A	reg. no.	W/L		SCALE	1	B/0	I/0	BASE DISP.	0	OUTER DISP.

```
                                              00: Reserved.
                                              01: Null (0).
                                              10: Word.
                                              11: Long word.

                                              0: Include Index.
                                              1: Suppress Index.
                                              0: Include Base.
                                              1: Suppress Base.

                             00: Index * 1.
                             01: Index * 2.
                             10: Index * 4.
                             11: Index * 8.
                  0: Sign-extended index word.
                  1: Full 32-bit index.
                  Index register number.
                  0: Data register as index.
                  1: Address register as index.
```

0	000:	No outer displacement	Base Register Indexed Indirect.
0	001:	Null outer displacement	
0	010:	Word outer displacement	Pre-indexed Memory Indirect.
0	011:	Long outer displacement	
0	100:		Not used.
0	101:	Null outer displacement	
0	110:	Word outer displacement	Post-indexed Memory Indirect.
0	111:	Long outer displacement	
1	000:	No outer displacement	Base Register Indirect
1	001:	Null outer displacement	
1	010:	Word outer displacement	Memory Indirect (non-indexed).
1	011:	Long outer displacement	
1	100 to 111:		Not used.

Figure 3.7. 68020 full format index word.

long word). This register supplies the base address, possibly displaced and indexed, for the first level of memory indirection.

Base Displacement This displacement is added to the value obtained from the Base Register. It may be specified as null (i.e. not included, taken as a value of 0 in the index computation), as sign-extended word length or long word length. If included, it follows immediately after the index word in the instruction code. Note that if the Base Register is suppressed, the base displacement becomes the absolute address of the memory indirect location, possibly indexed.

Index Register This is specified, as in the brief index format, as the long word value or the sign-extended low order word of the Index Register (any of D0 to D7 or A0 to A7). It may be suppressed and the value 0 used in its stead. It is scaled by a factor of 1, 2, 4 or 8 before use. The index addend may be applied before (pre-index) or after (post-index) the first level of memory indirection in the memory and program indirect modes.

(Memory) The long word address at the indirect memory location is used, after displacement and (possibly) indexing, as the address of the operand data. The indirect memory address may be specified in two ways:

    (a) Pre-indexed indirect: (Base Register + Base displacement + Index Register)

    (b) Post-indexed indirect: (Base Register + Base displacement).

Outer displacement This displacement is added to the address obtained from memory in the memory and program indirect modes (after addition of the index in post-indexing) to complete the address of the operand data location. It may be specified as null (i.e. not included, taken as a value of 0 in the index computation), as sign-extended word length or long word length. If included, it follows immediately after the base displacement (after the index word when the base displacement is null) in the instruction code. The outer displacement is not allowed (it would be meaningless) in the Base Register indirect and base progam indirect modes which do not have memory indirection.

    The formation of the operand address from the index addends is shown diagrammatically in Appendix F. Note that in the full index format, any or all of the addends may be suppressed. Complete suppression results in direct addressing of data in location $00000000 or indirect addressing of data at the location specified by the 32-bit address held in location $00000000 – $00000003. Some of the full index format suppressed addend alternatives are not allowed: for verification, see Table E4.4 (Appendix E), which lists all possible and impossible assembler forms.

Chapter Four
The Supervisor State and Exception Processing

All 68000-series computers can operate in two states of privilege – User or Supervisor. The default state is the higher privileged Supervisor mode, and this is entered at power-up by a hard reset or by interrupt.

The Supervisor state

Supervisor mode exists principally as a superior operating state in which system management is protected from user interference and allowed access to all system functions. The programs normally inhabiting this domain fall into three basic categories:

(a) the operating system software, dealing with hardware management and general system housekeeping

(b) user task control, partitioning time and resources between multiple concurrent user programs

(c) error processing

Applications software is normally relegated to the lesser privileged User mode and allowed only restricted access to the system.

Whenever the cpu initiates a memory access cycle, to fetch instruction code or to read from or write to a data location, it outputs a 3-bit code to an external memory management device. This code, known as the function code (see Table 1.1 in Chapter 1), specifies the privilege mode currently in operation and whether the reference is to data or program memory.

The function code can be used by the memory management device to switch between memory banks. Although the switch could be made on the data or program memory state, it is more likely to be determined by the operating mode state. Supervisor programs, in RAM or ROM, may therefore reside at the same addresses as RAM available for User mode operation, or indeed at the same addresses as any user-accessible part of the system in ROM. This feature can be used to make Supervisor programs not merely operationally transparent but actually invisible to the user and so provide complete program protection.

Change of operating mode depends only on the state of the S bit in the Status Register. Whenever this bit is set (1) the processor operates in Supervisor mode, and when reset (∅) it operates in User mode; no other action is required for a change of mode. Programs operating in Supervisor mode are allowed access to the Status Register high order byte (system byte) and so may pass control to User mode simply by utilising any of the privileged instructions which write to or change the Status Register. The controlling system software, normally operating in Supervisor mode, will have to switch to User mode operation if it needs to access the separate User Stack Pointer. (A reason why the USP needs to be accessed in Supervisor mode is given in Chapter 1.)

Programs operating in User mode are denied write access to the system byte of the Status Register and so cannot simply step into Supervisor mode. This is another aspect of the protective field surrounding the Supervisor mode. Note that even system code, which has stepped down into User mode simply by writing to the SR, cannot just step back to Supervisor operation by the same method. Any attempt to write to or change the system byte of the SR while operating in User mode will result in an internally generated interrupt called an exception. In fact, the only method of switching to Supervisor from User mode is to cause an exception to occur.

Exceptions

An exception is, simply, an exception to normal sequential and orderly processing – it stands outside, or above, or beyond, or beneath, the programmed sequence of events and deals with the unforeseen error, the disallowed process, the unimplemented instruction or the action that may affect the system adversely. An exception will not check that an algorithm is sound, nor prevent program flow falling into an infinite loop, nor catch out spelling mistakes in word processor text flies. These latter abominations fall outside the purview of the processor's hardware self-consciousness. Nevertheless, program logic (software self-consciousness) can check for and trap such occurrences, utilising a small range of exception causing instructions specifically provided for this purpose (with the exception, perhaps, of the infinite loop).

Except in the case of bus cycle errors on the 68010 and 68020, the 68000-series hardware has no inbuilt mechanism for dealing with the problem which caused the exception interrupt to occur. The interrupt sequence of an exception merely saves the current machine state internally, sets the S bit in the Status Register to ensure Supervisor mode operation (exceptions may occur in either Supervisor or User mode but are always processed in Supervisor mode), transfers the machine state and sometimes other information to the Supervisor stack and passes control to an exception handler at a vectored address. A program to process the particular type of exception must be located at the correct address or no action will be taken. Lack of response to an exception could cause another exception to occur, or even cause the processor to halt until external reset.

Exception handling programs for some types of exceptions are normally provided as part of the operating system software. For system protection, these should be inaccessible to the user. Other types of exceptions really require vectoring to a user accessible location since they are designed for trapping errors in user program logic.

Exception types

Although the majority of exception types are internally generated, several types are generated externally. Not the least of these is the interrupt request from external or peripheral devices such as timer, keyboard, printer, and so on. Another externally generated exception is the hardware reset – a catastrophic type of interrupt which re-initialises machine state – and this, like the interrupt request, is found as a standard feature of most microprocessors. In the 68000 family these interrupts are included in the exception genus. Table 4.1 classifies the exception types.

Type	Internally generated	Externally generated
Error:	Address errors	Bus errors
	(68020: various coprocessor)	
Illegality:	Privilege violation Illegal op-code Unimplemented op-code	none
Instruction:	TRAP, TRAPV, CHK Division by zero	none
	(68020: BKPT, CALLM, CHK, CHK2 TRAPcc, and various coprocessor instructions)	
Interrupt:	Trace	Interrupt request Reset

Table 4.1. Exception types.

1. Error exceptions

Internally generated

Address errors occur when an attempt is made to fetch an instruction word or read from or write to a word or long word data location at an odd-byte address. Byte data may be accessed at odd byte addresses. The 68020 will allow word and long word data to be accessed on odd-byte boundaries but instruction words must be located on word boundaries to prevent addressing error exceptions. The system must deal with this situation and not vector control to the user. The exception process could deal with the situation by accessing the two memory words concerned and concatenating the required low and high order bytes (reads and fetches) or by splitting the data to two or three words (writes). It is more likely to report an error in the object program.

Various 68020 coprocessor instructions are capable of causing addressing errors.

Externally generated

Bus errors are basically address errors of a type transparent to the cpu but discovered by the external memory management devices employed. One obvious cause of a bus error is the absence of the memory page being accessed. The user software can do nothing about them and they must be dealt with by the system.

In the 68000 and 68008, bus errors are not recoverable at the instruction causing the error and so the exception will only diagnose and report. In the 68010 and 68020, it may be possible for the faulting instruction to be continued, possibly by software emulation of the cycle which generated the error. The system will normally retry the read or write cycle if that has not already been done by software emulation, and report the error if the retry fails.

2. Illegal exceptions

Internally generated

Privilege violations are attempts to use any of the special Supervisor mode instructions while operating in User mode. The system must determine what normally withheld resources it will allow to any particular user program – it may, for example, allow the RESET instruction (reset all external devices – *not* the same as the externally generated reset which restarts the processor) to a sub-system level user control program. In this case the system itself would execute the RESET instruction (without incurring a further privilege violation since it is operating in Supervisor mode) and then return control to the user program.

One privilege violation that could occur in the 68010 and 68020 but not in the 68000 or 68008 is a User mode attempt to MOVE from SR. This anomaly is discussed in Chapter 1. The 68010 or 68020 system should emulate a User mode allowable form of the instruction with the S bit always reset.

The system should report on privilege violation, since merely ignoring the faulting instruction could invalidate the user program's results or cause other errors.

Illegal op-codes are those instruction word bit patterns which are not recognised as forming a valid instruction. Less sophisticated processors often fail to decode instructions fully, with the result that unspecified codes are accepted and produce some processor effect. The 68000-series processors do fully decode all instructions (though not all extension words; see the discussion on the 68020 index extension words in Chapter 3) and initiate exception processing for unspecified codes.

The system may use the illegal code exception as a method of implementing a set of system call instructions from User mode. It could also vector the illegal instruction exception to a user accessible location and allow user defined pseudo-instructions, but this would be most unlikely.

Several op-codes that are illegal on earlier processors in the 68000-series are used in the extended 68020 instruction set. Systems built around the earlier processors may emulate the 68020 instructions by exception processing. One particular case in point is the set of op-codes, $4848 to $484F. These codes are illegal on the 68000 and 68008 but are used as rudimentary breakpoint codes on the 68010 and as the codes of the fully fledged breakpoint instruction, BKPT #n, on the 68020. Any decent 68000 system should acknowledge these codes as breakpoints.

Codes which are illegal – actually, unimplemented – may be used on current 68000-series processors for new instructions on future models. However, three codes are guaranteed as illegal on all current and future members of the family. These are $4AFA, $4AFB (both reserved for Motorola use) and $4AFC (the op-code of the ILLEGAL instruction).

There are two special groups of op-codes known as the A-line (op-code $Axxx) and

F-line (op-code $Fxxx). The 68020 uses a few of the F-line codes for its coprocessor instructions; apart from that the A-line and F-line codes are unassigned. Both groups generate special exception processing which may be used to emulate unimplemented instructions.

Externally generated
There are no externally generated illegal exceptions.

3. Instruction exceptions

Internally generated
There is a range of instructions designed to initiate exception processing as a guard against errors in program logic. These are TRAP, TRAPV and CHK (also BKPT, CHK2 and TRAPcc on the 68020). The division instructions will also fall to an exception if the divisor is zero and the 68020 CALLM instruction uses exception processing to build the module stack frame.

Apart from CALLM and, perhaps, BKPT, all exceptions caused by these instructions should be routed to user exception handler programs by the system.

Externally generated
There are no externally generated instruction exceptions.

4. Interrupt exceptions

Internally generated
The only internally generated (no error) interrupt is the Trace function. This is caused by setting the T bit in the SR system byte (two T bits on the 68020) which can be initiated only in Supervisor mode.

The single mode Trace of the 68000, 68008 and 68010 generates an interrupt immediately after the execution of every instruction. It may be used for single stepping or to produce a printed list of the program flow. The system is not likely to make the exception available to the user.

The 68020 Trace function has two modes of operation: it may be set to generate interrupts after every instruction, like the 68000's single mode Trace, or alternatively set to interrupt only after those instructions which break program sequence – branches, jumps and subroutine calls.

Externally generated
Reset should occur only *in extremis*. A system restart is made and the interrupted processing is not recoverable.

Interrupt requests are signals from external devices, often from peripherals such as printers, which request the processor to remove control from the currently executing program and divert it to a program that will handle the needs of the particular interrupting device. The requests may occur at any time during the execution of an instruction, but response is delayed until execution has finished. Even then, the request may not be honoured if the interrupt priority value, input on lines IPL2, IPL1 and IPL∅, is of the same or lower priority than the current program.

The 68000-series processors offer seven levels of interrupt priority – in ascending order 1 to 7. (The 68008 is restricted to the three priority levels, 2, 5 and 7.) Each program having access to the SR system byte may set the 3-bit priority mask in SR bits 1∅, 9 and 8 to prevent interruption from low priority interrupts. Value Ø on the IPL lines indicates no interrupt request and in the SR I bits Ø indicates that all interrupts are allowed. An interrupt with priority level 7 is treated as a special case and cannot be masked.

An interrupt may furnish an exception vector number, in which case control is passed to the exception processing program at the requested vectored address. Vectors 64 to 255 are reserved for User interrupt definition but, as no cpu protection exists on the other vectors, any vector Ø to 255 can be specified – see Table 4.4. Although the system software will use some of the user defined interrupt vectors, most should be available to the user. If the interrupt does not give a vector then the processor will route control to the vectored address associated with the interrupt's priority level. These 'autovectors' are unlikely to be user accessible.

Spurious interrupts may occur if any of the IPL lines goes high but external logic signals a bus error. There is a special exception for such cases.

Exception priorities

Not all exceptions have the same priority, since some obviously arise from more urgent needs than others. In the case of two or more exceptions occurring together, those with the higher priority, shown in Tables 4.2 and 4.3, will be processed first. Some exceptions, notably Reset, will cause other simultaneously occurring exceptions to be abandoned.

Priority	Exception	Process
0.0	Reset	Abort process and start Exception
0.1	Address error	within 2 clock cycles (the context
0.2	Bus error	is saved in the case of Address and Bus errors in the 68010).
1.0	Trace	Complete current instruction, if
1.1	Interrupt	possible, begin Exception process
1.2	Illegal	before next instruction.
1.3	Privilege	
2.0	Instruction	Instruction initiates Exception process. No priority difference exists between instructions types as simultaneous execution cannot occur.

Table 4.2. Exception priority: 68000, 68008 and 68010.

Exception vectors

All exceptions, after saving whatever part of the machine state or context is considered necessary, pass control to an appropriate exception handler program. This is done by loading the Program Counter with the exception program's address fetched from an exception vector table. Each type of exception has its own vector and some have several, which must be specified in some way – the TRAP #n instruction, for example, has sixteen

```
Priority        Exception               Process

0.0             Reset                   Abort process and start Exception.

1.0             Address error           Suspend process, save context and
1.1             Bus error               begin Exception immediately.

2.0             Instruction             Instruction initiates Exception
                                        process. No priority difference
                                        exists between instructions types as
                                        simultaneous execution cannot occur.

3.0             Illegal                 Start Exception before instruction
3.1             Unimplemented           is executed.
3.2             Privilege
3.3             cp pre-instruction

4.0             cp post-instruction     Complete current instruction and
4.1             Trace                   begin Exception before processing
4.2             Interrupt               next instruction.
```

Table 4.3. Exception priority: 68020.

vectors allotted to it (vector numbers 32 to 47) corresponding to each of the sixteen immediate data values, #0 to #15, and seven vectors are assigned for the seven levels of interrupt priority. The Reset exception is unusual in that it reinitialises the system and thus requires two vectors: the first, vector 0, is loaded to the Supervisor (Interrupt in the 68020) Stack Pointer and the second, vector 1, is loaded to the Program Counter. Table 4.4 gives the vector numbers in both decimal and hexadecimal, their table addresses in hexadecimal and their assignments.

Each entry in the vector table contains the long word address of the corresponding exception program – with the one exception of vector 0, which contains the long word Stack Pointer address for Reset. The exception vector thus acts as an index to the required address and is converted to a table byte offset by multiplying it by four.

In the 68000 and 68008 the exception vector table can only be located at addresses $00000000 to $000003FF. In the 68010 and 68020, however, the table is indexed by the value in the Vector Base Register and so may be located at any long word boundary. The rerouting of control to the exception handler program is shown in Figure 4.1.

Exception stack frames

Before the exception process transfers control to the address obtained from the vector table, it saves the interrupted context on the Supervisor stack – this may be the Interrupt or Master stack on the 68020. The amount of information stored in the exception stack frame depends on the type of exception and on the processor. The handler programs for address and bus error exceptions (priority group 0 in Table 4.2, group 1 in Table 4.3) require much more information than those of other exception types and so the stack frames for these exceptions are larger. For example, the contents of the decode and prefetch registers (pipeline on the 68020) are saved for bus cycle errors but not for other exceptions. The only exception type that does not build a stack frame is the Reset exception which reinitialises the system.

Vector no. dec	hex	Address	Assignment
0	$00	$000	Reset Initial Supervisor Stack Pointer
1	$01	$004	Reset Initial Program Counter
2	$02	$008	Bus error
3	$03	$00C	Address error
4	$04	$010	Illegal instruction
5	$05	$014	Division by zero
6	$06	$018	CHK (68020: CHK, CHK2)
7	$07	$01C	TRAPV (68020: TRAPV, TRAPcc, cpTRAPcc)
8	$08	$020	Privilege violation
9	$09	$024	Trace
10	$0A	$028	A-line (code $Axxx) emulator
11	$0B	$02C	F-line (code $Fxxx) emulator
12	$0C	$030	reserved for future Motorola use
13	$0D	$034	reserved for future Motorola use (68020: Coprocessor protocol violation)
14	$0E	$038	68000, 68008: reserved for future Motorola use 68010, 68020: Format error
15	$0F	$03C	Uninitialised interrupt
16 to 23	$10 to $17	$040 to $05C	reserved for future Motorola use (8 vectors)
24	$18	$060	Spurious interrupt
25	$19	$064	Priority level 1 interrupt autovector
26	$1A	$068	Priority level 2 interrupt autovector
27	$1B	$06C	Priority level 3 interrupt autovector
28	$1C	$070	Priority level 4 interrupt autovector
29	$1D	$074	Priority level 5 interrupt autovector
30	$1E	$078	Priority level 6 interrupt autovector
31	$1F	$07C	Priority level 7 interrupt autovector
32	$20	$080	TRAP #0
33	$21	$084	TRAP #1
34	$22	$088	TRAP #2
35	$23	$08C	TRAP #3
36	$24	$090	TRAP #4
37	$25	$094	TRAP #5
38	$26	$098	TRAP #6
39	$27	$09C	TRAP #7
40	$28	$0A0	TRAP #8
41	$29	$0A4	TRAP #9
42	$2A	$0A8	TRAP #10
43	$2B	$0AC	TRAP #11
44	$2C	$0B0	TRAP #12
45	$2D	$0B4	TRAP #13
46	$2E	$0B8	TRAP #14
47	$2F	$0BC	TRAP #15
48 to 63	$30 to $3F	$0C0 to $0FC	reserved for future Motorola use (16 vectors)
64 to 255	$40 to $FF	$100 to $3FC	User defined interrupt vectors (192 vectors)

Notes. 1. Reset requires a new Supervisor Stack Pointer as well as a new Program Counter value.
2. Vector 0 (Reset SSP) is loaded to the Interrupt Stack Pointer in the 68020 — the M (Master) bit of SR is cleared.
3. Vectors 0 and 1 (Reset) are in Supervisor Program space, all other vectors are in Supervisor Data space.
4. 68010, 68020: The vector address is an offset from the VBR.

Table 4.4. Exception vectors.

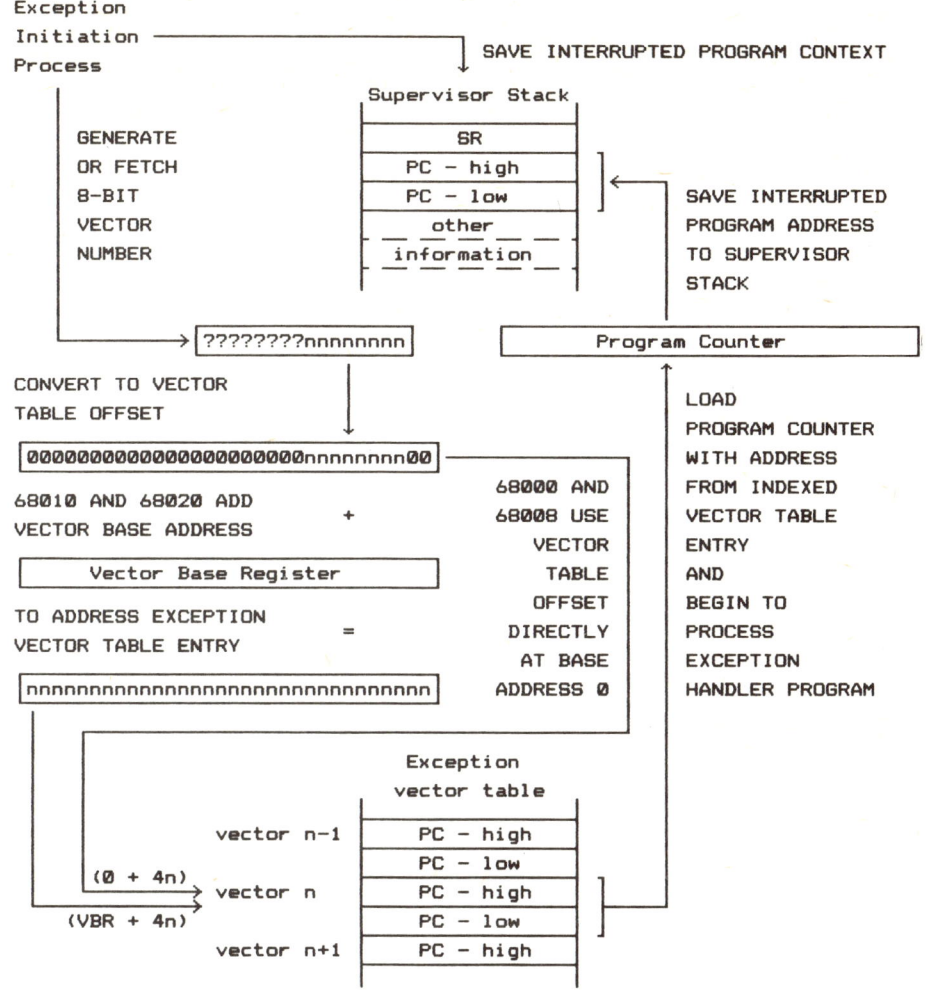

Exception
Initiation ───┐
Process   SAVE INTERRUPTED PROGRAM CONTEXT

Supervisor Stack

GENERATE
OR FETCH
8-BIT
VECTOR
NUMBER

| SR |
| PC – high |
| PC – low |
| other |
| information |

SAVE INTERRUPTED
PROGRAM ADDRESS
TO SUPERVISOR
STACK

→ ????????nnnnnnnn   Program Counter

CONVERT TO VECTOR
TABLE OFFSET

00000000000000000000000nnnnnnnn00 ──────────

68010 AND 68020 ADD   +
VECTOR BASE ADDRESS

Vector Base Register

TO ADDRESS EXCEPTION   =
VECTOR TABLE ENTRY

nnnnnnnnnnnnnnnnnnnnnnnnnnnnnnnn

68000 AND
68008 USE
VECTOR
TABLE
OFFSET
DIRECTLY
AT BASE
ADDRESS 0

LOAD
PROGRAM COUNTER
WITH ADDRESS
FROM INDEXED
VECTOR TABLE
ENTRY
AND
BEGIN TO
PROCESS
EXCEPTION
HANDLER PROGRAM

Exception
vector table

	vector n–1	PC – high
		PC – low
(0 + 4n)		PC – high
(VBR + 4n)	vector n	PC – low
	vector n+1	PC – high

Figure 4.1. Exception vectoring of control.

Figure 4.2 shows the two stack frame formats used in the 68000 and 68008. The smaller format (a) is used for all exception types with priority levels 1 and 2 (see Table 4.2) and only the minimum information about the interrupted program, its execution address (PC) and status (SR), is saved. The address stored in the stack frame depends on the exception: it may be that of a faulting instruction that cannot be fully processed before exception is initiated (illegal instruction or privilege violation) or it could be the address of the next sequential instruction to which control will pass on return from the exception (Trace, interrupt and instruction). The larger format (b) comprises the PC and SR and an additional four words. The PC value is moved past the instruction causing the error before being saved. The contents of the instruction decode register are stacked above the SR and the faulting access address stacked above that. Finally, bus cycle information in the lower order five bits of a word are placed on top of stack – bits 2-0 give the function code (FC2, FC1 and FC0), bit 4 is reset for a write cycle or set for a read cycle, and bit 3 is reset to show that an instruction was being processed when the exception occurred

(a) Supervisor Stack

SSP	SR
SSP + 2	PC – high
SSP + 4	PC – low

PC: Program Counter.
SR: Status Register.
IR: Instruction Register.
FA: Faulting Address.
fff: Function Code (FC2, FC1, FC0).
i = 0: Instruction being processed.
i = 1: Instruction not being processed.
b = 0: Write bus cycle.
b = 1: Read bus cycle.

(b) Supervisor Stack

SSP	00000000000bifff
SSP + 2	AA – high
SSP + 4	AA – low
SSP + 6	IR
SSP + 8	SR
SSP + 10	PC – high
SSP + 12	PC – low

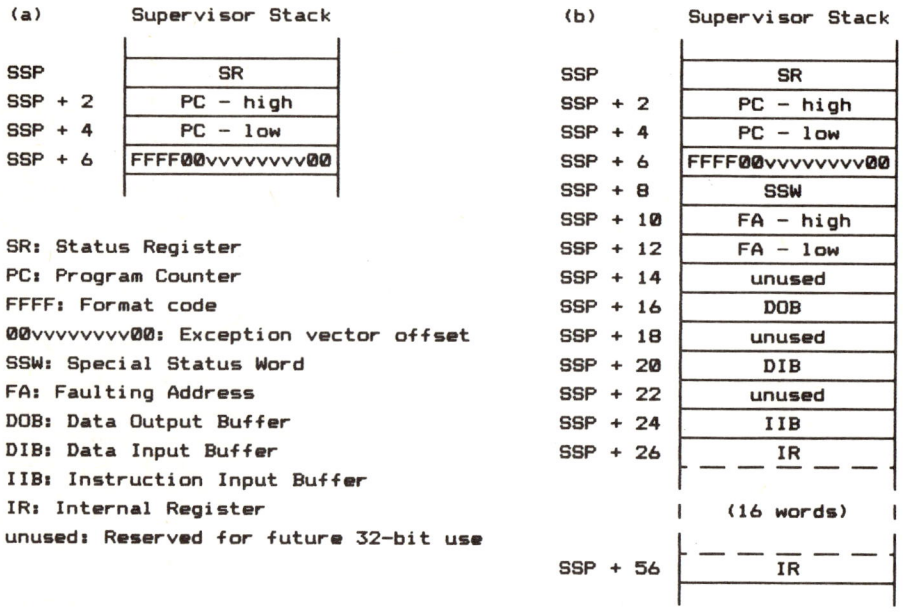

Figure 4.2. 68000 and 68008 exception stack frames, (a) group 1 and 2, (b) address and bus error.

(a) Supervisor Stack

SSP	SR
SSP + 2	PC – high
SSP + 4	PC – low
SSP + 6	FFFF00vvvvvvvv00

SR: Status Register
PC: Program Counter
FFFF: Format code
00vvvvvvvv00: Exception vector offset
SSW: Special Status Word
FA: Faulting Address
DOB: Data Output Buffer
DIB: Data Input Buffer
IIB: Instruction Input Buffer
IR: Internal Register
unused: Reserved for future 32-bit use

(b) Supervisor Stack

SSP	SR
SSP + 2	PC – high
SSP + 4	PC – low
SSP + 6	FFFF00vvvvvvvv00
SSP + 8	SSW
SSP + 10	FA – high
SSP + 12	FA – low
SSP + 14	unused
SSP + 16	DOB
SSP + 18	unused
SSP + 20	DIB
SSP + 22	unused
SSP + 24	IIB
SSP + 26	IR
	(16 words)
SSP + 56	IR

Figure 4.3. 68010 short format (a) and long format (b) exception stack frames.

(normal state or priority group 2 exception) or set for no instruction processing (priority group Ø and 1 exceptions)

The stack frames of the 68010 are quite different from those of the 68000, as can be seen in Figure 4.3, which gives the 68010 stack frames that correspond to those of the 68000 in Figure 4.2. Being a 'virtual' machine and thus liable to a great deal of software emulation, the 68010 requires more information about the exception to be provided in the stack frame, particularly for address and bus errors. Unlike the 68000, which can only diagnose and report on a bus cycle error, the 68010 can rerun the cycle, either by software emulation or by a processor retry on exit from the exception handler program. More of the context, particularly internal 68010 registers, has to be placed on stack for this error resolution and buffers are provided for instruction fetch or data read/write on the bus cycle retry. The fault information needed to process the cycle rerun is provided in a Special Status Word, Figure 4.4.

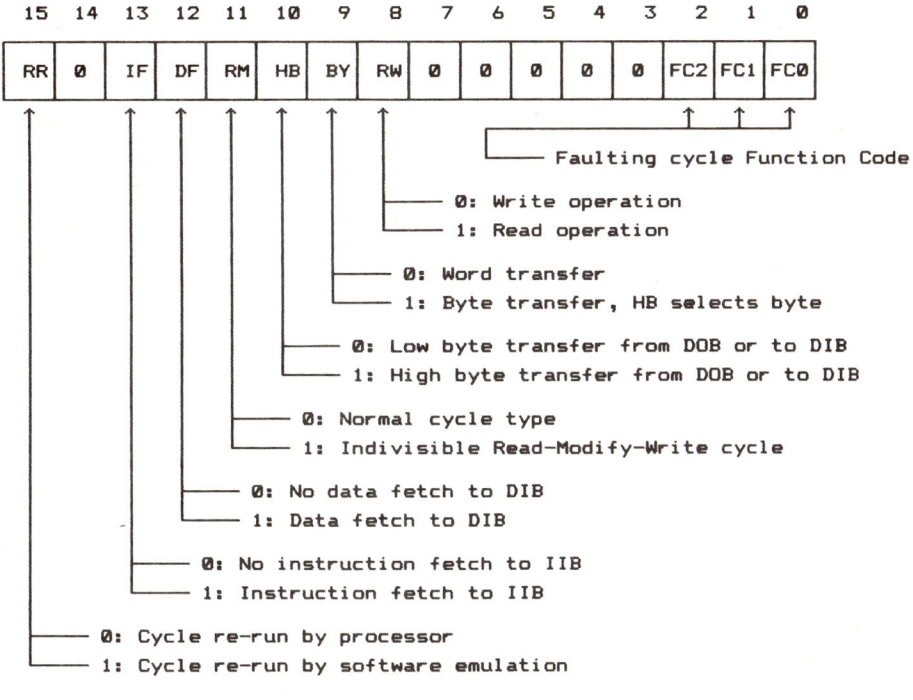

Figure 4.4. 68010 Special Status Word (SSW).

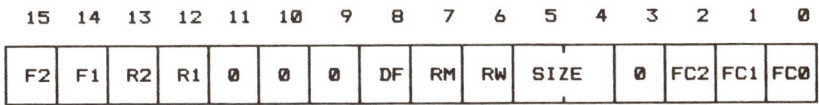

F2: Set if fault on instruction pipe second stage
F1: Set if fault on instruction pipe first stage
R2: Set for processor re-run of second stage fetch cycle
R1: Set for processor re-run of first stage fetch cycle
DF: Set for a Data Fault and processor re-run of data access
RM: Set for indivisible Read-Modify-Write cycle
RW: Reset for write cycle, set for read cycle
SIZE: Data cycle fault data size - 00 = byte, 01 = word, 10 = long word
FC2,FC1,FC0: Faulting cycle Function Code

Figure 4.5. 68020 Special Status Word (SSW).

So that the return from exception process (RTE) can act correctly on the stack frame, the 68010 and 68020 include frame format code as part of the frame information. The possible formats are shown in Table 4.5. Note that the 68010 is allowed only two formats: the family 4-word format (code %0000) and the unique 68010 bus fault format (code

%1000). Any other format code, or a wrongly sized stack frame, will cause a format error exception on RTE.

Format Code bin	hex	dec	Length (words)	Frame format
0000	0	0	4	68000-series Short format
0001	1	1	4	68020 Interrupt Stack throwaway
0010	2	2	6	68020 Instruction exception
0011	3	3	–	Reserved for future use
0100	4	4	–	Reserved for future use
0101	5	5	–	Reserved for future use
0110	6	6	–	Reserved for future use
0111	7	7	–	Reserved for future use
1000	8	8	29	68010 Long format (bus fault)
1001	9	9	10	68020 Coprocessor mid-instruction
1010	A	10	16	68020 Short bus fault (instr. boundary)
1011	B	11	44	68020 long bus fault (not instr. boundary)
1100	C	12	–	Reserved for future use
1101	D	13	–	Reserved for future use
1110	E	14	–	Reserved for future use
1111	F	15	–	Reserved for future use

Table 4.5. 68010 and 68020 exception stack frame format codes.

The 68020 has six exception stack frame formats two of which, the 'Throwaway' and the 'Coprocessor mid-instruction', are really special versions of the other interrupt and instruction exception formats shown in Figure 4.6.

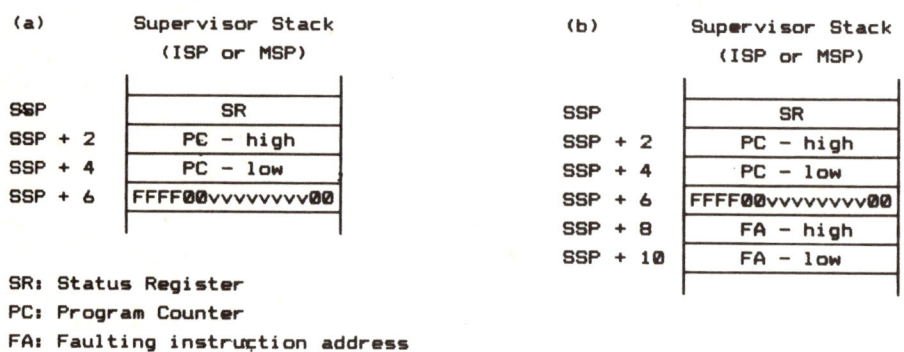

SR: Status Register
PC: Program Counter
FA: Faulting instruction address
FFFF: Format code
00vvvvvvvv00: Exception vector offset

Figure 4.6. 68020 4-word (a) and 6-word (b) exception stack frames.

The 4-word stack frame format is identical in the 68010 and 68020. It results from interrupts, illegal instructions, privilege violations, A-line and F-line traps, format errors (illegal frame format discovered by RTE process) and the TRAP #n instruction. The value stored as the Program Counter depends on the exception type: if the instruction causing the exception is processable then it addresses the next instruction, otherwise it addresses the exception causing instruction.

The 6-word stack frame is used for CHK, CHK2, TRAPV, TRAPcc, cpTRAPcc and

Trace exceptions. It is similar to the 4-word format but includes the address of the faulting instruction. The Program Counter in this case always addresses the next instruction to be executed on exit from the exception.

The Throwaway stack frame is identical to the 4-word frame except for the format code. If an interrupt occurs while the processor is in the multi-task Master state (M bit set), the initial stack frame is built on the Master stack, the M bit is reset, changing the operating mode to Interrupt, and the stack frame is copied to the Interrupt stack before control is routed to the interrupt processing program.

The Coprocessor mid-instruction stack frame is similar to the 6-word frame but has four additional words below the faulting instruction address (i.e. at higher addresses). These contain the contents of the internal registers dealing with coprocessor communication.

(a)	Supervisor Stack (ISP or MSP)		(b)	Supervisor Stack (ISP or MSP)
SSP	SR		SSP	SR
SSP + 2	PC – high		SSP + 2	PC – high
SSP + 4	PC – low		SSP + 4	PC – low
SSP + 6	FFFF00vvvvvvvvv00		SSP + 6	FFFF00vvvvvvvvv00
SSP + 8	IR		SSP + 8	IR
SSP + 10	SSW		SSP + 10	SSW
SSP + 12	IP2		SSP + 12	IP2
SSP + 14	IP1		SSP + 14	IP1
SSP + 16	DF – high		SSP + 16	DF – high
SSP + 18	DF – low		SSP + 18	DF – low
SSP + 20	IR		SSP + 20	IR
SSP + 22	IR		SSP + 22	IR
SSP + 24	DOB – high		SSP + 24	IR
SSP + 26	DOB – low		SSP + 26	IR
SSP + 28	IR		SSP + 28	IR
SSP + 30	IR		SSP + 30	IR
			SSP + 32	IPA1 – high
			SSP + 34	IPA1 – low
			SSP + 36	IR
SR: Status Register			SSP + 38	IR
PC: Program Counter			SSP + 40	DOB – high
FFFF: Format code			SSP + 42	DOB – low
00vvvvvvvv00: Exception vector offset			SSP + 44	DIB – high
SSW: Special Status Word			SSP + 46	DIB – low
DF: Data Fault address			SSP + 48	— — IR — —
DOB: Data Output Buffer				
DIB: Data Input Buffer				(20 words)
IP2: Pipeline second stage				
IP1: Pipeline first stage				— — — — —
IPA1: Pipeline first stage address			SSP + 86	IR
IR: Internal Register				

Figure 4.7. 68020 Short (a) and long (b) bus cycle fault exception stack frames.

Figure 4.7. shows the two stack frames that may be created for address and bus error exceptions. The short format is formed when a bus cycle error occurs at an instruction boundary; the long format occurs in mid instruction when a greater number of processes could be at fault. Like the 68010, the bus cycle can be retried by either software emulation or processor rerun, after the condition which caused the error has been corrected. A Special Status Word (Figure 4.5) is provided in the frame giving information about the fault.

Return from exception

After the interrupt, error, emulation or other exception has been dealt with, control is returned to the interrupted program by the RTE instruction.

RTE on the 68000 and 68008 merely restores the Status Register and Program Counter from Supervisor stack and resumes execution at the restored PC address – whether in Supervisor or User space depends on the state of the S bit in the restored Status Register. Programs handling address and bus error exceptions, which stack five words of further information above the Status Register, must clean up the stack in preparation for RTE by removing the five additional words or a stacking error will result. In fact, bus error exceptions on the 68000 or 68008 are more likely to result in a warm restart, with stack reinitialised by the system, than in resumption of the interrupted program.

RTE on the 68010 and 68020 first checks the stack frame format code. If this is invalid then a format error exception ensues. If the format is valid and indicates a short or 4-word frame, then the SR and PC are restored as in the 68000 RTE process but with the SSP incremented by 8 to clear the format/vector word. The 6-word and Coprocessor frames of the 68020 are similarly cleared. Since the Throwaway frame is a second frame created to deal with interrupts, the RTE process must first clear the Throwaway frame and then clear the original frame.

When the format code indicates a bus cycle frame, data in the stack frame is checked for validity. Any anomaly in the data is classed as a format error and causes further exception processing. Only when the format code and data are validated does the RTE process continue to restore the context from stack. Should another bus cycle fault occur during context restoration the processor treats it as a sign of catastrophic system failure and enters the abnormal HALT state until external reset. Once the context has been restored successfully, the processor may rerun the faulting bus cycle if that has not already been emulated by the exception processing software – that it has is indicated by the Special Status Word (see Figures 4.4 and 4.5). A bus cycle fault occurring on the retry will cause further exception processing.

Chapter Five
Assembly Language Programming

Unlike high level languages which are, on the whole, portable across computer systems based on different processors, a machine code language is specific to one particular processor. Writing code that will control the processor's actions simply cannot be done without a preliminary basic knowledge of the machine's hardware features and the methods used for data organisation and access: this and other information specific to the 68000 family of processors has been the subject of preceding chapters. However, such system specific information cannot be used effectively or efficiently without the more conceptual knowledge of the software tools and techniques available to the machine code programmer. This more generally applicable aspect of assembly language programming is the subject of this chapter. Section A is about assemblers and section B discusses methods of program development.

A. ASSEMBLERS

Machine code is rarely written direct, even for those simple 8-bit processors which support relatively few addressing modes and consequently have very few instruction codes. For the 68000 it would be quite an impossible task to code directly more than the shortest subroutine: the number of possible permutations of source or destination Effective Address 3-bit modes and source or destination register numbers runs into many thousands, as a quick glance at Appendix D or E will show.

The normal method of producing machine code programs is initially to write a 'source program' in assembly (or assembler) language. This is a mnemonic language which utilises labels, arithmetic expressions, assembler directives and other features to make the task far less of a numerical nightmare. The source program is then run through an assembler program to generate the 'object program' machine code.

The standard assembler

Most processor manufacturers publish a set of assembler mnemonics to represent the numeric machine codes. Most also produce an assembler program which tends to standardise the forms and syntax used in programming their processor; standard 68000-series assembler conventions are given in Appendix C. However, there is no intrinsic reason why the standards published by the manufacturer should be followed by the writers of editor-assemblers and other machine level software. Provided that an assembler will produce the correct machine codes (i.e. those which cause the processor to effect the desired action), it may use any mnemonic or follow any syntactical rule.

In general, an assembler must conform to the basic rule of one assembly language instruction to a single machine code instruction. If not, the language stops being an assembler and becomes a compiler. An exception to this rule occurs with a class of assemblers known as 'macroassemblers', which allow multi-instruction 'macros' to be defined. At assembly, the macroassembler inserts the entire string of predefined instructions into the program for each occurrence of the macro command. Ultimately, if all instructions used in a program are macros, then it is virtually a compiled program.

Assemblers written for any processor rarely introduce new mnemonics, since those published by the manufacturers are universally accepted, and an attempt to do so would be commercial suicide. Other aspects of the assembly language are not so rigorously followed, however, and it is not uncommon to find that one assembler limits the size of labels to six upper-case alphabetic characters, whilst others allow labels of any length composed of any valid ASCII characters, or that the three letters EQU are used by one assembler to equate a numeric value to a label but the symbol '=' is required by another assembler for the same purpose. Generally speaking, the conventions used by any assembler are loosely based on the standard forms used by the manufacturer of the processor concerned but with additions and enhancements.

Assembler fields

Assembly language programs are usually written in a tabular style with columns known as 'fields'. These are normally of a fixed width and start at a fixed character position on the line. More sophisticated assemblers allow some latitude in both width and position of the fields provided that the correct 'delimiters' (characters used to separate the fields) are

```
Object program        Source program

LOCATION   CODE        LINE NO.  LABEL  MNEMONIC OPERAND   COMMENT


000010FA               00108     SB     EQU      #1        Set shift count.
000010FA               00109     *
000010FA   9355        00110     LOOP   SUB.W    D1,(A5)   Sub divisor
000010FC   6402        00111            BCC      TEST      skip if gone
000010FE   D355        00112            ADD.W    D1,(A5)   else add back.
00001100               00113     *
00001100   E398        00114     TEST   ROL.L    #SB,D0    Repeat for
00001102   65F6        00115            BCS      LOOP      dividend bits.
00001104               00116     *
00001104   4E75        00117            RTS                Exit when done.
```

Figure 5.1. Sample assembler listing showing all fields.

used. A minimum of two fields is essential but four or five are usual, and there may be as many as seven fields in the listing of a complete source-cum-object program (see Figure 5.1). The first two fields, Location and Code, are not part of the source program and can only be listed after assembly.

Location

This field belongs to the object program and gives the address of the first word, high order byte, of the machine code instruction. It is usually given in hexadecimal.

Code

This is the actual object program consisting entirely of machine code instructions. It is usually given in hexadecimal and often listed in word format, split into the instruction word, or words, and extension words.

Line number

This is optional but if present is the first field in the source program. It is mainly for the convenience of the programmer during writing, editing and debugging and is often produced automatically by the assembler rather than needing to be typed in. Some assemblers accept several instructions on one line but most do not.

  Assembler directives, full comment lines and blank lines are each numbered. The number is usually given in decimal.

Label

This is the first necessary field in the source program. Programs may be written without the use of labels but they do make life easier. A label may be placed against any instruction or programmed data, or it may be equated to a value. At assembly, the label is used as the address of the instruction or data, or as the equated data.

Mnemonic

This is the abbreviated name of the operation effected by an instruction, e.g. ADDX. Assemblers also expect any directives, such as **ORG** (origin) to appear in this field. See Appendices D and E for the standard mnemonics of 68000-series instructions.

Operand or address

This gives the source and destination immediate data, register or memory reference part of the assembler instruction, e.g. $-(A5),D\emptyset$. In certain cases no operand or only the source or destination operand need be given. Operand expressions may include labels (which must appear somewhere in the label field) as the equivalent of addresses or immediate data. See Appendix C for the symbols which may be used in the operand field and Appendices D and E for standard allowed operand forms.

Comment

This field is an entirely optional part of the source program but one to which any programmer should pay the most attention – it is absolutely essential for understanding the program during debugging and later updating. Apart from comments restricted to the comment field, most assemblers accept complete comment lines if preceded by a distinguishing character, e.g. the asterisk '*'.

Delimiters and terminators

All assemblers recognise certain characters as delimiters, separating fields or parts of fields, or terminators, denoting that no more characters are to be found in a field or on a line. Some are common to all assemblers but others vary.

Space ( ) Required after a label, after the mnemonic and after the operand field if followed by a comment. At least one space is needed before any instruction mnemonic not preceded by a label, though usually mnemonics are written in a column starting some 9 or 10 characters from the beginning of the line.

Colon (:) May be required to terminate a label which does not start in the first character position on the line. The colon is used in the 68020 operand field to join two operands (see DIVSL, Table E7.8). Some assemblers may use the colon to terminate each instruction on a multi-instruction line.

Comma (,) Always used to separate the source from the destination operand. No spaces are allowed before or after the comma. The comma is also used to separate the operand addends (i.e. those registers and immediate data which are added to form the effective address) in indexed forms.

Semicolon (;) May be used in obscure 68000 assemblers to precede comments – a standard set by assemblers of Z80, 8086 and other popular codes.

Slash (/) or backslash (\) May be used in other obscure assemblers to precede comments, though use of the slash character is unwise in this context since it is used in the operand field to delimit a list of registers for the MOVEM instruction (see Table D7.2 and The operand field, below).

Period (.) May be required to begin a label. A period is used to append a single letter operation size code to mnemonics, viz.B, .W and .L for byte, word and long word.

Asterisk (*) Used to indicate a full line comment. An asterisk may also be used to denote that the address should be computed relative to the current location counter (the assembler variable which keeps track of instruction location during assembly and acts as the equivalent of the Program Counter).

At cost (@) or other ASCII symbols may be required by obscure assemblers to begin labels.

Carriage return Terminates a line.

The label field

An assembler will usually set an upper limit to the character length of labels. It may also not accept certain characters. Most assemblers will accept a label beginning with an upper-case letter and composed of letters and numbers. Some will accept (or demand) an initial period (.) or other special character. Other characters acceptable to most assemblers are those commonly used to delimit filenames, such as period (.), dash (–), underline (_), dollar ($) or backslash (\). Spaces are generally not accepted, since most assemblers recognise a space as a label terminator. Some assemblers will not accept labels that begin with (or sometimes that contain) a standard instruction mnemonic.

Some assemblers accept labels of any length and composed of any valid ASCII character (see Appendix A). Others place restrictions on what will be allowed. Since invalid labels will be thrown out as errors during assembly, no great harm ensues (usually) by trying everything – though a great deal of time can be wasted.

● Beware of the assembler which accepts labels such as END-OF-FILE, END-OF-DATA and END-OF-GOODNESS-KNOWS-WHAT but uses only the first six characters.

● Beware of using ADDX, DIVSL and other instruction mnemonics as labels, or even embedded within labels. Your current assembler might accept them but your next one certainly won't.

●Beware of labels such as LØØØ1, LØØØ2, etc. They might be short and sequential but you'll wonder why you put them there. Write labels that help to document the program, such as UPDATE-LINE.

●Beware of incorporating obscure and little used ASCII characters like PART` SECTION^LOOP. Few assemblers accept these characters and, perhaps, you meant to type PART^SECTIONLOOP` .

●Beware of the labels XXXXX and XXXXXX – if you don't confuse them your assembler will!

● Do standardise your label usage. If possible, name subroutines with a label that describes their action. Begin all labels used in a subroutine with the first two or three letters of the subroutine name label. Use labels terminating in LOOP or LP at the start of loops. Use labels terminating in X, XIT, END, ND, OUT or RET for the single exit point from each of your structured subroutines, sticking to one form throughout the program.

●Do not be afraid to assign more than one label to a single instruction or datum, always provided that your assembler will allow the practice. If embedded loops have a common start location, use one label to designate the outer loop followed by a second to designate the inner loop, as is done with OUTLOOP and INLOOP in Figure 5.2. The subroutine call label, SEND, also addresses the instruction MOVE.B (AØ),DØ, and so three labels, all with separate uses, are converted to one address at assembly. SEND may be assembled as an absolute address or used to calculate a displacement, depending on the addressing mode used for the subroutine call; OUTLOOP and INLOOP are used only in the calculation of branch displacements. The label READY, which appears between SEND and OUTLOOP, converts to the equated value $A4, and not to an address.

Figure 5.3. demonstrates the value of multiple labelling when used to address the same data in different ways. Each block of eight bytes, used as the pixel codes for playing card symbols, could be individually addressed by the labels HEART, DIAMOND, CLUB and SPADE. Some games, however, might need to choose one at random and this would be better done by generating a random number, Ø to 3, multiplying it by 8 and adding it to the base address CARDS. Should only a black card or a red card be wanted, it can be found by adding a randomly generated Ø or 1, multiplied by 8, to base address BLACK or RED.

The mnemonic field

All instruction mnemonics (see Appendices D and E) properly belong to the mnemonic field but so do various other words. These are the pseudo-operations or assembler

```
* "SEND" - Data output subroutine.
* (A0 + 0): input port, (A0 + 2): ouput port.
* (A1 + 0): start of data block.
*
SEND                                   Subroutine call label
*
* Define constants
*
READY    EQU.B    #$A4                 Device ready value at input port.
*
* Loop, outputting one data byte until null terminator found.
*
OUTLOOP                                Fall into inner wait loop.
*
* Loop, waiting until device ready: port read = READY constant.
*
INLOOP   MOVE.B   (A0),D0              Read device input port and
         CMPI.B   #READY,D0            test if READY signal received,
         BNE      INLOOP               looping until it is.
*
* Ready signal is received, send output data byte and address next byte,
* repeat until all data sent and null terminator found then exit SEND.
*
         MOVE.B   (A1)+,2(A0)          Output one data byte, index next
         TST.B    (A1)                 and test for null terminator,
         BNE      OUTLOOP              continue until full block output.
*
         RTS                           Exit, all data sent, (A1) = 0.
```

Figure 5.2. Multiple labelling in program loops.

```
*
* Set up graphics character bit pattern table for CARDS.
*
CARDS                                  Card graphics table base address.
*
RED                                    Red cards base address.
*
HEART     DC.L     #$44EEFEFE          Address HEART or CARDS + (8*0)
          DC.L     #$7C381000          or RED + (8*0).
*
DIAMOND   DC.L     #$10387CFE          Address DIAMOND or CARDS + (8*1)
          DC.L     #$7C381000          or RED + (8*1).
*
BLACK                                  Black cards base address.
*
CLUB      DC.L     #$103854FE          Address CLUB or CARDS + (8*2)
          DC.L     #$54101000          or BLACK + (8*0).
*
SPADE     DC.L     #$10387CFE          Address SPADE or CARDS + (8*3)
          DC.L     #$FE541000          or BLACK + (8*1).
*
```

Figure 5.3. Multiple labelling in data reference.

directives which are used to communicate to the assembler, initialise data in memory or assign values to labels. Many of these directives require some form of operand, usually immediate data or addresses, in the operand field. They are not part of the program proper. Standard 68000-series assembler directives are given in Table C2. in Appendix C.

The list is not definitive but forms the core of the pseudo operations expected from a good assembler.

There is little room for creative expression in the mnemonic field of ordinary assemblers since only entries of a clearly defined form are allowed. If you are using a macroassembler, the macro command names appear in the mnemonic field: the same care should be taken with them as with labels, perhaps more so since mnemonic strings are certainly not allowed as macro names.

The operand field

The expressions found in the operand field are either values transmitted to the assembler by way of directives or the source and destination operands pertaining to an instruction. Directives require immediate data (numeric or ASCII), or arithmetic expressions which reduce to a usable data form, or labels which equate to an address or data. Instruction operands may take any of the allowed forms given in Appendices D and E.

Numeric data may be given in base 1Ø (decimal), base 16 (hexadecimal), base 8 (octal) or base 2 (binary). Decimal is the default case and is usually accepted without a preceding symbol, though the ampersand (&) may be used for clarity. Hexadecimal data should begin with the dollar symbol ($), octal with the at cost symbol (@) and binary with the percent symbol (%).

Character data may be given, and the assembler will convert to the ASCII codes (or any other internal coding system that may be in use). Character strings should be enclosed in single quotes, e.g. 'CHARACTERS'. Note that the single quote symbol (') cannot be included in character form but must be specified as the ASCII code 39 ($27).

Immediate data must be preceded by the number sign (#). Data not preceded by this sign are taken as address. Some assemblers may allow the number sign to be omitted where immediate data are expected.

The use of parentheses to indicate indirect addressing differs between the 68020 and earlier 68000-series processors. In the earlier implementations, displacements to the indirect address expression are given outside the parentheses, e.g. #$FF(A1), whereas the 68020 demands that the parentheses enclose both displacement and Base Register, e.g. (#$FF,A1). Both forms given in the example subtract 1 from (actually, add −1 to) the contents of register A1 and use the resultant value as the memory address of the operand data, but the 68000 form would suggest that the displacement is added to the value fetched from memory at the indirect address. Nevertheless, the form demanded by the particular assembler must be used.

Most assemblers accept some sort of arithmetic or logical expression written in the operand field. At assembly, the expression is resolved, truncated to the operation size if too large, and used as a single integer value, either as data or as an address. Previously defined labels may be used as parts of the expression. You should keep such expressions simple – it is the computer's job, not the assembler's, to perform arithmetic.

The comment field

Almost every assembler allows comments to be written in the source program after each instruction, usually also as complete lines of program information. This facility should be neither neglected nor abused. Although it may be, and very often is, tedious to include plain English explanations for every instruction in a long program, especially when the actions caused by single instructions are virtually insignificant compared with the overall program operation, it is more tedious weeks or months later, when the program needs updating, to spend hours trying to understand what task is performed by a particular section of the program or even discover why you included it in the first place. It is yet more arduous trying to understand the actions of another programmer's uncommented source program.

Badly commented code can be just as difficult to understand as uncommented code. Comments should describe effects wrought on the program environment by individual instructions and by identifiably separate parts of the program – from sections varying in size from two word loops, through page length subroutines to complete modules. Each section of program may be introduced by one or more full line comments that explain the overall effect of the section and its role as part of the complete program. Comments written after each instruction then clarify the method used to obtain the desired effect.

Comments that refer specifically to register names and processor actions are, on the whole, bad comments. The explanation of what the program is doing at any particular point should use whatever meaning has been assigned to the register values, and the description should be of the changes made to those values. Above all, comments should not seek to expand the meaning implicit in the mnemonic and operands of an instruction. Instructions like 'ADD.LD∅,D2' commented as 'add 32-bit value from Data Register ∅ to 32-bit value in Data Register 2' superbly explain an action that any competent programmer could work out, given time, but they don't tell anyone that D∅ contains the character position along a screen line, that D2 contains the address of the first character on that line and that the result is the address of the required character position. A comment like 'add char offset to line start giving char pos' would be far more useful. Comments used educationally are, of course, an exception to this rule.

B. PROGRAM DEVELOPMENT

The art (some would say science) of program development is a subject that has filled many multi-volume books. This section can do no more than provide a few reasons why the writing of programs should follow a logical sequence of development and offer one tried and tested system.

No programmer should rush straight into coding his or her ideas, either on paper or directly into the computer. Even small programs are the complex interactions of a set or sets of values, and unless those interactions are carefully planned and the results controlled, errors will occur. At the level of specific action (i.e. machine code operation) the possibility for error is practically limitless but, thinking in terms only of general processes, the coding of unplanned ideas can give rise to many types of error, among which are:

● processes are omitted

- processes are carried out on the wrong data
- incorrect processes are performed
- incomplete processes are performed
- unworkable processes are attempted
- inefficient processes are performed
- unnecessary processes are written into the program
- separate processes are inextricably tangled together
- processes are split and scattered through the program

The possibility of gross structural errors occurring in any program can be minimised, if not completely avoided, by following a planned sequence of program definition and design. There are four stages to the sequence which effect a gradual transition from analysis of the problem, or job to be done, to coding of the program.

1. Job definition

The essential first step in writing a program is to produce a clear definition of purpose. The purpose may appear obvious: word processors, chess programs and pools forecasters do what their names suggest, on the whole, but what specific task does an accounts program perform? Does it stop at bookkeeping or go on to produce a trading account, revenue accounts and balance sheets? Does it, or should it, analyse and forecast future profits? Coming back to the word processor – do you need it only for writing letters of a few pages or for writing a book with hundreds of manuscript pages and large numbers of tables and line figures, like this one? Is it, in fact, a word processor that you require or a graphics processor? Only by analysing the extent of the job can you begin to specify the type of program required.

A good maxim to follow when defining any program is that it should do just one job and should do that job properly. You are less likely to win a fortune by combining a football pools forecaster with a horse racing form selection program (the chances of Leeds United Football Club winning the 3.30 at Cheltenham are quite slim) than by writing entirely separate programs. If need be you can always write a higher level program with the sole task of offering other programs on a menu and calling them up when selected.

Job definition should produce quite a lot of documentation. This should be in three parts:

1. *The initial state* – a definition of the raw data, the input or the state of the system before the action takes place.
2. *The transformation* – a definition of the job or process (or processes), which could be used on the content of part 1 to give the desired result in part 3.
3. *The terminal state* – a definition of the finished information, or output, from the transformation process.

To put it concisely, the job definition should describe what we've got, what we want and how we set about getting it. As an example, applying the three-part analysis to chess gives:

1. The initial board state: a formal definition of a chess board, of each piece and its start location on the board.
2. The playing rules: a formal statement of all legal chess moves.
3. The game finished state: a formal definition of checkmate, draw, resign and upset board. The latter may be a problem in computerised chess.

Referring to a game of chess as a transformational process with initial input of a laid out chess board and terminal output of a draw or win position may be a strange concept but it is the best method of defining the job that the program must do. However, as defined so far the program would play a rather poor game; knowledge of which moves are legal is not enough to transform the initial state to the required terminal state. Although the object of the complete program has been defined, there is still not enough information to begin designing a computer program that will play chess. The process has to be subdivided into smaller tasks and, within the context of the complete game, the job of each task must also be defined – again with the three-part analysis of input or initial state, process, and output or terminal state. The compilation of all sub-task definitions gives a more detailed description of the overall task; the description of the overall task is a summary of the sub-task definitions.

A complete specification of the program's job will be structured, giving first the overall purpose, then the purpose of each task, then of each sub-task. The process of subdividing and formally specifying the transformation that must be applied to the subdivision is repeated until a bottom layer is reached, below which no transformation process can be defined without resorting to actual computational processes.

2. Structured design

If the job definition has been carried out correctly and fully, it will have a structure that can be mapped directly on to a program design. Each task and sub-task will correspond to a discrete program section and there will be a system of task dependency similar to the structure chart shown in Figure 5.4. Every job definition is translated into a formal description of the computational process required to produce the transformation: no regard is yet paid to the target code.

The most important point about structure in a computer program is that it exists solely for the benefit of the programmer. The structural awareness of the cpu is generally limited to the extent of processing a single instruction (but see the description of the 68010 loop mode in Chapter 1). Structure is a device which allows the programmer to see clearly the dependence of some process on another and to isolate program sections and levels of

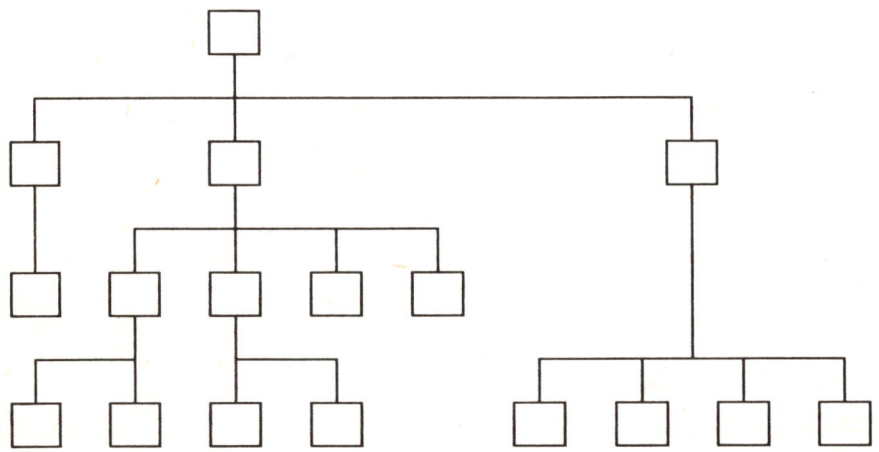

Figure 5.4. Part of a structure chart.

operation during all the stages of definition, design, coding, testing, debugging and later updating. The method implies the production of good documentation at each stage, and this acts like a route map through the finished program – the documentation from the several stages being rather like overlays giving different types of information.

Every program has a natural structure which is entirely dependent on the necessary transformations discovered in the job definition and which owes nothing to the code in which the program will finally be written. However, the natural structure may be ill-balanced, with some processes giving rise to a large number of offspring sub-processes. If the number of processes extending from a parent process is greater than about seven or eight, the structure will be difficult to follow (see Figure 5.5 (a)). This is the stage at which to give nature a helping hand and insert one or more intermediate level processes to aid clarity, shown in Figure 5.5(b).

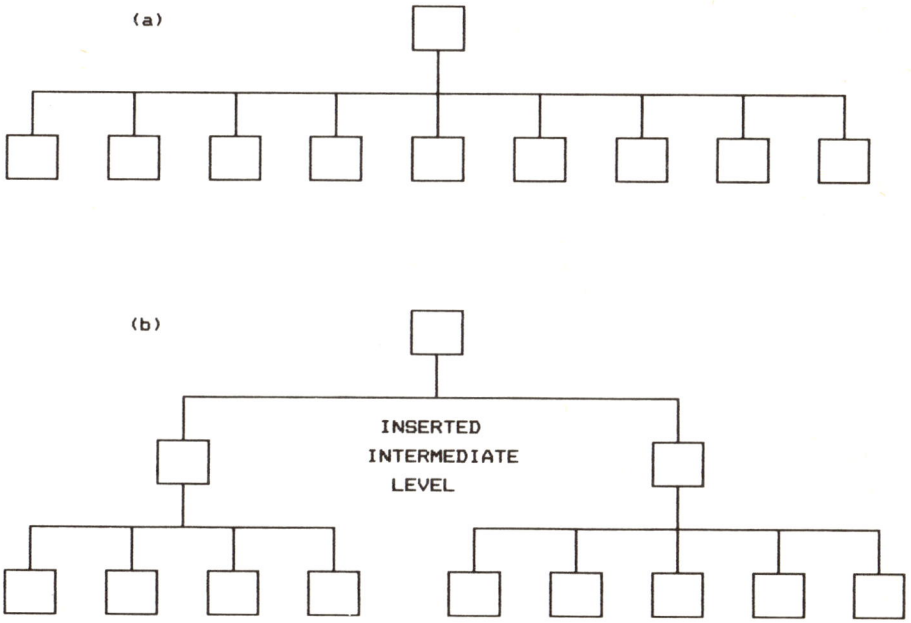

Figure 5.5. Structure (a) crowded, (b) clearer.

3. Program flow: sequence, iteration, selection

The method used to define the program's main job and its sub-tasks, and translate those definitions into descriptions of computational processes, is basically data driven. The design structure is based more on the structure of the input data, or initial state, than on the flow of that data through the various processes. Some notion of the order in which transformations are applied is given by the dependency structure of the design charts, if the convention of reading from left to right is followed, but on the whole program flow notation cannot be superimposed directly on the structure charts – and this is essential for coding. The structure charts have to be converted into program flow charts (or flow diagrams).

Flow charts generally display far more detail than the structure charts. They are diagrams of how control is to flow through the finished program and each of its parts. Not only do they delineate the order in which the transformational processes shown in the structure chart are executed, but they also identify the purely computer directed processes of input, output, module and subroutine call and, most importantly, decision.

All flow charts are built from a standard set of open box shapes with connecting lines of flow. Templates are available, which contain about twenty of the standard symbols labelled with the normal meanings, and should conform to ISO standard 1028, ANSI X3.5-1970 or BS4058. Figure 5.6 shows the more important of these symbols.

Flow lines in flow charts are commonly supplied with arrowheads to show the direction of flow. These are totally unnecessary and lead to unconventional and pathological program design. Omitting arrowheads from the flow charts means that only a very limited

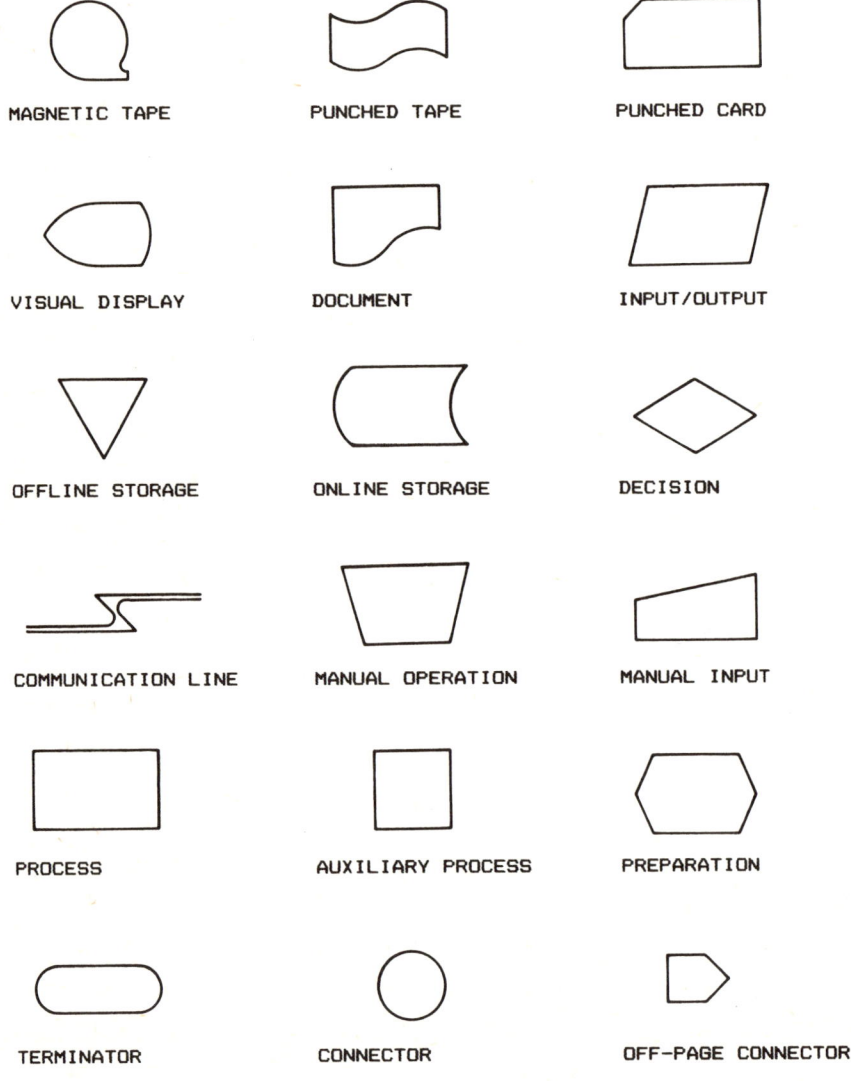

Figure 5.6. Flow chart symbols.

set of program constructs, with standardised flow directions, can be used, and these ensure that the subsequent coding will be clear, simple and quick to write.

The three basic types of construct are sequence, iteration and selection. Each of these is a discrete entity and could be replaced in a less detailed chart by a single box with flow entering at the top and leaving at the bottom. Internally, flow may be split (selection and iteration) and may flow upwards (iteration) but it does so only by standard rules which produce unique, easily readable flow chart patterns.

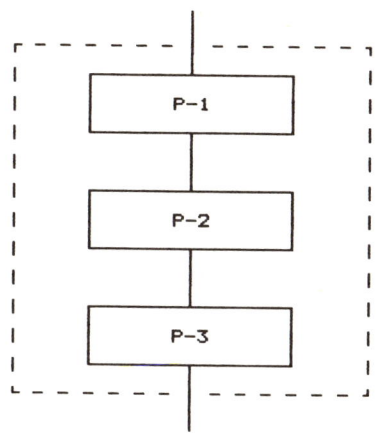

Figure 5.7. Sequence of three processes.

Sequence is shown in Figure 5.7. Flow goes straight down through all included processes in turn. The broken line shows the extent of the construct.

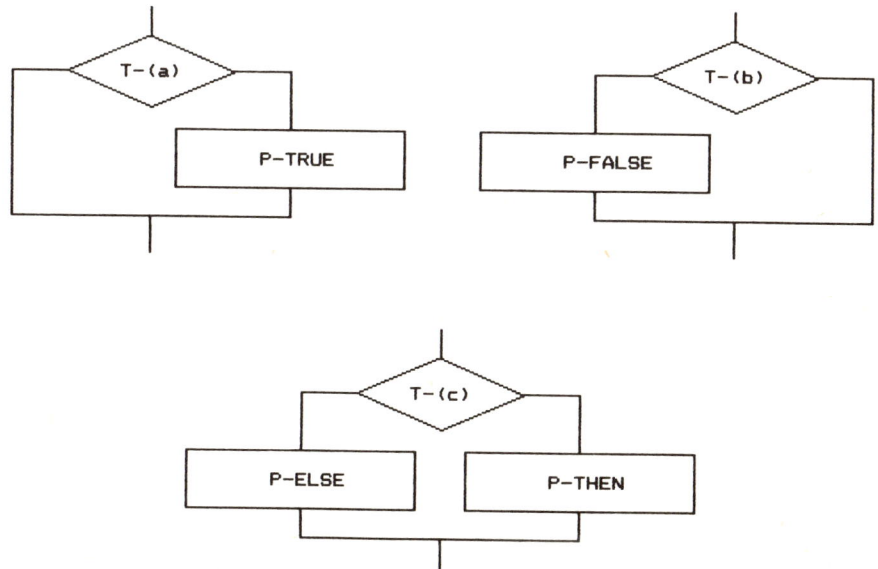

Figure 5.8. Selection: (a) skip if false, (b) skip if true, (c) IF...THEN...ELSE....

Selection is a rather more complex phenomenon. It may involve a selection between two mutually exclusive processes or a decision whether or not to execute a single process. The decision is purely binary with only two possible results, and these determine left and right paths. The left flow path is taken if the test result is false and the right path if the result is true. Only one flow path can be taken at any one occurrence of the selection. Diagrammatically the flow paths join before exit from the construct, symbolising program continuation at the same point whatever decision is taken; flow line T-junctions always indicate the end of a selection construct. Figure 5.8 shows the three possible simple selection constructs.

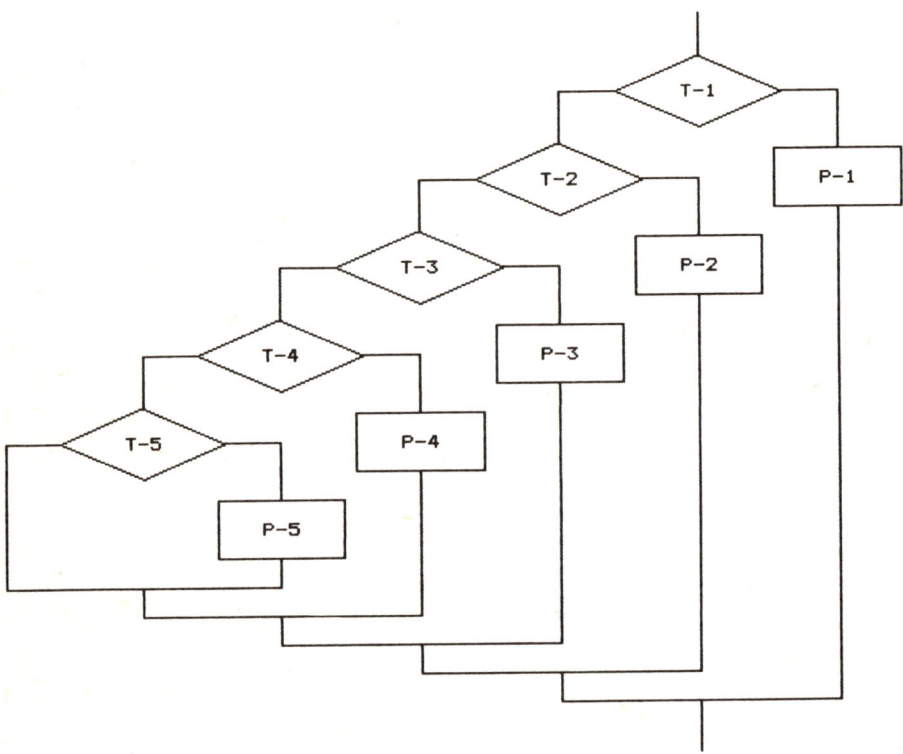

Figure 5.9. Case structure.

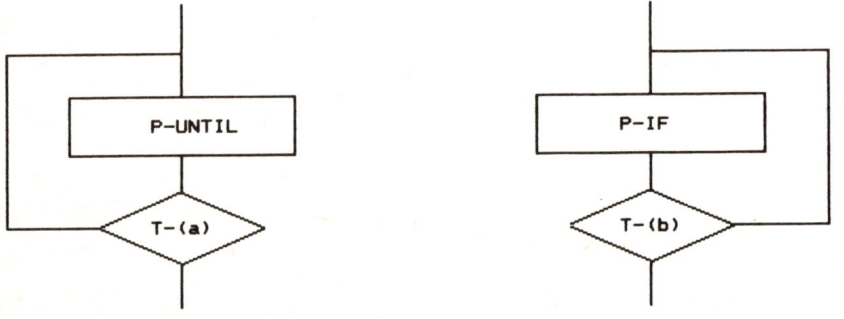

Figure 5.10. Iteration: (a) REPEAT UNTIL (true), (b) REPEAT IF (true).

A more complex decision structure selects between several processes on the state of some input variable. This is the Case structure, which corresponds to the ON...GOTO... or ON...GOSUB... command in Basic. Figure 5.9 shows that this is merely a group of embedded selection constructs – each successive selection being an expansion of one of the anonymous process boxes in Figure 5.8(b). The leftmost selection in the Case structure shows skipping for a no-match situation.

Iteration also involves a type of decision. In this case the decision is whether or not to repeat the process *just executed*. This means that all processes within the iteration construct are executed at least once. The structured language terms for this type of iteration are REPEAT UNTIL (i.e. loop back if the test result is false) and REPEAT IF (i.e. loop if the test result is true). Side joining of the flow lines always indicates the start of an iteration construct. The flow line leaving the bottom of the decision box is a 'fallthrough' line: REPEAT UNTIL gives the fallthrough condition and REPEAT IF gives the looping condition. The two forms are shown in Figure 5.10.

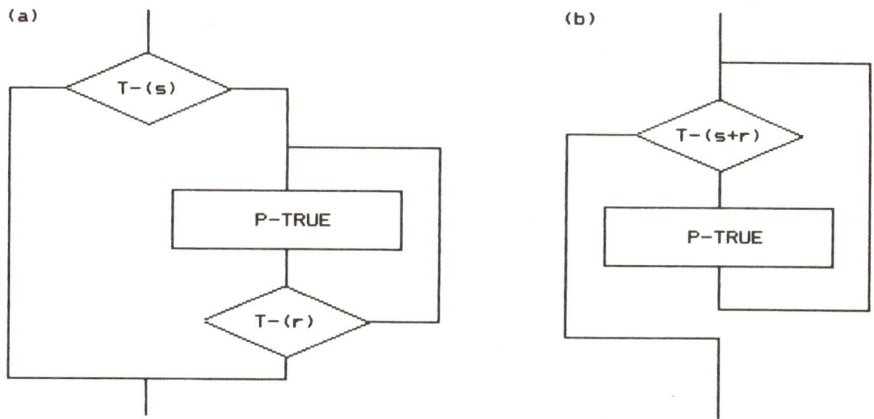

Figure 5.11. DO WHILE (true): (a) well structured, (b) pathological.

One other type of iteration often found in structured languages is the DO WHILE, which allows execution of the process to be skipped initially or to take place repeatedly until some specified condition fails to hold. It is, as Figure 5.11 (a) shows, a composite of a selection construct with an embedded REPEAT IF construct. The DO WHILE shown in Figure 5.11 (b) is the pathological form of the same construct: the flow line loops back without any decision having been made, and the exit flow is from the side of the construct.

A more pathological form of DO WHILE which may develop from the form of Figure 5.11 (b) is shown in Figure 5.12 (a). The bad structure makes it difficult to determine just how many times each of the two processes (P1 and P2) may be executed and exactly what the tests T1 and T2 determine – it appears that T2 tests a result of P1 and overrides T1. A more readable structure is given in Figure 5.12(b), where T2 determines only whether P2 is performed and a compound third test (T3 = T1 *and* T2) decides if the REPEAT IF condition still holds. Because of the singularity of most machine code decision tests, several test-and-branch combinations may have to be performed in sequence to implement a single compound decision shown at the flow chart stage.

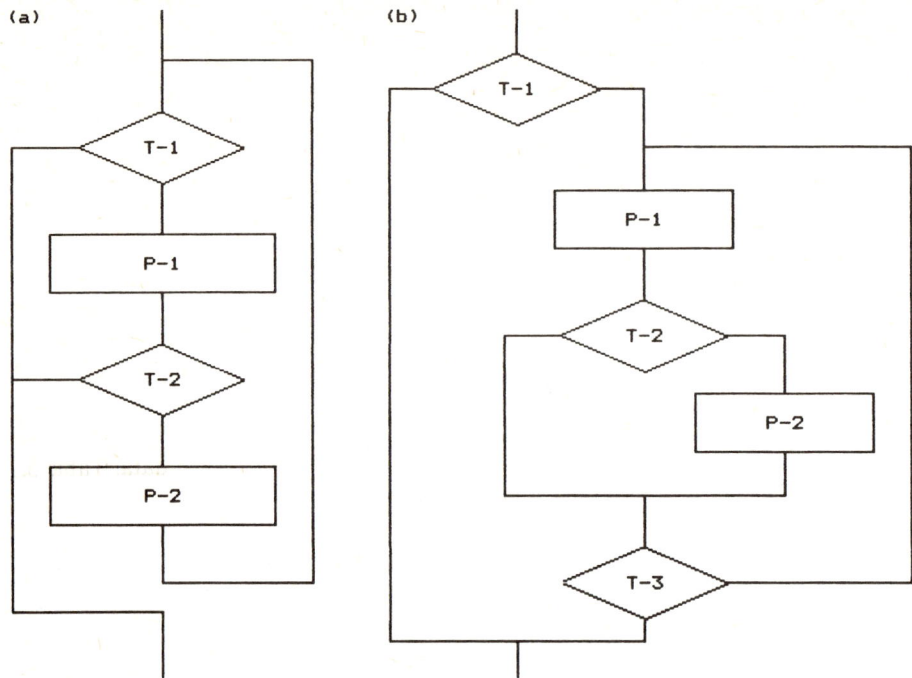

Figure 5.12. DO WHILE compound tests: (a) pathological, (b) structured.

4. Coding, testing, debugging

Transition from flow chart to actual program code should be quite straightforward. The lowest level boxes in the flow chart will correspond to no more than a dozen or so instructions in even the least sophisticated processor languages, but in 68000-series code most will translate to a single instruction. This level contains the basic action of the program, effecting transformation on data fed from the next higher level and passing the result back. The higher levels of the structure deal mostly with testing of conditions and control of the program.

This distinction between levels is important in coding and testing programs. The process should begin at the topmost level with all called processes written as 'stubs' returning pseudo-result data, or sometimes merely returning control to the calling process. In many cases setting of the condition codes to different configurations will show whether or not the calling process operates correctly. Testing the top levels virtually guarantees that the control logic of the program is correct before too much work has gone into coding the low level transformation processes. It is far easier to correct any error discovered in the program logic at this stage than when large sections of detailed program have already been written. Coding continues downwards, level by level, expanding the stubs to full processes and opening up the processes of next lower level as new stubs. With all higher levels already proven, any problem can occur only in the level under test and, furthermore, can be isolated to a single branch of the structure – in effect, one process box of the structure chart.

Testing of each section should use test data at the extremes of the range of data which will be encountered. For example, a program section acting on ASCII hexadecimal digits and not on other values would need to be tested with:

$2F (/) $3Ø (Ø) as low end of group Ø-9
$39 (9) $3A (:) as high end of group Ø-9
$4Ø (@) $41 (A) as low end of group A-F
$46 (F) $47 (G) as high end of group A-F

This should ensure that all valid ASCII digit codes within the two groups produce the correct response. It also determines the response to invalid codes, though only those with bit 7 reset. Corresponding codes with bit 7 set (i.e. $AF,$BØ,$B9,$BA,$CØ,$C1,$C6 and $C7) should also be used in the test to ensure that the code will not accept invalid ASCII codes.

The standard tool for testing and debugging a machine code program is the machine code monitor. Unlike editor-assemblers, which allow changes to be made only to the source program, the monitor is used on the already assembled object program or object code to alter the contents of individual memory locations and registers. Selected program sections may thus be tested in isolation with a range of initial or test data. Table 5.1 describes the normal features of machine code monitors.

Command	Meaning
Breakpoint	Insert software interrupt at a given address to cause monitor interrupt of program.
Copy	Transfer contents of a specified block of memory to a specified location.
Disassemble	Produce source code equivalent of the object code beginning at a specified location.
Dump	Display contents of a specified block of memory, usually as hexadecimal values.
Enter	Direct keyboard entry of code or data, usually either as hexadecimal values or as ASCII.
Exit	Exit monitor to the operating system or other system software.
Fill	Fill a specified block of memory with input value (or sequence of values).
Go	Execute program at address contained in displayed Program Counter.
Jump	Execute program at input address.
Load	Load machine code program or data file from tape or disk to memory.
Register	Display contents of user accessible registers.
Save	Save machine code program or data file from memory to tape or disk.
Single-Step	Execute program one instruction at a time, on key press, displaying all register contents and current instruction at each step.
System	Alter computer system parameters, e.g. print speed, input/output rate, display mode, etc.
Trace	Print out the control path of the program during its execution – either the address of every instruction executed or the address of each branch, jump and subroutine call destination.

Table 5.1. Machine code monitor commands.

General purpose subroutines

Coding can often be speeded up by recourse to a library of general purpose subroutines. These are not subroutines capable of performing many tasks, but rather single task routines which are useful in many different programs – for example, square root calculation, random number generation and graphics screen access. When such a routine is first written, if it is designed to operate correctly not only in the current situation but in any situation, it can be saved as an independent program and used without the need to retest in subsequent programs having different conditions.

For multi-program use of this kind, a library routine must meet certain standards of operation which ensure that it will work correctly in different contexts without corrupting any part of the program or system. Its job, actions and input and output requirements have to be clearly documented to show exactly what it does and how it can be fitted in to a program. For several years, routines of this description, written for many different processors including the 68000-series, have been published as 'datasheets' in the *Personal Computer World* magazine feature, Sub Set. The datasheet documentation is of a standard form designed to be written as part of the source program listing. The sort of information it contains is practically identical to that produced by the four stage development of complete programs – though obviously less extensive. Figure 5.13 shows the datasheet documentation format written to 68000 assembler standards and describes the type of information included in each section.

```
*****************************************************************
*
* = NAME          Label by which the routine is named and called, with
*                 a short verbal expansion explaining the name.
*
*****************************************************************
*
*                 (General definition and structure)
*
* JOB             A definition of the task performed by the routine,
*                 including any special considerations such as whether
*                 or not the routine is time critical. This corresponds
*                 to stage 1 of the four-stage sequence.
*
* ACTION          The algorithm or method used in the routine, usually
*                 written in a structured language. This corresponds to
*                 stages 2 and 3 of the four-stage sequence.
*
*---------------------------------------------------------------
*
*                 (System implementation)
*
* CPU             The processor (or processors) for which the routine is
*                 written. This may include essential details such as
*                 clock frequency specification.
*
* HARDWARE        Any particular computer or hardware configuration
*                 required by the routine, specifying exactly what
*                 hardware is used and affected.
*
* SOFTWARE        The name and necessary details of any other software
*                 used by the routine (e.g. subroutines called by it).
*
*---------------------------------------------------------------
```

Figure 5.13. Datasheet documentation format.

```
*
*                      (Operation details)
*
* INPUT                All variables, parameters and other data passed to the
*                      routine by the calling program, this includes the
*                      contents of registers, information on stack, condition
*                      codes or specified memory contents.
*
* OUTPUT               All result information passed back from the routine to
*                      the calling program. Also all registers, condition
*                      codes, stack and memory changed by the routine.
*
* ERRORS               Any possible error which could result from wrong use
*                      of the routine - e.g. input of invalid data if the
*                      routine does not check input, interrupts causing stack
*                      overwrite if the routine manipulates the hardware
*                      stack pointer.
*
* REG USE              All registers (including CCR) disturbed by the use of
*                      the routine, either for passing data or information or
*                      corrupted during execution of the routine.
*
* STACK USE            The maximum number of BYTES that could be added to the
*                      hardware stack during execution of the routine. This
*                      includes all register saves to stack and all deeper
*                      subroutine calls. It does not include the 4-byte
*                      return address to the calling program.
*                      If input Address registers are used as software stack
*                      pointers, the software stack use should also be
*                      included here.
*
* RAM USE              Any directly addressed read/write memory used either
*                      for passing information to or from the routine or as
*                      workspace by the routine.
*
* LENGTH               The total number of bytes occupied by the assembled
*                      object code, including any data or workspace appended
*                      to the routine.
*
* CYCLES               This section is optional for routines which are not
*                      time critical (most aren't - those which are include
*                      printer, disk and other peripheral drivers, delays and
*                      time sensitive machine or system control routines).
*                      For critical timing, the exact number of clock periods
*                      taken by the process must be given (if input is
*                      variable then a variable expression must be used).
*                      For non-critical timing, a maximum and/or close
*                      approximation will suffice.
*
*-----------------------------------------------------------------------------
*
*                      (Classification - see notes in next section)
*
* CLASS 2              -discreet        *interruptable      *promable
* -**---               -reentrant       -relocatable        -robust
*
*****************************************************************************
*
* ... The source program (and assembled object code) listing appears in
* ... this section, commented and interspersed with full line comments.
*
*
* Further notes:  CLASS
*
*                 Six criteria indicating situations where the routine
*                 may be safely used as written - either as object code
*                 or source code. Only if all criteria are met is the
*                 routine designated CLASS 1.
*
*                 '*' indicates the condition is satisfied.
*                 '-' indicates the condition is not satisfied.
*
```

Figure 5.13 (contd)

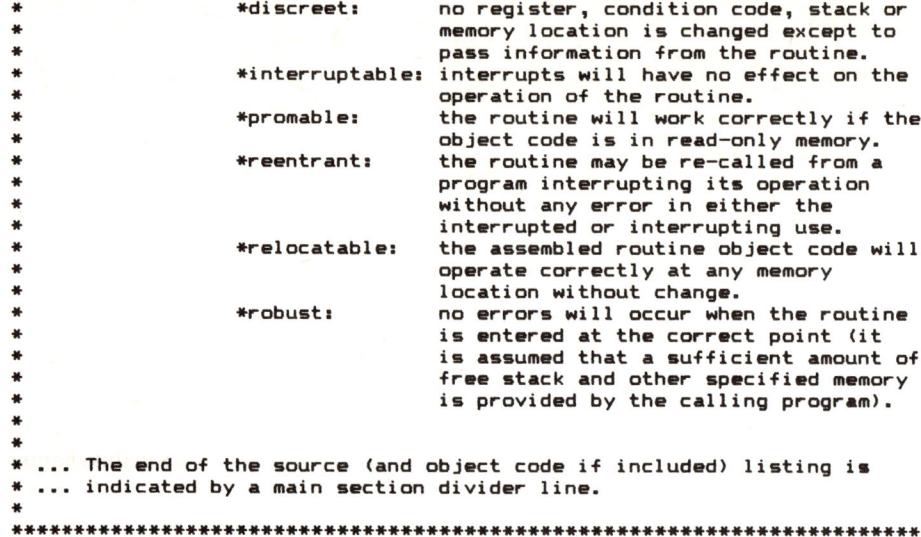

```
*
*                  *discreet:      no register, condition code, stack or
*                                  memory location is changed except to
*                                  pass information from the routine.
*                  *interruptable: interrupts will have no effect on the
*                                  operation of the routine.
*                  *promable:      the routine will work correctly if the
*                                  object code is in read-only memory.
*                  *reentrant:     the routine may be re-called from a
*                                  program interrupting its operation
*                                  without any error in either the
*                                  interrupted or interrupting use.
*                  *relocatable:   the assembled routine object code will
*                                  operate correctly at any memory
*                                  location without change.
*                  *robust:        no errors will occur when the routine
*                                  is entered at the correct point (it
*                                  is assumed that a sufficient amount of
*                                  free stack and other specified memory
*                                  is provided by the calling program).
*
*
* ... The end of the source (and object code if included) listing is
* ... indicated by a main section divider line.
*
******************************************************************************
```

Figure 5.13 (contd)

Library routines of this sort cannot always be slotted into programs without any changes having to be made. One reason why this might be so is that the registers used for input and output by the subroutine do not match those used by the calling program. This can be rectified either by using 'interface' routines between the program and the subroutine to exchange register contents or by changing the registers used in the subroutine itself. If only the actual registers are changed without any other alteration to instructions, then the routine should operate correctly without the need for extensive tests.

Chapter Six
Data Structures

Much code is written to address, store or retrieve data, or key information pertaining to data, held in various forms usually referred to as structures. The routines in this chapter act on some of the basic structures used for data storage: the stack, the queue and the array.

The routines are not necessarily the quickest, or shortest, or the most elegant, or the easiest to follow – but neither are they the slowest, longest, most clumsy or most obscure methods available. They do have the redeeming quality of being structured, and so there is no jumping in and out and around the program flow which makes so many machine code programs virtually impossible to follow. However, they are composed of parts which implement conceptually different methods of performing similar tasks, and any experienced programmer will undoubtedly see them as patchwork programs. All of these remarks also apply to the emulatory programs to be found in the next chapter.

There are several good reasons for this hybrid approach taken in writing the routines. Without necessarily assuming any priority in the order of these points, the routines are designed to:

● Show some methods of data storage, retrieval or address – not only those which are the object of the program's operation but also the register contents and addresses used by the program.
● Demonstrate the usefulness and necessity of extensive documentation in showing system and input/output requirements, overall program structure, the translation of design features into specific code and in clarifying obscure or conceptually difficult manipulative methods.
● Demonstrate the operation of a reasonably wide range of 68000 instructions and addressing modes within a limited amount of program space and show a selection of the different uses to which they can be put.
● Show a few of the many manipulative tricks available to the machine code programmer.
● Show that no one method must always be used to perform a particular task: there is always a large reservoir of alternative ways of performing any job and, although the simplest and most direct method is usually the best one to use, particular applications may require or benefit from the implementation of alternative approaches; knowledge of the different methods is part and parcel of a programmer's skill.
● Provide an ideal source for experimentation in finding better ways to code the program – by substituting methods which operate quicker, or are shorter (i.e. which have less

machine code), that use less stack space (most of the routines are heavy users of stack storage), are easier to adapt to an enhanced or altered purpose, or utilise less complex and more direct data manipulation and reference. Work on improving existing fully documented and understood routines is one of the best ways of extending skill at programming.

The first suite of routines, STAK, is excessively documented and explains points which would be very obvious to an experienced programmer. Normally, such information as, '... as stack grows downwards in memory, the address in the stack pointer must increase with a pull, whereas the stack byte count must decrease with a pull', would not be necessary. The convention that stacks (almost) always do grow downwards in memory is accepted as a law of nature by most programmers. (The phenomenon of a stack growing upwards would need to be commented upon!) The remaining routines are more soberly commented.

Multi-byte data stacks

The simplest use of a stack is for storing the current contents of the Program Counter before it is loaded with the address of a subroutine during execution of a subroutine call instruction (**BSR** or **JSR**). At the end of the subroutine, the return from subroutine instruction (**RTS**) reloads the saved address to the PC and causes execution to resume at the original location. A refinement of **RTS** is also possible: the instruction **RTR** (return and restore condition codes) loads both CCR and PC from values stored at the 'top of stack'. Unfortunately, there is no corresponding subroutine call instruction which saves the CCR as part of its operation – this has to be done by a **MOVE CCR,–(A7)** instruction in the subroutine and before any other registers or data are saved on stack.

A set of nested subroutines will cause the PC's current value to be put to the top of stack for every call. All the stored values will be transferred back to the PC (by the **RTS** instructions at the end of each subroutine) in the correct order. The last value stored is the first to be restored: the hardware stack is a type of data structure commonly called a 'last in first out', or 'LIFO' list.

Apart from the PC and CCR, the contents of registers are usually saved temporarily on the hardware stack while the registers themselves are used for other purposes. If register use is heavy, or nesting of subroutines is carried out to any appreciable depth, the same registers may be 'pushed' more than once, resulting in massive stack use. Because the hardware stack can grow at an alarming rate, it is common practice to set up separate 'software' or 'user' stacks if LIFO storage of large data is needed.

The STAK suite of routines (Listing 6.1) controls 16 stacks for the LIFO storage and retrieval of large blocks of byte data. The maximum data size is 255 bytes plus one byte giving the size (a size byte value of 0 means that the size byte only is pushed or pulled). Uses for the stack suite include manipulation of character strings, or of variable length file records, perhaps in sorting or search processes. Word and long word data blocks can also be accommodated, as can records consisting of different fields, provided that the lengths are expressed in terms of bytes and the blocks, strings or records begin with a size byte.

Each stack needs a set of parameters for its control. These are the stack pointer, which is incremented or decremented to always address the last byte of data stacked, and a count of the number of bytes on the stack. The stack count is used to determine when the stack is empty and when full. The problem of empty or full stack does not normally occur for hardware stacking of return addresses and register contents, since programs are written with an awareness of what exactly is on the stack.

This stack awareness is often not present in the type of program which needs LIFO data block storage. Although such a program could use variables to keep a check on its stack use, it is easier and usually less complex for that function to be provided by the stack control suite. Keeping a count of stack byte size is not the only method that could be used: one alternative is to provide maximum and minimum addresses for stack memory, which provides greater flexibility than the count method but requires three more parameter words for each stack.

```
***********************************************************************
*
* = STAK              Variable length data string stacks suite.
* > STAK-DEF          Define new stack address.
* > STAK-PSH          Push data string (block) to numbered stack.
* > STAK-PUL          Pull data string (block) from numbered stack.
*
***********************************************************************
*
* JOB                 STAK-DEF: To define a data string stack from an input
*                               address and stack index, returning error
*                               information if stack is defined and in use.
*                     STAK-PSH: To push an addressed block of data on to an
*                               indexed data string stack and update stack
*                               parameters, returning error information if
*                               stack is undefined or full.
*                     STAK-PUL: To pull a block of data from the top of an
*                               indexed data string stack and store in
*                               memory at an input address, returning error
*                               information if stack is undefined or empty.
*
* ACTION              STAK-DEF:
*                     Address indexed stack parameter block:
*                     [ Block offset = index * block size.
*                       Block address = parameter base + offset. ]
*                     IF stack size parameter =< 0
*                     THEN [ clear stack size.
*                            set stack pointer = input address + 1.
*                            set stack defined flags. ]
*                     ELSE [ set stack defined and in use flags. ]
*
*                     STAK-PSH:
*                     Address indexed stack parameter block.
*                     IF stack size parameter >= 0
*                     THEN [ Read data block size.
*                            IF stack size + data block size < 0 (2's compl)
*                            THEN [ Write new stack size.
*                                   FOR data block bytes
*                                   [ decrement stack pointer.
*                                     move data byte to (stack pointer). ]
*                                   set push completed flags. ]
*                            ELSE [ set stack full flag. ] ]
*                     ELSE [ set stack undefined flag. ]
*
*                     STAK-PUL:
*                     Address indexed stack parameter block.
*                     IF stack size > 0
```

Listing 6.1. Large-data stacks.

```
*                       THEN [ Read top of stack data block size.
*                              Stack pointer = stack pointer + block size.
*                              Stack size = stack size - data block size.
*                              FOR data block bytes
*                              [ move byte from stack to addressed memory. ]
*                              set pull completed flags. ]
*                       ELSE [ IF stack size < 0
*                              THEN [ set stack undefined flag. ]
*                              ELSE [ set stack empty flag. ]
*
*-----------------------------------------------------------------------
*
* CPU             68000-series
*
* HARDWARE        Stacks RAM. (STAK-PAR RAM if STAK-PAR is not attached
*                 to the suite but defined elsewhere in memory.)
*
* SOFTWARE        Local subroutine "STAK-AD" to address stack parameter
*                 block, get stack pointer and test if empty/undefined.
*
*
*-----------------------------------------------------------------------
*
* INPUT           All:                   D0 = Stack number (0 to 15).
*                 STAK-DEF:              A0 = Highest stack address.
*                 STAK-PSH & STAK-PUL:  A0 = address of data block size
*                                        byte (lowest address).
*
* OUTPUT          STAK-DEF: N,Z = 1: Stack number D0 defined with
*                                    stack pointer = A0 + 1.
*                           N,Z = 0: Stack in use, not redefined.
*                 STAK-PSH: N,Z = 0: Data block (A0) pushed to stack D0.
*                                    Stack D0 parameters updated.
*                                    A0 is unchanged.
*                           N = 1:   Stack undefined - no push.
*                           Z = 1:   Stack full - no push.
*                 STAK-PUL: N,Z = 0: Data block on top of stack D0
*                                    pulled to memory at (A0).
*                                    A0 is unchanged.
*                           N = 1:   Stack undefined - no pull.
*                           Z = 1:   Stack empty - no pull.
*                 Flags X,V,C are changed.
*
* ERRORS          No check is made for any stack overflowing other
*                 stack areas.
*
* REG USE         D0 A0 CCR
*
* STACK USE       (A7): STAK-DEF  8.  STAK-PSH  16.  STAK-PUL  16.
*
* RAM USE         STAK-PAR: 96 bytes for stack parameters.
*
* LENGTH          276 (including stack parameter storage)
*                 STAK-PAR: 96.  STAK-DEF: 48.
*                 STAK-PSH: 58.  STAK-PUL: 48.  STAK-AD: 26.
*
* CYCLES          Not given.
*
*-----------------------------------------------------------------------
*
* CLASS 2         -discreet       *interruptable       -promable
* -*----          -reentrant      -relocatable         -robust
*
*                 Promable and relocatable if STAK-PAR is not appended
*                 to the object code but defined elswhere in memory.
*
```

Listing 6.1 (contd)

```
********************************************************************
*
*
STAK      TRAP      #n
*
* ... The suite name STAK may be used for reference to the suite but
* ... subroutine calls to the address STAK cannot be allowed. Any such
* ... false calls should be trapped - the trap number should cause a
* ... user processed exception.
* ... If TRAP #n is not available for user exception processing, then
* ... a jump may be made to a user error handling routine:
* ...    STAK      JMP       ERRORLBL
* ... Alernatively, STAK could be made equivalent to STAK-DEF, STAK-PSH
* ... or STAK-PUL by a JMP but this could cause errors on wrong input.
*
*
STAK-PAR                                Stack parameters base address.
*
* ... Initialise 16 stack parameters: 2 words to contain stack pointer
* ... and third word to hold number of bytes on stack (0 to 32767).
* ... Bit 15 of the stack count is set to indicate an undefined stack.
*
* ... Each set of parameters is labelled to allow direct progam
* ... reference. The suite uses only the base address STAK-PAR with an
* ... index 0 - 15 ($0 - $F) in D0.B.
*
STAK-P-0 DC.W     0,0,$8000            Initialise stack $0 parameters.
STAK-P-1 DC.W     0,0,$8000            Initialise stack $1 parameters.
STAK-P-2 DC.W     0,0,$8000            Initialise stack $2 parameters.
STAK-P-3 DC.W     0,0,$8000            Initialise stack $3 parameters.
STAK-P-4 DC.W     0,0,$8000            Initialise stack $4 parameters.
STAK-P-5 DC.W     0,0,$8000            Initialise stack $5 parameters.
STAK-P-6 DC.W     0,0,$8000            Initialise stack $6 parameters.
STAK-P-7 DC.W     0,0,$8000            Initialise stack $7 parameters.
STAK-P-8 DC.W     0,0,$8000            Initialise stack $8 parameters.
STAK-P-9 DC.W     0,0,$8000            Initialise stack $9 parameters.
STAK-P-A DC.W     0,0,$8000            Initialise stack $A parameters.
STAK-P-B DC.W     0,0,$8000            Initialise stack $B parameters.
STAK-P-C DC.W     0,0,$8000            Initialise stack $C parameters.
STAK-P-D DC.W     0,0,$8000            Initialise stack $D parameters.
STAK-P-E DC.W     0,0,$8000            Initialise stack $E parameters.
STAK-P-F DC.W     0,0,$8000            Initialise stack $F parameters.
*
*------------------------------------------------------------------
*
* > STAK-DEF       Define new stack, flagging attempt to define stack
*                  already in use.
*
*
STAK-DEF MOVEM.L  D0/A1,-(A7)          Save regs for use in STAK-DEF.
*
* ... The required stack parameters must be addressed. The count word is
* ... checked to see if stack is in use (0 < count < $8000) and if so,
* ... no definition is allowed but an error is flagged.
*
         ANDI.L   #%1111,D0            Isolate stack number by masking
*                                      out unwanted bits.
         MULU     #6,D0               Change stack index number to
*                                      offset of required 3-word block
*                                      from parameter base.
         MOVEA.L  #STAK-PAR,A1         Get stack parameter base address.
         TST.W    #4(A1,D0.L)          Check count word to see if stack
*                                      is in use (positive) and exit if
         BGT      S-DF-END             it is with flags NZ reset.
*
* ... Stack is defined only if stack count msb was set, showing stack
* ... was not in use, or count = 0, showing an empty stack. Definition
* ... must clear the count, including the msb to show stack now in use,
* ... and set pointer value to 1 higher than next free stack byte.
* ... Finally the valid definition must be flagged.
```

Listing 6.1 (contd)

```
*
           CLR.W      #4(A1,D0.L)         Clear stack count.
           MOVE.L     A0,(A1,D0.L)        Move address of highest usable
           ADDQ.L     #1,(A1,D0.L)        byte to pointer and add 1 so that
*                                         it addresses "last byte stacked".
           ORI        #%1100,CCR          Set NZ flags to show stack
*                                         definition completed.
*
S-DF-END MOVEM.L     (A7)+,D0/A1         Restore saved registers and exit
           RTS                            with NZ flagging okay or error.
*
*----------------------------------------------------------------------
*
* > STAK-PSH         Push next block of data to stack from (A0) or flag
*                    error if stack full or undefined.
*
*
STAK-PSH MOVEM.L     D0/A1/A2,-(A7)      Save regs for use in STAK-PSH
*
           BSR        STAK-AD             Go compute parameter block
*                                         address, get stack pointer and
*                                         test if stack is undefined.
           BMI        S-PH-END            Skip, no push if undefined.
*
*
* ... Stack not undefined, so get block length byte (at data block
* ... pointer (A0)), and calculate new stack byte size by adding old
* ... size to number of bytes to be pushed. Check for overflow of stack
* ... (greater than $7FFF) and skip straight out, flagging stack full
* ... (Z = 1), if overflow would occur.
*
           MOVEQ      #0,D0               Clear full register, then
           MOVE.B     (A0),D0             get data block size.
           ADD.W      #4(A1),D0           Compute new stack count word by
           ADDQ.W     #1,D0               adding old count to number of
*                                         bytes to be pushed, plus 1 for
*                                         the size byte also pushed.
*
           EORI       #%1100              Change state of both N and Z
*                                         flags so N will be clear but Z
*                                         set if overflow will occur, and
           BPL        S-PH-NP             skip, flagging stack full, if so.
*
* ... Stack will not overflow, so write new stack size and get data
* ... block size as count and to adjust stack pointer in A2 and in the
* ... parameters past the size of data block to be pushed. Note that, as
* ... stack grows downwards in memory, the address in the stack pointer
* ... must decrease with a stack push, whereas the stack byte count must
* ... increase with a push. A program interrupting after this part
* ... cannot re-enter to pull data from the same stack without error.
*
           MOVE.W     D0,#4(A1)           Write new stack byte size.
*
           MOVEQ      #0,D0               Get data block size as
           MOVE.B     (A0),D0             before, this time for count.
*
* ... Block move. Loop transferring bytes starting at highest address
* ... in data block memory to next free stack byte. Last byte to be
* ... moved is the data block size byte, from (A2 + 0). A2 is adjusted
* ... down by 1 before each byte transfer and addresses the stacked
* ... size byte on exit from the loop.
* ... A0 is not changed by this operation.
S-PH-LP  MOVE.B     (A0,D0.L),-(A2)     Decrement stack pointer A2 by 1
*                                         and transfer one byte to stack.
           DBF        D0,S-PH-LP          Always decrement D0, repeat until
*                                         D0 = -1 and all data transferred.
*
* ... Loop leaves A2 at new top of stack, so write it to parameter SP.
```

Listing 6.1 (contd)

```
*
          MOVE.L     A2,(A1)                   Write new stack pointer.
*
          ANDI       #0,CCR                    Finally, clear N and Z flags to
*                                              show push successful.
*
S-PH-NP                                        This label exists only as the end
*                                              of the construct which selects
*                                              between push or no-push on the
*                                              overflow possibility. S-PH-NP
*                                              assembles as the same address as
*                                              S-PH-END. Consequently, the
*                                              instruction "BPL S-PH-NP" could
*                                              be replaced by "BPL S-PH-END".
*
S-PH-END MOVEM.L    (A7)+,D0/A1/A2            Restore saved registers and exit
          RTS                                  with NZ flagging okay or error.
*
*-------------------------------------------------------------------
*
*  > STAK-PUL        Pull next block of data from stack to (A0) or flag
*                    error if stack empty or undefined.
*
*
STAK-PUL MOVEM.L    D0/A1/A2,-(A7)           Save regs for use in STAK-PUL
*
          BSR        STAK-AD                  Go compute parameter block
*                                             address, get stack pointer and
*                                             test if stack empty or undefined.
          BLE        S-PL-END                 Skip, no pull if empty/undefined.
*
* ... Stack not empty or undefined, so set up data byte count using the
* ... data block length byte (first on stack, top of stack, at (A2)),
* ... and adjust stack pointer in parameters past the size of data block
* ... to be pulled. Also adjust stack byte size by number of bytes
* ... pulled. Note that, as stack grows downwards in memory, the address
* ... in the stack pointer must increase with a stack pull, whereas the
* ... stack byte count must decrease with a pull. A program interrupting
* ... after this part cannot re-enter and push data to the same stack
* ... without overwriting the data which is not yet pulled.
*
          MOVEQ      #0,D0                     Clear for count register, then
          MOVE.B     (A2),D0                   get data block size as count.
*
          ADD.L      D0,(A1)                   Correct stored pointer for data
          ADDQ.L     #1,(A1)                   bytes then add 1 more to correct
*                                              for size byte. Stack pointer in
*                                              parameters now addresses next
*                                              entry (data block) on stack.
          SUB.W      D0,#4(A1)                 Correct stack count word by same
          SUBQ.W     #1,#4(A1)                 amount as stack pointer.
*
* ... Block move. Loop transferring bytes starting at highest address
* ... from stack memory to destination. Last byte to be moved is the
* ... data block size byte, from (A2 + 0) to (A0 + 0).
* ... Neither A0 nor A2 are changed by this operation.
*
S-PL-LP  MOVE.B     (A2,D0.L),(A0,D0.L)      Transfer one byte.
          DBF        D0,S-PL-LP               Always decrement D0, repeat until
*                                             D0 = -1 and all data transferred.
*
          ANDI       #0,CCR                    Finally, clear N and Z flags to
*                                              show pull successful.
*
S-PL-END MOVEM.L    (A7)+,D0/A1/A2           Restore saved registers and exit
          RTS                                  with NZ flagging okay or error.
*
*-------------------------------------------------------------------
```

Listing 6.1 (contd)

```
* ... LOCAL SUBROUTINE "STAK-AD" to address stack parameters, get stack
* ... pointer and check for empty/undefined stack.
* ... A1 addresses stack parameters.  A2 = stack pointer.
* ... Z set if stack empty.  N set if stack undefined.
*
STAK-AD  ANDI.L   #%1111,D0           Isolate stack number by masking
                                      out unwanted bits.
         MULU     #6,D0               Change stack index number to
                                      offset of required 3-word block
                                      from parameter base.
         ADD.L    #STAK-PAR,D0        Add to parameter base address and
         MOVEA.L  D0,A1               move to parameter address reg.
         MOVEA.L  (A1),A2             Get stack pointer, A2.
         TST.W    #4(A1)              Check count word, setting flags
*                                     for undefined (N) or empty (Z)
*                                     stack, then
         RTS                          return to STAK-PSH or STAK-PUL.
*
****************************************************************************
```

Listing 6.1 (contd)

Queueing information

A queue could be described as 'last in last out' storage (LILO) but is more often referred to as 'first in first out' (FIFO), although both mean virtually the same.

Queues need two pointers; one to where the next datum is to be stored (the tail) and one to the next datum to be retrieved (the head). The terminology suggests that as each retrieval takes place, all stored data are shuffled up in memory, like would-be passengers queueing for a bus. This would be a slow process. Instead, the data remains where it is and the queue head and queue tail pointers are incremented as data are retrieved and stored. Where no other parameters are involved, the queue will creep through all memory and eventually wraparound to the address at which it started.

Normally, the addresses of the highest and lowest memory locations available to the queue are included as parameters, with the head and tail pointers checked at each increment and, if found to be at highest memory, reset to the lowest address. Some means of preventing storage to a full queue, or retrieval from an empty queue, (in both cases the head and tail pointers contain the same address) must also be provided and this is often done by setting or resetting a parameter flag.

QUEUE (Listing 6.2.) demonstrates methods of structuring the program around the format of the data acted on, minimising the number of parameters needed and simplifying address control. Routines written for specific applications, where there is no possibility of a change in data format, can be optimised to make full use of all or any opportunity afforded by the type and number of data.

The structure inherent in the data (not the data itself) is used to store program information and to control program operation. This is often done to cut down program length and increase execution speed, or to make life easier for the programmer who can omit or reduce program control structures by not considering all other data formats which may or may not be used in the future. The fault with this attitude is that any change in usage – longer data, larger amounts of data or a change in data type, such as replacing 7-bit ASCII decimal digit codes by 8-bit packed BCD codes – will require a complete rewrite of the routine. Conversely, a generally applicable queue suite, designed to use full parameters and control structures not dependent on the type and length of data acted on, could take longer to write, be slower in operation and take up more program space. Once written, however, it would be available for use with almost any data, whether in new programs or in updated use of the original program.

The special conditions applying in QUEUE are:

1. The queue is to hold a maximum of 256 entries.
2. 1Ø bytes of information need to be stored in each entry but 4 of those bytes contain ASCII decimal digits.
3. Bytes Ø and 1 contain only ASCII letters (i.e. 7-bit codes).

Condition 1 immediately suggests using single byte index values for the head and tail pointers instead of full long word addresses. The advantages will be:

(a) The index byte can simply be incremented by 1 for each entry stored (tail) or retrieved (head). This allows the shorter and quicker ADDQ instruction to be used in 68000 code (in other codes an INC instruction is usually shorter and quicker than an ADD instruction).

(b) The wraparound nature of unsigned binary arithmetic will automatically reset a byte length index to Ø on increment past 255. This removes the need to store minimum and maximum queue addresses, to compare head and tail pointers with the maximum address at every access and to reset the pointers to the minimum address when found to be at the maximum.

(c) Using a single byte index saves three bytes of parameter storage over using a full address. The parameter storage in QUEUE is reduced from 16 to 6 bytes.

The disadvantage is that the index value must be multiplied by the entry length before use, but if the entry byte length is a power of 2 (i.e. 1, 2, 4, 8, 16, and so on) the multiplication is easily and quickly achieved by shifting. Furthermore, if the length is any of 1, 2, 4 or 8 bytes, the index multiplication corresponds to the index scaling allowed in 68020 code.

Condition 2 suggests that the 10 bytes of each entry can easily be reduced to 8 by squashing the four ASCII decimal digits into two packed BCD bytes before storage and re-expanding on retrieval. In 68020 code this can be done by the special instructions **PACK** and **UNPK**; in 68000 code the emulatory routines ER-Pack and ER-UNPK must be used (given in Chapter 7). Packing of data before storage is quite common, but is normally done to increase capacity rather than reduce data to a friendlier size. If data packing is done at all, it really ought to be carried out by a separate routine before calling the queue control routines.

Condition 3 means that the most significant bit (bit 7) of both the first and second bytes in each entry (bytes Ø and 1 as indexed from the start of the entry) is not needed for data storage. The msb of the first byte can, therefore, be used to validate the entry by setting it (to 1) if the entry is not used. Storing any ASCII character to the byte will clear bit 7 and validate the entry as being in use. This system does mean that the queue has to be initialised by setting the msb in the first byte of every entry, and that retrieval of data must invalidate the entry, but it removes the need to set up and maintain parameter flags to indicate if the entire queue is full or empty and the need to compare head and tail pointers in testing for these two states. The queue is empty when the entry indexed by the head pointer is invalid; it is full when the entry indexed by the tail pointer is valid (in use).

QUEUE entries are not data but information relating to data (unlike STAK, which does manage the data itself). The 2-letter, 4-digit code is a reference key to the data block, file or record and is taken from a 6-byte field at the start of the record. The second part of each queue entry is the address from which the reference key was taken. Q-OUT is not an exact inverse process of Q-IN: the reference key is not written to memory but is output in registers, to be used by the calling program as a reference to the record stored elsewhere in memory or on some other medium, such as tape or disk. Manipulation of short keys, instead of an entire possibly very long record, is usual and is cost efficient in terms of processing time and memory usage.

Queues are used when processing of data or execution of a program must wait for information or for an external event. The current context is saved and the job is queued, allowing other tasks to be carried out. Eventually the pending job reaches the head of the queue and processing of it resumes. The queue system is used in time-sharing of one processor by several user programs.

```
***************************************************************************
*
* = QUEUE         Queue clear, write and read suite.
* > Q-CLEAR       Clear (invalidate) all entries in Queue space.
* > Q-IN          Write information to Queue.
* > Q-OUT         Read information from Queue.
*
***************************************************************************
*
* JOB             To initially clear a Queue area, to write Record
*                 information from an addressed record to the next end
*                 of Queue entry, to read record information into
*                 registers from the next start of Queue entry, or
*                 return Queue full or empty information.
*
*                 Record format:    (A0+0,1): 2-letter i/d
*                                (A0+2,3,4,5): 4-digit i/d (ASCII dec)
*                                   (A0+6,,?): content (not queued)
*
* ACTION          Q-CLEAR:
*                 Address Q highest entry + 1
*                 FOR number of Q-entries
*                 [ Address next lower Q-entry.
*                   Set Q-entry invalid flag. ]
*                 Initialise Q-head index to Q-entry 0.
*                 Initialise Q-tail index to Q-entry 0.
*
*                 Q-IN:
*                 Address Q-tail
*                 IF Q-tail entry invalid
*                 THEN [ Read 4-digit ASCII i/d.
*                        Pack 4-digit ASCII i/d to BCD.
*                        Write BCD i/d to Q-entry.
*                        Copy record 2-letter i/d to Q-entry.
*                        Write record address to Q-entry
*                        Set Q-tail entry valid flag.
*                        Increment Q-tail index.
*                        Set valid entry put flag. ]
*                 ELSE [ Set Q-full flag. ]
*
*                 Q-OUT:
*                 Address Q-head
*                 IF Q-head entry valid
*                 THEN [ Read record address.
```

Listing 6.2. Queueing keys.

```
*                              Read record 2-letter i/d.
*                              Read packed BCD 4-digit i/d.
*                              Unpack BCD i/d to 4-digit ASCII.
*                              Set Q-head entry invalid flag.
*                              Increment Q-head index.
*                              Set valid entry got flag. ]
*                     ELSE [ Set Q-empty flag. ]
*
*------------------------------------------------------------------------
*
* CPU            Q-CLEAR: 68000, 68008.
*                Q-IN, Q-OUT: 68000-series.
*
* HARDWARE       Queue RAM, Queue parameters RAM, Records RAM.
*
* SOFTWARE       ER-PACK, ER-UNPK: Routines to emulate the actions of
*                68020 PACK, UNPK instructions.
*
*------------------------------------------------------------------------
*
* INPUT          All:    A6 addresses Queue parameters.
*                Q-IN:   A0 addresses record (low address).
*
*                Q-parameters: (A6+0,1,2,3):  Q-start address.
*                                    (A6+4):  Q-head index (0 - 255)
*                                    (A6+5):  Q-tail index (0 - 255)
*
*                Q-entry format:   byte 0,1: 2-letter i/d
*                                       2,3: packed BCD 4-digit i/d
*                                       4,5,6,7: record address.
*
*                Q-entry invalid flag: bit 7, byte 0 = 1.
*
* OUTPUT         Q-CLEAR: All Q-entries invalidated.
*                         Q-head & Q-tail indexes zeroised.
*                         No registers changed.
*                Q-IN:  No registers changed.
*                       CCR = %11111: Record i/d and address written
*                                     to Q-tail entry.
*                                     Q-tail index incremented.
*                       CCR = %00000: Queue full - no entry made.
*                Q-OUT: CCR = %00000: A0 = Record address.
*                                     D0.W = Record 2-letter i/d.
*                                     D1.L = Record 4-digit i/d.
*                                     Q-entry invalidated,
*                                     Q-head index incremented.
*                       CCR = %11111: Queue empty - no entry got.
*
* ERRORS         Record i/d not validated:
*                  Invalid ASCII Record i/d could cause Queue error.
*
* REG USE        D0 D1 A0 A6 CCR
*
* STACK USE      (A7): Q-CLEAR  10.
*                      Q-IN  16 + ER-PACK stack use.
*                      Q-OUT 16 + ER-UNPK stack use.
*
* RAM USE        None.
*
* LENGTH         Not given.
*
* CYCLES         Not given.
*
*------------------------------------------------------------------------
*
* CLASS 2        *discreet        *interruptable       *promable
* ***-*-         -reentrant       *relocatable         -robust
*
*************************************************************************
*
```

Listing 6.2 (contd)

```
Q-CLEAR   MOVE      SR,-(A7)            Save flags and registers used
          MOVEM.L   D2/A1,-(A7)         in Q-CLEAR.
*
          MOVEA.L   (A6),A1             Get Q start address and index
          MOVE.W    #$0800,D2           highest entry + 1, 1st byte.
*
Q-C-LP    SUBQ.W    #8,D2               Index next lower entry, 1st byte
          SPL       #0(A1,D2.W)         and set always (especially bit 7)
          BNE       Q-C-LP              repeat until lowest entry set.
*
          MOVE.W    D2,#4(A6)           Set Q-head & Q-tail to 0.
*
          MOVEM.L   (A7)+,D2/A1         Restore registers and
          RTR                           exit, restoring flags.
*
*------------------------------------------------------------------------
*
Q-IN      MOVEM.L   D6/A1,-(A7)         Save registers (long or word)
          MOVEM.W   D2/D7,-(A7)         used in Q-IN.
*
          MOVEA.L   (A6),A1             Get Q start address.
          CLR.W     D2                  Clear index, get Q-tail index
          MOVE.B    #5(A6),D2           byte and multiply by 8 to give
          ASL.W     #3,D2               Q-tail entry offset from start.
*
          TST.B     #0(A1,D2.W)         Get entry validity (okay if msb
          ANDI      #01000,CCR          is 1), clear all CCR except N and
          BPL       Q-I-END             skip, all CCR = 0, if Q full.
*
*
          MOVE.L    #2(A0),D6           Else, get 4-digit ASCII i/d
*
Q-I-LP    JSR       ER-PACK             Pack 2 digits to one byte with
          DC.W      #0                  zero adjustment.
          SWAP      D6                  Access next 2 digits of ASCII
          ROR.W     #8,D7               and next destination byte.
          EORI.B    #$80,#0(A1,D2.W)    Change validity flag as loop test
          BPL       Q-I-LP              and loop only once.
*
          MOVE.W    D7,#2(A1,D2.W)      Write packed 4 digits to entry.
*
          MOVE.W    (A0),#0(A1,D2.W)    Move 2-letter i/d to entry, also
*                                       clearing bit 7, byte 0 (valid).
          MOVE.L    A0,#4(A1,D2.W)      Write record address.
*
          ADDQ.B    #1,#5(A6)           Increment Q-tail index byte, with
*                                       wraparound arithmetic (255+1=0).
          MOVE      #%11111,CCR         Set entry queued okay flags.
*
*
Q-I-END   MOVEM.W   (A7)+,D2/D7         Restore stacked registers in
          MOVEM.L   (A7)+,D6/A1         correct size and order.
          RTS                           Exit Q-IN.
*
*------------------------------------------------------------------------
*
Q-OUT     MOVEM.L   D6/A1,-(A7)         Save registers (long or word)
          MOVEM.W   D2/D7,-(A7)         used in Q-OUT.
*
          MOVEA.L   (A6),A1             Get Q start address.
          CLR.W     D2                  Clear index, get Q-head index
          MOVE.B    #4(A6),D2           byte and multiply by 8 to give
          ASL.W     #3,D2               Q-head entry offset from start.
*
          TST.B     #0(A1,D2.W)         Get entry validity (okay if msb
          ORI       #10111,CCR          is 0), set all CCR except N and
          BMI       Q-O-END             skip, all CCR = 1, if Q empty.
*
*
```

Listing 6.2 (contd)

```
        MOVEA.L   #4(A1,D2.W),A0      Read record address and
        MOVE.W    #0(A1,D2.W),D0      2-letter i/d to output registers.
*
        MOVE.L    #2(A1,D2.W),D7      Read packed BCD 4-digit i/d.
*
Q-O-LP  JSR       ER-UNPK             Unpack 2 digits to two bytes and
        DC.W      #$3030              adjust to ASCII decimal.
        SWAP      D6                  Access next destination word and
        ROR.W     #8,D7               and next 2-digits byte.
        TAS.B     #0(A1,D2.W)         Set invalid flag as loop test
        BPL       Q-O-LP              causing only one loop.
*
        MOVE.L    D6,D1               Move 4-digit i/d to output reg.
*
        ADDQ.B    #1,#4(A6)           Increment Q-head index byte, with
*                                     wraparound arithmetic (255+1=0).
        MOVE      #%00000,CCR         Set entry recovered okay flags.
*
*
Q-O-END MOVEM.W   (A7)+,D2/D7         Restore stacked registers in
        MOVEM.L   (A7)+,D6/A1         correct size and order.
        RTS                           Exit Q-OUT.
*
*******************************************************************************
```

Listing 6.2 (contd)

Data arrays

ARRAY (Listing 6.3) is different from both STAK and QUEUE in that it does not actually store or retrieve data but merely converts an array base address and a series of subscipts into the address of a single byte array element. This allows any byte, word or long word operation to be performed on any source or destination operand data at or in the vicinity of the element address.

The method used in ARRAY, of passing both array base address and subscripts, offers a great deal of flexibility to the programmer. The base address may be contained in any Address Register and the number of that register is passed to ARRAY as one word data embedded immediately following the subroutine call instruction (if the specified register is A7 then the array is stored on top of stack). The following embedded word gives the number of subscripts: this is essential for the routine to know how many embedded data there are in order to return to the instruction immediately after the last subscript. Each embedded subscript word is coded to indicate whether the subscript number is contained in the word as immediate data or in the specified high or low order word of any of the eight Data Registers. Thus array addressing is always dynamic, whereas subscripting may be static (programmed in as immediate data) or dynamic (computed and held in registers). There is no limit to the number of subscripts that may be used, except that the final index must be in the range $0 - 65534$.

The successfully found element address is output from ARRAY on top of stack and can be pulled to any Address Register by the calling program. Alternatively, an output Address Register number could be given as a further embedded parameter and the specified register loaded with the element address in the same way as the base address is copied to A1 by the case structure in ARRAY.

Storage of data in the array follows normal subscript forward indexing. Regard the subscript sequence as an ordered sequence of digits, with the last subscript having lowest order. Then, repeatedly adding 1 to the last subscript, with a carry to the next higher (i.e. preceding) subscript when any incremented subscript reaches maximum value and is reset to 0, will cause the subscript sequence to index every element sequentially upwards through array memory. In addition to the stored data, the array has several word length data giving header information – the number of dimensions and the maximum subscript size for each dimension. The formula used in addressing element ARRAY(a,b,c,...,n), where 0 is a valid subscript, is:

$$\text{Address} = [\text{Array base address}]$$
$$+ [2 * (\text{number of dimensions} + 1)]$$
$$+ [(a+1)(b+1)(c+1) * ... * (n+1) - 1]$$

Three types of error are identified as being possible in the use of ARRAY. If any of these occurs, control passes to a section of the routine which sets the appropriate error flag and causes a **TRAP** exception to a user defined error handling routine (if **TRAP** is not available for user definition, a **JMP** or **JSR** could be used). Apart from changing the address in the Program Counter and the status shown in the Condition Codes Register, no registers are changed. The error handling routine can thus diagnose and report on the cause of the error. An alternative method of dealing with errors would be to quit processing, restore all registers and return to the program with the type of error flagged. The program would then have the responsibility of checking whether the operation had been successful and jumping to the error handler if not.

```
****************************************************************************
*
* = ARRAY
*
****************************************************************************
*
* JOB            To address a specified byte element in a multi-
*                dimensional array, the array address and subscript
*                parameters given as program embedded data after the
*                subroutine call instruction, or to interrupt the
*                routine and divert control to error handler routine.
*
*                ARRAY FORMAT:
*                    Header information: Word 0: No. of dimensions (n).
*                                        Word 1: Dimensions,
*                                          to   : max. subscript size
*                                        Word n:
*                    Array data: Stored in subscript forward order.
*
* ACTION         Stack all possible subscript registers in right order.
*                Get return address as embedded parameter pointer.
*                Read 1st embedded parameter, incrementing pointer.
*                Use A-register number as index to array register.
*                Get array address to array pointer.
*                Compare no. of subscripts given in array with that
*                2nd embedded word, incrementing parameter pointer, and
*                exit to error routine if no match.
*                Initialise accumulator to 1.
*                IF no. of subscripts > 1
*                THEN [ FOR each subscript
*                        [ Read embedded parameter.
*                          Increment parameter pointer.
*                          IF register flag in parameter set
*                          THEN [ Convert parameter to stack index.
*                                  Subscript = indexed stacked
*                                             Data register value. ]
```

Listing 6.3. Array access.

```
*                              ELSE [ Subscript = parameter value. ]
*                              Compare subscript with subscript maximum
*                              value in array, incrementing array pointer,
*                              and exit to error routine if too big.
*                              Accumulator = accumulator * (subscript + 1).
*                              Exit to error routine on overflow. ] ]
*                    ELSE [ Skip. ]
*                    Element index = accumulator - 1.
*                    Element address = array pointer + element index.
*                    Store element address to ARRAY exit stack top.
*                    Restore subscript registers.
*
*------------------------------------------------------------------------
*
* CPU               68000, 68008
*
* HARDWARE          Array in memory.
*
* SOFTWARE          Unspecified routine(s) to handle various categories of
*                   error, entered by way of TRAP #vector.
*
*------------------------------------------------------------------------
*
* INPUT             All parameters are embedded after the subroutine call
*                   instruction:
*                      Word 0: Number of Address register which contains
*                              address of array header 1st word.
*                      Word 1: Number of subscripts, giving number of
*                              following embedded words.
*                      Word 2: Subscripts, either:
*                        to  : bit 15 = 0: Immediate data (0 to 32767)
*                      Word n: bit 15 = 1: Data register word index,
*                                          bits 2-0 = register number
*                                          bit 7 = 0: low order word
*                                          bit 7 = 1: high order word
*
*                   Indexed Address and Data registers must contain the
*                   appropriate array address or subscript.
*
*                   Maximum array size: 65536 bytes.
*
* OUTPUT            Valid exit: Address of specified byte element is on
*                               stack top.
*                               Return is to instruction following the
*                               embedded parameters.
*                   Error exit: All register contents (except PC and CCR)
*                               and stack are as at discovery of error.
*                               Error codes:
*                                  C = 1: Wrong number of dimensions.
*                                  N = 1: Subscript out of range.
*                                  V = 1: Array element index overflow.
*
* ERRORS            None.
*
* REG USE           As specified by embedded parameters.
*
* STACK USE         46 added above return address during ARRAY,
*                   On return, stack is 4 bytes greater than before call
*                   to ARRAY.
*
* RAM USE           None.
*
* LENGTH            Not given.
*
* CYCLES            Not given.
*
```

Listing 6.3 (contd)

```
*-------------------------------------------------------------------
*
* CLASS 1           *discreet      *interruptable    *promable
* ******            *reentrant     *relocatable      *robust
*
*********************************************************************
*
ARRAY     SUBQ.L    #4,A7              Make space for replacement of
*                                      incremented return address, the
*                                      element address will be stored to
*                                      current PC stack location.
          MOVE      SR,-(A7)           Save condition codes.
          MOVEM.L   D0-D7,-(A7)        Save Data registers, making them
*                                      stack-index accessible.
          MOVEM.L   A0/A1,-(A7)        Save A0 & A1 for use in ARRAY.
          MOVEA.L   #46(A7),A0         Get return address to A0, serving
*                                      as embedded parameter pointer.
*
          MOVE.W    (A0)+,D0           Get 1st embedded word, giving no.
*                                      of Address register containing
*                                      address of array.
          ANDI.W    #7,D0              Mask out any intrusive bits and
          ASL.W     #2,D0              multiply by 4, converting it to
*                                      index of the case list.
          JMP       ARR-A-0(PC,D0.W)   Jump to correct case.
*
* ... Case list of address registers containing array address. Indexed
* ... jump passes control to required MOVE.L An,A1 instruction. A0 is on
* ... stack top and A7 contents need adjusting for all stack storage.
*
ARR-A-0   MOVEA.L   (A7),A1            Get input A0 contents from stack
          BRA       ARR-A-OK           (= array address), go case-end.
*
ARR-A-1   MOVEA.L   A1,A1              Get A1 contents (= array address)
          BRA       ARR-A-OK           and go to case-end.
*
ARR-A-2   MOVEA.L   A2,A1              Get A2 contents (= array address)
          BRA       ARR-A-OK           and go to case-end.
*
ARR-A-3   MOVEA.L   A3,A1              Get A3 contents (= array address)
          BRA       ARR-A-OK           and go to case-end.
*
ARR-A-4   MOVEA.L   A4,A1              Get A4 contents (= array address)
          BRA       ARR-A-OK           and go to case-end.
*
ARR-A-5   MOVEA.L   A5,A1              Get A5 contents (= array address)
          BRA       ARR-A-OK           and go to case-end.
*
ARR-A-6   MOVEA.L   A6,A1              Get A6 contents (= array address)
          BRA       ARR-A-OK           and go to case-end.
*
ARR-A-7   MOVEA.L   A7,A1              Get SP contents and adjust for
          ADDA.W    #50,A1             all ARRAY stacking (= array
*                                      address) then fall through to
*                                      case-end.
*
* ... A1 now contains the array start address, i.e. of the word giving
* ... number of dimensions. A0 addresses instruction dimension word.
*
ARR-A-OK  MOVE.W    (A1)+,D0           Get no. of dimensions from array
          CMP.W     (A0)+,D0           and compare with dimensions given
*                                      by 2nd program embedded word and
          BNE       ARR-TRP0           error exit if different.
*
          MOVEQ     #1,D1              Initialise index accumulator.
*
          SUBQ.W    #1,D0              Convert dimensions to DBcc loop
*                                      count of dimensions.
```

Listing 6.3 (contd)

```
          BCS       ARR-FA             Skip if no dimensions: array is
*                                      a single byte.
*
ARR-M-LP MOVE.W    (A0)+,D2            Get next program embedded word.
          BPL       ARR-S-C            Skip if subscript value in word.
*
* ... Word read from program indexes the high or low order Data register
* ... word containing the subscript value. Manipulation of the word bits
* ... is needed to form the correct index.
*
          EORI.B    #$80,D2            Change state of hi/lo bit 7,
          ROL.B     #1,D2              D2 = reg no. * 2 + hi/lo * 1,
          ASL.B     #1,D2              D2 = reg no. * 4 + hi/lo * 2.
          ANDI.W    #$001E,D2          Isolate value as index to stacked
*                                      high or low word of register.
*
          MOVE.W    #8(A7,D2.W),D2     Get subscript from stacked
*                                      register high or low word.
*
ARR-S-C  CMP.W     (A1)+,D2           Compare subscript with maximum
*                                      value in array dimensions and do
          BHI       ARR-TRP1           error exit if out of range.
*
          ADDQ.W    #1,D2              Convert subscript index to number
          BCS       ARR-TRP1           but error exit if subscript is
*                                      out of range.
*
          MULU      D2,D1              Partial index * (subscript + 1),
          CMPI.L    #$10000,D1         test for word overflow and if so
          BCC       ARR-TRP2           do error exit on index overflow.
*
          DBF       D0,ARR-M-LP        Repeat for all subscripts.
*
* ... A1 is the address of the first element in the array. D1 is 1 more
* ... than the index of the required element from the 1st element.
*
ARR-FA   SUBQ.W    #1,D1              Index required element, and add
          ADDA.L    D1,A1              to address of first element to
*                                      give address of indexed element.
          MOVE.L    A1,#46(A7)         Store element address on top of
*                                      exit stack, replacing old PC.
          MOVE.L    A0,#42(A7)         Stack incremented PC, for return,
*                                      above address of element.
*
          MOVEM.L   (A7)+,A0/A1        Restore Address registers.
          MOVEM.L   (A7)+,D0-D7        Restore all Data registers.
          RTR                          Exit, restoring CCR, and leaving
*                                      element address on stack top.
*
*------------------------------------------------------------------------
*
* ... This section corresponds to ON ERROR GOTO .... Entry to this
* ... section is achieved only by breaking out of normal program flow,
* ... leaving registers (except CCR) and stack in the error state for
* ... the error handler routine to correct or report on.
* ... Set flag to show which error occurred and cause a TRAP to deal
* ... with the error. Alternatively, the TRAP instruction could be
* ... replaced by a JMP to the error handler, or the error handler could
* ... be written at the end of this section.
*
ARR-TV   EQU       #n                 Define trap vector number which
*                                      passes control to a user defined
*                                      error handler routine.
*
ARR-TRP0 MOVE      #%00001,CCR        Set flag for no. of dimensions
          BRA       ARR-TRPE           wrong and go error exit.
```

Listing 6.3 (contd)

```
*
ARR-TRP1 MOVE      #%01000,CCR            Set subscript out of range flag
         BRA       ARR-TRPE               and go error exit.
*
ARR-TRP2 MOVE      #%00010.CCR            Set array index overflow flag and
         BRA       ARR-TRPE               go error exit.
*
ARR-TRPE TRAP      #ARR-TV                Cause trap to vectored handler.
*
**********************************************************************
```

Listing 6.3 (contd)

Chapter Seven
Emulation

Like the routines given in Chapter 6, those in this chapter are designed to be educational rather than efficient: there is room for much improvement.

Emulation means mimicking the operations of other computers, either the instructions of different processors or the operation of non-implemented devices. The object is to run programs that would run on the emulated system. In this chapter, emulation is used in a less strict sense and refers to the writing of routines that will produce similar results to those given by individual instructions of another processor – in particular, the 68020.

With true instruction emulation, the program is written in the code of the emulated processor. The emulation program, or emulator, must act as the mimicked processor, performing all instruction fetch and decoding, all source and destination operand address calculation, read and write and, of course, the arithmetic or logical manipulation of the data involved. The program written in emulated code is not executed directly by the processor.

True emulated programs run quite slowly, since no emulator can operate as quickly as a processor. The main use of this sort of emulation is to write and test software for systems that are designed but not yet functional, or that are ordered but not yet delivered. Another major use is to run good software written for one system on a system for which it is not yet available. Quite powerful systems often emulate smaller systems.

With 'emulatory routines' the program is written in the code of the processor on which it runs. Emulation of non-implemented instructions is achieved normally by system calls or subroutine calls to routines which produce the desired effect. Both the 'pseudo-emulatory' program and the 'pseudo-emulation' routines are executed directly by the processor.

Emulatory routines also run slowly but, as these form only a small part of the program, most of which is executed directly by the processor, the program as a whole is barely affected. It may even be speeded up by the use of efficient emulatory methods – were emulation routines not used, some other method would have to have been. Speed, however, is not the most important aspect when writing code to emulate the actions of another processor. The main object is to provide functions that operate efficiently and so ease the task of programming. The programming concepts behind the functions exist independently and could be utilised without reference to their implementation on the emulated system but describing the routines as emulatory recognises that the implementation is efficient and worth copying. It may be also that the program is written so as to be easily converted to run on the emulated system merely by exchanging the subroutine call instructions for the emulated instructions.

BCD packing

ER-PACK and ER-UNPK (Listing 7.1) perform the same operations as the 68020 instructions **PACK** and **UNPK** but use a restricted form of operand addressing. The source data for **PACK** is Data Register 6 and the destination is Data Register 7. These same registers assume the reverse roles in **UNPK**, which is more or less the reverse process to **PACK**.

In keeping with the 68020 instruction forms which have the adjustment word as immediate data, the routines both require the adjustment word to be embedded in the program immediately following the subroutine call instruction. The return address is, of course, incremented past the embedded word before exit.

These routines could be made to act more like the 68020 originals by using the method given in ARRAY (Chapter 6) to access any specified Data Register, or even any Address Register for the –(AS),–(Ad),#data addressing form. Complete emulation would require that the routines are not called but that the actual 68020 codes are trapped by an illegal exception with control passed to the routines.

An example of ER-PACK and ER-UNPK use for squashing and expanding ASCII decimal data is shown in the QUEUE suite in Chapter 6.

```
*******************************************************************************
*
* = ER-PACK        68020 instruction PACK restricted emulator.
* > ER-UNPK        68020 instruction UNPK restricted emulator.
*
*******************************************************************************
*
* JOB             To provide simple emulation of the 68020 instructions,
*                 PACK and UNPK, for the 68000 and 68008, acting only on
*                 specific registers.
*
* ACTION          ER-PACK:
*                 Move unpacked Word source to accumulator.
*                 Read Return Address as embedded adjustment pointer.
*                 Add adjustment Word to accumulator.
*                 Increment adjustment pointer past adjustment Word.
*                 Stack adjustment pointer as new Return Address.
*                 Shift low order digit up against high order digit.
*                 Shift two packed digits down to low order byte.
*                 Move packed Byte from accumulator to destination.
*                 Exit, return to instruction after embedded adjustment.
*
*                 ER-UNPK:
*                 Move packed Byte source to destination.
*                 Shift packed digits up, high order going to 2nd byte.
*                 Shift low order digit down to low nibble, 1st byte.
*                 Clear high order nibbles of 1st and 2nd bytes.
*                 Read Return Address as embedded adjustment pointer.
*                 Add adjustment Word to destination.
*                 Increment adjustment pointer past adjustment Word.
*                 Stack adjustment pointer as new Return Address.
*                 Exit, return to instruction after embedded adjustment.
*
```

Listing 7.1. 68020 PACK/UNPK emulation.

```
*-------------------------------------------------------------
*
* CPU             68000, 68008
*
* HARDWARE        None.
*
* SOFTWARE        None.
*
*-------------------------------------------------------------
*
* INPUT           ER-PACK: D6.W contains 2 unpacked decimal digits.
*                 ER-UNPK: D7.B contains 2 packed BCD digits.
*                 Both:    Adjustment Word embedded after call instr.
*
* OUTPUT          ER-PACK: D7.B = D6+adj.[11-8] / 16 + D6+adj.[3-0]
*                 ER-UNPK: D6.W = D7[7-4] * 16 + D7[3-0] + adj.
*                 Both:    D6 high word and D7 high 3 bytes not changed.
*                          Exit to location after adjustment word.
*                          No other registers or flags changed.
*
* ERRORS          None.
*
* REG USE         D6.W D7.B
*
* STACK USE       ER-PACK: 10.  ER-UNPK: 6.
*
* RAM USE         None.
*
* LENGTH          ER-PACK: 30.  ER-UNPK: 32.
*
* CYCLES          Not given.
*
*-------------------------------------------------------------
*
* CLASS 1         *discreet       *interruptable      *promable
* ******          *reentrant      *relocatable        *robust
*
*************************************************************************
*
ER-PACK  MOVE      SR,-(A7)          Save CCR - no output flags.
         MOVEM.L   D0/A0,-(A7)       Save temporary accumulator and
*                                    adjustment word address register.
*
         MOVE.W    D6,D0             Get 2 unpacked digits to D0.
*
         MOVEA.L   #10(A7),A0        Read stacked return address (=
*                                    address of adjustment word) and
         ADD.W     (A0)+,D0          add adjustment to unpacked digits
*                                    incrementing A0 past adj. word.
         MOVE.L    A0,#10(A7)        Stack new return address.
*
         ASL.B     #4,D0             Butt low digit against high and
         ASR.W     #4,D0             move both to low byte of D0.
*
         MOVE.B    D0,D7             Copy packed digits to D7 lo-byte.
*
         MOVEM.L   (A7)+,D0/A0       Restore regs. and exit (restoring
         RTR                         CCR) to new return address.
*
*-------------------------------------------------------------
*
ER-UNPK  MOVE      SR,-(A7)          Save CCR - no output flags.
         MOVEM.L   A0,-(A7)          Save adj. word address register.
*
         MOVE.B    D7,D6             Move packed 2-digits to D6.
*
```

Listing 7.1 (contd)

```
        ASL.W    #4,D6              Move high digit up to low nibble
*                                   of 2nd byte in D6.
        ASR.B    #4,D6              Move low digit back down to low
*                                   nibble of 1st byte in D6.
        ANDI.W   #$0F0F,D6          Clear high nibbles of both bytes.
*
        MOVEA.L  #6(A7),A0          Read stacked return address (=
*                                   address of adjustment word) and
        ADD.W    (A0)+,D6           add adjustment to unpacked digits
*                                   incrementing A0 past adj. word.
        MOVE.L   A0,#6(A7)          Stack new return address.
*
        MOVEM.L  (A7)+,A0           Restore reg. and exit (restoring
        RTR                         CCR) to new return address.
*
*************************************************************************
```

Listing 7.1 (contd)

Module control

The routines in Listing 7.2, ER-CALLM and ER-RTM, emulate the operation of the 68020 module control instructions – but only type $00, option %000. Type $01 (the only other legal type) operates in conjunction with external hardware to assign access rights to the module, and option %100 indicates that the argument list is not on stack but in separate memory addressed by a pointer in the module descriptor. These other module classifications may also cause a change of stack pointer, with arguments transferred from the original to the new stack. The type $00, option %000 is, then, the most simple form and the only one which can easily be emulated in 68000 user mode operation.

Modules are glorified subroutines. Information about a module is contained in a module descriptor and this contains a minimum of two and a maximum of three addresses used by **CALLM:** the address of the module program code, the address of a data area used by the module, and an optional module stack pointer address. ER-CALLM uses only the first two of these addresses. Apart from the addresses, the descriptor also contains one word giving type, option and access level (all ignored by ER-CALLM and may contain additional information at the discretion of the user.

Module descriptors can be queued in the same way as the record keys in the QUEUE suite (Chapter 6) to share out processing time between several user tasks, or applications, apparently running concurrently. More usually, modules are discrete parts of a large program which cannot all exist in memory simultaneously. The main control section of the program is always resident and so are the module descriptors, but individual modules are called up from external storage (disk) only when needed – the descriptor containing enough information to load and pass control to its module.

Like ER-Pack and ER-UNPK, the module control routines are entered by subroutine calls, but if access to the illegal exception handler is allowed by the system the 68020 **CALLM** and **RTM** codes could be used. Both routines require embedded data words: since a jump or branch would not supply an address by which the data can be accessed, a subroutine call must be used to enter ER-RTM, even though no retun is made to the following location.

The actions of ER-CALLM and ER-RTM consist mainly of transferring data and addresses into and out of the correct places in the module stack frame. Data is also transferred between memory and any specified register. This problem is resolved in ER-CALLM by stacking all registers and using the input register number as a stack index in much the same way as the subscripts are accessed in ARRAY (Chapter 6). A different and somewhat unusual method is used in ER-RTM. A short subroutine is built up on stack, inside the stack frame, by ER-RTM, to perform the single job of transferring one long word stored in the stack frame to the specified register, and the address in the stack pointer is used, with an appropriate displacement, as the effective subroutine address. One word of warning would be in order here: in a strictly regulated system the interchangeable use of memory as program space or data space may not be possible.

```
*************************************************************************
*
* = ER-CALLM      68020 instruction CALLM restricted emulator.
* > ER-RTM        68020 instruction RTM restricted emulator.
*
*************************************************************************
*
* JOB             To provide simple emulation of the 68020 instructions,
*                 CALLM and RTM, for the 68000 and 68008, acting only on
*                 the direct address mode.
*
* ACTION          ER-CALLM:
*                 Adjust Stack pointer by frame size and for stacking
*                 all registers above frame.
*                 Store condition codes and Program Counter to frame.
*                 Adjust stored PC to address instruction following
*                 program embedded argument count and module descriptor
*                 address.
*                 Move embedded argument count and descriptor address to
*                 module stack frame.
*                 Address module descriptor.
*                 Move Opt-type-access Word to stack frame.
*                 Get address of Module Entry Word.
*                 Store MEW + 2 to stack as module entry address.
*                 Read MEW Module Data Area Pointer register number.
*                 Use register number as index to stacked registers and
*                 move stacked register value to stack frame, replace by
*                 new Module Data Area Pointer from module descriptor.
*                 Restore stacked registers and "return" to module.
*
*                 ER-RTM:
*                 Move frame-PC (return address to program that called
*                 the module) to deepest frame-cum-arguments stack
*                 location, saving its address within the frame.
*                 Use return address to module which called ER-RTM as
*                 address of embedded Data Area Pointer register number.
*                 Read DAP register number.
*                 IF register number NOT Stack Pointer (A7)
*                 THEN [ Use register number as destination register
*                         number (Rn) and build the instruction word for
*                         "MOVE.L #disp(A7),Rn".
*                         Store instruction word in stack frame, followed
*                         by displacement to frame Data Area Pointer, and
*                         by the code for "RTS".
*                         Execute subroutine built in stack frame to move
*                         DAP value to required register. ]
*                 ELSE [ Skip ... DAP lost if register is A7. ]
*                 Restore frame condition codes to CCR.
*                 Read frame-PC address to SP and execute "RTS" to set
*                 SP at stack below frame-cum-arguments and return
*                 control to program that originally called the module.
*
```

Listing 7.2. 68020 CALLM/RTM emulation.

```
*-------------------------------------------------------------------
*
* CPU            68000, 68008
*
* HARDWARE       None.
*
* SOFTWARE       None.
*
*-------------------------------------------------------------------
*
* INPUT          ER-CALLM: JSR ER-CALLM instruction must be followed by
*                          embedded data:
*                             word 1:  Argument count (0 to 254), even
*                                      numbers only, this gives the
*                                      number of arguments passed to
*                                      the module on stack.
*                             word 2,3: Address of module descriptor.
*                          Module descriptor must comply with the 68020
*                          type $00, option %000 descriptor of CALLM.
*                          The module entry word (immediately preceding
*                          the module object code) must comply with the
*                          68020 module entry word.
*                ER-RTM:   JSR ER-RTM instruction must be followed by
*                          embedded data:
*                             one word: Must correspond to the 68020
*                                       instruction RTM.
*
* OUTPUT         ER-CALLM: Type $00, option %000 module stack frame
*                          built above stacked arguments.
*                          Control passed to module address found in
*                          module descriptor.
*                ER-RTM:   Module stack frame and arguments removed
*                          from stack. Control returned to program
*                          address contained in stack frame.
*
* ERRORS         Errors will occur if any of the format standards are
*                not complied with.
*
* REG USE        One register is usd for the Data Area Pointer, this
*                is named in the Module Entry Word and the RTM word
*                and is preserved in the module stack frame.
*
* STACK USE      ER-CALLM: Stack frame, passed to module, 24,
*                          for register manipulation, 68 (above frame).
*                ER-RTM:   Return address above stack frame, 4,
*                          all frame and arguments removed from stack.
*
* RAM USE        None.
*
* LENGTH         Not given.
*
* CYCLES         Not given.
*
*-------------------------------------------------------------------
*
* CLASS 2        *discreet       *interruptable     *promable
* ***-*-         -reentrant      *relocatable       -robust
*
*******************************************************************************
*
ER-CALLM SUBA.W    #88,A7                      Make space for frame + regs.
*
         MOVE      SR,#70(A7)                  Save CCR to frame, clearing
         ANDI.W    #$00FF,#70(A7)              high byte of SR.
*
         MOVEA.L   #88(A7),#80(A7)             Move PC to correct frame place &
         ADDQ.L    #6,#80(A7)                  adjust for call parameters, then
         CLR.L     #88(A7)                     clear unused SP store in frame.
```

Listing 7.2 (contd)

```
          MOVEM.L   D0-A7,(A7)             Stack all regs for index access,
          ADDI.L    #68,#60(A7)            adjust stacked SP to frame top.
*
          MOVEA.L   #80(A7),A0             Use return address to address
          MOVE.W    #-6(A0),#72(A7)        arg count, move it to frame, &
          MOVEA.L   #-4(A0),A0             module descriptor pointer, copy
          MOVE.L    A0,#76(A7)             it to frame.
*
          MOVE.W    (A0),#68(A7)           Move Opt-type-access to frame.
*
          MOVEA.L   #4(A0),#64(A7)         Move Entry Word Pointer to space
                                           reserved for ER-CALLM exit PC and
          ADDQ.L    #2,#64(A7)             adjust to address 1st code word.
*
          MOVEA.L   #64(A7),A1             Address module and get
          MOVE.W    #-2(A1),D1             entry word for MDAP reg number.
          ROL.W     #4,D1                  Move reg number to low nibble
          ANDI.W    #$000F,D1              and mask out unwanted bits.
*
          MOVE.L    #0(A7,D1.W),#84(A7)    Move saved MDAP reg to frame &
          MOVE.L    #8(A0),#0(A7,D1.W)     put new DAP to stacked reg.
*
          MOVEM.L   (A7)+,D0-A6            Restore all regs except stacked
          CLR.L     (A7)+                  SP (= A7) which is discarded.
          MOVE      #6(A7),CCR             Restore condition codes and
          RTS                              "return" to called module.
*
*-------------------------------------------------------------------------------
*
ER-RTM    MOVE.L    A0,#10(A7)             Save A0 as ER-RTM pointer.
          MOVEA.L   A7,A0                  Address stack, add frame + ret
          ADDA.W    #28,A0                 addr size to address arguments,
          ADDA.W    #8(A7),A0              add args to address exit stack.
*
          MOVE.L    #16(A7),-(A0)          Move frame-PC to top of exit
          MOVE.L    A0,#16(A7)             stack and store pre-exit SP.
*
          MOVE.L    (A7),A0                Get the JSR ER-RTM ret addr as
                                           pointer to MDAP reg. no. word.
          MOVE.L    D7,(A7)                Save D7 for reg. no. operations.

          MOVE.W    (A0),D7                Get MDAP reg. number to D7
          MOVEA.L   #10(A7),A0             and restore A0.
*
          ANDI.W    #$000F,D7              Isolate register number, and
          CMPI.W    #$000F,D7              ignore if A7 (= SP) is
          BEQ       ER-R-END               destination register.
*
          ADDI.W    #$1FF8,D7              Shift bit 3 (A/D) to bit 13
          ANDI.W    #$2007,D7              mask out all but A/D and reg no.
          ROR.W     #7,D7                  rotate to MOVE dest. EA field,
          ADDI.W    #$202F,D7              add size and source EA codes for
*                                          Long move from #d(A7) to reg.
*
          MOVE.W    D7,#10(A7)             Store as MOVE.L d(A7),Rn instr.,
          MOVE.W    #20,#12(A7)            followed by disp to stacked MDAP,
          MOVE.W    #$4E75,#14(A7)         followed by RTS as a subroutine
*                                          built up in the stack frame.
*
          MOVE.L    (A7)+,D7               Restore D7 for possible load by
*                                          stack subroutine, adjusting SP.
*
          JSR       #10(A7)                Call stack subroutine, with
*                                          disp allowing for saved PC.
*
          MOVE.L    D7,-(A7)               Re-stack D7 for ER-R-END restore.
*
```

Listing 7.2 (contd)

```
ER-R-END MOVE.L    (A7),D7              Restore D7.
         MOVE      #6(A7),CCR           Restore module frame CCR to CCR.
         MOVEA.L   #16(A7),A7           Get address of exit-PC as SP.
*
         RTS                            Return to program that called
*                                       module which called ER-RTM.
**********************************************************************
```

Listing 7.2 (contd)

Appendix A
ASCII

ASCII (American Standard Code for Information Interchange) control codes ($00 to $1F and $7F) were designed for terminal control and may be used for intercomputer and computer-peripheral communications. Most have no internal use within stand-alone microcomputers, although several are often used as cursor control codes.

ASCII character codes ($20 to $7E) are almost always used for intercomputer communicating and often for file storage on tape or disk. They are often but not always used for internal character representation. Variations on the standard US set may occur in different countries – for example, one of the lesser used codes may be replaced by the pound symbol (£) to produce a UK version in British computers and peripherals.

ASCII control codes

Table A1 gives the ASCII control codes in hexadecimal, the two- or three-letter standard abbreviations and their meanings.

Hex	Abbr.	Meaning	Hex	Abbr.	Meaning
00	NUL	Null	10	DLE	Data Link Escape
01	SOH	Start of Heading	11	DC1	Direct Control 1
02	STX	Start Text	12	DC2	Direct Control 2
03	ETX	End Text	13	DC3	Direct Control 3
04	EOT	End of Transmission	14	DC4	Direct Control 4
05	ENQ	Enquiry	15	NAK	Negative Acknowledge
06	ACK	Acknowledge	16	SYN	Synchronous Idle
07	BEL	Bell	17	ETB	End Transmission Block
08	BS	Backspace	18	CAN	Cancel
09	HT	Horizontal Tab	19	EM	End of Medium
0A	LF	Line Feed	1A	SUB	Substitute
0B	VT	Vertical Tab	1B	ESC	Escape
0C	FF	Form Feed	1C	FS	Form Separator
0D	CR	Carriage Return	1D	GS	Group Separator
0E	SO	Shift Out	1E	RS	Record Separator
0F	SI	Shift In	1F	US	Unit Separator
7F	DEL	Delete	20	SP	Space

Table A1. ASCII control codes – abbreviations and meanings.

Standard ASCII codes

Standard ASCII codes use 7-bit values ($00 to $7F) and are usually represented as 8-bit (byte) values with bit 7 reset.

Table A2 gives the standard USASCII codes in hexadecimal and decimal notation, showing the four main groups: control codes (CTRL), symbols and decimal digits (S/D), upper-case letters (U.C.), and lower-case letters (L.C.).

Hex	Dec	CTRL	Hex	Dec	S/D	Hex	Dec	U.C.	Hex	Dec	L.C.
00	0	NUL	20	32	SP	40	64	@	60	96	`
01	1	SOH	21	33	!	41	65	A	61	97	a
02	2	STX	22	34	"	42	66	B	62	98	b
03	3	ETX	23	35	#	43	67	C	63	99	c
04	4	EOT	24	36	$	44	68	D	64	100	d
05	5	ENQ	25	37	%	45	69	E	65	101	e
06	6	ACK	26	38	&	46	70	F	66	102	f
07	7	BEL	27	39	'	47	71	G	67	103	g
08	8	BS	28	40	(	48	72	H	68	104	h
09	9	HT	29	41	)	49	73	I	69	105	i
0A	10	LF	2A	42	*	4A	74	J	6A	106	j
0B	11	VT	2B	43	+	4B	75	K	6B	107	k
0C	12	FF	2C	44	,	4C	76	L	6C	108	l
0D	13	CR	2D	45	−	4D	77	M	6D	109	m
0E	14	SO	2E	46	.	4E	78	N	6E	110	n
0F	15	SI	2F	47	/	4F	79	O	6F	111	o
10	16	DLE	30	48	0	50	80	P	70	112	p
11	17	DC1	31	49	1	51	81	Q	71	113	q
12	18	DC2	32	50	2	52	82	R	72	114	r
13	19	DC3	33	51	3	53	83	S	73	115	s
14	20	DC4	34	52	4	54	84	T	74	116	t
15	21	NAK	35	53	5	55	85	U	75	117	u
16	22	SYN	36	54	6	56	86	V	76	118	v
17	23	ETB	37	55	7	57	87	W	77	119	w
18	24	CAN	38	56	8	58	88	X	78	120	x
19	25	EM	39	57	9	59	89	Y	79	121	y
1A	26	SUB	3A	58	:	5A	90	Z	7A	122	z
1B	27	ESC	3B	59	;	5B	91	[	7B	123	{
1C	28	FS	3C	60	<	5C	92	\	7C	124	!
1D	29	GS	3D	61	=	5D	93	]	7D	125	}
1E	30	RS	3E	62	>	5E	94	^	7E	126	~
1F	31	US	3F	63	?	5F	95	_	7F	127	DEL

Table A2. ASCII hexadecimal and decimal codes (bit 7 reset).

Alternative ASCII codes

When ASCII codes are implemented internally, an equivalent range utilising the code group $80 to $FF (bit 7 set) is sometimes used to represent inverse characters or some other alternative font. Dot matrix printers often have a set of predefined graphics characters which may be accessed by sending codes above $80.

Table A3 demonstrates the graphics characters and alternate (italic) font of one of the most popular dot matrix printers – the Epson RX-80 F/T – accessed by codes $80 to $FF. Hexadecimal and decimal notation is given and the tabulation shows the four main groups: special character generator (CG), symbols and decimal digits (S/D), upper-case letters (U.C.), and lower-case letters (L.C.).

Hex	Dec	CG	Hex	Dec	S/D	Hex	Dec	U.C.	Hex	Dec	L.C.
80	128	+	A0	160		C0	192	@	E0	224	`
81	129	⊥	A1	161	!	C1	193	A	E1	225	a
82	130	τ	A2	162	"	C2	194	B	E2	226	b
83	131	⊣	A3	163	#	C3	195	C	E3	227	c
84	132	⊦	A4	164	$	C4	196	D	E4	228	d
85	133	−	A5	165	%	C5	197	E	E5	229	e
86	134			A6	166	&	C6	198	F	E6	230	f
87	135	⌐	A7	167	'	C7	199	G	E7	231	g
88	136	⌐	A8	168	(	C8	200	H	E8	232	h
89	137	∟	A9	169	)	C9	201	I	E9	233	i
8A	138	⌐	AA	170	*	CA	202	J	EA	234	j
8B	139	▓	AB	171	+	CB	203	K	EB	235	k
8C	140	■	AC	172	,	CC	204	L	EC	236	l
8D	141	▬	AD	173	−	CD	205	M	ED	237	▮
8E	142	▌	AE	174	.	CE	206	N	EE	238	n
8F	143	●	AF	175	/	CF	207	O	EF	239	o
90	144	○	B0	176	0	D0	208	P	F0	240	p
91	145	♠	B1	177	1	D1	209	Q	F1	241	q
92	146	♥	B2	178	2	D2	210	R	F2	242	r
93	147	♦	B3	179	3	D3	211	S	F3	243	s
94	148	♣	B4	180	4	D4	212	T	F4	244	t
95	149	♪	B5	181	5	D5	213	U	F5	245	u
96	150	♬	B6	182	6	D6	214	V	F6	246	v
97	151	✦	B7	183	7	D7	215	W	F7	247	ⱳ
98	152	#	B8	184	8	D8	216	X	F8	248	x
99	153	☿	B9	185	9	D9	217	Y	F9	249	y
9A	154	☆	BA	186	:	DA	218	Z	FA	250	z
9B	155	↑	BB	187	;	DB	219	[	FB	251	{
9C	156	↓	BC	188	<	DC	220	\	FC	252	/
9D	157	×	BD	189	=	DD	221	]	FD	253	}
9E	158	÷	BE	190	>	DE	222	^	FE	254	~
9F	159	±	BF	191	?	DF	223	_	FF	255	

Table A3. Epson ASCII codes (bit 7 set).

Appendix B
Registers

TYPE	MODE	REGISTER	SIZE	IMPLEMENTATIONS
DATA	USER	D0 D1 D2 D3 D4 D5 D6 D7	32 32 32 32 32 32 32 32	all
ADDRESS	USER	A0 A1 A2 A3 A4 A5 A6 A7	32 32 32 32 32 32 32 32	all
CONTROL	USER	CCR PC USP (A7)	8 32 32	all
	SUPERVISOR	SR (inc. CCR)	16	all
		SSP (A7')	32	68000, 68008, 68010
		ISP (A7') MSP (A7")	32 32	68020
		VBR SFC DFC	32 3 3	68010, 68020
		CACR CAAR	32 32	68020

Figure B1. 68000-series registers by type, mode and bit size.

All processors in the 68000-series have a set of eight Data Registers. These are the equivalent of both accumulators and general purpose data storage registers in other computers. In addition, there are eight Address Registers designed for use in indirectly addressing memory, although these too may be used for data storage.

Of the registers used for program and system control, the 68000 and 68008 have a Program Counter, Status Register and two stack pointers. The Status Register includes the Condition Codes Register containing operation result flags, and the system byte containing system control bits. The two stack pointers each correspond to Address Register A7; the User Stack Pointer obtains in User mode and the Supervisor Stack Pointer in Supervisor mode.

The 68010, along with all the registers provided in the 68000, also has a Vector Base Register and two 3-bit Address Space Registers, the Source Function Code Register and the Destination Function Code Register.

The 68020 exceeds the 68010 with two registers to control its on-chip cache memory, the Cache Control Register and Cache Address Register. It also contains one extra stack pointer, the Master Stack Pointer, used for internal task handling, whilst the equivalent of the Supervisor Stack Pointer is transformed into an Interrupt Stack Pointer, used for the processing of external and asynchronous events.

Figure B1 shows an arrangement by type, mode accessibility and bit size, of all the 68000, 68008, 68010 and 68020 registers that are available to the applications programmer (User mode only) or systems programmer (Supervisor and User modes).

Function

The modes in which they may be accessed and the type of operation allowed on them regulates and constrains the functions of 68000-series registers. Figure B2 shows a categorisation of all registers according to these functions. The use of both Data and Address Registers as Index Registers is a secondary function.

Operand size

The 32-bit Data Registers may be used as 32-bit (long word) operands. They may also be used as 16-bit (word) operands, in which case operations affect only the 16 low order bits (15 through $\emptyset$); the 16 high order bits (31 through 16) are disregarded (not changed). Similarly, use of Data Registers as 8-bit (byte) operands affects only bits 7 through $\emptyset$, leaving bits 31 through 8 unaffected. This is shown in Figure B3.

Operations performed on Address Registers are intended only for address manipulation. Consequently, the complete 32-bit destination Address Register is affected by an operation. Word length sources are sign extended to 32-bit operands before the operation occurs. Byte length sources and operations are not allowed.

Accumulator and General Storage		
D0 to D7	Data Registers 0 to 7	(User and Supervisor Modes)

Memory Reference		
A0 to A7	Address Registers 0 to 7	(User and Supervisor Modes)

Index		
D0 to D7, A0 to A7	Data and Address Registers (all Modes)	

Stack Pointer		
USP (A7)	User Stack Pointer	(User Mode only)
SSP (A7')	Supervisor Stack Pointer	(Supervisor Mode, not 68020)
ISP (A7')	Interrupt Stack Pointer	(68020 Supervisor State)
MSP (A7")	Master Stack Pointer	(68020 Supervisor & Master State)

Program Status and Control		
CCR	Condition Codes Register	(User & Supervisor Modes)
PC	Program Counter	(User & Supervisor Modes)

System Status and Control		
SR	Status Register	(Supervisor Mode only)
VBR	Vector Base Register	(68010/68020 Supervisor Mode)
SFC	Source Function Code Register	(68010/68020 Supervisor Mode)
DFC	Destination Function Code Register	(68010/68020 Supervisor Mode)

Cache Memory Control		
CACR	Cache Control Register	(68020 Supervisor Mode)
CAAR	Cache Address Register	(68020 Supervisor Mode)

Figure B2. 68000-series registers by function.

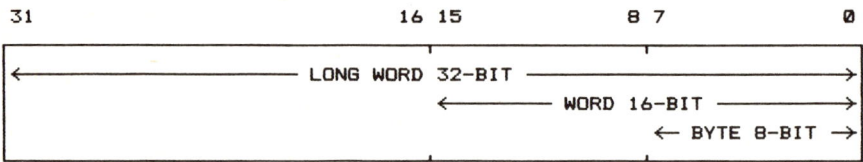

Figure B3. Register operand sizes.

Addressing capabilities

Although all Address Registers, Stack Pointers (all Stack Pointers are Address Register A7 or its alternatives in Supervisor mode), the Vector Base Register and the Program Counter are 32 bits wide, only the 68020 supports the full width address bus. The other processors, having sawn-off address buses, are restricted in the amount of memory they may address directly.

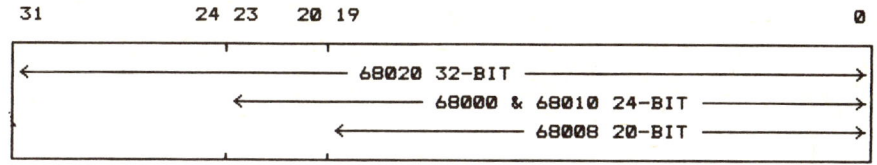

Figure B4. 68000-series maximum address capabilities.

Figure B4 shows the extent of validity in any register used for memory addressing in the 68000, 68008, 68010 and 68020. It is likely that most systems will not contain the maximum addressable memory and valid limits will be several bits lower. However, both the 68010 and 68020 are virtual machines and the system could support full addressing capability with limited on-board memory.

The Status Register

Figure B5 shows the 16-bit Status Register. The high order byte (bits 15 through 8) is accessible only in Supervisor mode and controls some aspects of the system. These are:

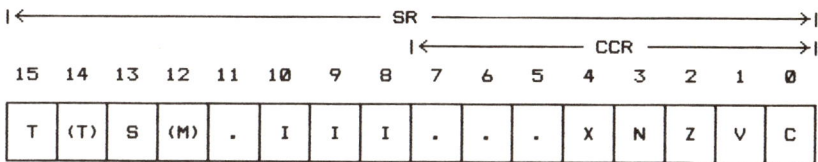

Figure B5. Status Register and Condition Codes Register.

T: Trace mode (four Trace modes in the 68020, switched by two T bits)
S: Supervisor or User mode
M: (68020 only) Master or Interrupt state for Supervisor mode
I: 3-bit Interrupt priority – seven levels

The low order byte, the Condition Codes Register, is accessible in both User and Supervisor modes. The CCR flags the operation results:

N: Negative
Z: Zero
V: Overflow
C: Carry

The CCR also contains one bit, **X** (Extend), which is used as the carry-over bit in extended length operations.

Further information about the Status Register may be found in Tables D5.1, D5.2 and E5 in Appendices D and E.

Appendix C
Standard Assembler Conventions

The standard assembler for 68000-series processors allows the four fields, label, mnemonic, operand and comment. Variable start position and termination of each field is allowed.

Label

Table C1. gives the standard conventions for label attributes. Note particularly that labels longer than the number of characters used by the assembler are allowed to be written.

Label attribute	68000-series assembler convention
Length	optional
Significant characters	1-8
Start character	(A-Z) or period (.)
Terminator	<space> or colon (:) for indented label
Valid characters	(A-Z), (1-9), ($), (-), (.), (_)
Mnemonic strings	allowed
Multi-labelling	allowed

Table C1. Label attributes.

Mnemonic

The mnemonic field is to the right of the label field and must be preceded by at least one space. It is terminated by one or more spaces. Standard 68000-series mnemonics are given in Appendices D and E.

Table C2. lists the usual forms of the basic 68000 assembler directives. The list may be vastly extended in particular assemblers.

Form	Meaning
ORG	Origin – program, subroutine, stack or data area start address.
EQU	Equate label to data value.
DC	Define Constant data – initialise memory to given data. Multiple data may be assigned if each datum is separated by a comma.
DCB	Define Constant data Block – initialise block of memory locations to given data.
DS	Define Storage – reserve a given number of memory locations.
END	End of source program.

Notes. 1. EQU, DC, DCB and DS may be specified as byte, word or long word by appending a size code (.B, .W or .L).
2. The need to keep instruction words on an even byte boundary may result in one extra byte being assigned (skipped or initialised to zero) by DC.B, DCB.B and DS.B.
3. Character string data should be enclosed in single quotes, a comma between each character is not necessary.

Table C2. Assembler directives.

Operand

Instruction source operands precede destination operands and are separated by a comma. The operand field is terminated by one or more spaces. The standard forms of instruction operands may be found in Appendices D and E in Tables D2 and E2. Note that the use of parentheses to denote indirect addressing differs between the 68020 and earlier 68000-series assembler conventions.

Table C3 gives standard symbolic notation for entries in the operand field.

Comment

Comments occupy the rightmost field when occurring on the same line as a label or instruction, but may occupy the entire line. If following an instruction then the space terminator after the operand(s), or after the mnemonic if no operands are required, is a sufficient delimeter. Full line comments, or comments succeeding a label require an initial asterisk (*). No other limitations are placed on comments.

Symbol	Meaning
!	OR in arithmetic and logical expressions.
#	Immediate data (initial character).
$	Hexadecimal data (initial character).
%	Binary data (initial character).
&	(1) AND in arithmetic and logical expressions.
	(2) Optional initial character to decimal data.
' '	Single quotes enclosing ASCII character string.
( )	Encloses indirect address expression.
( )+	Post-increment indirect addressing.
-( )	Pre-decrement indirect addressing.
*	(1) MULTIPLY in arithmetic and logical expressions.
	(2) To denote the contents of the assembler location counter for program relative offset addressing.
+	(1) ADD in arithmetic and logical expressions.
	(2) To denote a positive displacement or offset.
,	(1) Delimiter for source and destination operands.
	(2) Delimiter for index address forms operand addends.
	(3) Delimiter for multiple data.
-	(1) MINUS in arithmetic and logical expressions.
	(2) To denote a negative displacement or offset.
	(3) To identify a register list range.
.	To append a size code (W or L) to registers in index modes.
/	(1) DIVIDE in arithmetic and logical expressions.
	(2) Delimiter in a register list.
:	To conjoin two operands as source or destination.
<<	To denote left shift in a logical expression.
>>	To denote right shift in a logical expression.
@	Octal data (initial character).
[]	Encloses first level of indirection in memory indirect addressing.
^	Exponential symbol in arithmetic and logical expressions.

Notes. 1. Decimal data is the default case and requires no numerical base initial character symbol.
2. Arithmetic and logical expressions are truncated to the specified operand size.

Table C3. Operand symbols.

Appendix D
68000, 68008 and 68010 Instructions

This appendix gives the mnemonic, allowed operand forms, action caused, object code (machine code), result condition codes (flags) and the timing in clock cycles for all instructions that are valid in both User and Supervisor modes on the 68000, 68008 and 68010 microprocessors. Similar information for the 68020 is given in Appendix E.

The 68000 has many thousands of distinct instruction forms when all the various methods of addressing memory and use of sixteen Data and Address Registers are taken into account. Consequently, it is no simple matter to provide reference tables showing their 2-byte to 1∅-byte machine codes clearly in a few pages. Luckily, most codes beyond the 2-byte instruction word have standard 'extension' forms corresponding to the addressing mode used as operand. Nevertheless, the instruction word itself can contain an assortment of register, mode, address, size, condition and data fields. In many cases, to aid clarity and quick reference, these fields are expanded fully in the object code table and given as separate instructions. In some cases expansion would amount to a veritable explosion of instruction forms, and symbolic notation has been used to prevent this.

Tables D1.1 and D1.2 provide reference to the main instruction group tables D7.1. to D7.22. For assistance in writing upward compatible programs or for writing code to emulate the more advanced 68020 instructions they also indicate those instructions supported on the 68020 but not on earlier processors. Table D1.1 may be used when searching for a particular instruction, Table D1.2 when searching for an instruction to perform a particular task.

Table D2 lists the groups of effective address forms contained in each of several categories. The 68000-series processors are designed to regulate operand access as part of the concept of structured programming with differentiated data space and program space. Memory addressed relative to the Program Counter may be read but not written to since this could involve instruction code changes during run time. Likewise, the forms which stipulate an address are distinguished from those which stipulate data. Use of invalid effective address operand forms, if not caught during assembly, will initiate exception processing.

Tables D3.1 to D3.5 give the full digit or double digit (byte) hexadecimal expansions for the symbolic forms used in the code word columns of the main instruction tables.

Tables D4.1 and D4.2 list the number and type of effective address extension words. The high order byte of the index extension word is given in full for each possible form.

Tables D5.1 and D5.2 explain the principal result flag states and describe the system byte of the Status Register which is affected by some instructions.

Table D6.1 gives the basic time used in calculating (and fetching) the effective address, which must be added to the times shown against many instruction forms in the main instruction tables. Table D6.2 gives the minimum timing for exception processing. This is the number of clock cycles consumed in stacking the machine state and prefetching the first two instruction words of the exception handler routine; it does not include the processing to sort out the problem which caused the exception.

Tables D7.1 to D7.22 give all instruction forms, their action, code, flag results and timing. D7.21 (coprocessor) and D7.22 (bit field) are null tables in this appendix (none of those types of instruction are implemented on processors designed earlier than the 68020), but are noted to enable full cross-processor correspondence with the 68020 instruction tables in Appendix E.

Table D8. gives the allowed forms with iteration timing for the special loop mode operation of the 68010.

Instruction	General Operation Description	Ref:
ABCD	Add Binary Coded Decimal with Extend.	D.7.09.
ADD	Add Binary.	D.7.05.
ADDA	Add Binary to Address Register.	D.7.05.
ADDI	Add Immediate Binary Data.	D.7.05.
ADDQ	Add Quick Immediate Binary Data.	D.7.05.
ADDX	Add Binary with Extend.	D.7.05.
AND	Logical AND.	D.7.10.
ANDI	Logical AND Immediate Data.	D.7.10.
ANDI to CCR	Logical AND Immediate Data to CCR.	D.7.16.
ANDI to SR	Logical AND Immediate Data to SR.	D.7.17.
ASL	Arithmetic Shift Left.	D.7.11.
ASR	Arithmetic Shift Right.	D.7.11.
Bcc	Branch on Condition True.	D.7.15.
BCHG	Bit Test then Change.	D.7.13.
BCLR	Bit Test then Clear.	D.7.13.
BFCHG	Bit Field Test then Change.	*E.7.22.
BFCLR	Bit Field Test then Clear.	*E.7.22.
BFEXTS	Move Sign extended Bit Field to Data Register.	*E.7.22.
BFEXTU	Move Zero-extended Bit Field to Data Register.	*E.7.22.
BFFFO	Find First One (msb) in Bit Field.	*E.7.22.
BFINS	Move Data Register to Bit Field.	*E.7.22
BFSET	Bit Field Test then Set.	*E.7.22.
BFTST	Bit Field Test.	*E.7.22.
BKPT	Breakpoint.	D.7.19.
BRA	Branch Always.	D.7.15.
BSET	Bit Test then Set.	D.7.13.
BSR	Branch to Subroutine.	D.7.15.
BTST	Bit Test.	D.7.13.
CALLM	Call Module, passing parameters.	*E.7.14.
CAS	Compare and Swap Single Update Operand.	*E.7.20.
CAS2	Compare and Swap Dual Update Operand.	*E.7.20.
CHK	Check Register, TRAP if <0 or >bound.	D.7.19.
CHK2	Check Register, TRAP if out of bounds.	*E.7.19.
CLR	Clear.	D.7.03.
CMP	Compare.	D.7.07.
CMP2	Compare Register against bounds.	*E.7.07.
CMPA	Compare Address Register with Operand.	D.7.07.
CMPI	Compare Operand with Immediate Data.	D.7.07.
CMPM	Compare Memory Operands.	D.7.07.
cpBcc	Branch on Coprocessor Condition True.	*E.7.21.
cpDBcc	Decrement & Branch on Coprocessor Condition False.	*E.7.21.

Table D1.1. Instruction Set Table Reference: 68000-series instructions alphabetically listed.

cpGEN	Pass General Function Command to Coprocessor.	*E.7.21.
cpRESTORE	Restore Coprocessor Internal State.	*E.7.21.
cpSAVE	Save Coprocessor Internal State.	*E.7.21.
cpScc	Set if Coprocessor Condition True, Clear if False.	*E.7.21.
cpTRAPcc	TRAP if Coprocessor Condition True.	*E.7.21.
DBcc	Decrement and Branch on Condition False.	D.7.15.
DIVS	Two's Complement Signed Divide.	D.7.08.
DIVSL	Longer Two's Complement Signed Divide.	*E.7.08.
DIVU	Unsigned Binary Divide.	D.7.08.
DIVUL	Longer Unsigned Binary Divide.	*E.7.08.
EOR	Logical Exclusive-OR.	D.7.10.
EORI	Logical EOR Immediate Data.	D.7.10.
EORI to CCR	Logical EOR Immediate Data to CCR.	D.7.16.
EORI to SR	Logical EOR Immediate Data to SR.	D.7.17.
EXG	Exchange Register with Register.	D.7.03.
EXT	Sign Extend Data Register.	D.7.03.
EXTB	Sign Extend Data Register byte to long word.	*E.7.03.
ILLEGAL	Cause Illegal Instruction Exception.	D.7.19.
JMP	Jump.	D.7.14.
JSR	Jump to Subroutine.	D.7.14.
LEA	Load Effective Address to Address Register.	D.7.04.
LINK	Link and Allocate Workspace.	D.7.04.
LSL	Logical Shift Left.	D.7.11.
LSR	Logical Shift Right.	D.7.11.
MOVE	Move Data.	D.7.01.
MOVE from CCR	Move from Condition Codes.	D.7.16.
MOVE to CCR	Move Data to CCR.	D.7.16.
MOVE from SR	Move from Status Register.	D.7.17.
MOVE to SR	Move Data to SR.	D.7.17.
MOVE USP	Move USP to/from Address Register.	D.7.17.
MOVEA	Move Address to Address Register.	D.7.01.
MOVEC	Move to/from Control Register.	D.7.18.
MOVEM	Move Data to/from Multiple Registers.	D.7.02.
MOVEP	Move Peripheral Data to/from Data Register.	D.7.02.
MOVEQ	Move Quick Immediate Data to Data Register.	D.7.01.
MOVES	Move to/from alternate address space.	D.7.18.
MULS	Two's Complement Signed Multiply.	D.7.08.
MULU	Unsigned Binary Multiply.	D.7.08.
NBCD	Negate Binary Coded Decimal with Extend.	D.7.09.
NEG	Negate Binary.	D.7.07.
NEGX	Negate Binary with Extend.	D.7.07.
NOP	No Operation.	D.7.14.
NOT	Logical Complement.	D.7.10.
OR	Logical Inclusive-OR.	D.7.10.
ORI	Logical OR Immediate Data.	D.7.10.
ORI to CCR	Logical OR Immediate Data to CCR.	D.7.16.
ORI to SR	Logical OR Immediate Data to SR.	D.7.17.
PACK	Pack unpacked Binary Coded Decimal.	*E.7.09.
PEA	Push Effective Address.	D.7.04.
RESET	Reset External Devices.	D.7.18.
ROL	Rotate Left.	D.7.12.
ROR	Rotate Right.	D.7.12.
ROXL	Rotate Left through Extend.	D.7.12.
ROXR	Rotate Right through Extend.	D.7.12.
RTD	Return and Deallocate Stack Parameters.	D.7.14.
RTE	Return from Exception.	D.7.18.
RTM	Return from Module.	*E.7.14.
RTR	Restore CCR and Return from Subroutine.	D.7.14.
RTS	Return from Subroutine.	D.7.14.
SBCD	Subtract Binary Coded Decimal with Extend.	D.7.09.
Scc	Set Byte if Condition True, or Clear if False.	D.7.15.
STOP	Move Immediate Data to SR then Stop.	D.7.18.
SUB	Subtract Binary.	D.7.06.
SUBA	Subtract Binary from Address Register.	D.7.06.
SUBI	Subtract Immediate Binary Data.	D.7.06.
SUBQ	Subtract Quick Immediate Binary Data.	D.7.06.
SUBX	Subtract Binary with Extend.	D.7.06.
SWAP	Swap Data Register Low and High Order Words.	D.7.03.

Table D1.1. (contd)

TAS	Test Byte and Set Most Significant Bit.	D.7.20.
TRAP	Cause TRAP Exception.	D.7.19.
TRAPcc	Cause TRAP on Condition True.	*E.7.19.
TRAPV	Cause TRAP on Overflow True.	D.7.19.
TST	Test, Compare Operand with Zero.	D.7.07.
UNLK	Unlink and De-allocate Workspace.	D.7.04.
UNPK	Unpack packed Binary Coded Decimal.	*E.7.09.

Notes. 1. Instructions with D.7.xx. references are implemented on all or some of the 68000, 68008 and 68010; refer to this appendix.
2. Instructions with *E.7.xx. references are 68020 instructions not implemented on the 68000, 68008 and 68010; they are to be found in Appendix E.
3. 68020 implementations of instructions common to all or some processors in the series may differ; refer to the corresponding table in Appendix E.

Table D1.1. (contd)

Instruction Group	Instructions	Ref:
Data transfer (1)	MOVE, MOVEA, MOVEQ.	D.7.01.
Data transfer (2)	MOVEM, MOVEP.	D.7.02.
Data transfer (3)	CLR, EXT, *EXTB, SWAP, EXG.	D.7.03.
Data transfer (4)	LEA, PEA, LINK, UNLK.	D.7.04.
Arithmetic (1)	ADD, ADDA, ADDI, ADDQ, ADDX.	D.7.05.
Arithmetic (2)	SUB, SUBA, SUBI, SUBQ, SUBX.	D.7.06.
Arithmetic (3)	CMP, *CMP2, CMPA, CMPI, CMPM, NEG, NEGX, TST.	D.7.07.
Arithmetic (4)	DIVS, *DIVSL, DIVU, *DIVUL, MULS, MULU.	D.7.08.
Binary Coded Decimal	ABCD, SBCD, NBCD, *PACK, *UNPK.	D.7.09.
Logic	AND, ANDI, EOR, EORI, OR, ORI, NOT.	D.7.10.
Shift	ASL, ASR, LSL, LSR.	D.7.11.
Rotate	ROL, ROR, ROXL, ROXR.	D.7.12.
Bit manipulation	BCHG, BCLR, BSET, BTST.	D.7.13.
Program Control (1)	*CALLM, JMP, JSR, NOP, RTD, *RTM, RTR, RTS.	D.7.14.
Program Control (2)	BRA, BSR, Bcc, DBcc, Scc.	D.7.15.
System Control (1)	MOVE to/from CCR, ANDI to CCR, EORI to CCR, ORI to CCR.	D.7.16.
System Control (2)	MOVE to/from SR, ANDI to CCR, EORI to CCR, ORI to SR, MOVE USP.	D.7.17.
System Control (3)	MOVEC, MOVES, RESET, STOP, RTE.	D.7.18.
System Control (4)	BKPT, CHK, ILLEGAL, TRAP, TRAPV, *CHK2, *TRAPcc.	D.7.19.

Table D1.2. Instruction Set Table Reference: grouped 68000-series instructions.

Multiprocessor	TAS, *CAS, *CAS2.		D.7.20.
Coprocessor	*cpBcc, *cpDBcc, *cpGEN, *cpRESTORE, *cpSAVE, *cpScc, *cpTRAPcc.		D.7.21.
Bit Field	*BFCHG, *BFCLR, *BFEXTS, *BFEXTU, *BFFFO, *BFINS, *BFSET, *BFTST.		D.7.22.

Notes. 1. A few instructions are implemented on the 68010 but not on the 68000 or 68008; see the appropriate table in this appendix.
2. * prefix: Instructions prefixed with '*' are not implemented on the 68000, 68008 and 68010; refer to the corresponding table in Appendix E.
3. 68020 implementations of instructions common to all or some processors in the series may differ; refer to the corresponding table in Appendix E.

Table D1.2. (contd)

EA	read allowed set				write allowed set			
	raEA	rcEA	rdEA	rmEA	waEA	wcEA	wdEA	wmEA
Dn	✓	–	✓	–	✓	–	✓	–
An	✓	–	–	–	✓	–	–	–
(An)	✓	✓	✓	✓	✓	✓	✓	✓
(An)+	✓	–	✓	✓	✓	–	✓	✓
-(An)	✓	–	✓	✓	✓	–	✓	✓
sdw(An)	✓	✓	✓	✓	✓	✓	✓	✓
sdb(An,Xx)	✓	✓	✓	✓	✓	✓	✓	✓
addr.W	✓	✓	✓	✓	✓	✓	✓	✓
addr.L	✓	✓	✓	✓	✓	✓	✓	✓
sdw(PC)	✓	✓	✓	✓	–	–	–	–
sdb(PC,Xx)	✓	✓	✓	✓	–	–	–	–
#data.B	✓	–	✓	✓	–	–	–	–
#data.W	✓	–	✓	✓	–	–	–	–
#data.L	✓	–	✓	✓	–	–	–	–

Notes. 1. a = all forms. c = control. d = data. m = memory.
2. ✓ form allowed. – form not allowed.

Table D2. 68000, 68008 and 68010 Effective Address categories.

Symbol	3-bit field (s or d) =	000	001	010	011	100	101	110	111
0s or 0d		0	1	2	3	4	5	6	7
1s or 1d		8	9	A	B	C	D	E	F
s0 or d0		0	2	4	6	8	A	C	E
s1 or d1		1	3	5	7	9	B	D	F

Notes. 1. 3-bit field (s or d) is used variously as:
(a) Register number: 0 1 2 3 4 5 6 7
(b) Quick data value: 8 1 2 3 4 5 6 7
(c) Shift/rotate count: 8 1 2 3 4 5 6 7
   and (68010 only),
(d) Breakpoint number: 0 1 2 3 4 5 6 7

Table D3.1. Complete 1-digit hexadecimal codes for the binary/symbolic forms 0s 0d 1s 1d s0 d0 s1 d1.

EA	00mn	00m000	00m001	00m010	00m011	00m100	00m101	00m110	00m111
Dn	00000n	00	01	02	03	04	05	06	07
An	00001n	08	09	0A	0B	0C	0D	0E	0F
(An)	00010n	10	11	12	13	14	15	16	17
(An)+	00011n	18	19	1A	1B	1C	1D	1E	1F
-(An)	00100n	20	21	22	23	24	25	26	27
sdw(An)	00101n	28	29	2A	2B	2C	2D	2E	2F
sdb(An,Xx)	00110n	30	31	32	33	34	35	36	37
addr.W	00111n	38	–	–	–	–	–	–	–
addr.L	00111n	–	39	–	–	–	–	–	–
sdw(PC)	00111n	–	–	3A	–	–	–	–	–
sdb(PC,Xx)	00111n	–	–	–	3B	–	–	–	–
#data.B	00111n	–	–	–	–	3C	–	–	–
#data.W	00111n	–	–	–	–	3C	–	–	–
#data.L	00111n	–	–	–	–	3C	–	–	–

Notes. 1. 00mn refers to three binary fields –
00 (bits 7 and 6): ususally denotes byte size operation.
m (bits 5, 4 and 3): Effective Address mode field.
n (bits 2, 1 and 0): Register number field.
2. 00mn is shown in tables D.7.01 to D.7.22. as 00ms or 00md (referring to source and destination operands).

Table D3.2. Complete 2-digit hexadecimal codes for the 68000, 68008 and 68010 Effective Address binary/symbolic forms 00ms and 00md.

EA	01mn	01m000	01m001	01m010	01m011	01m100	01m101	01m110	01m111
Dn	01000n	40	41	42	43	44	45	46	47
An	01001n	48	49	4A	4B	4C	4D	4E	4F
(An)	01010n	50	51	52	53	54	55	56	57
(An)+	01011n	58	59	5A	5B	5C	5D	5E	5F
-(An)	01100n	60	61	62	63	64	65	66	67
sdw(An)	01101n	68	69	6A	6B	6C	6D	6E	6F
sdb(An,Xx)	01110n	70	71	72	73	74	75	76	77
addr.W	01111n	78	–	–	–	–	–	–	–
addr.L	01111n	–	79	–	–	–	–	–	–
sdw(PC)	01111n	–	–	7A	–	–	–	–	–
sdb(PC,Xx)	01111n	–	–	–	7B	–	–	–	–
#data.B	01111n	–	–	–	–	7C	–	–	–
#data.W	01111n	–	–	–	–	7C	–	–	–
#data.L	01111n	–	–	–	–	7C	–	–	–

Notes. 1. 01mn refers to three binary fields –
01 (bits 7 and 6): ususally denotes word size operation.
m (bits 5, 4 and 3): Effective Address mode field.
n (bits 2, 1 and 0): Register number field.
2. 01mn is shown in tables D.7.01 to D.7.22. as 01ms or 01md (referring to source and destination operands).

Table D3.3. Complete 2-digit hexadecimal codes for the 68000, 68008 and 68010 Effective Address binary/symbolic forms 01ms and 01md.

EA	10mn	10m000	10m001	10m010	10m011	10m100	10m101	10m110	10m111
Dn	10000n	80	81	82	83	84	85	86	87
An	10001n	88	89	8A	8B	8C	8D	8E	8F
(An)	10010n	90	91	92	93	94	95	96	97
(An)+	10011n	98	99	9A	9B	9C	9D	9E	9F
-(An)	10100n	A0	A1	A2	A3	A4	A5	A6	A7
sdw(An)	10101n	A8	A9	AA	AB	AC	AD	AE	AF
sdb(An,Xx)	10110n	B0	B1	B2	B3	B4	B5	B6	B7
addr.W	10111n	B8	-	-	-	-	-	-	-
addr.L	10111n	-	B9	-	-	-	-	-	-
sdw(PC)	10111n	-	-	BA	-	-	-	-	-
sdb(PC,Xx)	10111n	-	-	-	BB	-	-	-	-
#data.B	10111n	-	-	-	-	BC	-	-	-
#data.W	10111n	-	-	-	-	BC	-	-	-
#data.L	10111n	-	-	-	-	BC	-	-	-

Notes. 1. 10mn refers to three binary fields —
10 (bits 7 and 6): ususally denotes long word size operation.
m (bits 5, 4 and 3): Effective Address mode field.
n (bits 2, 1 and 0): Register number field.
2. 10mn is shown in tables D.7.01 to D.7.22. as 10ms or 10md
(referring to source and destination operands).

Table D3.4. Complete 2-digit hexadecimal codes for the 68000, 68008 and 68010 Effective Address binary/symbolic forms 10ms and 10md.

EA	11mn	11m000	11m001	11m010	11m011	11m100	11m101	11m110	11m111
Dn	11000n	C0	C1	C2	C3	C4	C5	C6	C7
An	11001n	C8	C9	CA	CB	CC	CD	CE	CF
(An)	11010n	D0	D1	D2	D3	D4	D5	D6	D7
(An)+	11011n	D8	D9	DA	DB	DC	DD	DE	DF
-(An)	11100n	E0	E1	E2	E3	E4	E5	E6	E7
sdw(An)	11101n	E8	E9	EA	EB	EC	ED	EE	EF
sdb(An,Xx)	11110n	F0	F1	F2	F3	F4	F5	F6	F7
addr.W	11111n	F8	-	-	-	-	-	-	-
addr.L	11111n	-	F9	-	-	-	-	-	-
sdw(PC)	11111n	-	-	FA	-	-	-	-	-
sdb(PC,Xx)	11111n	-	-	-	FB	-	-	-	-
#data.B	11111n	-	-	-	-	FC	-	-	-
#data.W	11111n	-	-	-	-	FC	-	-	-
#data.L	11111n	-	-	-	-	FC	-	-	-

Notes. 1. 11mn refers to three binary fields —
11 (bits 7 and 6): is ususally word or long word operation.
m (bits 5, 4 and 3): Effective Address mode field.
n (bits 2, 1 and 0): Register number field.
2. 11mn is shown in tables D.7.01 to D.7.22. as 11ms or 11md
(referring to source and destination operands).

Table D3.5. Complete 2-digit hexadecimal codes for the 68000, 68008 and 68010 Effective Address binary/symbolic forms 11ms and 11md.

EA	Extension Words	
	No.	Type
Dn	0	–
An	0	–
(An)	0	–
(An)+	0	–
-(An)	0	–
sdw(An)	1	16-bit signed displacement, high order byte first.
sdb(An,Xx)	1	Index register/size + 8-bit signed displacement.
addr.W	1	16-bit sign-extended address, high order byte first.
addr.L	2	32-bit absolute address, high order word first.
sdw(PC)	1	16-bit signed displacement, high order byte first.
sdb(PC,Xx)	1	Index register/size + 8-bit signed displacement.
#data.B	1	8-bit immediate data, (high order byte of word = 0).
#data.W	1	16-bit immediate data, high order byte first.
#data.L	2	32-bit immediate data, high order word first.

Notes. 1. Source extensions always precede destination extensions.
2. See Table D.4.2. for Index extension word.

Table D4.1. Number and type of extension words required for each 68000, 68008 and 68010 Effective Address form.

Index form	x = 0	1	2	3	4	5	6	7
#disp(An,Dx.W)	00sd	10sd	20sd	30sd	40sd	50sd	60sd	70sd
#disp(An,Dx.L)	08sd	18sd	28sd	38sd	48sd	58sd	68sd	78sd
#disp(An,Ax.W)	80sd	90sd	A0sd	B0sd	C0sd	D0sd	E0sd	F0sd
#disp(An,Ax.L)	88sd	98sd	A8sd	B8sd	C8sd	D8sd	E8sd	F8sd
label(PC,Dx.W)	00sd	10sd	20sd	30sd	40sd	50sd	60sd	70sd
label(PC,Dx.L)	08sd	18sd	28sd	38sd	48sd	58sd	68sd	78sd
label(PC,Ax.W)	80sd	90sd	A0sd	B0sd	C0sd	D0sd	E0sd	F0sd
label(PC,Ax.L)	88sd	98sd	A8sd	B8sd	C8sd	D8sd	E8sd	F8sd

Notes. 1. Dx, Ax are given as Xx throughout this appendix.
2. Xx.L: full 32-bit value in index register used.
3. Xx.W: sign extended value of the index low order word used.
4. sd: 8-bit signed displacement:
   (a) programmed as an immediate data offset from the address contained in the Address base register.
   (b) assembler calculated distance from the Program Counter (i.e. address of the index word) to address of 'label'.

Table D4.2. Complete index extension word hexadecimal codes for the 68000, 68008 and 68010.

CCR bit	Flag	Name	Operation result condition indicated
7	–	–	(Not used).
6	–	–	(Not used).
5	–	–	(Not used).
4	X	Extend	carry/borrow out in extended operations, (generally a copy of Carry flag).
3	N	Negative	2's complement sign, (copy of the result most significant bit).
2	Z	Zero	set if zero result, else reset, (in extended operations, cleared for a non-zero result, else unchanged).
1	V	Overflow	set if 2's complement overflow, else reset, (overflow defined as carry into most significant bit ≠ carry out of msb).
0	C	Carry	set if carry/borrow out, else reset, (also receives the last bit shifted out of an operand in a shift or rotate operation).

Notes. 1. Throughout this appendix:
Flag names (XNZVC) show normal condition flagging.
B (Borrow) replaces C for subtract and compare operations.
E is used for the extended operation Zero flag result.
0 indicates that the bit is always reset (cleared).
1 indicates that the bit is always set.
? indicates that the bit state is undefined.
– indicates that the bit is unaffected.
Other conditions are explained in footnotes.

Table D5.1. 68000, 68008 and 68010 Condition Codes Register (Status Register user byte).

SR bit	Flag	Name	Operation result condition indicated
15	T	Trace Mode	When set, causes interrupt to occur for each instruction, allowing program flow to be charted.
14	–	–	(Not used).
13	S	Supervisor Mode	When set, programs operate in a higher privilege state, with access to the full system resources and a wider range of instructions.
12	–	–	(Not used).
11	–	–	(Not used).
10	I_2	Interrupt mask 2	Bits 10, 9 and 8 form a 3-bit interrupt
9	I_1	Interrupt mask 1	priority mask: %000 (0) = no interrupt,
8	I_0	Interrupt mask 0	%001 (1) to %111 (7) give seven levels of priority with %111 (7) the highest.

Notes. 1. System byte bits are unaffected by most instructions, they are not given in tables D.7.01. to D.7.22.
2. The Supervisor mode deals with all privilege violations, bus errors, illegal instruction codes, etc.
3. 68008 interrupt priorities are restricted to 0, 2, 5 and 7.

Table D5.2. 68000, 68008 and 68010 Status Register (system byte).

EA	68000			68008			68010 no-fetch			68010 fetch		
	.B	.W	.L	.B	.W	.L	.B	.W	.L	.B	.W	.L
Dn	0	0	0	0	0	0	–	–	–	0	0	0
An	0	0	0	0	0	0	–	–	–	0	0	0
(An)	4	4	8	4	8	16	2	2	2	4	4	8
(An)+	4	4	8	4	8	16	4	4	4	4	4	8
-(An)	6	6	10	6	10	18	4	4	4	6	6	10
sdw(An)	8	8	12	12	16	24	4	4	4	8	8	12
sdb(An,Xx)	10	10	14	14	18	26	8	8	8	10	10	14
addr.W	8	8	12	12	16	24	4	4	4	8	8	12
addr.L	12	12	16	20	24	32	8	8	8	12	12	16
sdw(PC)	8	8	12	12	16	24	–	–	–	8	8	12
sdb(PC,Xx)	10	10	14	14	18	26	–	–	–	10	10	14
#data.B	4	–	–	8	–	–	–	–	–	4	–	–
#data.W	–	4	–	–	8	–	–	–	–	–	4	–
#data.L	–	–	8	–	–	16	–	–	–	–	–	8

Notes. 1. 68010 no-fetch calculation time is used for the instructions,
MOVE from CCR, MOVE from SR, Scc and TAS, all others use the
fetch calculation time.
2. In these and all other timings in this appendix, it is assumed
that read, write and other bus cycles take 4 clock cycles.

Table D6.1. 68000, 68008 and 68010 Effective Address calculation times.

Exception	68000	68008	68010
Address error	50	94	126
BKPT, breakpoint	–	–	42
Bus error	50	94	126
CHK, out of bounds	44+	68+	44+
DIVS, DIVU, division by zero	42	66	42
Illegal instruction (including ILLEGAL)	34	62	38
Interrupt	44	72	46
MOVEC, illegal Control register	–	–	46
Privilege violation	34	62	38
Reset (N.B. CPU reset, not RESET instruction)	40	68	40
RTE, illegal stack format code	–	–	50
RTE, illegal stacked data revision	–	–	70
Trace	34	62	38
TRAP	38	62	38
TRAPV	34	66	40

Notes. 1. This timing includes all processor exception related actions
including fetch of the first two instruction words of the
exception handler routine.
2. Some of these exception times will also be found against the
appropriate instructions in Tables D.7.01 to D.7.22.
3. + Add Effective Address calculation time.

Table D6.2. 68000, 68008 and 68010 exception timing.

Key to Tables D7.1 to D7.22 – 68000, 68008 and 68010 instructions.

Mnemonic	Standard assembler acronym (where necessary, and for clarity sometimes where not, operation size suffixes, .B, .W and .L are appended).
Operands	Register or memory acted on (source operands precede destination operands).
Action	Generalised symbolic description of the operation caused by the instruction.
Code Word 1	Four-digit hexadecimal machine code instruction word.
Code Word 2	Where applicable, precedes any extension words.
Extension	Number of possible source and destination extension words (source operand extensions precede those of destination operands).
Condition	Operation result status shown in the five condition codes, X N Z V C.
Execution Time	Clock cycles taken to perform the operation (assuming no wait states for memory access, each read and write bus cycle takes 4 clock cycles). Non-implemented instructions are indicated by '–' in the appropriate processor column.
As and Ad	Source and destination Address registers.
Ds and Dd	Source and destination Data registers.
Es and Ed	Source and destination Effective Address operands, (in all instructions except JMP, JSR, LEA and PEA, which use the actual Effective Address as data, the data affected is located at the address, or contained in the register, specified by Es or Ed).
←	Assign arrow – the value of the expression on the right is moved or assigned to the destination operand on the left.
↔	Exchange arrows – data is exchanged between operands.
Subscripts e.g. $15{\sim}0$	Used to indicate an operand bit number or inclusive bit-fields within an operand, example: bits 15 to 0 inclusive as a 16-bit word operand.
sgn.ext.operand	Source operand is sign-extended (i.e. the most significant bit of the source is replicated) to the length of the destination operand, or that required by the operation.

Other symbols and abbreviations are explained in the preceeding tables or in footnotes to tables D.7.01. to D.7.22.

MOVE, MOVEA, MOVEQ

Mnemonic	Operands src,dst	Action
MOVE.B	rdEA,Dn	Dd ← Es
	rdEA,(An)	(Ad) ← Es
	rdEA,(An)+	(Ad) ← Es
		Ad ← Ad + 1
	rdEA,-(An)	Ad ← Ad − 1
		(Ad) ← Es
	rdEA,sdw(An)	(Ad+sdw) ← Es
	rdEA,sdb(An,Xx)	(Ad+Xx+sdb) ← Es
	rdEA,addr.W	(sgn.ext.addrW) ← Es
	rdEA,addr.L	(addrL) ← Es
MOVE.W	raEA,Dn	Dd ← Es
	raEA,(An)	(Ad) ← Es
	raEA,(An)+	(Ad) ← Es
		Ad ← Ad + 2
	raEA,-(An)	Ad ← Ad − 2
		(Ad) ← Es
	raEA,sdw(An)	(Ad+sdw) ← Es
	raEA,sdb(An,Xx)	(Ad+Xx+sdb) ← Es
	raEA,addr.W	(sgn.ext.addrW) ← Es
	raEA,addr.L	(addrL) ← Es
MOVE.L	raEA,Dn	Dd ← Es
	raEA,(An)	(Ad) ← Es
	raEA,(An)+	(Ad) ← Es
		Ad ← Ad + 4
	raEA,-(An)	Ad ← Ad − 4
		(Ad) ← Es
	raEA,sdw(An)	(Ad+sdw) ← Es
	raEA,sdb(An,Xx)	(Ad+Xx+sdb) ← Es
	raEA,addr.W	(sgn.ext.addrW) ← Es
	raEA,addr.L	(addrL) ← Es
MOVEA.W	raEA,An	Ad ← sgn.ext.Es
MOVEA.L	raEA,An	Ad ← Es
MOVEQ	#data.B,Dn	$Dd_{31\sim0}$ ← sgn.ext.#byte

Notes. 1. MOVE.B rdEA,(A7)+ or -(A7) increment/decrement is by 2 to
keep A7 (the Stack Pointer) on a word boundary.

Table D7.1. Data transfer (1)

MOVE, MOVEA, MOVEQ

Code Word 1 1 2 3 4	Code Word 2 1 2 3 4	Extension src dst	Condition X N Z V C	Execution Time 68000 68008 68010
1 d0 00ms	— — — —	012 0	— N Z 0 0	4+ 8+ 4+
1 d0 10ms	— — — —	012 0	— N Z 0 0	8+ 12+ 8+
1 d0 11ms	— — — —	012 0	— N Z 0 0	8+ 12+ 8+
1 d1 00ms	— — — —	012 0	— N Z 0 0	8+ 12+ 8+
1 d1 01ms	— — — —	012 1	— N Z 0 0	12+ 20+ 12+
1 d1 10ms	— — — —	012 1	— N Z 0 0	14+ 22+ 14+
1 1 11ms	— — — —	012 1	— N Z 0 0	12+ 20+ 12+
1 3 11ms	— — — —	012 2	— N Z 0 0	16+ 28+ 16+
3 d0 00ms	— — — —	012 0	— N Z 0 0	4+ 8+ 4+
3 d0 10ms	— — — —	012 0	— N Z 0 0	8+ 16+ 8+
3 d0 11ms	— — — —	012 0	— N Z 0 0	8+ 16+ 8+
3 d1 00ms	— — — —	012 0	— N Z 0 0	8+ 16+ 8+
3 d1 01ms	— — — —	012 1	— N Z 0 0	12+ 24+ 12+
3 d1 10ms	— — — —	012 1	— N Z 0 0	14+ 26+ 14+
3 1 11ms	— — — —	012 1	— N Z 0 0	12+ 20+ 12+
3 3 11ms	— — — —	012 2	— N Z 0 0	16+ 32+ 16+
2 d0 00ms	— — — —	012 0	— N Z 0 0	4+ 8+ 4+
2 d0 10ms	— — — —	012 0	— N Z 0 0	12+ 24+ 12+
2 d0 11ms	— — — —	012 0	— N Z 0 0	12+ 24+ 12+
2 d1 00ms	— — — —	012 0	— N Z 0 0	12+ 24+ 12+*
2 d1 01ms	— — — —	012 1	— N Z 0 0	16+ 32+ 16+
2 d1 10ms	— — — —	012 1	— N Z 0 0	18+ 34+ 18+
2 1 11ms	— — — —	012 1	— N Z 0 0	16+ 32+ 16+
2 3 11ms	— — — —	012 2	— N Z 0 0	20+ 40+ 20+
3 d0 01ms	— — — —	012 0	— — — — —	4+ 8+ 4+
2 d0 01ms	— — — —	012 0	— — — — —	4+ 8+ 4+
7 d0 data8	— — — —	0 0	— N Z 0 0	4 8 4

Notes. 2. + Add source Effective Address calculation times.
3. * Add 2 clock cycles if source is Data or Address register.

Table D7.1. (contd)

MOVEM, MOVEP

Mnemonic	Operands src,dst	Action
MOVEM.W	regs,wcEA	dst ← Ed FOR registers Rs on list(D0–A7): (dst) ← $Rs_{15\sim0}$, dst ← dst+2.
	regs,-(An)	FOR registers Rs on list(A7–D0): Ad ← Ad-2, (Ad) ← $Rs_{15\sim0}$.
	rcEA,regs	src ← Es FOR registers Rd on list(D0–A7): $Rd_{31\sim0}$ ← s.x.(src), src ← src+2.
	(An)+,regs	FOR registers Rd on list(D0–A7): $Rd_{31\sim0}$ ← s.x.(As), As ← As+2.

MOVEM.L	regs,wcEA	dst ← Ed
		FOR registers Rs on list(D0–A7):
		  (dst) ← $Rs_{31\sim16}$, dst ← dst+2.
		  (dst) ← $Rs_{15\sim0}$, dst ← dst+2.

	regs,-(An)	FOR registers Rs on list(A7–D0):
		  Ad ← Ad-2, (Ad) ← $Rs_{15\sim0}$.
		  Ad ← Ad-2, (Ad) ← $Rs_{31\sim16}$.

	rcEA,regs	src ← Es
		FOR registers Rd on list(D0–A7):
		  $Rd_{31\sim16}$ ← (src), src ← src+2.
		  $Rd_{15\sim0}$ ← (src), src ← src+2.

	(An)+,regs	FOR registers Rd on list(D0–A7):
		  $Rd_{31\sim16}$ ← (As), As ← As+2.
		  $Rd_{15\sim0}$ ← (As), As ← As+2.

MOVEP.W	Dn,sdw(An)	$(Ad+sdw)$ ← $Ds_{15\sim8}$ $(Ad+sdw+2)$ ← $Ds_{7\sim0}$
	sdw(An),Dn	$Dd_{15\sim8}$ ← $(As+sdw)$ $Dd_{7\sim0}$ ← $(As+sdw+2)$
MOVEP.L	Dn,sdw(An)	$(Ad+sdw)$ ← $Ds_{31\sim24}$ $(Ad+sdw+2)$ ← $Ds_{23\sim16}$ $(Ad+sdw+4)$ ← $Ds_{15\sim8}$ $(Ad+sdw+6)$ ← $Ds_{7\sim0}$
	sdw(An),Dn	$Dd_{31\sim24}$ ← $(As+sdw)$ $Dd_{23\sim16}$ ← $(As+sdw+2)$ $Dd_{15\sim8}$ ← $(As+sdw+4)$ $Dd_{7\sim0}$ ← $(As+sdw+6)$

Notes. 1. MOVEM regs - list(D0–A7) or (A7–D0) - specified as:
   (1) named and separated by (/), for example -
     A1/A5/D0/A7 specifies registers D0, A1, A5 and A7.
   (2) inclusive bounded by (-), for example -
     A2–A5 specifies registers A2, A3, A4 and A5.
  2. MOVEP data may be moved to/from even or odd byte addresses.

Table D7.2. Data transfer (2)

MOVEM, MOVEP

Code Word 1 (1 2 3 4)	Code Word 2 (1 2 3 4)	Ext src	Ext dst	X	N	Z	V	C	68000	68008	68010
4 8 10md	reg mask	0	012	–	–	–	–	–	4+ (+4n)	8+ (+8n)	4+ (+4n)
4 8 A 0d	reg mask	0	0	–	–	–	–	–	8 (+4n)	16 (+8n)	8 (+4n)
4 C 10ms	reg mask	012	0	–	–	–	–	–	8+ (+4n)	16+ (+8n)	8+ (+4n)
4 C 9 1s	reg mask	0	0	–	–	–	–	–	12 (+4n)	24 (+8n)	12 (+4n)
4 8 11md	reg mask	0	012	–	–	–	–	–	4+ (+8n)	8+ (+16n)	4+ (+8n)
4 8 E 0d	reg mask	0	0	–	–	–	–	–	8 (+8n)	16 (+16n)	8 (+8n)
4 C 11ms	reg mask	012	0	–	–	–	–	–	8+ (+8n)	16+ (+16n)	8+ (+8n)
4 C D 1s	reg mask	0	0	–	–	–	–	–	12 (+8n)	24 (+16n)	12 (+8n)
0 s1 8 1d	dispword	0	0	–	–	–	–	–	16	24	16
0 d1 0 1s	dispword	0	0	–	–	–	–	–	16	24	16
0 s1 C 1d	dispword	0	0	–	–	–	–	–	24	32	24
0 d1 4 1s	dispword	0	0	–	–	–	–	–	24	32	24

Notes. 3. MOVEM reg mask: AND-mask (move register if bit set):

mask bit: 15 14 13 12 11 10 9 8 7 6 5 4 3 2 1 0

EA or (An)+: A7 A6 A5 A4 A3 A2 A1 A0 D7 D6 D5 D4 D3 D2 D1 D0
−(An): D0 D1 D2 D3 D4 D5 D6 D7 A0 A1 A2 A3 A4 A5 A6 A7

The register represented by mask bit 0 is transferred first.
4. MOVEM time: + Add word Effective Address calculation time.
5. MOVEM time: (+kn) Add k × [no. of registers moved] cycles.

Table D7.2. (contd)

CLR, EXT, SWAP, EXG

Mnemonic	Operands src,dst	Action
CLR.B	Dn	Dd ← 0
	wmEA	Ed ← 0
CLR.W	Dn	Dd ← 0
	wmEA	Ed ← 0
CLR.L	Dn	Dd ← 0
	wmEA	Ed ← 0
EXT.W	Dn	$Dd_{15\sim0}$ ← sgn.ext.$Dd_{7\sim0}$
EXT.L	Dn	$Dd_{31\sim0}$ ← sgn.ext.$Dd_{15\sim0}$
SWAP	Dn	$Dd_{31\sim16}$ ↔ $Dd_{15\sim0}$
EXG	Dn,Dn	Dd ↔ Ds
	Dn,An	Ad ↔ Ds
	An,An	Ad ↔ As

Table D7.3. Data transfer (3)

LEA, PEA, LINK, UNLK

Mnemonic	Operands src,dst	Action
LEA	rcEA,An	Ad ← \<Es\>
PEA	rcEA	SP ← SP − 4
		(SP) ← \<Es\>
LINK	An,#disp16	SP ← SP − 4
		(SP) ← As
		As ← SP
		SP ← SP + sgn.ext.#word
UNLK	An	SP ← As
		As ← (SP)
		SP ← SP + 4

Notes. 1. LINK displacement should be negative to provide stack space for frame parameters. A positive displacement will cause stacked return addresses to be overwritten on further pushes.
2. \<Es\>: Effective Address (not data at EA) is loaded or pushed.

Table D7.4. Data transfer (4)

CLR, EXT, SWAP, EXG

Code Word 1 1 2 3 4	Code Word 2 1 2 3 4	Extension src dst	Condition X N Z V C	Execution Time 68000 68008 68010		
4 2 0 0d	– – – –	– 0	– N Z 0 0	4	8	4
4 2 00md	– – – –	– 012	– N Z 0 0	8+	12+	8+*
4 2 4 0d	– – – –	– 0	– N Z 0 0	4	8	4
4 2 01md	– – – –	– 012	– N Z 0 0	8+	16+	8+*
4 2 8 0d	– – – –	– 0	– N Z 0 0	6	10	6
4 2 10md	– – – –	– 012	– N Z 0 0	12+	24+	12+*
4 8 8 0d	– – – –	– 0	– N Z 0 0	4	8	4
4 8 C 0d	– – – –	– 0	– N Z 0 0	4	8	4
4 8 4 0d	– – – –	– 0	– N Z 0 0	4	8	4
C s1 4 0d	– – – –	0 0	– – – – –	6	10	6
C s1 8 1d	– – – –	0 0	– – – – –	6	10	6
C s1 4 1d	– – – –	0 0	– – – – –	6	10	6

Notes. 1. Time: + Add Effective Address calculation time.
2. Time: * Index modes, add 2 clock cycles.
3. SWAP: CCR flags the full 32-bit result.

Table D7.3. (contd)

LEA, PEA, LINK, UNLK

Code Word 1 1 2 3 4	Code Word 2 1 2 3 4	Extension src dst	Condition X N Z V C	Execution Time 68000 68008 68010		
4 d1 11ms	– – – –	012 0	– – – – –	0+*	0+*	0+*
4 8 01ms	– – – –	012 –	– – – – –	8+*	16+*	8+*
4 E 5 0s	dispword	0 0	– – – – –	16	32	16
4 E 5 1s	– – – –	0 –	– – – – –	12	24	12

Notes. 3. Time: + Add word Effective Address calculation time.
4. Time: * Index modes, add 2 clock cycles.

Table D7.4. (contd)

ADD, ADDA, ADDI, ADDQ, ADDX

Mnemonic	Operands src,dst	Action
ADD.B	rdEA,Dn	Dd ← Dd + Es
	Dn,wmEA	Ed ← Ed + Ds
ADD.W	raEA,Dn	Dd ← Dd + Es
	Dn,wmEA	Ed ← Ed + Ds
ADD.L	raEA,Dn	Dd ← Dd + Es
	Dn,wmEA	Ed ← Ed + Ds
ADDA.W	raEA,An	Ad ← Ad + sgn.ext.Es
ADDA.L	raEA,An	Ad ← Ad + Es
ADDI.B	#data.B,Dn	Dd ← Dd + #byte
	#data.B,wmEA	Ed ← Ed + #byte
ADDI.W	#data.W,Dn	Dd ← Dd + #word
	#data.W,wmEA	Ed ← Ed + #word
ADDI.L	#data.L,Dn	Dd ← Dd + #long
	#data.L,wmEA	Ed ← Ed + #long
ADDQ.B	#Qdata,Dn	Dd ← Dd + #quick
	#Qdata,wmEA	Ed ← Ed + #quick
ADDQ.W	#Qdata,Dn	Dd ← Dd + #quick
	#Qdata,An	Ad.L ← Ad.L + #quick
	#Qdata,wmEA	Ed ← Ed + #quick
ADDQ.L	#Qdata,Dn	Dd ← Dd + #quick
	#Qdata,An	Ad.L ← Ad.L + #quick
	#Qdata,wmEA	Ed ← Ed + #quick
ADDX.B	Dn,Dn	Dd ← Dd + Ds + X
	-(An),-(An)	Ad ← Ad - 1, As ← As - 1
		(Ad) ← (Ad) + (As) + X
ADDX.W	Dn,Dn	Dd ← Dd + Ds + X
	-(An),-(An)	Ad ← Ad - 2, As ← As - 2
		(Ad) ← (Ad) + (As) + X
ADDX.L	Dn,Dn	Dd ← Dd + Ds + X
	-(An),-(An)	Ad ← Ad - 4, As ← As - 4
		(Ad) ← (Ad) + (As) + X

Notes. 1. #quick data is 3-bit data (0, 1 to 7) with value (8, 1 to 7).
2. ADDX.B -(An),-(An) if either An is A7 then decrement is by 2 to keep A7 (the Stack Pointer) on a word boundary.

Table D7.5. Arithmetic (1)

ADD, ADDA, ADDI, ADDQ, ADDX

Code Word 1				Code Word 2				Extension		Condition					Execution Time		
1	2	3	4	1	2	3	4	src	dst	X	N	Z	V	C	68000	68008	68010
D	d0	00ms		−	−	−	−	012	0	X	N	Z	V	C	4+	8+	4+
D	s1	00md		−	−	−	−	0	012	X	N	Z	V	C	8+	12+	8+
D	d0	01ms		−	−	−	−	012	0	X	N	Z	V	C	4+	8+	4+
D	s1	01md		−	−	−	−	0	012	X	N	Z	V	C	8+	16+	8+
D	d0	10ms		−	−	−	−	012	0	X	N	Z	V	C	6+*	10+*	6+
D	s1	10md		−	−	−	−	0	012	X	N	Z	V	C	12+	24+	12+
D	d0	11ms		−	−	−	−	012	0	−	−	−	−	−	8+	12+	8+
D	d1	11ms		−	−	−	−	012	0	−	−	−	−	−	6+*	10+*	6+
0	6	0	0d	−	−	−	−	1	0	X	N	Z	V	C	8	16	8
0	6	00md		−	−	−	−	1	012	X	N	Z	V	C	12+	20+	12+
0	6	4	0d	−	−	−	−	1	0	X	N	Z	V	C	8	16	8
0	6	01md		−	−	−	−	1	012	X	N	Z	V	C	12+	24+	12+
0	6	8	0d	−	−	−	−	2	0	X	N	Z	V	C	16	28	14
0	6	10md		−	−	−	−	2	012	X	N	Z	V	C	20+	40+	20+
5	s0	0	0d	−	−	−	−	0	0	X	N	Z	V	C	4	8	4
5	s0	00md		−	−	−	−	0	012	X	N	Z	V	C	8+	12+	8+
5	s0	4	0d	−	−	−	−	0	0	X	N	Z	V	C	4	8	4
5	s0	4	1d	−	−	−	−	0	0	−	−	−	−	−	8	12	4
5	s0	01md		−	−	−	−	0	012	X	N	Z	V	C	8+	16+	8+
5	s0	8	0d	−	−	−	−	0	0	X	N	Z	V	C	8	12	8
5	s0	8	1d	−	−	−	−	0	0	−	−	−	−	−	8	12	8
5	s0	10md		−	−	−	−	0	012	X	N	Z	V	C	12+	24+	12+
D	d1	0	0s	−	−	−	−	0	0	X	N	E	V	C	4	8	4
D	d1	0	1s	−	−	−	−	0	0	X	N	E	V	C	18	22	18
D	d1	4	0s	−	−	−	−	0	0	X	N	E	V	C	4	8	4
D	d1	4	1s	−	−	−	−	0	0	X	N	E	V	C	18	34	18
D	d1	8	0s	−	−	−	−	0	0	X	N	E	V	C	8	12	6
D	d1	8	1s	−	−	−	−	0	0	X	N	E	V	C	30	58	30

Notes. 3. Time: + Add Effective Address calculation time.
 4. Time: * Add 2 clock cycles if raEA is Dn, An or #long.
 5. Z flag: E Cleared for a non-zero result, else unchanged.

Table D7.5. (contd)

SUB, SUBA, SUBI, SUBQ, SUBX

Mnemonic	Operands src,dst	Action
SUB.B	rdEA,Dn Dn,wmEA	Dd ← Dd − Es Ed ← Ed − Ds
SUB.W	raEA,Dn Dn,wmEA	Dd ← Dd − Es Ed ← Ed − Ds
SUB.L	raEA,Dn Dn,wmEA	Dd ← Dd − Es Ed ← Ed − Ds
SUBA.W	raEA,An	Ad ← Ad − sgn.ext.Es
SUBA.L	raEA,An	Ad ← Ad − Es
SUBI.B	#data.B,Dn #data.B,wmEA	Dd ← Dd − #byte Ed ← Ed − #byte
SUBI.W	#data.W,Dn #data.W,wmEA	Dd ← Dd − #word Ed ← Ed − #word
SUBI.L	#data.L,Dn #data.L,wmEA	Dd ← Dd − #long Ed ← Ed − #long
SUBQ.B	#Qdata,Dn #Qdata,wmEA	Dd ← Dd − #quick Ed ← Ed − #quick
SUBQ.W	#Qdata,Dn #Qdata,An #Qdata,wmEA	Dd ← Dd − #quick Ad.L ← Ad.L − #quick Ed ← Ed − #quick
SUBQ.L	#Qdata,Dn #Qdata,An #Qdata,wmEA	Dd ← Dd − #quick Ad.L ← Ad.L − #quick Ed ← Ed − #quick
SUBX.B	Dn,Dn −(An),−(An)	Dd ← Dd − Ds − X Ad ← Ad − 1, As ← As − 1 (Ad) ← (Ad) − (As) − X
SUBX.W	Dn,Dn −(An),−(An)	Dd ← Dd − Ds − X Ad ← Ad − 2, As ← As − 2 (Ad) ← (Ad) − (As) − X
SUBX.L	Dn,Dn −(An),−(An)	Dd ← Dd − Ds − X Ad ← Ad − 4, As ← As − 4 (Ad) ← (Ad) − (As) − X

Notes. 1. #quick data is 3-bit data (0, 1 to 7) with value (8, 1 to 7).
2. SUBX.B −(An),−(An) if either An is A7 then decrement is by 2 to keep A7 (the Stack Pointer) on a word boundary.

Table D7.6. Arithmetic (2)

SUB, SUBA, SUBI, SUBQ, SUBX

Code Word 1				Code Word 2				Extension		Condition					Execution Time		
1	2	3	4	1	2	3	4	src	dst	X	N	Z	V	C	68000	68008	68010
9	d0	00ms		–	–	–	–	012	0	X	N	Z	V	B	4+	8+	4+
9	s1	00md		–	–	–	–	0	012	X	N	Z	V	B	8+	12+	8+
9	d0	01ms		–	–	–	–	012	0	X	N	Z	V	B	4+	8+	4+
9	s1	01md		–	–	–	–	0	012	X	N	Z	V	B	8+	16+	8+
9	d0	10ms		–	–	–	–	012	0	X	N	Z	V	B	6+*	10+*	6+
9	s1	10md		–	–	–	–	0	012	X	N	Z	V	B	12+	24+	12+
9	d0	11ms		–	–	–	–	012	0	–	–	–	–	–	8+	12+	8+
9	d1	11ms		–	–	–	–	012	0	–	–	–	–	–	6+*	10+*	6+
0	4	0	0d	–	–	–	–	1	0	X	N	Z	V	B	8	16	8
0	4	00md		–	–	–	–	1	012	X	N	Z	V	B	12+	20+	12+
0	4	4	0d	–	–	–	–	1	0	X	N	Z	V	B	8	16	8
0	4	01md		–	–	–	–	1	012	X	N	Z	V	B	12+	24+	12+
0	4	8	0d	–	–	–	–	2	0	X	N	Z	V	B	16	28	14
0	4	10md		–	–	–	–	2	012	X	N	Z	V	B	20+	40+	20+
5	s1	0	0d	–	–	–	–	0	0	X	N	Z	V	B	4	8	4
5	s1	00md		–	–	–	–	0	012	X	N	Z	V	B	8+	12+	8+
5	s1	4	0d	–	–	–	–	0	0	X	N	Z	V	B	4	8	4
5	s1	4	1d	–	–	–	–	0	0	–	–	–	–	–	8	12	4
5	s1	01md		–	–	–	–	0	012	X	N	Z	V	B	8+	16+	8+
5	s1	8	0d	–	–	–	–	0	0	X	N	Z	V	B	8	12	8
5	s1	8	1d	–	–	–	–	0	0	–	–	–	–	–	8	12	8
5	s1	10md		–	–	–	–	0	012	X	N	Z	V	B	12+	24+	12+
9	d1	0	0s	–	–	–	–	0	0	X	N	E	V	B	4	8	4
9	d1	0	1s	–	–	–	–	0	0	X	N	E	V	B	18	22	18
9	d1	4	0s	–	–	–	–	0	0	X	N	E	V	B	4	8	4
9	d1	4	1s	–	–	–	–	0	0	X	N	E	V	B	18	34	18
9	d1	8	0s	–	–	–	–	0	0	X	N	E	V	B	8	12	6
9	d1	8	1s	–	–	–	–	0	0	X	N	E	V	B	30	58	30

Notes. 3. Time: + Add Effective Address calculation time.
4. Time: * Add 2 clock cycles if raEA is Dn, An or #long.
5. Z flag: E Cleared for a non-zero result, else unchanged.

Table D7.6. (contd)

CMP, CMPA, CMPI, CMPM, NEG, NEGX, TST

Mnemonic	Operands src,dst	Action
CMP.B	rdEA,Dn	CCR ← status(Dd − Es)
CMP.W	raEA,Dn	CCR ← status(Dd − Es)
CMP.L	raEA,Dn	CCR ← status(Dd − Es)
CMPA.W	raEA,An	CCR ← status(Ad − sgn.ext.Es)
CMPA.L	raEA,An	CCR ← status(Ad − Es)
CMPI.B	#data.B,Dn	CCR ← status(Dd − #byte)
	#data.B,wmEA	CCR ← status(Ed − #byte)
CMPI.W	#data.W,Dn	CCR ← status(Dd − #word)
	#data.W,wmEA	CCR ← status(Ed − #word)
CMPI.L	#data.L,Dn	CCR ← status(Dd − #long)
	#data.L,wmEA	CCR ← status(Ed − #long)
CMPM.B	(An)+,(An)+	CCR ← status((Ad) − (As)) As ← As + 1, Ad ← Ad + 1
CMPM.W	(An)+,(An)+	CCR ← status((Ad) − (As)) As ← As + 2, Ad ← Ad + 2
CMPM.L	(An)+,(An)+	CCR ← status((Ad) − (As)) As ← As + 4, Ad ← Ad + 4
NEG.B	Dn	Dd ← 0 − Dd
	wmEA	Ed ← 0 − Ed
NEG.W	Dn	Dd ← 0 − Dd
	wmEA	Ed ← 0 − Ed
NEG.L	Dn	Dd ← 0 − Dd
	wmEA	Ed ← 0 − Ed
NEGX.B	Dn	Dd ← 0 − Dd − X
	wmEA	Ed ← 0 − Ed − X
NEGX.W	Dn	Dd ← 0 − Dd − X
	wmEA	Ed ← 0 − Ed − X
NEGX.L	Dn	Dd ← 0 − Dd − X
	wmEA	Ed ← 0 − Ed − X
TST.B	wdEA	CCR ← status(Ed − 0)
TST.W	wdEA	CCR ← status(Ed − 0)
TST.L	wdEA	CCR ← status(Ed − 0)

Notes. 1. CMPM.B (An)+,(An)+ if either An is A7 then increment is by 2 to keep A7 (the Stack Pointer) on a word boundary.

Table D7.7. Arithmetic (3)

CMP, CMPA, CMPI, CMPM, NEG, NEGX, TST

Code Word 1 1	2	3	4	Code Word 2 1	2	3	4	Extension src	dst	Condition X	N	Z	V	C	Execution Time 68000	68008	68010
B	d0	0	0ms	-	-	-	-	012	0	-	N	Z	V	B	4+	8+	4+
B	d0	0	1ms	-	-	-	-	012	0	-	N	Z	V	B	4+	8+	4+
B	d0	1	0ms	-	-	-	-	012	0	-	N	Z	V	B	6+	10+	6+
B	d0	1	1ms	-	-	-	-	012	0	-	N	Z	V	B	6+	10+	6+
B	d1	1	1ms	-	-	-	-	012	0	-	N	Z	V	B	6+	10+	6+
0	C	0	0d	-	-	-	-	1	0	-	N	Z	V	B	8	16	8
0	C	0	0md	-	-	-	-	1	012	-	N	Z	V	B	8+	16+	8+
0	C	4	0d	-	-	-	-	1	0	-	N	Z	V	B	8	16	8
0	C	0	1md	-	-	-	-	1	012	-	N	Z	V	B	8+	16+	8+
0	C	8	0d	-	-	-	-	2	0	-	N	Z	V	B	14	26	12
0	C	1	0md	-	-	-	-	2	012	-	N	Z	V	B	12+	24+	12+
B	d1	0	1s	-	-	-	-	0	0	-	N	Z	V	B	12	24	12
B	d1	4	1s	-	-	-	-	0	0	-	N	Z	V	B	12	24	12
B	d1	8	1s	-	-	-	-	0	0	-	N	Z	V	B	20	40	20
4	4	0	0d	-	-	-	-	-	0	X	N	Z	V	B	4	8	4
4	4	0	0md	-	-	-	-	-	012	X	N	Z	V	B	8+	12+	8+
4	4	4	0d	-	-	-	-	-	0	X	N	Z	V	B	4	8	4
4	4	0	1md	-	-	-	-	-	012	X	N	Z	V	B	8+	16+	8+
4	4	8	0d	-	-	-	-	-	0	X	N	Z	V	B	6	10	6
4	4	1	0md	-	-	-	-	-	012	X	N	Z	V	B	12+	24+	12+
4	0	0	0d	-	-	-	-	-	0	X	N	E	V	B	4	8	4
4	0	0	0md	-	-	-	-	-	012	X	N	E	V	B	8+	12+	8+
4	0	4	0d	-	-	-	-	-	0	X	N	E	V	B	4	8	4
4	0	0	1md	-	-	-	-	-	012	X	N	E	V	B	8+	16+	8+
4	0	8	0d	-	-	-	-	-	0	X	N	E	V	B	6	10	6
4	0	1	0md	-	-	-	-	-	012	X	N	E	V	B	12+	24+	12+
4	A	0	0md	-	-	-	-	-	012	-	N	Z	0	0	4+	8+	4+
4	A	0	1md	-	-	-	-	-	012	-	N	Z	0	0	4+	8+	4+
4	A	1	0md	-	-	-	-	-	012	-	N	Z	0	0	4+	8+	4+

Notes. 2. Z flag: E Cleared for a non-zero result, else unchanged.
3. Time: + Add Effective Address calculation time.

Table D 7.7. (contd)

DIVS, DIVU, MULS, MULU

Mnemonic	Operands src,dst	Action
DIVS	rdEA,Dn	IF Es = 0 THEN TRAP. IF overflow occurs THEN Dd is unchanged ELSE $Dd_{15\sim0}$ ← quotient Dd.L / Es.W $Dd_{31\sim16}$ ← remainder Dd.L / Es.W
DIVU	rdEA,Dn	IF Es = 0 THEN TRAP. IF overflow occurs THEN Dd is unchanged ELSE $Dd_{15\sim0}$ ← quotient Dd.L ÷ Es.W $Dd_{31\sim16}$ ← remainder Dd.L ÷ Es.W
MULS	rdEA,Dn	Dd.L ← Dd.W * Es.W
MULU	rdEA,Dn	Dd.L ← Dd.W × Es.W

Notes. 1. Operators * / denote signed multiplication and division.
2. Operators × ÷ denote unsigned multiplication and division.
3. DIVS: Quotient sign = dividend sign ∀ divisor sign.
4. DIVS: Remainder sign = dividend sign, unless zero.
5. MULS: Product sign = multiplicand sign ∀ multiplier sign.

Table D7.8. Arithmetic (4)

ABCD, SBCD, NBCD

Mnemonic	Operands src,dst	Action
ABCD	Dn,Dn -(An),-(An)	Dd ← Dd [+] Ds [+] X As ← As - 1, Ad ← Ad - 1 (Ad) ← (Ad) [+] (As) [+] X
SBCD	Dn,Dn -(An),-(An)	Dd ← Dd [-] Ds [-] X As ← As - 1, Ad ← Ad - 1 (Ad) ← (Ad) [-] (As) [-] X
NBCD	wdEA	Ed ← 0 [-] Ed [-] X

Notes. 1. [+], [-]: packed BCD add, subtract on byte operands.
2. -(An),-(An) if either An is A7 then decrement is by 2 to keep A7 (the Stack Pointer) on a word boundary.

Table D7.9. Binary Coded Decimal

DIVS, DIVU, MULS, MULU

Code Word 1 1 2 3 4	Code Word 2 1 2 3 4	Extension src dst	Condition X N Z V C	Execution Time 68000 68008 68010		
8 d1 11ms	– – – –	012 0	– n z v 0	158+	162+	122+
8 d0 11ms	– – – –	012 0	– n z v 0	140+	144+	108+
C d1 11ms	– – – –	012 0	– N Z 0 0	70+	74+	42+
C d0 11ms	– – – –	012 0	– N Z 0 0	70+	74+	40+

Notes. 6. Flag n: Copies quotient bit 15, undefined on overflow.
       7. Flag z: Flags quotient zero status, undefined on overflow.
       8. Flag v: Set if division overflow occurs, else reset.
       9. Time: + Add Effective Address calculation time.
      10. Time: Maximum values given, minimum values are unlikely to
              better 90% (DIVS, DIVU) or 60% (MULS, MULU).

Table D7.8. (contd)

ABCD, SBCD, NBCD

Code Word 1 1 2 3 4	Code Word 2 1 2 3 4	Extension src dst	Condition X N Z V C	Execution Time 68000 68008 68010		
C d1 0 0s	– – – –	0 0	X ? E ? C	6	10	6
C d1 0 1s	– – – –	0 0	X ? E ? C	18	20	18
8 d1 0 0s	– – – –	0 0	X ? E ? B	6	10	6
8 d1 0 1s	– – – –	0 0	X ? E ? B	18	20	18
4 8 00md	– – – –	– 012	X ? E ? B	8+*	12+*	8+*

Notes. 4. NBCD time: + Add byte Effective Address calculation time.
       5. NBCD time: * subtract 2 clock cycles for Data register.
       6. Z flag: E Cleared for a non-zero result, else unchanged.

Table D7.9. (contd)

AND, ANDI, EOR, EORI, OR, ORI, NOT

Mnemonic	Operands src,dst	Action
AND.B	rdEA,Dn	Dd ← Dd ∧ Es
	Dn,wmEA	Ed ← Ed ∧ Ds
AND.W	raEA,Dn	Dd ← Dd ∧ Es
	Dn,wmEA	Ed ← Ed ∧ Ds
AND.L	raEA,Dn	Dd ← Dd ∧ Es
	Dn,wmEA	Ed ← Ed ∧ Ds
ANDI.B	#data.B,Dn	Dd ← Dd ∧ #byte
	#data.B,wmEA	Ed ← Ed ∧ #byte
ANDI.W	#data.W,Dn	Dd ← Dd ∧ #word
	#data.W,wmEA	Ed ← Ed ∧ #word
ANDI.L	#data.L,Dn	Dd ← Dd ∧ #long
	#data.L,wmEA	Ed ← Ed ∧ #long
EOR.B	Dn,Dn	Dd ← Dd ∀ Ds
	Dn,wmEA	Ed ← Ed ∀ Ds
EOR.W	Dn,Dn	Dd ← Dd ∀ Ds
	Dn,wmEA	Ed ← Ed ∀ Ds
EOR.L	Dn,Dn	Dd ← Dd ∀ Ds
	Dn,wmEA	Ed ← Ed ∀ Ds
EORI.B	#data.B,Dn	Dd ← Dd ∀ #byte
	#data.B,wmEA	Ed ← Ed ∀ #byte
EORI.W	#data.W,Dn	Dd ← Dd ∀ #word
	#data.W,wmEA	Ed ← Ed ∀ #word
EORI.L	#data.L,Dn	Dd ← Dd ∀ #long
	#data.L,wmEA	Ed ← Ed ∀ #long
OR.B	rdEA,Dn	Dd ← Dd V Es
	Dn,wmEA	Ed ← Ed V Ds
OR.W	raEA,Dn	Dd ← Dd V Es
	Dn,wmEA	Ed ← Ed V Ds
OR.L	raEA,Dn	Dd ← Dd V Es
	Dn,wmEA	Ed ← Ed V Ds
ORI.B	#data.B,Dn	Dd ← Dd V #byte
	#data.B,wmEA	Ed ← Ed V #byte
ORI.W	#data.W,Dn	Dd ← Dd V #word
	#data.W,wmEA	Ed ← Ed V #word
ORI.L	#data.L,Dn	Dd ← Dd V #long
	#data.L,wmEA	Ed ← Ed V #long
NOT.B	Dn	Dd ← ¬Dd
	wmEA	Ed ← ¬Ed
NOT.W	Dn	Dd ← ¬Dd
	wmEA	Ed ← ¬Ed
NOT.L	Dn	Dd ← ¬Dd
	wmEA	Ed ← ¬Ed

Notes. 1. AND, EOR and OR are bit to bit operations:
A = %0011, B = %0101, A∧B – %0001, A∀B = %0110, AVB = %0111.
2. NOT is the logical complement: A = %01, ¬A = %10.

Table D7.10. Logic

AND, ANDI, EOR, EORI, OR, ORI, NOT

Code Word 1				Code Word 2				Extension		Condition					Execution Time		
1	2	3	4	1	2	3	4	src	dst	X	N	Z	V	C	68000	68008	68010
C	d0	00ms		–	–	–	–	012	0	–	N	Z	0	0	4+	8+	4+
C	s1	00md		–	–	–	–	0	012	–	N	Z	0	0	8+	12+	8+
C	d0	01ms		–	–	–	–	012	0	–	N	Z	0	0	4+	8+	4+
C	s1	01md		–	–	–	–	0	012	–	N	Z	0	0	8+	16+	8+
C	d0	10ms		–	–	–	–	012	0	–	N	Z	0	0	6+*	10+*	6+
C	s1	10md		–	–	–	–	0	012	–	N	Z	0	0	12+	24+	12+
0	2	0	0d	–	–	–	–	1	0	–	N	Z	0	0	8	16	8
0	2	00md		–	–	–	–	1	012	–	N	Z	0	0	12+	20+	12+
0	2	4	0d	–	–	–	–	1	0	–	N	Z	0	0	8	16	8
0	2	01md		–	–	–	–	1	012	–	N	Z	0	0	12+	24+	12+
0	2	8	0d	–	–	–	–	2	0	–	N	Z	0	0	16	28	14
0	2	10md		–	–	–	–	2	012	–	N	Z	0	0	20+	40+	20+
B	s1	0	0d	–	–	–	–	0	0	–	N	Z	0	0	4	8	4
B	s1	00md		–	–	–	–	0	012	–	N	Z	0	0	8+	12+	8+
B	s1	4	0d	–	–	–	–	0	0	–	N	Z	0	0	4	8	4
B	s1	01md		–	–	–	–	0	012	–	N	Z	0	0	8+	16+	8+
B	s1	8	0d	–	–	–	–	0	0	–	N	Z	0	0	8	12	6
B	s1	10md		–	–	–	–	0	012	–	N	Z	0	0	12+	24+	12+
0	A	0	0d	–	–	–	–	1	0	–	N	Z	0	0	8	16	8
0	A	00md		–	–	–	–	1	012	–	N	Z	0	0	12+	20+	12+
0	A	4	0d	–	–	–	–	1	0	–	N	Z	0	0	8	16	8
0	A	01md		–	–	–	–	1	012	–	N	Z	0	0	12+	24+	12+
0	A	8	0d	–	–	–	–	2	0	–	N	Z	0	0	16	28	14
0	A	10md		–	–	–	–	2	012	–	N	Z	0	0	20+	40+	20+
8	d0	00ms		–	–	–	–	012	0	–	N	Z	0	0	4+	8+	4+
8	s1	00md		–	–	–	–	0	012	–	N	Z	0	0	8+	12+	8+
8	d0	01ms		–	–	–	–	012	0	–	N	Z	0	0	4+	8+	4+
8	s1	01md		–	–	–	–	0	012	–	N	Z	0	0	8+	16+	8+
8	d0	10ms		–	–	–	–	012	0	–	N	Z	0	0	6+*	10+*	6+
8	s1	10md		–	–	–	–	0	012	–	N	Z	0	0	12+	24+	12+
0	0	0	0d	–	–	–	–	1	0	–	N	Z	0	0	8	16	8
0	0	00md		–	–	–	–	1	012	–	N	Z	0	0	12+	20+	12+
0	0	4	0d	–	–	–	–	1	0	–	N	Z	0	0	8	16	8
0	0	01md		–	–	–	–	1	012	–	N	Z	0	0	12+	24+	12+
0	0	8	0d	–	–	–	–	2	0	–	N	Z	0	0	16	28	14
0	0	10md		–	–	–	–	2	012	–	N	Z	0	0	20+	40+	20+
4	6	0	0d	–	–	–	–	–	0	–	N	Z	0	0	4	8	4
4	6	00md		–	–	–	–	–	012	–	N	Z	0	0	8+	12+	8+
4	6	4	0d	–	–	–	–	–	0	–	N	Z	0	0	4	8	4
4	6	01md		–	–	–	–	–	012	–	N	Z	0	0	8+	16+	8+
4	6	8	0d	–	–	–	–	–	0	–	N	Z	0	0	6	10	6
4	6	10md		–	–	–	–	–	012	–	N	Z	0	0	12+	24+	12+

Notes. 3. Time: + Add Effective Address calculation time.
4. Time: * Add 2 clock cycles if raEA is Dn or #long.

Table D7.10. (contd)

ASL, ASR, LSL, LSR

Mnemonic	Operands src,dst	Action
ASL.B	Dn,Dn	FOR $Ds_{5\sim0}$: X & C ← Dd_7 ←←$_0$ ← 0
	#count,Dn	FOR #count: X & C ← Dd_7 ←←$_0$ ← 0
ASL.W	Dn,Dn	FOR $Ds_{5\sim0}$: X & C ← Dd_{15} ←←$_0$ ← 0
	#count,Dn	FOR #count: X & C ← Dd_{15} ←←$_0$ ← 0
	wmEA	X & C ← Ed_{15} ←←$_0$ ← 0
ASL.L	Dn,Dn	FOR $Ds_{5\sim0}$: X & C ← Dd_{31} ←←$_0$ ← 0
	#count,Dn	FOR #count: X & C ← Dd_{31} ←←$_0$ ← 0
ASR.B	Dn,Dn	FOR $Ds_{5\sim0}$: Dd_7 → Dd_7 →→$_0$ → X & C
	#count,Dn	FOR #count: Dd_7 → Dd_7 →→$_0$ → X & C
ASR.W	Dn,Dn	FOR $Ds_{5\sim0}$: Dd_{15} → Dd_{15} →→$_0$ → X & C
	#count,Dn	FOR #count: Dd_{15} → Dd_{15} →→$_0$ → X & C
	wmEA	Ed_{15} → Ed_{15} →→$_0$ → X & C
ASR.L	Dn,Dn	FOR $Ds_{5\sim0}$: Dd_{31} → Dd_{31} →→$_0$ → X & C
	#count,Dn	FOR #count: Dd_{31} → Dd_{31} →→$_0$ → X & C
LSL.B	Dn,Dn	FOR $Ds_{5\sim0}$: X & C ← Dd_7 ←←$_0$ ← 0
	#count,Dn	FOR #count: X & C ← Dd_7 ←←$_0$ ← 0
LSL.W	Dn,Dn	FOR $Ds_{5\sim0}$: X & C ← Dd_{15} ←←$_0$ ← 0
	#count,Dn	FOR #count: X & C ← Dd_{15} ←←$_0$ ← 0
	wmEA	X & C ← Ed_{15} ←←$_0$ ← 0
LSL.L	Dn,Dn	FOR $Ds_{5\sim0}$: X & C ← Dd_{31} ←←$_0$ ← 0
	#count,Dn	FOR #count: X & C ← Dd_{31} ←←$_0$ ← 0
LSR.B	Dn,Dn	FOR $Ds_{5\sim0}$: 0 → Dd_7 →→$_0$ → X & C
	#count,Dn	FOR #count: 0 → Dd_7 →→$_0$ → X & C
LSR.W	Dn,Dn	FOR $Ds_{5\sim0}$: 0 → Dd_{15} →→$_0$ → X & C
	#count,Dn	FOR #count: 0 → Dd_{15} →→$_0$ → X & C
	wmEA	0 → Ed_{15} →→$_0$ → X & C
LSR.L	Dn,Dn	FOR $Ds_{5\sim0}$: 0 → Dd_{31} →→$_0$ → X & C
	#count,Dn	FOR #count: 0 → Dd_{31} →→$_0$ → X & C

Notes. 1. The actions of ASL and LSL are identical.
2. #count: 3-bit data (0, 1 to 7) with value (8, 1 to 7).
3. ←←: Left shift all operand bits by one bit (low to high).
4. →→: Right shift all operand bits by one bit (high to low).

Table D7.11. Shift

ASL, ASR, LSL, LSR

Code Word 1				Code Word 2				Extension		Condition					Execution Time		
1	2	3	4	1	2	3	4	src	dst	X	N	Z	V	C	68000	68008	68010
E	s1	2	0d	-	-	-	-	0	0	X	N	Z	M	R	6*	10*	6*
E	s1	0	0d	-	-	-	-	0	0	X	N	Z	M	R	6*	10*	6*
E	s1	6	0d	-	-	-	-	0	0	X	N	Z	M	R	6*	10*	6*
E	s1	4	0d	-	-	-	-	0	0	X	N	Z	M	R	6*	10*	6*
E	1	11md		-	-	-	-	-	012	X	N	Z	M	R	8+	16+	8+
E	s1	A	0d	-	-	-	-	0	0	X	N	Z	M	R	8*	12*	8*
E	s1	8	0d	-	-	-	-	0	0	X	N	Z	M	R	8*	12*	8*
E	s0	2	0d	-	-	-	-	0	0	X	N	Z	M	R	6*	10*	6*
E	s0	0	0d	-	-	-	-	0	0	X	N	Z	M	R	6*	10*	6*
E	s0	6	0d	-	-	-	-	0	0	X	N	Z	M	R	6*	10*	6*
E	s0	4	0d	-	-	-	-	0	0	X	N	Z	M	R	6*	10*	6*
E	0	11md		-	-	-	-	-	012	X	N	Z	M	R	8+	16+	8+
E	s0	A	0d	-	-	-	-	0	0	X	N	Z	M	R	8*	12*	8*
E	s0	8	0d	-	-	-	-	0	0	X	N	Z	M	R	8*	12*	8*
E	s1	2	1d	-	-	-	-	0	0	X	N	Z	0	R	6*	10*	6*
E	s1	0	1d	-	-	-	-	0	0	X	N	Z	0	R	6*	10*	6*
E	s1	6	1d	-	-	-	-	0	0	X	N	Z	0	R	6*	10*	6*
E	s1	4	1d	-	-	-	-	0	0	X	N	Z	0	R	6*	10*	6*
E	3	11md		-	-	-	-	-	012	X	N	Z	0	R	8+	16+	8+
E	s1	A	1d	-	-	-	-	0	0	X	N	Z	0	R	8*	12*	8*
E	s1	8	1d	-	-	-	-	0	0	X	N	Z	0	R	8*	12*	8*
E	s0	2	1d	-	-	-	-	0	0	X	N	Z	0	R	6*	10*	6*
E	s0	0	1d	-	-	-	-	0	0	X	N	Z	0	R	6*	10*	6*
E	s0	6	1d	-	-	-	-	0	0	X	N	Z	0	R	6*	10*	6*
E	s0	4	1d	-	-	-	-	0	0	X	N	Z	0	R	6*	10*	6*
E	2	11md		-	-	-	-	-	012	X	N	Z	0	R	8+	16+	8+
E	s0	A	1d	-	-	-	-	0	0	X	N	Z	0	R	8*	12*	8*
E	s0	8	1d	-	-	-	-	0	0	X	N	Z	0	R	8*	12*	8*

Notes. 5. Flag M: Set if operand msb changed during shift, else reset.
6. Flag R: Carry is reset if zero shift count (Ds mod 64 = 0).
7. Time: + Add Effective Address calculation time.
8. Time: * Add 2n clock cycles, where n = shift count.

Table D7.11. (contd)

ROL, ROR, ROXL, ROXR

Mnemonic	Operands src,dst	Action
ROL.B	Dn,Dn	FOR $Ds_{5\sim0}$: $C \leftarrow Dd_7 \twoheadleftarrow_0 \leftarrow Dd_7$
	#count,Dn	FOR #count: $C \leftarrow Dd_7 \twoheadleftarrow_0 \leftarrow Dd_7$
ROL.W	Dn,Dn	FOR $Ds_{5\sim0}$: $C \leftarrow Dd_{15} \twoheadleftarrow_0 \leftarrow Dd_{15}$
	#count,Dn	FOR #count: $C \leftarrow Dd_{15} \twoheadleftarrow_0 \leftarrow Dd_{15}$
	wmEA	$C \leftarrow Ed_{15} \twoheadleftarrow_0 \leftarrow Ed_{15}$
ROL.L	Dn,Dn	FOR $Ds_{5\sim0}$: $C \leftarrow Dd_{31} \twoheadleftarrow_0 \leftarrow Dd_{31}$
	#count,Dn	FOR #count: $C \leftarrow Dd_{31} \twoheadleftarrow_0 \leftarrow Dd_{31}$
ROR.B	Dn,Dn	FOR $Ds_{5\sim0}$: $Dd_0 \rightarrow Dd_7 \twoheadrightarrow_0 \rightarrow C$
	#count,Dn	FOR #count: $Dd_0 \rightarrow Dd_7 \twoheadrightarrow_0 \rightarrow C$
ROR.W	Dn,Dn	FOR $Ds_{5\sim0}$: $Dd_0 \rightarrow Dd_{15} \twoheadrightarrow_0 \rightarrow C$
	#count,Dn	FOR #count: $Dd_0 \rightarrow Dd_{15} \twoheadrightarrow_0 \rightarrow C$
	wmEA	$Ed_0 \rightarrow Ed_{15} \twoheadrightarrow_0 \rightarrow C$
ROR.L	Dn,Dn	FOR $Ds_{5\sim0}$: $Dd_0 \rightarrow Dd_{31} \twoheadrightarrow_0 \rightarrow C$
	#count,Dn	FOR #count: $Dd_0 \rightarrow Dd_{31} \twoheadrightarrow_0 \rightarrow C$
ROXL.B	Dn,Dn	FOR $Ds_{5\sim0}$: $X \& C \leftarrow Dd_7 \twoheadleftarrow_0 \leftarrow X$
	#count,Dn	FOR #count: $X \& C \leftarrow Dd_7 \twoheadleftarrow_0 \leftarrow X$
ROXL.W	Dn,Dn	FOR $Ds_{5\sim0}$: $X \& C \leftarrow Dd_{15} \twoheadleftarrow_0 \leftarrow X$
	#count,Dn	FOR #count: $X \& C \leftarrow Dd_{15} \twoheadleftarrow_0 \leftarrow X$
	wmEA	$X \& C \leftarrow Ed_{15} \twoheadleftarrow_0 \leftarrow X$
ROXL.L	Dn,Dn	FOR $Ds_{5\sim0}$: $X \& C \leftarrow Dd_{31} \twoheadleftarrow_0 \leftarrow X$
	#count,Dn	FOR #count: $X \& C \leftarrow Dd_{31} \twoheadleftarrow_0 \leftarrow X$
ROXR.B	Dn,Dn	FOR $Ds_{5\sim0}$: $X \rightarrow Dd_7 \twoheadrightarrow_0 \rightarrow X \& C$
	#count,Dn	FOR #count: $X \rightarrow Dd_7 \twoheadrightarrow_0 \rightarrow X \& C$
ROXR.W	Dn,Dn	FOR $Ds_{5\sim0}$: $X \rightarrow Dd_{15} \twoheadrightarrow_0 \rightarrow X \& C$
	#count,Dn	FOR #count: $X \rightarrow Dd_{15} \twoheadrightarrow_0 \rightarrow X \& C$
	wmEA	$X \rightarrow Ed_{15} \twoheadrightarrow_0 \rightarrow X \& C$
ROXR.L	Dn,Dn	FOR $Ds_{5\sim0}$: $X \rightarrow Dd_{31} \twoheadrightarrow_0 \rightarrow X \& C$
	#count,Dn	FOR #count: $X \rightarrow Dd_{31} \twoheadrightarrow_0 \rightarrow X \& C$

Notes. 1. ROL and ROR are 8, 16 or 32 bit rotations,
ROXL and ROXR are 9, 17 or 33 bit rotations.
2. #count: 3-bit data (0, 1 to 7) with value (8, 1 to 7).
3. $\twoheadleftarrow$: Left shift all operand bits by one bit (low to high).
4. $\twoheadrightarrow$: Right shift all operand bits by one bit (high to low).

Table D7.12. Rotate

ROL, ROR, ROXL, ROXR

Code Word 1				Code Word 2				Extension		Condition					Execution Time		
1	2	3	4	1	2	3	4	src	dst	X	N	Z	V	C	68000	68008	68010
E	s1	3	1d	-	-	-	-	0	0	-	N	Z	0	R	6*	10*	6*
E	s1	1	1d	-	-	-	-	0	0	-	N	Z	0	R	6*	10*	6*
E	s1	7	1d	-	-	-	-	0	0	-	N	Z	0	R	6*	10*	6*
E	s1	5	1d	-	-	-	-	0	0	-	N	Z	0	R	6*	10*	6*
E	7	11md		-	-	-	-	-	012	-	N	Z	0	R	8+	16+	8+
E	s1	B	1d	-	-	-	-	0	0	-	N	Z	0	R	8*	12*	8*
E	s1	9	1d	-	-	-	-	0	0	-	N	Z	0	R	8*	12*	8*
E	s0	3	1d	-	-	-	-	0	0	-	N	Z	0	R	6*	10*	6*
E	s0	1	1d	-	-	-	-	0	0	-	N	Z	0	R	6*	10*	6*
E	s0	7	1d	-	-	-	-	0	0	-	N	Z	0	R	6*	10*	6*
E	s0	5	1d	-	-	-	-	0	0	-	N	Z	0	R	6*	10*	6*
E	6	11md		-	-	-	-	-	012	-	N	Z	0	R	8+	16+	8+
E	s0	B	1d	-	-	-	-	0	0	-	N	Z	0	R	8*	12*	8*
E	s0	9	1d	-	-	-	-	0	0	-	N	Z	0	R	8*	12*	8*
E	s1	3	0d	-	-	-	-	0	0	X	N	Z	0	x	6*	10*	6*
E	s1	1	0d	-	-	-	-	0	0	X	N	Z	0	x	6*	10*	6*
E	s1	7	0d	-	-	-	-	0	0	X	N	Z	0	x	6*	10*	6*
E	s1	5	0d	-	-	-	-	0	0	X	N	Z	0	x	6*	10*	6*
E	5	11md		-	-	-	-	-	012	X	N	Z	0	x	8+	16+	8+
E	s1	B	0d	-	-	-	-	0	0	X	N	Z	0	x	8*	12*	8*
E	s1	9	0d	-	-	-	-	0	0	X	N	Z	0	x	8*	12*	8*
E	s0	3	0d	-	-	-	-	0	0	X	N	Z	0	x	6*	10*	6*
E	s0	1	0d	-	-	-	-	0	0	X	N	Z	0	x	6*	10*	6*
E	s0	7	0d	-	-	-	-	0	0	X	N	Z	0	x	6*	10*	6*
E	s0	5	0d	-	-	-	-	0	0	X	N	Z	0	x	6*	10*	6*
E	4	11md		-	-	-	-	-	012	X	N	Z	0	x	8+	16+	8+
E	s0	B	0d	-	-	-	-	0	0	X	N	Z	0	x	8*	12*	8*
E	s0	9	0d	-	-	-	-	0	0	X	N	Z	0	x	8*	12*	8*

Notes. 5. Flag X: Unchanged if zero shift count (Ds mod 64 = 0).
6. Flag R: Carry is reset if zero shift count (Ds mod 64 = 0).
7. Flag x: Carry = Extend if zero shift count (Ds mod 64 = 0).
8. Time: + Add Effective Address calculation time.
9. Time: * Add 2n clock cycles, where n = shift count.

Table D7.12. (contd)

BCHG, BCLR, BSET, BTST

Mnemonic	Operands src,dst	Action		
BCHG	Dn,wmEA	Z ← ¬Ed$_{Ds}$,	Ed$_{Ds}$ ← ¬Ed$_{Ds}$	
	#bitno,wmEA	Z ← ¬Ed$_{\#b}$,	Ed$_{\#b}$ ← ¬Ed$_{\#b}$	
	Dn,Dn	Z ← ¬Dd$_{Ds}$,	Dd$_{Ds}$ ← ¬Dd$_{Ds}$	
	#bitno,Dn	Z ← ¬Dd$_{\#b}$,	Dd$_{\#b}$ ← ¬Dd$_{\#b}$	
BCLR	Dn,wmEA	Z ← ¬Ed$_{Ds}$,	Ed$_{Ds}$ ← 0	
	#bitno,wmEA	Z ← ¬Ed$_{\#b}$,	Ed$_{\#b}$ ← 0	
	Dn,Dn	Z ← ¬Dd$_{Ds}$,	Dd$_{Ds}$ ← 0	
	#bitno,Dn	Z ← ¬Dd$_{\#b}$,	Dd$_{\#b}$ ← 0	
BSET	Dn,wmEA	Z ← ¬Ed$_{Ds}$,	Ed$_{Ds}$ ← 1	
	#bitno,wmEA	Z ← ¬Ed$_{\#b}$,	Ed$_{\#b}$ ← 1	
	Dn,Dn	Z ← ¬Dd$_{Ds}$,	Dd$_{Ds}$ ← 1	
	#bitno,Dn	Z ← ¬Dd$_{\#b}$,	Dd$_{\#b}$ ← 1	
BTST	Dn,rmEA	Z ← ¬Ed$_{Ds}$		
	#bitno,rmEA	Z ← ¬Ed$_{\#b}$		
	Dn,Dn	Z ← ¬Dd$_{Ds}$		
	#bitno,Dn	Z ← ¬Dd$_{\#b}$		

Notes. 1. Ds, #bitno: Range 0-31 for Dd and 0-7 for EA operations.
2. BTST #bitno,rmEA: The #byte form of rmEA is not allowed.
3. ¬ (NOT) is the logical complement: A = %01, ¬A = %10.

Table D7.13. Bit manipulation

JMP, JSR, NOP, RTD, RTR, RTS

Mnemonic	Operands src,dst	Action
JMP	rcEA	PC ← <Es>
JSR	rcEA	SP ← SP - 4, (SP) ← PC, PC ← <Es>
NOP		No Operation
RTD	#disp16	PC ← (SP), SP ← SP + 4 SP ← SP + sgn.ext.#word
RTR		CCR ← (SP), SP ← SP + 2 PC ← (SP), SP ← SP + 4
RTS		PC ← (SP), SP ← SP + 4

Notes. 1. <Es>: Effective Address (not data at EA) is moved to the PC.
2. RTD is not implemented on the 68000 and 68008.
3. RTR: High order byte of word pulled from stack is ignored.

Table D7.14. Program control (1)

BCHG, BCLR, BSET, BTST

Code Word 1 1 2 3 4	Code Word 2 1 2 3 4	Extension src dst	Condition X N Z V C	Execution Time 68000 68008 68010
0 s1 01md	– – – –	0 012	– – Z – –	8+ 12+ 8+
0 8 01md	0 0 bitno	0 012	– – Z – –	12+ 20+ 12+
0 s1 4 0d	– – – –	0 0	– – Z – –	8* 12* 8*
0 8 4 0d	0 0 bitno	0 0	– – Z – –	12* 20* 12*
0 s1 10md	– – – –	0 012	– – Z – –	8+ 12+ 8+
0 8 10md	0 0 bitno	0 012	– – Z – –	12+ 20+ 12+
0 s1 8 0d	– – – –	0 0	– – Z – –	10* 14* 10*
0 8 8 0d	0 0 bitno	0 0	– – Z – –	14* 22* 14*
0 s1 11md	– – – –	0 012	– – Z – –	8+ 12+ 8+
0 8 11md	0 0 bitno	0 012	– – Z – –	12+ 20+ 12+
0 s1 C 0d	– – – –	0 0	– – Z – –	8* 12* 8*
0 8 C 0d	0 0 bitno	0 0	– – Z – –	12* 20* 12*
0 s1 00md	– – – –	0 012	– – Z – –	4+ 8+ 4+
0 8 00md	0 0 bitno	0 012	– – Z – –	8+ 16+ 8+
0 s1 0 0d	– – – –	0 0	– – Z – –	6 10 6
0 8 0 0d	0 0 bitno	0 0	– – Z – –	10 18 10

Notes. 4. Time: + Add Effective Address calculation time.
     5. Time: * Maximum time – may be bettered by 2 clock cycles.

Table D7.13. (contd)

JMP, JSR, NOP, RTD, RTR, RTS

Code Word 1 1 2 3 4	Code Word 2 1 2 3 4	Extension src dst	Condition X N Z V C	Execution Time 68000 68008 68010
4 E 11ms	– – – –	012 –	– – – – –	* * *
4 E 10ms	– – – –	012 –	– – – – –	8+ 16+ 8+
4 E 7 1	– – – –	– –	– – – – –	4 8 4
4 E 7 4	dispword	– –	– – – – –	– – 16
4 E 7 7	– – – –	– –	d d d d d	20 40 20
4 E 7 5	– – – –	– –	– – – – –	16 32 16

Notes. 4. Flag d: Data on stack top is moved to CCR.
     5. JMP Time: * (An) d(An) d(An,Xx) addr.W addr.L d(PC) d(PC,Xx)
        68000/68010: 8   10   14   10   12   10   14
        68008: 16   18   22   18   24   18   22
     6. JSR Time: + Add Effective Address JMP time.

Table D7.14. (contd)

BRA, BSR, Bcc, DBcc, Scc

Mnemonic	Operands src,dst	Action
BRA.S	label	PC ← PC + pbd
BRA	label	PC ← PC + pwd
BSR.S	label	SP ← SP − 4, (SP) ← PC, PC ← PC + pbd
BSR	label	SP ← SP − 4, (SP) ← PC, PC ← PC + pwd
Bcc.S	label	IF cc true THEN PC ← PC + pbd ELSE PC ← PC + 0
Bcc	label	IF cc true THEN PC ← PC + pwd ELSE PC ← PC + 2
DBcc	Dn,label	IF cc false THEN Ds.W ← Ds.W − 1 IF Ds.W ≠ \$FFFF THEN PC ← PC + pwd ELSE PC ← PC + 2 ELSE PC ← PC + 2
Scc	Dn	IF cc true THEN Dd$_{7\sim0}$ ← %11111111 ELSE Dd$_{7\sim0}$ ← %00000000
Scc	wmEA	IF cc true THEN Ed.B ← %11111111 ELSE Ed.B ← %00000000

Notes. 1. pbd, pwd: Byte or word signed displacement calculated as [address of 'label'] − [address of instruction + 2].

2. cc: State of one or more configurations of N Z V C flags:

	cc	meaning, true if:	N	Z	V	C		cc	meaning, true if:	N	Z	V	C
(a) *Unconditional*													
	T	True (always)	–	–	–	–		F	False (never)	–	–	–	–
(b) *Unsigned conditional*													
	HI	Higher	–	0	–	0		LS	Lower or Same	–	–	–	1
									(or)	–	1	–	–
(c) *Simple conditional*													
	CC	Carry Clear	–	–	–	0		CS	Carry Set	–	–	–	1
	NE	Not Equal	–	0	–	–		EQ	Equal	–	1	–	–
	VC	Overflow Clear	–	–	0	–		VS	Overflow Set	–	–	1	–
	PL	Plus (positive)	0	–	–	–		MI	Minus (negative)	1	–	–	–
(d) *Signed conditional*													
	GE	Greater or Equal	0	–	0	–		LT	Less Than	0	–	1	–
		(or)	1	–	1	–			(or)	1	–	0	–
	GT	Greater Than	0	0	0	–		LE	Less or Equal	–	1	–	–
		(or)	1	0	1	–			(or)	0	–	1	–
									(or)	1	–	0	–

3. BRA replaces BT and BSR replaces BF

Table D7.15. Program control (2)

BRA, BSR, Bcc, DBcc, Scc

Code Word 1 1 2 3 4	Code Word 2 1 2 3 4	Extension src	dst	Condition X N Z V C	68000	68008	68010
6 0 disp8 - - - -		-	0	- - - - -	10	18	10
6 0 0 0	dispword	-	0	- - - - -	10	18	10
6 1 disp8 - - - -		-	0	- - - - -	18	34	18
6 1 0 0	dispword	-	0	- - - - -	18	34	18
6 cd disp8 - - - -		-	0	- - - - -	10 / 8	18 / 12	10 / 6
6 cd 0 0	dispword	-	0	- - - - -	10 / 12	18 / 20	10 / 10
5 cd C 1s	dispword	0	0	- - - - -	10 / 14 / 12	18 / 26 / 20	10 / 16 / 10
5 cd C 0d - - - -		-	0	- - - - -	6 / 4	10 / 8	4 / 4
5 cd 11md - - - -		-	012	- - - - -	8+ / 8+	12+ / 12+	8* / 8*

Notes. 4. cd: Digit depending on condition:

```
cc: T  F  HI LS CC CS NE EQ VC VS PL MI GE LT GT LE
cd: 0  1  2  3  4  5  6  7  8  9  A  B  C  D  E  F
```

5. cc time: Timing is given against the action taken.
6. Time: + Add Effective Address calculation time.
7. Time: * Add no-fetch Effective Address calculation time.

Table D7.15. (contd)

MOVE from CCR, MOVE to CCR, ANDI to CCR, EORI to CCR, ORI to CCR

Mnemonic	Operands src,dst	Action
MOVE	CCR,Dn	$Dd_{15\sim0} \leftarrow CCR$
	CCR,wmEA	$Ed.W \leftarrow CCR$
MOVE	Dn,CCR	$CCR \leftarrow Ds_{15\sim0}$
	rmEA,CCR	$CCR \leftarrow Es.W$
ANDI	#data.B,CCR	$CCR \leftarrow CCR \wedge \#byte$
EORI	#data.B,CCR	$CCR \leftarrow CCR \veebar \#byte$
ORI	#data.B,CCR	$CCR \leftarrow CCR \vee \#byte$

Notes. 1. MOVE from CCR: Not implemented on 68000/08 (See MOVE from SR).
        2. MOVE from CCR: Word operation, destination high byte cleared.
        3. MOVE to CCR: Word operation, destination high byte unaffected.
        4. AND, EOR and OR are bit to bit operations:
            A = %0011, B = %0101, A∧B = %0001, A∀B = %0110, A∨B = %0111.

Table D7.16. System control (1)

MOVE from SR, MOVE to SR, ANDI to SR, EORI to SR, ORI to SR, MOVE USP

Mnemonic	Operands src,dst	Action
MOVE	SR,Dn	<<IF S=0 THEN TRAP ELSE>> $Dd_{15\sim0} \leftarrow SR$
	SR,wmEA	<<IF S=0 THEN TRAP ELSE>> $Ed.W \leftarrow SR$
MOVE	Dn,SR ·	IF S=0 THEN TRAP ELSE $SR \leftarrow Ds_{15\sim0}$
	rmEA,SR	IF S=0 THEN TRAP ELSE $SR \leftarrow Es.W$
ANDI	#data.W,SR	IF S=0 THEN TRAP ELSE $SR \leftarrow SR \wedge \#word$
EORI	#data.W,SR	IF S=0 THEN TRAP ELSE $SR \leftarrow SR \veebar \#word$
ORI	#data.W,SR	IF S=0 THEN TRAP ELSE $SR \leftarrow SR \vee \#word$
MOVE	An,USP	IF S=0 THEN TRAP ELSE $USP \leftarrow As$
	USP,An	IF S=0 THEN TRAP ELSE $Ad \leftarrow USP$

Notes. 1. All these instructions are Privileged (with the exception of
            MOVE from SR on the 68000 and 68008).
        2. See MOVE from CCR for 68010 condition code access.
        3. <<...>>: Ignore for 68000 and 68008, include for 68010.
        4. S=0: Not in Supervisor mode of operation.
        5. AND, EOR and OR are bit to bit operations:
            A = %0011, B = %0101, A∧B = %0001, A∀B = %0110, A∨B = %0111.

Table D7.17. System control (2)

MOVE from CCR, MOVE to CCR, ANDI to CCR, EORI to CCR, ORI to CCR

Code Word 1				Code Word 2				Extension		Condition					Execution Time		
1	2	3	4	1	2	3	4	src	dst	X	N	Z	V	C	68000	68008	68010
4	2	C	0d	–	–	–	–	0	0	–	–	–	–	–	–	–	4
4	2	11md		–	–	–	–	0	012	–	–	–	–	–	–	–	8*
4	4	C	0s	–	–	–	–	0	0	d	d	d	d	d	12	18	12
4	4	11ms		–	–	–	–	012	0	d	d	d	d	d	12+	18+	12+
0	2	3	C	0	0	#data		0	0	a	a	a	a	a	20	32	16
0	A	3	C	0	0	#data		0	0	e	e	e	e	e	20	32	16
0	0	3	C	0	0	#data		0	0	o	o	o	o	o	20	32	16

Notes. 5. Flag: d, Always changed to corresponding moved data bit.
6. Flag: a, Reset if corresponding #data bit 0, else unchanged.
7. Flag: e, Changed if corresponding #data bit 1, else unchanged.
8. Flag: o, Set if corresponding #data bit 1, else unchanged.
9. Time: + Add Effective Address calculation time.
10. Time: * Add non-fetch EA calculation time.

Table D7.16. (contd)

MOVE from SR, MOVE to SR, ANDI to SR, EORI to SR, ORI to SR, MOVE USP

Code Word 1				Code Word 2				Extension		Condition					Execution Time		
1	2	3	4	1	2	3	4	src	dst	X	N	Z	V	C	68000	68008	68010
4	0	C	0d	–	–	–	–	0	0	–	–	–	–	–	6	10	4
4	0	11md		–	–	–	–	0	012	–	–	–	–	–	8+	16+	8*
4	6	C	0s	–	–	–	–	0	0	d	d	d	d	d	12	18	12
4	6	11ms		–	–	–	–	012	0	d	d	d	d	d	12+	18+	12+
0	2	7	C	#worddata				0	0	a	a	a	a	a	20	32	16
0	A	7	C	#worddata				0	0	e	e	e	e	e	20	32	16
0	0	7	C	#worddata				0	0	o	o	o	o	o	20	32	16
4	E	6	0s	–	–	–	–	0	0	–	–	–	–	–	4	8	6
4	E	6	1d	–	–	–	–	0	0	–	–	–	–	–	4	8	6

Notes. 6. Flags: d, a, e, o, All bits of SR may be affected.
7. Flag: d, Always changed to corresponding moved data bit.
8. Flag: a, Reset if corresponding #data bit 0, else unchanged.
9. Flag: e, Changed if corresponding #data bit 1, else unchanged.
10. Flag: o, Set if corresponding #data bit 1, else unchanged.
11. Time: + Add Effective Address calculation time.
12. Time: * Add non-fetch EA calculation time.

Table D7.17. (contd)

MOVEC, MOVES, RESET, STOP, RTE

Mnemonic	Operands src,dst	Action
MOVEC	Cr,Dn	IF S=0 THEN TRAP ELSE Dd ← Cs
	Cr,An	IF S=0 THEN TRAP ELSE Ad ← Cs
	Dn,Cr	IF S=0 THEN TRAP ELSE Cd ← Ds
	An,Cr	IF S=0 THEN TRAP ELSE Cd ← As
MOVES.B	Dn,wmEA	IF S=0 THEN TRAP ELSE DFC:Ed ← $Ds_{7\sim0}$
	An,wmEA	IF S=0 THEN TRAP ELSE DFC:Ed ← $As_{7\sim0}$
	wmEA,Dn	IF S=0 THEN TRAP ELSE $Dd_{7\sim0}$ ← SFC:Es
	wmEA,An	IF S=0 THEN TRAP ELSE Ad ← sgn.ext.SFC:Es
MOVES.W	Dn,wmEA	IF S=0 THEN TRAP ELSE DFC:Ed ← $Ds_{15\sim0}$
	An,wmEA	IF S=0 THEN TRAP ELSE DFC:Ed ← $As_{15\sim0}$
	wmEA,Dn	IF S=0 THEN TRAP ELSE $Dd_{15\sim0}$ ← SFC:Es
	wmEA,An	IF S=0 THEN TRAP ELSE Ad ← sgn.ext.SFC:Es
MOVES.L	Dn,wmEA	IF S=0 THEN TRAP ELSE DFC:Ed ← Ds
	An,wmEA	IF S=0 THEN TRAP ELSE DFC:Ed ← As
	wmEA,Dn	IF S=0 THEN TRAP ELSE Dd ← SFC:Es
	wmEA,An	IF S=0 THEN TRAP ELSE Ad ← SFC:Es
RESET		IF S=0 THEN TRAP ELSE External Reset
STOP	#data.W	IF S=0 THEN TRAP ELSE SR ← #word WAIT UNTIL Trace, Interrupt or Reset.
RTE		IF S=0 THEN TRAP ELSE SR ← (SP), PC ← (SP+2) SP ← SP + 6, run
RTE		IF S=0 THEN TRAP ELSE SR ← (SP), PC ← (SP+2) Read stack format code [short] SP ← SP + 8, run [long] read stack data SP ← SP + 58, run

Notes. 1. All these instructions are Privileged.
    2. S=0: Not in Supervisor mode of operation.
    3. Control registers:
        SFC Source Function Code   DFC Destination Function Code
        USP User Stack Pointer   VBR Vector Base Register
    4. Function codes (SFC, DFC):
        %000 Not used.   %100 Not used.
        %001 User Data space.   %101 Supervisor Data space.
        %010 User Program space. %110 Supervisor Program space.
        %011 Not used.   %111 CPU space.

Table D7.18. System control (3)

MOVEC, MOVES, RESET, STOP, RTE

Code Word 1 1	2	3	4	Code Word 2 1	2	3	4	Extension src	dst	Condition X	N	Z	V	C	Execution Time 68000	68008	68010
4	E	7	A	0d	control			0	0	–	–	–	–	–	–	–	12
4	E	7	A	1d	control			0	0	–	–	–	–	–	–	–	12
4	E	7	B	0s	control			0	0	–	–	–	–	–	–	–	10
4	E	7	B	1s	control			0	0	–	–	–	–	–	–	–	10
0	E	00md		0s	8	0	0	0	012	–	–	–	–	–	–	–	4+*
0	E	00md		1s	8	0	0	0	012	–	–	–	–	–	–	–	4+*
0	E	00ms		0d	0	0	0	012	0	–	–	–	–	–	–	–	4+*
0	E	00ms		1d	0	0	0	012	0	–	–	–	–	–	–	–	4+*
0	E	01md		0s	8	0	0	0	012	–	–	–	–	–	–	–	4+*
0	E	01md		1s	8	0	0	0	012	–	–	–	–	–	–	–	4+*
0	E	01ms		0d	0	0	0	012	0	–	–	–	–	–	–	–	4+*
0	E	01ms		1d	0	0	0	012	0	–	–	–	–	–	–	–	4+*
0	E	10md		0s	8	0	0	0	012	–	–	–	–	–	–	–	4+*
0	E	10md		1s	8	0	0	0	012	–	–	–	–	–	–	–	4+*
0	E	10ms		0d	0	0	0	012	0	–	–	–	–	–	–	–	4+*
0	E	10ms		1d	0	0	0	012	0	–	–	–	–	–	–	–	4+*
4	E	7	0	–	–	–	–	–	–	–	–	–	–	–	132	136	130
4	E	7	2	#worddata				0	–	d	d	d	d	d	4*	4*	4*
4	E	7	3	–	–	–	–	–	–	d	d	d	d	d	20	40	–
4	E	7	3	–	–	–	–	–	–	d	d	d	d				
															–	–	24
															–	–	110~

Notes. 5. Code Word 2: control, 3-digit control register codes:
    SFC $000   DFC $001   USP $800   VBR $801.
  6. Flag: d All bits of SR are changed to corresponding moved or
     pulled data bit.
  7. Time: + Add corresponding MOVE Rn,wmEA or MOVE wmEA,Rn times.
  8. Time: * Minimum time.
  9. Time: ~ Add 2 clock cycles for read or write retry.

Table D7.18. (contd)

BKPT, CHK, ILLEGAL, TRAP, TRAPV

Mnemonic	Operands src,dst	Action
BKPT	#number	Signal external hardware SSP ← SSP − 4, (SSP) ← PC SSP ← SSP − 2, (SSP) ← SR PC ← illegal instruction vector

CHK	rdEA,Dn	IF Dd < 0:
		THEN: N ← 1, TRAP
		ELSE: IF Dd > Es:
		    THEN: N ← 0, TRAP
		    ELSE: N ← ?

ILLEGAL		SSP ← SSP − 4, (SSP) ← PC SSP ← SSP − 2, (SSP) ← SR PC ← illegal instruction vector
TRAP	#vector	SSP ← SSP − 4, (SSP) ← PC SSP ← SSP − 2, (SSP) ← SR PC ← vector
TRAPV		IF V = 1 THEN TRAP ELSE continue

Notes. 1. ILLEGAL code is guaranteed to initiate illegal instruction exception processing in all future 68xxx implementations.
2. #vector references one of the 16 trap vectors 32 to 47.

Table D7.19. System control (4)

TAS

Mnemonic	Operands src,dst	Action
TAS	Dn wmEA	CCR ← status($Dd_{7 \sim 0}$ − 0) and Dd_7 ← 1 CCR ← status(Ed.B − 0) and Ed_7 ← 1

Notes. 1. TAS operation is indivisible for synchronisation purposes in a multiprocessor environment.

Table D7.20. Multiprocessor environment

Table D7.21. Coprocessor and *Table D7.22* bit field addressing

Neither of these two instruction types are implemented on the 68000, 68008 and 68010. As with other non-implemented instructions, they may be emulated in Supervisor mode by an illegal instruction exception routine.

BKPT, CHK, ILLEGAL, TRAP, TRAPV

Code Word 1				Code Word 2				Extension		Condition					Execution Time		
1	2	3	4	1	2	3	4	src	dst	X	N	Z	V	C	68000	68008	68010
4	8	4	1s	-	-	-	-	-	-	-	-	-	-	-	-	-	42
4	d1	10ms		-	-	-	-	012	0	-	N	?	?	?			
															44+	68+	44+
															44+	68+	44+
															10+	14+	8+
4	A	F	C	-	-	-	-	-	-	-	-	-	-	-	34	62	38
4	E	4	vv	-	-	-	-	0	-	-	-	-	-	-	38	62	38
4	E	7	6	-	-	-	-	-	-	-	-	-	-	-	34	66	40
															4	8	4

Notes. 3. $4AFA and $4AFB are Motorola reserved `ILLEGAL´ codes.
4. Code digit: vv, 0-F trap vector number.
5. Time: + Add Effective Address calculation time.

Table D7.19. (contd)

TAS

Code Word 1				Code Word 2				Extension		Condition					Execution Time		
1	2	3	4	1	2	3	4	src	dst	X	N	Z	V	C	68000	68008	68010
4	A	C	0d	-	-	-	-	-	0	-	N	Z	0	0	4	8	4
4	A	11md		-	-	-	-	-	012	-	N	Z	0	0	10+	14+	14*

Notes. 2. Time: + Add Effective Address calculation time.
3. Time: * Add no-fetch EA calculation time.

Table D7.20. (contd)

Instruction form		Byte			Word			Long		
		−1	cT	cF	−1	cT	cF	−1	cT	cF
ABCD	−(An),−(An)	28	30	24	not allowed			not allowed		
ADD	Dn,(An)	20	22	16	20	22	16	28	30	24
ADD	Dn,(An)+	20	22	16	20	22	16	28	30	24
ADD	Dn,−(An)	22	24	18	22	24	18	30	32	26
ADD	(An),Dn	20	22	16	20	22	16	26	28	22
ADD	(An)+,Dn	20	22	16	20	22	16	26	28	22
ADD	−(An),Dn	22	24	18	22	24	18	28	30	24
ADDA	(An),An	not allowed			22	24	18	26	28	22
ADDA	(An)+,An	not allowed			22	24	18	26	28	22
ADDA	−(An),An	not allowed			24	26	20	28	30	24
ADDX	−(An),−(An)	26	28	22	26	28	22	36	38	32
AND	Dn,(An)	20	22	16	20	22	16	28	30	24
AND	Dn,(An)+	20	22	16	20	22	16	28	30	24
AND	Dn,−(An)	22	24	18	22	24	18	30	32	26
AND	(An),Dn	20	22	16	20	22	16	26	28	22
AND	(An)+,Dn	20	22	16	20	22	16	26	28	22
AND	−(An),Dn	22	24	18	22	24	18	28	30	24
ASL	(An)	not allowed			22	24	18	not allowed		
ASL	(An)+	not allowed			22	24	18	not allowed		
ASL	−(An)	not allowed			24	26	20	not allowed		
ASR	(An)	not allowed			22	24	18	not allowed		
ASR	(An)+	not allowed			22	24	18	not allowed		
ASR	−(An)	not allowed			24	26	20	not allowed		
CLR	(An)	16	18	10	16	18	10	20	22	14
CLR	(An)+	16	18	10	16	18	10	20	22	14
CLR	−(An)	18	20	12	18	20	12	22	24	16
CMP	(An),Dn	16	18	12	16	18	12	20	24	18
CMP	(An)+,Dn	16	18	12	16	18	12	20	24	18
CMP	−(An),Dn	18	20	14	18	20	14	22	26	20
CMPA	(An),An	not allowed			16	18	12	20	24	18
CMPA	(An)+,An	not allowed			16	18	12	20	24	18
CMPA	−(An),An	not allowed			18	20	14	22	26	20
CMPM	(An)+,(An)+	18	20	14	18	20	14	26	30	24
EOR	Dn,(An)	20	22	16	20	22	16	28	30	24
EOR	Dn,(An)+	20	22	16	20	22	16	28	30	24
EOR	Dn,−(An)	22	24	18	22	24	18	30	32	26
LSL	(An)	not allowed			22	24	18	not allowed		
LSL	(An)+	not allowed			22	24	18	not allowed		
LSL	−(An)	not allowed			24	26	20	not allowed		
LSR	(An)	not allowed			22	24	18	not allowed		
LSR	(An)+	not allowed			22	24	18	not allowed		
LSR	−(An)	not allowed			24	26	20	not allowed		

Table D8. 68010 loop mode – allowed instruction forms and timing.

MOVE	Dn,(An)	16	18	10	16	18	10	18	20	14
MOVE	Dn,(An)+	16	18	10	16	18	10	18	20	14
MOVE	Dn,-(An)	not	allowed		not	allowed		not	allowed	
MOVE	An,(An)	not	allowed		16	18	10	18	20	14
MOVE	An,(An)+	not	allowed		16	18	10	18	20	14
MOVE	An,-(An)	not	allowed		not	allowed		not	allowed	
MOVE	(An),(An)	18	20	14	18	20	14	24	28	22
MOVE	(An),(An)+	18	20	14	18	20	14	24	28	22
MOVE	(An),-(An)	20	22	16	20	22	16	26	30	24
MOVE	(An)+,(An)	18	20	14	18	20	14	24	28	22
MOVE	(An)+,(An)+	18	20	14	18	20	14	24	28	22
MOVE	(An)+,-(An)	20	22	16	20	22	16	26	30	24
MOVE	-(An),(An)	20	22	16	20	22	16	26	30	24
MOVE	-(An),(An)+	20	22	16	20	22	16	26	30	24
MOVE	-(An),-(An)	22	24	18	22	24	18	28	32	26
NBCD	(An)	22	24	18	not	allowed		not	allowed	
NBCD	(An)+	22	24	18	not	allowed		not	allowed	
NBCD	-(An)	24	26	20	not	allowed		not	allowed	
NEG	(An)	20	22	16	20	22	16	28	30	24
NEG	(An)+	20	22	16	20	22	16	28	30	24
NEG	-(An)	22	24	18	22	24	18	30	22	36
NEGX	(An)	20	22	16	20	22	16	28	30	24
NEGX	(An)+	20	22	16	20	22	16	28	30	24
NEGX	-(An)	22	24	18	22	24	18	30	22	36
NOT	(An)	20	22	16	20	22	16	28	30	24
NOT	(An)+	20	22	16	20	22	16	28	30	24
NOT	-(An)	22	24	18	22	24	18	30	22	36
OR	Dn,(An)	20	22	16	20	22	16	28	30	24
OR	Dn,(An)+	20	22	16	20	22	16	28	30	24
OR	Dn,-(An)	22	24	18	22	24	18	30	32	26
OR	(An),Dn	20	22	16	20	22	16	26	28	22
OR	(An)+,Dn	20	22	16	20	22	16	26	28	22
OR	-(An),Dn	22	24	18	22	24	18	28	30	24
ROL	(An)	not	allowed		22	24	18	not	allowed	
ROL	(An)+	not	allowed		22	24	18	not	allowed	
ROL	-(An)	not	allowed		24	26	20	not	allowed	
ROR	(An)	not	allowed		22	24	18	not	allowed	
ROR	(An)+	not	allowed		22	24	18	not	allowed	
ROR	-(An)	not	allowed		24	26	20	not	allowed	
ROXL	(An)	not	allowed		22	24	18	not	allowed	
ROXL	(An)+	not	allowed		22	24	18	not	allowed	
ROXL	-(An)	not	allowed		24	26	20	not	allowed	
ROXR	(An)	not	allowed		22	24	18	not	allowed	
ROXR	(An)+	not	allowed		22	24	18	not	allowed	
ROXR	-(An)	not	allowed		24	26	20	not	allowed	
SBCD	-(An),-(An)	28	30	24	not	allowed		not	allowed	
SUB	Dn,(An)	20	22	16	20	22	16	28	30	24
SUB	Dn,(An)+	20	22	16	20	22	16	28	30	24
SUB	Dn,-(An)	22	24	18	22	24	18	30	32	26
SUB	(An),Dn	20	22	16	20	22	16	24	26	20
SUB	(An)+,Dn	20	22	16	20	22	16	24	26	20

Table D8. (contd)

		-1	cT	cF	-1	cT	cF	-1	cT	cF
SUB	-(An),Dn	22	24	18	22	24	18	26	28	22
SUBA	(An),An	not allowed			22	24	18	26	28	22
SUBA	(An)+,An	not allowed			22	24	18	26	28	22
SUBA	-(An),An	not allowed			24	26	20	28	30	24
SUBX	-(An),-(An)	26	28	22	26	28	22	36	38	32
TST	(An)	16	18	12	16	18	12	20	24	18
TST	(An)+	16	18	12	16	18	12	20	24	18
TST	-(An)	18	20	14	18	20	14	22	26	20

Notes. 1. Instruction form: Only the forms shown are allowed, each
generates a single word of instruction machine code.
2. -1 cT cF: Clock cycles for the three possible cases of DBcc
operation:-
-1: Count register low order word decrements to -1 ($FFFF),
the condition is not tested, loop terminates.
cT: Decremented count is not equal to -1, the condition is
tested and found to be true, loop terminates.
cF: Decremented count is not equal to -1, the condition is
tested and found to be false, looping continues.
3. The only displacement allowed for the DBcc instruction is -4,
other displacements will not initiate loop mode processing.
4. On entry to the loop, the looped instruction word and the
first word of the DBcc instruction are fetched twice, no other
instruction fetches occur until loop termination.
5. The timing given against each instruction includes all operand
reads and writes in one iteration and the time taken to loop
or to exit the loop and fetch the next two instruction words.
6. The order of DBcc operations in loop mode is different to that
in non-loop mode but for all practical purposes the results
are equivalent.
7. Interrupts are acknowledged only after the DBcc operation and
not after the looped instruction.

Table D8. (contd)

Appendix E
68020 Instructions

This appendix gives the mnemonic, allowed operand forms, action caused, object code (machine code), result condition codes (flags) and the maximum timing in clock cycles for all instructions that are valid in both User and Supervisor modes on the 68020 microprocessor. Similar information for the 68000, 68008 and 68010 is given in Appendix D.

Tables E1.1 and E1.2 provide reference to the main instruction group tables E7.1 to E7.22. For assistance in writing programs that are compatible with other processors in the 68000-series, they also indicate those instructions supported on the 68020 but not on earlier processors. Table E1.1 may be used when searching for a particular instruction, Table E1.2 when searching for an instruction to perform a particular task.

Table E2 lists the groups of effective address forms contained in each of several categories. The 68020 is designed to regulate operand access as part of the concept of structured programming with differentiated data space and program space. Memory addressed relative to the Program Counter may be read but not written to, since this could involve instruction code changes during run time. Likewise, the forms which stipulate an address are distinguished from those which stipulate data. Use of invalid Effective Address operand forms, if not caught during assembly, will initiate exception processing. Note that the use of parentheses with displacements and offsets in many of the Effective Address forms is not the same as that of earlier 68000-series processors (see Table D2).

Tables E3.1 to E3.5 give the full digit or double digit (byte) hexadecimal expansions for the symbolic forms used in the code word columns of the main instruction tables.

Tables E4.1 to E4.4 list the number and type of Effective Address extension words and give full expansions for both index formats supported by the 68020.

Table E5 explains the principal result flag states and describes the system byte of the Status Register which is affected by some instructions.

Table E6.1 gives the standard effective address calculation (and fetch) timing which must be added to the times shown against many instruction forms in the main instruction tables. Table E6.2, gives the minimum timing for exception processing. This is the number of clock cycles consumed in stacking the machine state and prefetching the first two instruction words of the exception handler routine; it does not include the processing to sort out the problem which caused the exception.

Tables E7.1 to E7.22 give all instruction forms, their action, code, flag results and maximum timing.

Instruction	General Operation Description	Ref:
ABCD	Add Binary Coded Decimal with Extend.	E.7.09.
ADD	Add Binary.	E.7.05.
ADDA	Add Binary to Address Register.	E.7.05.
ADDI	Add Immediate Binary Data.	E.7.05.
ADDQ	Add Quick Immediate Binary Data.	E.7.05.
ADDX	Add Binary with Extend.	E.7.05.
AND	Logical AND.	E.7.10.
ANDI	Logical AND Immediate Data.	E.7.10.
ANDI to CCR	Logical AND Immediate Data to CCR.	E.7.16.
ANDI to SR	Logical AND Immediate Data to SR.	E.7.17.
ASL	Arithmetic Shift Left.	E.7.11.
ASR	Arithmetic Shift Right.	E.7.11.
Bcc	Branch on Condition True.	E.7.15.
BCHG	Bit Test then Change.	E.7.13.
BCLR	Bit Test then Clear.	E.7.13.
BFCHG	Bit Field Test then Change.	*E.7.22.
BFCLR	Bit Field Test then Clear.	*E.7.22.
BFEXTS	Move Sign extended Bit Field to Data Register.	*E.7.22.
BFEXTU	Move Zero-extended Bit Field to Data Register.	*E.7.22.
BFFFO	Find First One (msb) in Bit Field.	*E.7.22.
BFINS	Move Data Register to Bit Field.	*E.7.22
BFSET	Bit Field Test then Set.	*E.7.22.
BFTST	Bit Field Test.	*E.7.22.
BKPT	Breakpoint.	E.7.19.
BRA	Branch Always.	E.7.15.
BSET	Bit Test then Set.	E.7.13.
BSR	Branch to Subroutine.	E.7.15.
BTST	Bit Test.	E.7.13.
CALLM	Call Module, passing parameters.	*E.7.14.
CAS	Compare and Swap Single Update Operand.	*E.7.20.
CAS2	Compare and Swap Dual Update Operand.	*E.7.20.
CHK	Check Register, TRAP if <0 or >bound.	E.7.19.
CHK2	Check Register, TRAP if out of bounds.	*E.7.19.
CLR	Clear.	E.7.03.
CMP	Compare.	E.7.07.
CMP2	Compare Register against bounds.	*E.7.07.
CMPA	Compare Address Register with Operand.	E.7.07.
CMPI	Compare Operand with Immediate Data.	E.7.07.
CMPM	Compare Memory Operands.	E.7.07.
cpBcc	Branch on Coprocessor Condition True.	*E.7.21.
cpDBcc	Decrement & Branch on Coprocessor Condition False.	*E.7.21.
cpGEN	Pass General Function Command to Coprocessor.	*E.7.21.
cpRESTORE	Restore Coprocessor Internal State.	*E.7.21.
cpSAVE	Save Coprocessor Internal State.	*E.7.21.
cpScc	Set if Coprocessor Condition True, Clear if False.	*E.7.21.
cpTRAPcc	TRAP if Coprocessor Condition True.	*E.7.21.
DBcc	Decrement and Branch on Condition False.	E.7.15.
DIVS	Two's Complement Signed Divide.	E.7.08.
DIVSL	Longer Two's Complement Signed Divide.	*E.7.08.
DIVU	Unsigned Binary Divide.	E.7.08.
DIVUL	Longer Unsigned Binary Divide.	*E.7.08.
EOR	Logical Exclusive-OR.	E.7.10.
EORI	Logical EOR Immediate Data.	E.7.10.
EORI to CCR	Logical EOR Immediate Data to CCR.	E.7.16.
EORI to SR	Logical EOR Immediate Data to SR.	E.7.17.
EXG	Exchange Register with Register.	E.7.03.
EXT	Sign Extend Data Register.	E.7.03.
EXTB	Sign Extend Data Register byte to long word.	*E.7.03.
ILLEGAL	Cause Illegal Instruction Exception.	E.7.19.
JMP	Jump.	E.7.14.

Table E1.1. Instruction Set Table Reference: 68000-series instructions alphabetically listed.

JSR	Jump to Subroutine.	E.7.14.
LEA	Load Effective Address to Address Register.	E.7.04.
LINK	Link and Allocate Workspace.	E.7.04.
LSL	Logical Shift Left.	E.7.11.
LSR	Logical Shift Right.	E.7.11.
MOVE	Move Data.	E.7.01.
MOVE from CCR	Move from Condition Codes.	E.7.16.
MOVE to CCR	Move Data to CCR.	E.7.16.
MOVE from SR	Move from Status Register.	E.7.17.
MOVE to SR	Move Data to SR.	E.7.17.
MOVE USP	Move USP to/from Address Register.	E.7.17.
MOVEA	Move Address to Address Register.	E.7.01.
MOVEC	Move to/from Control Register.	E.7.18.
MOVEM	Move Data to/from Multiple Registers.	E.7.02.
MOVEP	Move Peripheral Data to/from Data Register.	E.7.02.
MOVEQ	Move Quick Immediate Data to Data Register.	E.7.01.
MOVES	Move to/from alternate address space.	E.7.18.
MULS	Two's Complement Signed Multiply.	E.7.08.
MULU	Unsigned Binary Multiply.	E.7.08.
NBCD	Negate Binary Coded Decimal with Extend.	E.7.09.
NEG	Negate Binary.	E.7.07.
NEGX	Negate Binary with Extend.	E.7.07.
NOP	No Operation.	E.7.14.
NOT	Logical Complement.	E.7.10.
OR	Logical Inclusive-OR.	E.7.10.
ORI	Logical OR Immediate Data.	E.7.10.
ORI to CCR	Logical OR Immediate Data to CCR.	E.7.16.
ORI to SR	Logical OR Immediate Data to SR.	E.7.17.
PACK	Pack unpacked Binary Coded Decimal.	*E.7.09.
PEA	Push Effective Address.	E.7.04.
RESET	Reset External Devices.	E.7.18.
ROL	Rotate Left.	E.7.12.
ROR	Rotate Right.	E.7.12.
ROXL	Rotate Left through Extend.	E.7.12.
ROXR	Rotate Right through Extend.	E.7.12.
RTD	Return and Deallocate Stack Parameters.	E.7.14.
RTE	Return from Exception.	E.7.18.
RTM	Return from Module.	*E.7.14.
RTR	Restore CCR and Return from Subroutine.	E.7.14.
RTS	Return from Subroutine.	E.7.14.
SBCD	Subtract Binary Coded Decimal with Extend.	E.7.09.
Scc	Set Byte if Condition True, or Clear if False.	E.7.15.
STOP	Move Immediate Data to SR then Stop.	E.7.18.
SUB	Subtract Binary.	E.7.06.
SUBA	Subtract Binary from Address Register.	E.7.06.
SUBI	Subtract Immediate Binary Data.	E.7.06.
SUBQ	Subtract Quick Immediate Binary Data.	E.7.06.
SUBX	Subtract Binary with Extend.	E.7.06.
SWAP	Swap Data Register Low and High Order Words.	E.7.03.
TAS	Test Byte and Set Most Significant Bit.	E.7.20.
TRAP	Cause TRAP Exception.	E.7.19.
TRAPcc	Cause TRAP on Condition True.	*E.7.19.
TRAPV	Cause TRAP on Overflow True.	E.7.19.
TST	Test, Compare Operand with Zero.	E.7.07.
UNLK	Unlink and De-allocate Workspace.	E.7.04.
UNPK	Unpack packed Binary Coded Decimal.	*E.7.09.

Notes. 1. Instructions with E.7.xx. references are also implemented on all or some of the 68000, 68008 and 68010; see appendix D.

2. Instructions with *E.7.xx. references are 68020 instructions not implemented on the 68000, 68008 and 68010.

3. 68020 implementations of instructions common to all or some processors in the series may differ; for series compatibility, refer to the corresponding table in Appendix D.

Table E1.1. (contd)

Instruction Group	Instructions	Ref:
Data transfer (1)	MOVE, MOVEA, MOVEQ.	E.7.01.
Data transfer (2)	MOVEM, MOVEP.	E.7.02.
Data transfer (3)	CLR, EXT, *EXTB, SWAP, EXG.	E.7.03.
Data transfer (4)	LEA, PEA, LINK, UNLK.	E.7.04.
Arithmetic (1)	ADD, ADDA, ADDI, ADDQ, ADDX.	E.7.05.
Arithmetic (2)	SUB, SUBA, SUBI, SUBQ, SUBX.	E.7.06.
Arithmetic (3)	CMP, *CMP2, CMPA, CMPI, CMPM, NEG, NEGX, TST.	E.7.07.
Arithmetic (4)	DIVS, *DIVSL, DIVU, *DIVUL, MULS, MULU.	E.7.08.
Binary Coded Decimal	ABCD, SBCD, NBCD, *PACK, *UNPK.	E.7.09.
Logic	AND, ANDI, EOR, EORI, OR, ORI, NOT.	E.7.10.
Shift	ASL, ASR, LSL, LSR.	E.7.11.
Rotate	ROL, ROR, ROXL, ROXR.	E.7.12.
Bit manipulation	BCHG, BCLR, BSET, BTST.	E.7.13.
Program Control (1)	*CALLM, JMP, JSR, NOP, RTD, *RTM, RTR, RTS.	E.7.14.
Program Control (2)	BRA, BSR, Bcc, DBcc, Scc.	E.7.15.
System Control (1)	MOVE to/from CCR, ANDI to CCR, EORI to CCR, ORI to CCR.	E.7.16.
System Control (2)	MOVE to/from SR, ANDI to CCR, EORI to CCR, ORI to SR, MOVE USP.	E.7.17.
System Control (3)	MOVEC, MOVES, RESET, STOP, RTE.	E.7.18.
System Control (4)	BKPT, CHK, ILLEGAL, TRAP, TRAPV, *CHK2, *TRAPcc.	E.7.19.
Multiprocessor	TAS, *CAS, *CAS2.	E.7.20.
Coprocessor	*cpBcc, *cpDBcc, *cpGEN, *cpRESTORE, *cpSAVE, *cpScc, *cpTRAPcc.	E.7.21.
Bit Field	*BFCHG, *BFCLR, *BFEXTS, *BFEXTU, *BFFFO, *BFINS, *BFSET, *BFTST.	E.7.22.

Notes. 1. A few "virtual machine" instructions are also implemented on the 68010 but not on the 68000 or 68008.
2. * prefix: Instructions prefixed with '*' are not implemented on the 68000, 68008 and 68010.
3. 68020 implementations of instructions common to all or some processors in the series may differ; for series compatibility, refer to the corresponding table in Appendix D.

Table E1.2. Instruction Set Table Reference: grouped 68000-series instructions.

EA	read allowed set raEA	rcEA	rdEA	rmEA	write allowed set waEA	wcEA	wdEA	wmEA
Dn	✓	–	✓	–	✓	–	✓	–
An	✓	–	–	–	✓	–	–	–
(An)	✓	✓	✓	✓	✓	✓	✓	✓
(An)+	✓	–	✓	✓	✓	–	✓	✓
–(An)	✓	–	✓	✓	✓	–	✓	✓
(sdw,An)	✓	✓	✓	✓	✓	✓	✓	✓
(sdb,An,Xx)	✓	✓	✓	✓	✓	✓	✓	✓
(bsd,An,Xx)	✓	✓	✓	✓	✓	✓	✓	✓
([bsd,An],Xx,osd)	✓	✓	✓	✓	✓	✓	✓	✓
([bsd,An,Xx],osd)	✓	✓	✓	✓	✓	✓	✓	✓
addr.W	✓	✓	✓	✓	✓	✓	✓	✓
addr.L	✓	✓	✓	✓	✓	✓	✓	✓
(sdw,PC)	✓	✓	✓	✓	–	–	–	–
(sdb,PC,Xx)	✓	✓	✓	✓	–	–	–	–
(bsd,PC,Xx)	✓	✓	✓	✓	–	–	–	–
([bsd,PC],Xx,osd)	✓	✓	✓	✓	–	–	–	–
([bsd,PC,Xx],osd)	✓	✓	✓	✓	–	–	–	–
#data.B	✓	–	✓	✓	–	–	–	–
#data.W	✓	–	✓	✓	–	–	–	–
#data.L	✓	–	✓	✓	–	–	–	–

Notes. 1. a = all forms. c = control. d = data. m = memory.
2. ✓ form allowed. – form not allowed.
3. sdw, sdb: sign extended displacement – word, byte.
4. bsd: sign extended base displacement – null, word or long.
5. osd: sign extended outer displacement – null, word or long.
6. In base indexed forms, all EA addends are optional.

Table E2. 68020 Effective Address categories.

Symbol	3-bit field (s or d) = 000	001	010	011	100	101	110	111
0s or 0d	0	1	2	3	4	5	6	7
1s or 1d	8	9	A	B	C	D	E	F
s0 or d0	0	2	4	6	8	A	C	E
s1 or d1	1	3	5	7	9	B	D	F

Notes. 1. 3-bit field (s or d) is used variously as:
(a) Register number: 0 1 2 3 4 5 6 7
(b) Quick data value: 8 1 2 3 4 5 6 7
(c) Shift/rotate count: 8 1 2 3 4 5 6 7
(d) Breakpoint number: 0 1 2 3 4 5 6 7

Table E3.1. Complete 1-digit hexadecimal codes for the binary/symbolic forms 0s 0d 1s 1d s0 d0 s1 d1.

EA	00mn n = 000	001	010	011	100	101	110	111
Dn	00000n 00	01	02	03	04	05	06	07
An	00001n 08	09	0A	0B	0C	0D	0E	0F
(An)	00010n 10	11	12	13	14	15	16	17
(An)+	00011n 18	19	1A	1B	1C	1D	1E	1F
-(An)	00100n 20	21	22	23	24	25	26	27
(sdw,An)	00101n 28	29	2A	2B	2C	2D	2E	2F
(sdb,An,Xx)	00110n 30	31	32	33	34	35	36	37
(bsd,An,Xx)	00110n 30	31	32	33	34	35	36	37
([bsd,An],Xx,osd)	00110n 30	31	32	33	34	35	36	37
([bsd,An,Xx],osd)	00110n 30	31	32	33	34	35	36	37
addr.W	00111n 38	–	–	–	–	–	–	–
addr.L	00111n –	39	–	–	–	–	–	–
(sdw,PC)	00111n –	–	3A	–	–	–	–	–
(sdb,PC,Xx)	00111n –	–	–	3B	–	–	–	–
(bsd,PC,Xx)	00111n –	–	–	3B	–	–	–	–
([bsd,PC],Xx,osd)	00111n –	–	–	3B	–	–	–	–
([bsd,PC,Xx],osd)	00111n –	–	–	3B	–	–	–	–
#data.B	00111n –	–	–	–	3C	–	–	–
#data.W	00111n –	–	–	–	3C	–	–	–
#data.L	00111n –	–	–	–	3C	–	–	–

Notes. 1. 00 (bits 7 and 6): is ususally byte operation.
2. m (bits 5, 4 and 3): Effective Address mode field.
3. n (bits 2, 1 and 0): Register number field.
4. 00mn is shown in tables E.7.01 to E.7.22. as 00ms or 00md.

Table E3.2. Complete 2-digit hexadecimal codes for the 68020 Effective Address binary/symbolic forms 00ms and 00md.

EA	01mn n = 000	001	010	011	100	101	110	111
Dn	01000n 40	41	42	43	44	45	46	47
An	01001n 48	49	4A	4B	4C	4D	4E	4F
(An)	01010n 50	51	52	53	54	55	56	57
(An)+	01011n 58	59	5A	5B	5C	5D	5E	5F
-(An)	01100n 60	61	62	63	64	65	66	67
(sdw,An)	01101n 68	69	6A	6B	6C	6D	6E	6F
(sdb,An,Xx)	01110n 70	71	72	73	74	75	76	77
(bsd,An,Xx)	01110n 70	71	72	73	74	75	76	77
([bsd,An],Xx,osd)	01110n 70	71	72	73	74	75	76	77
([bsd,An,Xx],osd)	01110n 70	71	72	73	74	75	76	77
addr.W	01111n 78	–	–	–	–.	–	–	–
addr.L	01111n –	79	–	–	–	–	–	–
(sdw,PC)	01111n –	–	7A	–	–	–	–	–
(sdb,PC,Xx)	01111n –	–	–	7B	–	–	–	–
(bsd,PC,Xx)	01111n –	–	–	7B	–	–	–	–
([bsd,PC],Xx,osd)	01111n –	–	–	7B	–	–	–	–
([bsd,PC,Xx],osd)	01111n –	–	–	7B	–	–	–	–
#data.B	01111n –	–	–	–	7C	–	–	–
#data.W	01111n –	–	–	–	7C	–	–	–
#data.L	01111n –	–	–	–	7C	–	–	–

Notes. 1. 01 (bits 7 and 6): is ususally word operation.
2. m (bits 5, 4 and 3): Effective Address mode field.
3. n (bits 2, 1 and 0): Register number field.
4. 01mn is shown in tables E.7.01 to E.7.22. as 01ms or 01md.

Table E3.3. Complete 2-digit hexadecimal codes for the 6820 Effective Address binary/symbolic forms 01ms and 01md.

EA	10mn n = 000	001	010	011	100	101	110	111
Dn	10000n 80	81	82	83	84	85	86	87
An	10001n 88	89	8A	8B	8C	8D	8E	8F
(An)	10010n 90	91	92	93	94	95	96	97
(An)+	10011n 98	99	9A	9B	9C	9D	9E	9F
-(An)	10100n A0	A1	A2	A3	A4	A5	A6	A7
(sdw,An)	10101n A8	A9	AA	AB	AC	AD	AE	AF
(sdb,An,Xx)	10110n B0	B1	B2	B3	B4	B5	B6	B7
(bsd,An,Xx)	10110n B0	B1	B2	B3	B4	B5	B6	B7
([bsd,An],Xx,osd)	10110n B0	B1	B2	B3	B4	B5	B6	B7
([bsd,An,Xx],osd)	10110n B0	B1	B2	B3	B4	B5	B6	B7
addr.W	10111n B8	–	–	–	–	–	–	–
addr.L	10111n –	B9	–	–	–	–	–	–
(sdw,PC)	10111n –	–	BA	–	–	–	–	–
(sdb,PC,Xx)	10111n –	–	–	BB	–	–	–	–
(bsd,PC,Xx)	10111n –	–	–	BB	–	–	–	–
([bsd,PC],Xx,osd)	10111n –	–	–	BB	–	–	–	–
([bsd,PC,Xx],osd)	10111n –	–	–	BB	–	–	–	–
#data.B	10111n –	–	–	–	BC	–	–	–
#data.W	10111n –	–	–	–	BC	–	–	–
#data.L	10111n –	–	–	–	BC	–	–	–

Notes. 1. 10 (bits 7 and 6): is ususally long word operation.
2. m (bits 5, 4 and 3): Effective Address mode field.
3. n (bits 2, 1 and 0): Register number field.
4. 10mn is shown in tables E.7.01 to E.7.22. as 10ms or 10md.

Table E3.4. Complete 2-digit hexadecimal codes for the 68020 Effective Address binary/symbolic forms 10ms and 10md.

EA	11mn n = 000	001	010	011	100	101	110	111
Dn	11000n C0	C1	C2	C3	C4	C5	C6	C7
An	11001n C8	C9	CA	CB	CC	CD	CE	CF
(An)	11010n D0	D1	D2	D3	D4	D5	D6	D7
(An)+	11011n D8	D9	DA	DB	DC	DD	DE	DF
-(An)	11100n E0	E1	E2	E3	E4	E5	E6	E7
(sdw,An)	11101n E8	E9	EA	EB	EC	ED	EE	EF
(sdb,An,Xx)	11110n F0	F1	F2	F3	F4	F5	F6	F7
(bsd,An,Xx)	11110n F0	F1	F2	F3	F4	F5	F6	F7
([bsd,An],Xx,osd)	11110n F0	F1	F2	F3	F4	F5	F6	F7
([bsd,An,Xx],osd)	11110n F0	F1	F2	F3	F4	F5	F6	F7
addr.W	11111n F8	–	–	–	–	–	–	–
addr.L	11111n –	F9	–	–	–	–	–	–
(sdw,PC)	11111n –	–	FA	–	–	–	–	–
(sdb,PC,Xx)	11111n –	–	–	FB	–	–	–	–
(bsd,PC,Xx)	11111n –	–	–	FB	–	–	–	–
([bsd,PC],Xx,osd)	11111n –	–	–	FB	–	–	–	–
([bsd,PC,Xx],osd)	11111n –	–	–	FB	–	–	–	–
#data.B	11111n –	–	–	–	FC	–	–	–
#data.W	11111n –	–	–	–	FC	–	–	–
#data.L	11111n –	–	–	–	FC	–	–	–

Notes. 1. 11 (bits 7 and 6): is ususally word or long word operation.
2. m (bits 5, 4 and 3): Effective Address mode field.
3. n (bits 2, 1 and 0): Register number field.
4. 11mn is shown in tables E.7.01 to E.7.22. as 11ms or 11md.

Table E3.5. Complete 2-digit hexadecimal codes for the 68020 Effective Address binary/symbolic forms 11ms and 11md.

EA	Extension Words No. Type	

(a) Standard 68000-series forms.

Dn	0	-
An	0	-
(An)	0	-
(An)+	0	-
-(An)	0	-
(sdw,An)	1	16-bit signed displacement.
(sdb,An,Xx)	1	Brief Index Format.
addr.W	1	16-bit sign-extended address.
addr.L	2	32-bit absolute address.
(sdw,PC)	1	16-bit signed displacement.
(sdb,PC,Xx)	1	Brief Index Format.
#data.B	1	8-bit immediate data (high order byte = 0).
#data.W	1	16-bit immediate data.
#data.L	2	32-bit immediate data.

(b) 68020 base displacement index forms.

(BR,Xx)	1	Full Index Format with null base displacement.
(bsd.W,BR,Xx)	2	Full Index Format with word base displacement.
(bsd.L,BR,Xx)	3	Full Index Format with long base displacement.
([BR,Xx])	1	Full Index Format with null bsd & null osd.
([BR,Xx],osd.W)	2	Full Index Format with null bsd & word osd.
([BR,Xx],osd.L)	3	Full Index Format with null bsd & long osd.
([bsd.W,BR,Xx])	2	Full Index Format with word bsd & null osd.
([bsd.W,BR,Xx],osd.W)	3	Full Index Format with word bsd & word osd.
([bsd.W,BR,Xx],osd.L)	4	Full Index Format with word bsd & long osd.
([bsd.L,BR,Xx])	3	Full Index Format with long bsd & null osd.
([bsd.L,BR,Xx],osd.W)	4	Full Index Format with long bsd & word osd.
([bsd.L,BR,Xx],osd.L)	5	Full Index Format with long bsd & long osd.
([BR],Xx)	1	Full Index Format with null bsd & null osd.
([BR],Xx,osd.W)	2	Full Index Format with null bsd & word osd.
([BR],Xx,osd.L)	3	Full Index Format with null bsd & long osd.
([bsd.W,BR],Xx)	2	Full Index Format with word bsd & null osd.
([bsd.W,BR],Xx,osd.W)	3	Full Index Format with word bsd & word osd.
([bsd.W,BR],Xx,osd.L)	4	Full Index Format with word bsd & long osd.
([bsd.L,BR],Xx)	3	Full Index Format with long bsd & null osd.
([bsd.L,BR],Xx,osd.W)	4	Full Index Format with long bsd & word osd.
([bsd.L,BR],Xx,osd.L)	5	Full Index Format with long bsd & long osd.

Notes. 1. Source extensions always precede destination extensions.
2. Base Register (BR) is either An or PC.
3. See Table E.4.2. for Brief Index Format extension codes and Tables E.4.3. & E.4.4. for Full Index Format extension codes.
4. Word length base displacements, outer displacements, base registers and index registers are sign extended to 32-bits.
5. Base and Index register components may also be specified as null (i.e. disregarded) in the bsd-index modes but this does not affect instruction word length.
6. In all 32-bit addresses or data, the high order word precedes the low order word.
7. In all 16-bit addresses or data, the high order byte precedes the low order byte.

Table E4.1. Number and type of extension words required for each 68020 Effective Address form.

Index Register Sized & Scaled	Xx = D0	D1	D2	D3	D4	D5	D6	D7	A0	A1	A2	A3	A4	A5	A6	A7
Xx.W*1	00	10	20	30	40	50	60	70	80	90	A0	B0	C0	D0	E0	F0
Xx.L*1	08	18	28	38	48	58	68	78	88	98	A8	B8	C8	D8	E8	F8
Xx.W*2	02	12	22	32	42	52	62	72	82	92	A2	B2	C2	D2	E2	F2
Xx.L*2	0A	1A	2A	3A	4A	5A	6A	7A	8A	9A	AA	BA	CA	DA	EA	FA
Xx.W*4	04	14	24	34	44	54	64	74	84	94	A4	B4	C4	D4	E4	F4
Xx.L*4	0C	1C	2C	3C	4C	5C	6C	7C	8C	9C	AC	BC	CC	DC	EC	FC
Xx.W*8	06	16	26	36	46	56	66	76	86	96	A6	B6	C6	D6	E6	F6
Xx.L*8	0E	1E	2E	3E	4E	5E	6E	7E	8E	9E	AE	BE	CE	DE	EE	FE

Notes.
1. Dx, Ax are given as Xx throughout this appendix.
2. Xx.W: sign extended value of the index low order word used.
3. The index register is scaled by a factor of 1, 2, 4 or 8 (i.e. it is left shifted by 0, 1, 2 or 3 bits) before use — only a scale factor of 1 is downward compatible with the 68000, 68008 and 68010 processors.
4. The low order byte of this index format consists of an 8-bit signed displacement with the following assembler forms:
   (#byte,An,Xx.S*s) — programmed as an immediate data offset from the address in the Address base register.
   (#byte,PC,Xx.S*s) — programmed as an immediate data offset from the address of the index word.
   (label,PC,Xx.S*s) — assembler calculated distance from the Program Counter (i.e. index word address) to 'label' address.
5. The full 32-bit value of the base register (An or PC) is always included in computing the Effective Address.
6. The index form is identical for base register An or PC.

Table E4.2. High order byte hexadecimal codes for the 68020 brief index format extension word.

Index Register Sized & Scaled	Xx = D0	D1	D2	D3	D4	D5	D6	D7	A0	A1	A2	A3	A4	A5	A6	A7
Xx.W*1	01	11	21	31	41	51	61	71	81	91	A1	B1	C1	D1	E1	F1
Xx.L*1	09	19	29	39	49	59	69	79	89	99	A9	B9	C9	D9	E9	F9
Xx.W*2	03	13	23	33	43	53	63	73	83	93	A3	B3	C3	D3	E3	F3
Xx.L*2	0B	1B	2B	3B	4B	5B	6B	7B	8B	9B	AB	BB	CB	DB	EB	FB
Xx.W*4	05	15	25	35	45	55	65	75	85	95	A5	B5	C5	D5	E5	F5
Xx.L*4	0D	1D	2D	3D	4D	5D	6D	7D	8D	9D	AD	BD	CD	DD	ED	FD
Xx.W*8	07	17	27	37	47	57	67	77	87	97	A7	B7	C7	D7	E7	F7
Xx.L*8	0F	1F	2F	3F	4F	5F	6F	7F	8F	9F	AF	BF	CF	DF	EF	FF

Notes.
1. Dx, Ax are given as Xx throughout this appendix.
2. Xx.W: sign extended value of the index low order word used.
3. This format is not downward compatible with the 68000, 68008 and 68010 processors.
4. See Table E.4.4. for the low order byte for this format.
5. The high order byte is identical for base register An or PC.

Table E4.3. High order byte hexadecimal codes for the 68020 full index format extension word.

EA Assembler form	EA Addends				Extension words				
	bsd	BR	Xx	osd	1	2	3	4	5

(a) Register Indirect Indexed with various reduced addend forms.

EA Assembler form	bsd	BR	Xx	osd	1	2	3	4	5
(BR,Xx)	n	A/P	D/A	n	xx10	–	–	–	–
(BR)	n	A/P	d/a	n	xx50	–	–	–	–
(Xx)	n	a/z	D/A	n	xx90	–	–	–	–
(0)	n	a/z	d/a	n	xxD0	–	–	–	–
(bsd.W,BR,Xx)	W	A/P	D/A	n	xx20	bsdw	–	–	–
(bsd.W,BR)	W	A/P	d/a	n	xx60	bsdw	–	–	–
(bsd.W,Xx)	W	a/z	D/A	n	xxA0	bsdw	–	–	–
(bsd.W)	W	a/z	d/a	n	xxE0	bsdw	–	–	–
(bsd.L,BR,Xx)	L	A/P	D/A	n	xx30	bsdh	bsdl	–	–
(bsd.L,BR)	L	A/P	d/a	n	xx70	bsdh	bsdl	–	–
(bsd.L,Xx)	L	a/z	D/A	n	xxB0	bsdh	bsdl	–	–
(bsd.L)	L	a/z	d/a	n	xxF0	bsdh	bsdl	–	–

(b) Memory Indirect Pre-indexed with Indirect reduced addend forms.

EA Assembler form	bsd	BR	Xx	osd	1	2	3	4	5
([BR,Xx])	n	A/P	D/A	n	xx11	–	–	–	–
([BR])	n	A/P	d/a	n	xx51	–	–	–	–
([Xx])	n	a/z	D/A	n	xx91	–	–	–	–
([0])	n	a/z	d/a	n	xxD1	–	–	–	–
([BR,Xx],osd.W)	n	A/P	D/A	W	xx12	osdw	–	–	–
([BR],osd.W)	n	A/P	d/a	W	xx52	osdw	–	–	–
([Xx],osd.W)	n	a/z	D/A	W	xx92	osdw	–	–	–
([0],osd.W)	n	a/z	d/a	W	xxD2	osdw	–	–	–
([BR,Xx],osd.L)	n	A/P	D/A	L	xx13	osdh	osdl	–	–
([BR],osd.L)	n	A/P	d/a	L	xx53	osdh	osdl	–	–
([Xx],osd.L)	n	a/z	D/A	L	xx93	osdh	osdl	–	–
([0],osd.L)	n	a/z	d/a	L	xxD3	osdh	osdl	–	–
([bsd.W,BR,Xx])	W	A/P	D/A	n	xx21	bsdw	–	–	–
([bsd.W,BR])	W	A/P	d/a	n	xx61	bsdw	–	–	–
([bsd.W,Xx])	W	a/z	D/A	n	xxA1	bsdw	–	–	–
([bsd.W])	W	a/z	d/a	n	xxE1	bsdw	–	–	–
([bsd.W,BR,Xx],osd.W)	W	A/P	D/A	W	xx22	bsdw	osdw	–	–
([bsd.W,BR],osd.W)	W	A/P	d/a	W	xx62	bsdw	osdw	–	–
([bsd.W,Xx],osd.W)	W	a/z	D/A	W	xxA2	bsdw	osdw	–	–
([bsd.W],osd.W)	W	a/z	d/a	W	xxE2	bsdw	osdw	–	–
([bsd.W,BR,Xx],osd.L)	W	A/P	D/A	L	xx23	bsdw	osdh	osdl	–
([bsd.W,BR],osd.L)	W	A/P	d/a	L	xx63	bsdw	osdh	osdl	–
([bsd.W,Xx],osd.L)	W	a/z	D/A	L	xxA3	bsdw	osdh	osdl	–
([bsd.W],osd.L)	W	a/z	d/a	L	xxE3	bsdw	osdh	osdl	–
([bsd.L,BR,Xx])	L	A/P	D/A	n	xx31	bsdh	bsdl	–	–
([bsd.L,BR])	L	A/P	d/a	n	xx71	bsdh	bsdl	–	–
([bsd.L,Xx])	L	a/z	D/A	n	xxB1	bsdh	bsdl	–	–
([bsd.L])	L	a/z	d/a	n	xxF1	bsdh	bsdl	–	–
([bsd.L,BR,Xx],osd.W)	L	A/P	D/A	W	xx32	bsdh	bsdl	osdw	–
([bsd.L,BR],osd.W)	L	A/P	d/a	W	xx72	bsdh	bsdl	osdw	–
([bsd.L,Xx],osd.W)	L	a/z	D/A	W	xxB2	bsdh	bsdl	osdw	–
([bsd.L],osd.W)	L	a/z	d/a	W	xxF2	bsdh	bsdl	osdw	–

Table E4.4. Low order byte hexadecimal codes for the 68020 full index format extension word with allowed reduced addend forms and displacement extensions.

([bsd.L,BR,Xx],osd.L)	L	A/P	D/A	L	xx33	bsdh	bsdl	osdh	osdl
([bsd.L,BR],osd.L)	L	A/P	d/a	L	xx73	bsdh	bsdl	osdh	osdl
([bsd.L,Xx],osd.L)	L	a/z	D/A	L	xxB3	bsdh	bsdl	osdh	osdl
([bsd.L],osd.L)	L	a/z	d/a	L	xxF3	bsdh	bsdl	osdh	osdl

(c) Memory Indirect Post-indexed.

([BR],Xx)	n	A/P	D/A	n	xx15	–	–	–	–
([BR])	*								
([0],Xx)	n	a/z	D/A	n	xx95	–	–	–	–
([0])	*								
([BR],Xx,osd.W)	n	A/P	D/A	W	xx16	osdw	–	–	–
([BR],osd.W)	*								
([0],Xx,osd.W)	n	a/z	D/A	W	xx96	osdw	–	–	–
([0],osd.W)	*								
([BR],Xx,osd.L)	n	A/P	D/A	L	xx17	osdh	osdl	–	–
([BR],osd.L)	*								
([0],Xx,osd.L)	n	a/z	D/A	L	xx97	osdh	osdl	–	–
([0],osd.L)	*								
([bsd.W,BR],Xx)	W	A/P	D/A	n	xx25	bsdw	–	–	–
([bsd.W,BR])	*								
([bsd.W],Xx)	W	a/z	D/A	n	xxA5	bsdw	–	–	–
([bsd.W])	*								
([bsd.W,BR],Xx,osd.W)	W	A/P	D/A	W	xx26	bsdw	osdw	–	–
([bsd.W,BR],osd.W)	*								
([bsd.W],Xx,osd.W)	W	a/z	D/A	W	xxA6	bsdw	osdw	–	–
([bsd.W],osd.W)	*								
([bsd.W,BR],Xx,osd.L)	W	A/P	D/A	L	xx27	bsdw	osdh	osdl	–
([bsd.W,BR],osd.L)	*								
([bsd.W],Xx,osd.L)	W	a/z	D/A	L	xxA7	bsdw	osdh	osdl	–
([bsd.W],osd.L)	*								
([bsd.L,BR],Xx)	L	A/P	D/A	n	xx35	bsdh	bsdl	–	–
([bsd.L,BR])	*								
([bsd.L],Xx)	L	a/z	D/A	n	xxB5	bsdh	bsdl	–	–
([bsd.L])	*								
([bsd.L,BR],Xx,osd.W)	L	A/P	D/A	W	xx36	bsdh	bsdl	osdw	–
([bsd.L,BR],osd.W)	*								
([bsd.L],Xx,osd.W)	L	a/z	D/A	W	xxB6	bsdh	bsdl	osdw	–
([bsd.L],osd.W)	*								
([bsd.L,BR],Xx,osd.L)	L	A/P	D/A	L	xx37	bsdh	bsdl	osdh	osdl
([bsd.L,BR],osd.L)	*								
([bsd.L],Xx,osd.L)	L	a/z	D/A	L	xxB7	bsdh	bsdl	osdh	osdl
([bsd.L],osd.L)	*								

Notes. 1. n, W, L: Null Word or Long displacement.
Word displacements are sign extended before use.
2. A/P: Base Register may be specified as an Address register or the Program Counter in the Instruction word Effective Address field.
a/z: Base Register specified but suppressed (assembler Index form should specify 'ZPC' instead of '0' or blank for program space references).
3. D/A: Index register is Data or Address register.
d/a: Index register is specified but suppressed.
4. *: These reductions are not allowed.
5. xx: See Table E.4.3. for Index word high order byte.
6. bsdw, osdw: Word displacement.
7. bsdh bsdl, osdh osdl: Long displacement high and low words.

Table E4.4. (contd)

SR bit	Flag	Name	Condition indicated

(a) System byte.

15	T_1	Trace	4-state program flow trace function enable.
14	T_0	Modes	%00 Trace off, %01 Trace flow changes only, %10 Trace all instructions, %11 Reserved.
13	S	Supervisor state	When set, programs operate in a higher privilege state, with access to full system resources and a wider instruction range.
12	M	Master State	When set, SSP = Master stack pointer; when reset, SSP = Interrupt stack pointer. Controls multitasking.
11	–	–	(Not used, reset).
10	I_2	I mask 2	Bits 10, 9 and 8 form a 3-bit interrupt
9	I_1	I mask 1	priority mask: %000 (0) = no interrupt,
8	I_0	I mask 0	%001 (1) to %111 (7) give seven levels of priority with %111 (7) the highest.

(b) User byte (CCR).

7	–	–	(Not used, reset).
6	–	–	(Not used, reset).
5	–	–	(Not used, reset).
4	X	Extend	carry/borrow out in extended operations, (generally a copy of Carry flag).
3	N	Negative	2's complement sign, (copy of the result most significant bit).
2	Z	Zero	set if zero result, else reset, (in extended operations, cleared for a non-zero result, else unchanged).
1	V	Overflow	set if 2's complement overflow, else reset, (overflow defined as carry into most significant bit ≠ carry out of msb).
0	C	Carry	set if carry/borrow out, else reset, (also receives the last bit shifted out of an operand in a shift or rotate operation).

Notes. 1. System byte bits are unaffected by most instructions, they are not given in tables E.7.01. to E.7.22.
2. The Supervisor mode deals with all privilege violations, bus errors, illegal instruction codes, etc.
3. Throughout this appendix:
   Flag names (XNZVC) show normal condition flagging.
   B (Borrow) replaces C for subtract and compare operations.
   E is used for the extended operation Zero flag result.
   0 indicates that the bit is always reset (cleared).
   1 indicates that the bit is always set.
   ? indicates that the bit state is undefined.
   – indicates that the bit is unaffected.
   Other conditions are explained in footnotes.

Table E5. 68020 status Register, System byte and User byte (Condition Codes Register).

Effective Address Assembler Form	fetch EA times			no-fetch EA times			
	EA	#W,EA	#L,EA	EA	#W,EA	#L,EA	JMP-EA
Dn	0	3	5	0	3	5	—
An	0	3	5	0	3	5	—
(An)	4	4	7	2	3	5	2
(An)+	4	7	9	2	5	7	—
-(An)	5	6	8	2	4	6	—
(sdw,An)	6	7	10	2	5	8	4
(sdb,An,Xx)	8	11	13	5	8	10	6
addr.W	6	7	10	3	5	8	2
addr.L	7	10	12	5	6	10	2
(sdw,PC)	6	19	21	3	18	20	4
(sdb,PC,Xx)	8	11	13	5	8	10	6
#data.B	3	6	8	3	4	6	—
#data.W	3	6	8	3	4	6	—
#data.L	5	8	10	5	6	8	—
(BR,Xx)	9	12	14	7	10	12	6
(bsd.W,BR,Xx)	12	15	17	10	13	15	8
(bsd.L,BR,Xx)	16	19	21	15	18	20	12
([BR,Xx])	13	16	18	12	15	17	11
([BR,Xx],osd.W)	16	19	21	15	18	20	14
([BR,Xx],osd.L)	17	20	22	16	19	21	14
([bsd.W,BR,Xx])	16	19	21	15	18	20	14
([bsd.W,BR,Xx],osd.W)	19	22	24	18	21	23	17
([bsd.W,BR,Xx],osd.L)	20	23	25	19	22	24	17
([bsd.L,BR,Xx])	20	23	25	19	22	24	19
([bsd.L,BR,Xx],osd.W)	22	25	27	21	24	26	21
([bsd.L,BR,Xx],osd.L)	24	25	29	24	24	29	23
([BR],Xx)	13	16	18	12	15	17	11
([BR],Xx,osd.W)	16	19	21	15	18	20	14
([BR],Xx,osd.L)	17	20	22	16	19	21	14
([bsd.W,BR],Xx)	16	19	21	15	18	20	14
([bsd.W,BR],Xx,osd.W)	19	22	24	18	21	23	17
([bsd.W,BR],Xx,osd.L)	20	23	25	19	22	24	17
([bsd.L,BR],Xx)	20	23	25	19	22	24	19
([bsd.L,BR],Xx,osd.W)	22	25	27	21	24	26	21
([bsd.L,BR],Xx,osd.L)	24	25	29	24	24	29	23

Notes. 1. 68020 instruction timing varies with instruction sequence.
2. #W,EA and #L,EA: Immediate data.W or data.L source to EA.
3. See note on Time in Key to Tables E.7.xx.
4. No-fetch (Memory Indirect modes): The indirect address is fetched from memory but the data operand is not.
5. BR (Index modes): Base Register, either An or PC.
6. bsd-Index modes: Suppression of Base Register or Index addends and Index size and scaling does not affect timing.

Table E6.1. 68020 Standard Effective Address calculation times.

Exception	Time
A-line Trap (code word format $Axxx is reserved)	27
BKPT	10
Bus error (short)	50
Bus error (long)	86
F-line Trap (code word format $Fxxx is coprocessor)	27
Illegal instruction	27
Interrupt (ISP)	33
Interrupt (MSP)	48
Privilege violation	27
RESET	519
RTE (coprocessor)	33
RTE (long fault)	94
RTE (normal)	24
RTE (short fault)	45
RTE (six-word)	24
RTE (throwaway)	39+
STOP	8
Trace	32
TRAP #no.	27
TRAPcc (Trap)	32
TRAPcc (no Trap)	5
TRAPCC.W (Trap)	33
TRAPCC.W (no Trap)	7
TRAPCC.L (Trap)	33
TRAPCC.L (no Trap)	10
TRAPV (Trap)	32
TRAPV (no Trap)	5

Notes. 1. This timing includes all processor exception related actions.
2. See note on Time in Key to Tables E.7.xx.
3. Some of these exception times will also be found against the appropriate instructions in Tables E.7.01 to E.7.22.
4. + Add second RTE time.

Table E6.2. 68020 exception timing.

Key to Tables E7.1 to E7.22 – 68020 instructions.

Mnemonic	Standard assembler acronym (where necessary, and for clarity sometimes where not, operation size suffixes, .B, .W and .L are appended).
Operands	Register or memory acted on (source operands precede destination operands).
Action	Generalised symbolic description of the operation caused by the instruction.
Code Word 1 Code Word 2 Code Word 3	Four-digit hexadecimal machine code instruction word. Where applicable, 2nd and 3rd words precede any further extension words.
Extension	Number of possible source and destination extension words after the Code Word(s) (source operand extensions precede those of destination operands).
Condition	Operation result status shown in the five condition codes, X N Z V C.
Time	Execution time in clock cycles taken to perform the operation (assuming no wait states for memory access, each read and write bus cycle takes 3 clock cycles). The maximum time is given – this is for an instruction in external memory with no execution overlap. Under optimum conditions, with cache memory enabled and with overlap of processes within the instruction stream, average timing may be as little as 50% of maximum.
As and Ad	Source and destination Address registers.
Ds and Dd	Source and destination Data registers.
Es and Ed	Source and destination Effective Address operands, (in all instructions except JMP, JSR, LEA and PEA, which use the actual Effective Address as data, the data affected is located at the address, or contained in the register, specified by Es or Ed).
←	Assign arrow – the value of the expression on the right is moved or assigned to the destination operand on the left.
↔	Exchange arrows – data is exchanged between operands.
Subscripts e.g. $_{15\sim0}$	Used to indicate an operand bit number or inclusive bit-fields within an operand, example: bits 15 to 0 inclusive as a 16-bit word operand.
s.x.operand	Source operand is sign-extended (i.e. the most significant bit of the source is replicated) to the length of the destination operand, or that required by the operation.
z.x.operand	Source operand is zero-extended (i.e. high order bits are reset) to the length of the destination operand, or that required by the operation.

Other symbols and abbreviations are explained in the preceeding tables or in footnotes to tables E.7.01. to E.7.22.

MOVE, MOVEA, MOVEQ

Mnemonic	Operands source, destination	Action
MOVE.B	rdEA,Dn	Dd ← Es
	rdEA,(An)	(Ad) ← Es
	rdEA,(An)+	(Ad) ← Es, Ad ← Ad + 1
	rdEA,-(An)	Ad ← Ad - 1, (Ad) ← Es
	rdEA,(sdw,An)	(Ad+sdw) ← Es
	rdEA,(sdb,An,Xx)	(Ad+Xx+sdb) ← Es
	rdEA,(bsd,An,Xx)	(Ad+Xx+bsd) ← Es
	rdEA,([bsd,An,Xx],osd)	ADDR ← (Ad+Xx+bsd) (ADDR+osd) ← Es
	rdEA,([bsd,An],Xx,osd)	ADDR ← (Ad+bsd) (ADDR+Xx+osd) ← Es
	rdEA,addr.W	(s.x.addrW) ← Es
	rdEA,addr.L	(addrL) ← Es
MOVE.W	raEA,Dn	Dd ← Es
	raEA,(An)	(Ad) ← Es
	raEA,(An)+	(Ad) ← Es, Ad ← Ad + 2
	raEA,-(An)	Ad ← Ad - 2, (Ad) ← Es
	raEA,(sdw,An)	(Ad+sdw) ← Es
	raEA,(sdb,An,Xx)	(Ad+Xx+sdb) ← Es
	raEA,(bsd,An,Xx)	(Ad+Xx+bsd) ← Es
	raEA,([bsd,An,Xx],osd)	ADDR ← (Ad+Xx+bsd) (ADDR+osd) ← Es
	raEA,([bsd,An],Xx,osd)	ADDR ← (Ad+bsd) (ADDR+Xx+osd) ← Es
	raEA,addr.W	(s.x.addrW) ← Es
	raEA,addr.L	(addrL) ← Es
MOVE.L	raEA,Dn	Dd ← Es
	raEA,(An)	(Ad) ← Es
	raEA,(An)+	(Ad) ← Es, Ad ← Ad + 4
	raEA,-(An)	Ad ← Ad - 4, (Ad) ← Es
	raEA,(sdw,An)	(Ad+sdw) ← Es
	raEA,(sdb,An,Xx)	(Ad+Xx+sdb) ← Es
	raEA,(bsd,An,Xx)	(Ad+Xx+bsd) ← Es
	raEA,([bsd,An,Xx],osd)	ADDR ← (Ad+Xx+bsd) (ADDR+osd) ← Es
	raEA,([bsd,An],Xx,osd)	ADDR ← (Ad+bsd) (ADDR+Xx+osd) ← Es
	raEA,addr.W	(s.x.addrW) ← Es
	raEA,addr.L	(addrL) ← Es
MOVEA.W	raEA,An	Ad ← s.x.Es
MOVEA.L	raEA,An	Ad ← Es
MOVEQ	#data.B,Dn	$Dd_{31\sim0}$ ← s.x.#byte

Notes. 1. MOVE.B rdEA,(A7)+ or -(A7) increment/decrement is by 2 to
keep A7 (the Stack Pointer) on a word boundary.
2. ADDR: Memory Indirect component of EA.

Table E7.1. Data transfer (1)

MOVE, MOVEA, MOVEQ

Code Word 1				Code Word 2				Code Word 3				Extension		Condition					Time
1	2	3	4	1	2	3	4	1	2	3	4	src	dst	X	N	Z	V	C	
1	d0	00ms		−	−	−	−	−	−	−	−	0−5	0	−	N	Z	0	0	3+
1	d0	10ms		−	−	−	−	−	−	−	−	0−5	0	−	N	Z	0	0	5+
1	d0	11ms		−	−	−	−	−	−	−	−	0−5	0	−	N	Z	0	0	5+
1	d1	00ms		−	−	−	−	−	−	−	−	0−5	0	−	N	Z	0	0	5+
1	d1	01ms		−	−	−	−	−	−	−	−	0−5	1	−	N	Z	0	0	7+
1	d1	10ms		−	−	−	−	−	−	−	−	0−5	1	−	N	Z	0	0	7+
1	d1	10ms		−	−	−	−	−	−	−	−	0−5	1−3	−	N	Z	0	0	*+
1	d1	10ms		−	−	−	−	−	−	−	−	0−5	1−5	−	N	Z	0	0	#+
1	d1	10ms		−	−	−	−	−	−	−	−	0−5	1−5	−	N	Z	0	0	#+
1	1	11ms		−	−	−	−	−	−	−	−	0−5	1	−	N	Z	0	0	7+
1	3	11ms		−	−	−	−	−	−	−	−	0−5	2	−	N	Z	0	0	9+
3	d0	00ms		−	−	−	−	−	−	−	−	0−5	0	−	N	Z	0	0	3+
3	d0	10ms		−	−	−	−	−	−	−	−	0−5	0	−	N	Z	0	0	5+
3	d0	11ms		−	−	−	−	−	−	−	−	0−5	0	−	N	Z	0	0	5+
3	d1	00ms		−	−	−	−	−	−	−	−	0−5	0	−	N	Z	0	0	5+
3	d1	01ms		−	−	−	−	−	−	−	−	0−5	1	−	N	Z	0	0	7+
3	d1	10ms		−	−	−	−	−	−	−	−	0−5	1	−	N	Z	0	0	7+
3	d1	10ms		−	−	−	−	−	−	−	−	0−5	1−3	−	N	Z	0	0	*+
3	d1	10ms		−	−	−	−	−	−	−	−	0−5	1−5	−	N	Z	0	0	#+
3	d1	10ms		−	−	−	−	−	−	−	−	0−5	1−5	−	N	Z	0	0	#+
3	1	11ms		−	−	−	−	−	−	−	−	0−5	1	−	N	Z	0	0	7+
3	3	11ms		−	−	−	−	−	−	−	−	0−5	2	−	N	Z	0	0	9+
2	d0	00ms		−	−	−	−	−	−	−	−	0−5	0	−	N	Z	0	0	3+
2	d0	10ms		−	−	−	−	−	−	−	−	0−5	0	−	N	Z	0	0	5+
2	d0	11ms		−	−	−	−	−	−	−	−	0−5	0	−	N	Z	0	0	5+
2	d1	00ms		−	−	−	−	−	−	−	−	0−5	0	−	N	Z	0	0	5+
2	d1	01ms		−	−	−	−	−	−	−	−	0−5	1	−	N	Z	0	0	7+
2	d1	10ms		−	−	−	−	−	−	−	−	0−5	1	−	N	Z	0	0	7+
2	d1	10ms		−	−	−	−	−	−	−	−	0−5	1−3	−	N	Z	0	0	*+
2	d1	10ms		−	−	−	−	−	−	−	−	0−5	1−5	−	N	Z	0	0	#+
2	d1	10ms		−	−	−	−	−	−	−	−	0−5	1−5	−	N	Z	0	0	#+
2	1	11ms		−	−	−	−	−	−	−	−	0−5	1	−	N	Z	0	0	7+
2	3	11ms		−	−	−	−	−	−	−	−	0−5	2	−	N	Z	0	0	9+
3	d0	01ms		−	−	−	−	−	−	−	−	0−5	0	−	−	−	−	−	3+
2	d0	01ms		−	−	−	−	−	−	−	−	0−5	0	−	−	−	−	−	3+
7	d0	data8		−	−	−	−	−	−	−	−	0	0	−	N	Z	0	0	3

Notes. 3. Time *: 8+ (null bsd), 12+ (word bsd), 17+ (long bsd).
4. Time #:

bsd:	0	0	0	W	W	W	L	L	L
osd:	0	W	L	0	W	L	0	W	L
Time:	8+	15+	18+	15+	18+	21+	22+	23+	25+

5. Time +: Add source fetch EA calculation time with adjustments:
    (a) addr.W source to all modes: −1.
    (b) Dn, An or #data source to all modes: −3,
       then to all index modes: +2, then,
       (i) to (An): +1,
       (ii) to ([An],Xx) or ([An,Xx]): +4,
       (iii) to ([bsd.L,An],Xx) or ([bsd.L,An,Xx]): −2.

Table E7.1. (contd)

MOVEM, MOVEP

Mnemonic	Operands source, destination	Action
MOVEM.W	regs,wcEA	$dst \leftarrow Ed$ FOR registers Rs on list(D0–A7): $(dst) \leftarrow Rs_{15\sim0}$, $dst \leftarrow dst+2$.
	regs,-(An)	FOR registers Rs on list(A7–D0): $Ad \leftarrow Ad-2$, $(Ad) \leftarrow Rs_{15\sim0}$.
	rcEA,regs	$src \leftarrow Es$ FOR registers Rd on list(D0–A7): $Rd_{31\sim0} \leftarrow s.x.(src)$, $src \leftarrow src+2$.
	(An)+,regs	FOR registers Rd on list(D0–A7): $Rd_{31\sim0} \leftarrow s.x.(As)$, $As \leftarrow As+2$.
MOVEM.L	regs,wcEA	$dst \leftarrow Ed$ FOR registers Rs on list(D0–A7): $(dst) \leftarrow Rs_{31\sim16}$, $dst \leftarrow dst+2$. $(dst) \leftarrow Rs_{15\sim0}$, $dst \leftarrow dst+2$.
	regs,-(An)	FOR registers Rs on list(A7–D0): $Ad \leftarrow Ad-2$, $(Ad) \leftarrow Rs_{15\sim0}$. $Ad \leftarrow Ad-2$, $(Ad) \leftarrow Rs_{31\sim16}$.
	rcEA,regs	$src \leftarrow Es$ FOR registers Rd on list(D0–A7): $Rd_{31\sim16} \leftarrow (src)$, $src \leftarrow src+2$. $Rd_{15\sim0} \leftarrow (src)$, $src \leftarrow src+2$.
	(An)+,regs	FOR registers Rd on list(D0–A7): $Rd_{31\sim16} \leftarrow (As)$, $As \leftarrow As+2$. $Rd_{15\sim0} \leftarrow (As)$, $As \leftarrow As+2$.
MOVEP.W	Dn,(sdw,An)	$(Ad+sdw) \leftarrow Ds_{15\sim8}$ $(Ad+sdw+2) \leftarrow Ds_{7\sim0}$
	(sdw,An),Dn	$Dd_{15\sim8} \leftarrow (As+sdw)$ $Dd_{7\sim0} \leftarrow (As+sdw+2)$
MOVEP.L	Dn,(sdw,An)	$(Ad+sdw) \leftarrow Ds_{31\sim24}$ $(Ad+sdw+2) \leftarrow Ds_{23\sim16}$ $(Ad+sdw+4) \leftarrow Ds_{15\sim8}$ $(Ad+sdw+6) \leftarrow Ds_{7\sim0}$
	(sdw,An),Dn	$Dd_{31\sim24} \leftarrow (As+sdw)$ $Dd_{23\sim16} \leftarrow (As+sdw+2)$ $Dd_{15\sim8} \leftarrow (As+sdw+4)$ $Dd_{7\sim0} \leftarrow (As+sdw+6)$

Notes. 1. MOVEM regs – list(D0–A7) or (A7–D0) – specified as:
    (1) named and separated by (/), for example –
       A1/A5/D0/A7 specifies registers D0, A1, A5 and A7.
    (2) inclusive bounded by (–), for example –
       A2–A5 specifies registers A2, A3, A4 and A5.
  2. MOVEP data may be moved to/from even or odd byte addresses.

Table E7.2. Data transfer (2)

Code Word 1 1 2 3 4	Code Word 2 1 2 3 4	Code Word 3 1 2 3 4	Extension src	dst	Condition X N Z V C	Time
4 8 10md	reg mask	- - - -	0	0-5	- - - - -	5+3n+
4 8 A 0d	reg mask	- - - -	0	0	- - - - -	5+3n+
4 C 10ms	reg mask	- - - -	0-5	0	- - - - -	9+4n+
4 C 9 1s	reg mask	- - - -	0	0	- - - - -	9+4n+
4 8 11md	reg mask	- - - -	0	0-5	- - - - -	5+3n+
4 8 E 0d	reg mask	- - - -	0	0	- - - - -	5+3n+
4 C 11ms	reg mask	- - - -	0-5	0	- - - - -	9+4n+
4 C D 1s	reg mask	- - - -	0	0	- - - - -	9+4n+
0 s1 8 1d	dispword	- - - -	0	0	- - - - -	11
0 d1 0 1s	dispword	- - - -	0	0	- - - - -	12
0 s1 C 1d	dispword	- - - -	0	0	- - - - -	17
0 d1 4 1s	dispword	- - - -	0	0	- - - - -	18

Notes. 3. MOVEM reg mask: AND-mask (move register if bit set):

mask bit: 15 14 13 12 11 10 9 8 7 6 5 4 3 2 1 0

EA or (An)+: A7 A6 A5 A4 A3 A2 A1 A0 D7 D6 D5 D4 D3 D2 D1 D0
    -(An): D0 D1 D2 D3 D4 D5 D6 D7 A0 A1 A2 A3 A4 A5 A6 A7

The register represented by mask bit 0 is transferred first.
4. MOVEM time: + Add no-fetch #W,EA calculation time.
5. MOVEM time: (+kn) Add k × [no. of registers moved] cycles.

Table E7.2. (contd)

CLR, EXT, EXTB, SWAP, EXG

Mnemonic	Operands source, destination	Action
CLR.B	Dn	$Dd \leftarrow 0$
	wmEA	$Ed \leftarrow 0$
CLR.W	Dn	$Dd \leftarrow 0$
	wmEA	$Ed \leftarrow 0$
CLR.L	Dn	$Dd \leftarrow 0$
	wmEA	$Ed \leftarrow 0$
EXT.W	Dn	$Dd_{15 \sim 0} \leftarrow s.x.Dd_{7 \sim 0}$
EXT.L	Dn	$Dd_{31 \sim 0} \leftarrow s.x.Dd_{15 \sim 0}$
EXTB.L	Dn	$Dd_{31 \sim 0} \leftarrow s.x.Dd_{7 \sim 0}$
SWAP	Dn	$Dd_{31 \sim 16} \leftrightarrow Dd_{15 \sim 0}$
EXG	Dn,Dn	$Dd \leftrightarrow Ds$
	Dn,An	$Ad \leftrightarrow Ds$
	An,An	$Ad \leftrightarrow As$

Notes. 1. EXTB is not implemented on the 68000, 68008 or 68010.

Table E7.3. Data transfer (3)

LEA, PEA, LINK, UNLK

Mnemonic	Operands source, destination	Action
LEA	rcEA,An	$Ad \leftarrow <Es>$
PEA	rcEA	$SP \leftarrow SP - 4$
		$(SP) \leftarrow <Es>$
LINK.W	An,#disp16	$SP \leftarrow SP - 4, \quad (SP) \leftarrow As$
		$As \leftarrow SP$
		$SP \leftarrow SP + s.x.\#word$
LINK.L	An,#disp32	$SP \leftarrow SP - 4, \quad (SP) \leftarrow As$
		$As \leftarrow SP$
		$SP \leftarrow SP + \#long$
UNLK	An	$SP \leftarrow As$
		$As \leftarrow (SP)$
		$SP \leftarrow SP + 4$

Notes. 1. LINK displacement should be negative to provide stack space for frame parameters. A positive displacement will cause stacked return addresses to be overwritten on further pushes.
2. LINK.L is not implemented on the 68000, 68008 or 68010.
3. <Es>: Effective Address (not data at EA) is loaded or pushed.

Table E7.4. Data transfer (4)

CLR, EXT, EXTB, SWAP, EXG

Code Word 1				Code Word 2				Code Word 3				Extension		Condition					Time
1	2	3	4	1	2	3	4	1	2	3	4	src	dst	X	N	Z	V	C	
4	2	0	0d	–	–	–	–	–	–	–	–	–	0	–	N	Z	0	0	3
4	2	00md		–	–	–	–	–	–	–	–	–	0-5	–	N	Z	0	0	6+
4	2	4	0d	–	–	–	–	–	–	–	–	–	0	–	N	Z	0	0	3
4	2	01md		–	–	–	–	–	–	–	–	–	0-5	–	N	Z	0	0	6+
4	2	8	0d	–	–	–	–	–	–	–	–	–	0	–	N	Z	0	0	3
4	2	10md		–	–	–	–	–	–	–	–	–	0-5	–	N	Z	0	0	6+
4	8	8	0d	–	–	–	–	–	–	–	–	–	0	–	N	Z	0	0	4
4	8	C	0d	–	–	–	–	–	–	–	–	–	0	–	N	Z	0	0	4
4	9	C	0d	–	–	–	–	–	–	–	–	–	0	–	N	Z	0	0	4
4	8	4	0d	–	–	–	–	–	–	–	–	–	0	–	N	Z	0	0	4
C	s1	4	0d	–	–	–	–	–	–	–	–	0	0	–	–	–	–	–	3
C	s1	8	1d	–	–	–	–	–	–	–	–	0	0	–	–	–	–	–	3
C	s1	4	1d	–	–	–	–	–	–	–	–	0	0	–	–	–	–	–	3

Notes. 2. Time: + Add no-fetch EA calculation time.
3. SWAP: CCR flags the full 32-bit result.

Table E7.3. (contd)

LEA, PEA, LINK, UNLK

Code Word 1				Code Word 2				Code Word 3				Extension		Condition					Time
1	2	3	4	1	2	3	4	1	2	3	4	src	dst	X	N	Z	V	C	
4	d1	11ms		–	–	–	–	–	–	–	–	0-5	0	–	–	–	–	–	3+
4	8	01ms		–	–	–	–	–	–	–	–	0-5	–	–	–	–	–	–	6+
4	E	5	0s	dispword				–	–	–	–	0	0	–	–	–	–	–	7
4	8	0	1s	disp.L-hi				disp.L-lo				0	0	–	–	–	–	–	10
4	E	5	1s	–	–	–	–	–	–	–	–	0	–	–	–	–	–	–	7

Notes. 4. Time: + Add no-fetch EA calculation time.

Table E7.4. (contd)

ADD, ADDA, ADDI, ADDQ, ADDX

Mnemonic	Operands source, destination	Action
ADD.B	rdEA,Dn	Dd ← Dd + Es
	Dn,wmEA	Ed ← Ed + Ds
ADD.W	raEA,Dn	Dd ← Dd + Es
	Dn,wmEA	Ed ← Ed + Ds
ADD.L	raEA,Dn	Dd ← Dd + Es
	Dn,wmEA	Ed ← Ed + Ds
ADDA.W	raEA,An	Ad ← Ad + s.x.Es
ADDA.L	raEA,An	Ad ← Ad + Es
ADDI.B	#data.B,Dn	Dd ← Dd + #byte
	#data.B,wmEA	Ed ← Ed + #byte
ADDI.W	#data.W,Dn	Dd ← Dd + #word
	#data.W,wmEA	Ed ← Ed + #word
ADDI.L	#data.L,Dn	Dd ← Dd + #long
	#data.L,wmEA	Ed ← Ed + #long
ADDQ.B	#Qdata,Dn	Dd ← Dd + #quick
	#Qdata,wmEA	Ed ← Ed + #quick
ADDQ.W	#Qdata,Dn	Dd ← Dd + #quick
	#Qdata,An	Ad.L ← Ad.L + #quick
	#Qdata,wmEA	Ed ← Ed + #quick
ADDQ.L	#Qdata,Dn	Dd ← Dd + #quick
	#Qdata,An	Ad.L ← Ad.L + #quick
	#Qdata,wmEA	Ed ← Ed + #quick
ADDX.B	Dn,Dn	Dd ← Dd + Ds + X
	-(An),-(An)	Ad ← Ad - 1, As ← As - 1
		(Ad) ← (Ad) + (As) + X
ADDX.W	Dn,Dn	Dd ← Dd + Ds + X
	-(An),-(An)	Ad ← Ad - 2, As ← As - 2
		(Ad) ← (Ad) + (As) + X
ADDX.L	Dn,Dn	Dd ← Dd + Ds + X
	-(An),-(An)	Ad ← Ad - 4, As ← As - 4
		(Ad) ← (Ad) + (As) + X

Notes. 1. #quick data is 3-bit data (0, 1 to 7) with value (8, 1 to 7).
2. ADDX.B -(An),-(An) if either An is A7 then decrement is by 2 to keep A7 (the Stack Pointer) on a word boundary.

Table E7.5. Arithmetic (1)

ADD, ADDA, ADDI, ADDQ, ADDX

Code Word 1 (1 2 3 4)	Code Word 2 (1 2 3 4)	Code Word 3 (1 2 3 4)	Ext src	Ext dst	Condition X N Z V C	Time
D d0 00ms	- - - -	- - - -	0-5	0	X N Z V C	3+
D s1 00md	- - - -	- - - -	0	0-5	X N Z V C	6+
D d0 01ms	- - - -	- - - -	0-5	0	X N Z V C	3+
D s1 01md	- - - -	- - - -	0	0-5	X N Z V C	6+
D d0 10ms	- - - -	- - - -	0-5	0	X N Z V C	3+
D s1 10md	- - - -	- - - -	0	0-5	X N Z V C	6+
D d0 11ms	- - - -	- - - -	0-5	0	- - - - -	3+
D d1 11ms	- - - -	- - - -	0-5	0	- - - - -	6+
0 6 0 0d	0 0 #data	- - - -	0	0	X N Z V C	3*
0 6 00md	0 0 #data	- - - -	0	0-5	X N Z V C	6*
0 6 4 0d	#worddata	- - - -	0	0	X N Z V C	3*
0 6 01md	#worddata	- - - -	0	0-5	X N Z V C	6*
0 6 8 0d	#data.L-hi	#data.L-lo	0	0	X N Z V C	3*
0 6 10md	#data.L-hi	#data.L-lo	0	0-5	X N Z V C	6*
5 s0 0 0d	- - - -	- - - -	0	0	X N Z V C	3
5 s0 00md	- - - -	- - - -	0	0-5	X N Z V C	6+
5 s0 4 0d	- - - -	- - - -	0	0	X N Z V C	3
5 s0 4 1d	- - - -	- - - -	0	0	- - - - -	3
5 s0 01md	- - - -	- - - -	0	0-5	X N Z V C	6+
5 s0 8 0d	- - - -	- - - -	0	0	X N Z V C	3
5 s0 8 1d	- - - -	- - - -	0	0	- - - - -	3
5 s0 10md	- - - -	- - - -	0	0-5	X N Z V C	6+
D d1 0 0s	- - - -	- - - -	0	0	X N E V C	3
D d1 0 1s	- - - -	- - - -	0	0	X N E V C	13
D d1 4 0s	- - - -	- - - -	0	0	X N E V C	3
D d1 4 1s	- - - -	- - - -	0	0	X N E V C	13
D d1 8 0s	- - - -	- - - -	0	0	X N E V C	3
D d1 8 1s	- - - -	- - - -	0	0	X N E V C	13

Notes. 3. Time: + Add fetch Effective Address calculation time.
4. Time: * Add fetch #W,EA or #L,EA calculation time.
5. Z flag: E Cleared for a non-zero result, else unchanged.

Table E7.5. (contd)

SUB, SUBA, SUBI, SUBQ, SUBX

Mnemonic	Operands source, destination	Action
SUB.B	rdEA,Dn Dn,wmEA	Dd ← Dd − Es Ed ← Ed − Ds
SUB.W	raEA,Dn Dn,wmEA	Dd ← Dd − Es Ed ← Ed − Ds
SUB.L	raEA,Dn Dn,wmEA	Dd ← Dd − Es Ed ← Ed − Ds
SUBA.W	raEA,An	Ad ← Ad − s.x.Es
SUBA.L	raEA,An	Ad ← Ad − Es
SUBI.B	#data.B,Dn #data.B,wmEA	Dd ← Dd − #byte Ed ← Ed − #byte
SUBI.W	#data.W,Dn #data.W,wmEA	Dd ← Dd − #word Ed ← Ed − #word
SUBI.L	#data.L,Dn #data.L,wmEA	Dd ← Dd − #long Ed ← Ed − #long
SUBQ.B	#Qdata,Dn #Qdata,wmEA	Dd ← Dd − #quick Ed ← Ed − #quick
SUBQ.W	#Qdata,Dn #Qdata,An #Qdata,wmEA	Dd ← Dd − #quick Ad.L ← Ad.L − #quick Ed ← Ed − #quick
SUBQ.L	#Qdata,Dn #Qdata,An #Qdata,wmEA	Dd ← Dd − #quick Ad.L ← Ad.L − #quick Ed ← Ed − #quick
SUBX.B	Dn,Dn −(An),−(An)	Dd ← Dd − Ds − X Ad ← Ad − 1, As ← As − 1 (Ad) ← (Ad) − (As) − X
SUBX.W	Dn,Dn −(An),−(An)	Dd ← Dd − Ds − X Ad ← Ad − 2, As ← As − 2 (Ad) ← (Ad) − (As) − X
SUBX.L	Dn,Dn −(An),−(An)	Dd ← Dd − Ds − X Ad ← Ad − 4, As ← As − 4 (Ad) ← (Ad) − (As) − X

Notes. 1. #quick data is 3−bit data (0, 1 to 7) with value (8, 1 to 7).
2. SUBX.B −(An),−(An) if either An is A7 then decrement is by 2 to keep A7 (the Stack Pointer) on a word boundary.

Table E7.6. Arithmetic (2)

SUB, SUBA, SUBI, SUBQ, SUBX

Code Word 1				Code Word 2				Code Word 3				Extension		Condition					Time
1	2	3	4	1	2	3	4	1	2	3	4	src	dst	X	N	Z	V	C	
9	d0	00	ms	–	–	–	–	–	–	–	–	0-5	0	X	N	Z	V	B	3+
9	s1	00	md	–	–	–	–	–	–	–	–	0	0-5	X	N	Z	V	B	6+
9	d0	01	ms	–	–	–	–	–	–	–	–	0-5	0	X	N	Z	V	B	3+
9	s1	01	md	–	–	–	–	–	–	–	–	0	0-5	X	N	Z	V	B	6+
9	d0	10	ms	–	–	–	–	–	–	–	–	0-5	0	X	N	Z	V	B	3+
9	s1	10	md	–	–	–	–	–	–	–	–	0	0-5	X	N	Z	V	B	6+
9	d0	11	ms	–	–	–	–	–	–	–	–	0-5	0	–	–	–	–	–	3+
9	d1	11	ms	–	–	–	–	–	–	–	–	0-5	0	–	–	–	–	–	6+
0	4	0	0d	0	0	#data		–	–	–	–	0	0	X	N	Z	V	B	3*
0	4	00	md	0	0	#data		–	–	–	–	0	0-5	X	N	Z	V	B	6*
0	4	4	0d	#worddata				–	–	–	–	0	0	X	N	Z	V	B	3*
0	4	01	md	#worddata				–	–	–	–	0	0-5	X	N	Z	V	B	6*
0	4	8	0d	#data.L-hi				#data.L-lo				0	0	X	N	Z	V	B	3*
0	4	10	md	#data.L-hi				#data.L-lo				0	0-5	X	N	Z	V	B	6*
5	s1	0	0d	–	–	–	–	–	–	–	–	0	0	X	N	Z	V	B	3
5	s1	00	md	–	–	–	–	–	–	–	–	0	0-5	X	N	Z	V	B	6+
5	s1	4	0d	–	–	–	–	–	–	–	–	0	0	X	N	Z	V	B	3
5	s1	4	1d	–	–	–	–	–	–	–	–	0	0	–	–	–	–	–	3
5	s1	01	md	–	–	–	–	–	–	–	–	0	0-5	X	N	Z	V	B	6+
5	s1	8	0d	–	–	–	–	–	–	–	–	0	0	X	N	Z	V	B	3
5	s1	8	1d	–	–	–	–	–	–	–	–	0	0	–	–	–	–	–	3
5	s1	10	md	–	–	–	–	–	–	–	–	0	0-5	X	N	Z	V	B	6+
9	d1	0	0s	–	–	–	–	–	–	–	–	0	0	X	N	E	V	B	3
9	d1	0	1s	–	–	–	–	–	–	–	–	0	0	X	N	E	V	B	13
9	d1	4	0s	–	–	–	–	–	–	–	–	0	0	X	N	E	V	B	3
9	d1	4	1s	–	–	–	–	–	–	–	–	0	0	X	N	E	V	B	13
9	d1	8	0s	–	–	–	–	–	–	–	–	0	0	X	N	E	V	B	3
9	d1	8	1s	–	–	–	–	–	–	–	–	0	0	X	N	E	V	B	13

Notes. 3. Time: + Add fetch Effective Address calculation time.
       4. Time: * Add fetch #W,EA or #L,EA calculation time.
       5. Z flag: E Cleared for a non-zero result, else unchanged.

Table E7.6. (contd)

CMP, CMP2, CMPA, CMPI, CMPM, NEG, NEGX, TST

Mnemonic	Operands source, destination	Action
CMP.B	rdEA,Dn	CCR ← status(Dd − Es)
CMP.W	raEA,Dn	CCR ← status(Dd − Es)
CMP.L	raEA,Dn	CCR ← status(Dd − Es)
CMP2.B	rcEA,Dn	Z,C ← status(Dd − Es) IF Z V C = 0 THEN Z,C ← status(Dd − Es+1)
	rcEA,An	Z,C ← status(Ad − s.x.Es) IF Z V C = 0 THEN Z,C ← status(Ad − s.x.Es+1)
CMP2.W	rcEA,Dn	Z,C ← status(Dd − Es) IF Z V C = 0 THEN Z,C ← status(Dd − Es+2)
	rcEA,An	Z,C ← status(Ad − s.x.Es) IF Z V C = 0 THEN Z,C ← status(Ad − s.x.Es+2)
CMP2.L	rcEA,Dn	Z,C ← status(Dd − Es) IF Z V C = 0 THEN Z,C ← status(Dd − Es+4)
	rcEA,An	Z,C ← status(Ad − Es) IF Z V C = 0 THEN Z,C ← status(Ad − Es+1)
CMPA.W	raEA,An	CCR ← status(Ad − s.x.Es)
CMPA.L	raEA,An	CCR ← status(Ad − Es)
CMPI.B	#data.B,Dn #data.B,wmEA	CCR ← status(Dd − #byte) CCR ← status(Ed − #byte)
CMPI.W	#data.W,Dn #data.W,wmEA	CCR ← status(Dd − #word) CCR ← status(Ed − #word)
CMPI.L	#data.L,Dn #data.L,wmEA	CCR ← status(Dd − #long) CCR ← status(Ed − #long)
CMPM.B	(An)+,(An)+	CCR ← status((Ad) − (As)) As ← As + 1, Ad ← Ad + 1
CMPM.W	(An)+,(An)+	CCR ← status((Ad) − (As)) As ← As + 2, Ad ← Ad + 2
CMPM.L	(An)+,(An)+	CCR ← status((Ad) − (As)) As ← As + 4, Ad ← Ad + 4

Table E7.7. Arithmetic (3)

CMP, CMP2, CMPA, CMPI, CMPM, NEG, NEGX, TST

Code Word 1 (1 2 3 4)	Code Word 2 (1 2 3 4)	Code Word 3 (1 2 3 4)	Extension src	Extension dst	Condition X N Z V C	Time
B d0 00ms	– – – –	– – – –	0-5	0	– N Z V B	3+
B d0 01ms	– – – –	– – – –	0-5	0	– N Z V B	3+
B d0 10ms	– – – –	– – – –	0-5	0	– N Z V B	3+
0 0 11ms	0d 0 0 0	– – – –	0-5	0	– ? H ? W	18*
0 0 11ms	1d 0 0 0	– – – –	0-5	0	– ? H ? W	18*
0 2 11ms	0d 0 0 0	– – – –	0-5	0	– ? H ? W	18*
0 2 11ms	1d 0 0 0	– – – –	0-5	0	– ? H ? W	18*
0 4 11ms	0d 0 0 0	– – – –	0-5	0	– ? H ? W	18*
0 4 11ms	1d 0 0 0	– – – –	0-5	0	– ? H ? W	18*
B d0 11ms	– – – –	– – – –	0-5	0.	– N Z V B	4+
B d1 11ms	– – – –	– – – –	0-5	0	– N Z V B	4+
0 C 0 0d	0 0 #data	– – – –	0	0	– N Z V B	6
0 C 00md	0 0 #data	– – – –	0	0-5	– N Z V B	3*
0 C 4 0d	#worddata	– – – –	0	0	– N Z V B	6
0 C 01md	#worddata	– – – –	0	0-5	– N Z V B	3*
0 C 8 0d	#data.L-hi	#data.L-lo	0	0	– N Z V B	8
0 C 10md	#data.L-hi	#data.L-lo	0	0-5	– N Z V B	3*
B d1 0 1s	– – – –	– – – –	0	0	– N Z V B	10
B d1 4 1s	– – – –	– – – –	0	0	– N Z V B	10
B d1 8 1s	– – – –	– – – –	0	0	– N Z V B	10

Continued – NEG, NEGX, TST

Table E7.7. (contd)

CMP, CMP2, CMPA, CMPI, CMPM, NEG, NEGX, TST

Mnemonic	Operands source, destination	Action
NEG.B	Dn	Dd ← 0 − Dd
	wmEA	Ed ← 0 − Ed
NEG.W	Dn	Dd ← 0 − Dd
	wmEA	Ed ← 0 − Ed
NEG.L	Dn	Dd ← 0 − Dd
	wmEA	Ed ← 0 − Ed
NEGX.B	Dn	Dd ← 0 − Dd − X
	wmEA	Ed ← 0 − Ed − X
NEGX.W	Dn	Dd ← 0 − Dd − X
	wmEA	Ed ← 0 − Ed − X
NEGX.L	Dn	Dd ← 0 − Dd − X
	wmEA	Ed ← 0 − Ed − X
TST.B	wdEA	CCR ← status(Ed − 0)
TST.W	wdEA	CCR ← status(Ed − 0)
TST.L	wdEA	CCR ← status(Ed − 0)

Notes. 1. CMPM.B (An)+,(An)+ if either An is A7 then increment is by 2 to keep A7 (the Stack Pointer) on a word boundary.
2. CMP2 is a signed operation, the arithmetically smaller value should be at EA, the larger at EA+1, EA+2 or EA+4.
3. CMP2 is not implemented on the 68000, 68008 or 68010.

Table E7.7 (contd)

CMP, CMP2, CMPA, CMPI, CMPM, NEG, NEGX, TST

Code Word 1				Code Word 2				Code Word 3				Extension		Condition					Time
1	2	3	4	1	2	3	4	1	2	3	4	src	dst	X	N	Z	V	C	
4	4	0	0d	–	–	–	–	–	–	–	–	–	0	X	N	Z	V	B	3
4	4	00md		–	–	–	–	–	–	–	–	–	0-5	X	N	Z	V	B	6+
4	4	4	0d	–	–	–	–	–	–	–	–	–	0	X	N	Z	V	B	3
4	4	01md		–	–	–	–	–	–	–	–	–	0-5	X	N	Z	V	B	6+
4	4	8	0d	–	–	–	–	–	–	–	–	–	0	X	N	Z	V	B	3
4	4	10md		–	–	–	–	–	–	–	–	–	0-5	X	N	Z	V	B	6+
4	0	0	0d	–	–	–	–	–	–	–	–	–	0	X	N	E	V	B	3
4	0	00md		–	–	–	–	–	–	–	–	–	0-5	X	N	E	V	B	6+
4	0	4	0d	–	–	–	–	–	–	–	–	–	0	X	N	E	V	B	3
4	0	01md		–	–	–	–	–	–	–	–	–	0-5	X	N	E	V	B	6+
4	0	8	0d	–	–	–	–	–	–	–	–	–	0	X	N	E	V	B	3
4	0	10md		–	–	–	–	–	–	–	–	–	0-5	X	N	E	V	B	6+
4	A	00md		–	–	–	–	–	–	–	–	–	0-5	–	N	Z	0	0	3+
4	A	01md		–	–	–	–	–	–	–	–	–	0-5	–	N	Z	0	0	3+
4	A	10md		–	–	–	–	–	–	–	–	–	0-5	–	N	Z	0	0	3+

Notes. 4. Z flag: E Cleared for a non-zero result, else unchanged.
5. Z flag: H Set if Dn or An equal either bound, else reset.
6. C flag: W Set if Dn or An out of bounds, else reset.
7. Time: + Add fetch Effective Address calculation time.
8. Time: * Add fetch #W,EA or #L,EA calculation time.

Table E7.7. (contd)

DIVS, DIVSL, DIVU, DIVUL, MULS, MULU

Mnemonic	Operands source, destination	Action
DIVS.W	rdEA,Dn	IF Es = 0 THEN TRAP. IF overflow occurs THEN Dd is unchanged ELSE $Dd_{15 \sim 0}$ ← quotient Dd.L / Es.W $\quad\quad Dd_{31 \sim 16}$ ← remainder Dd.L / Es.W
DIVS.L	rdEA,Dq	as DIVS.W but... Dq.L ← quotient Dq.L / Es.L remainder is discarded.
DIVS.L	rdEA,Dr:Dq	as DIVS.W but... Dq.L ← quotient Dr.L:Dq.L / Es.L Dr.L ← remainder Dr.L:Dq.L / Es.L
DIVSL.L	rdEA,Dr:Dq	as DIVS.W but... Dq.L ← quotient Dq.L / Es.L Dr.L ← remainder Dq.L / Es.L
DIVU.W	rdEA,Dn	IF Es = 0 THEN TRAP. IF overflow occurs THEN Dd is unchanged ELSE $Dd_{15 \sim 0}$ ← quotient Dd.L ÷ Es.W $\quad\quad Dd_{31 \sim 16}$ ← remainder Dd.L ÷ Es.W
DIVU.L	rdEA,Dq	as DIVU.W but... Dq.L ← quotient Dq.L ÷ Es.L remainder is discarded.
DIVU.L	rdEA,Dr:Dq	as DIVU.W but... Dq.L ← quotient Dr.L:Dq.L ÷ Es.L Dr.L ← remainder Dr.L:Dq.L ÷ Es.L
DIVUL.L	rdEA,Dr:Dq	as DIVU.W but... Dq.L ← quotient Dq.L ÷ Es.L Dr.L ← remainder Dq.L ÷ Es.L
MULS.W	rdEA,Dn	Dd.L ← Dd.W * Es.W
MULS.L	rdEA,Dl	Dl.L ← (Dl.L * Es.L)MOD 2^{32}
MULS.L	rdEA,Dh:Dl	Dh.L:Dl.L ← Dl.L * Es.L
MULU.W	rdEA,Dn	Dd.L ← Dd.W × Es.W
MULU.L	rdEA,Dl	Dl.L ← (Dl.L × Es.L)MOD 2^{32}
MULU.L	rdEA,Dh:Dl	Dh.L:Dl.L ← Dl.L × Es.L

Notes. 1. Operators * / denote signed multiplication and division.
2. Operators × ÷ denote unsigned multiplication and division.
3. DIVS: Quotient sign = dividend sign ∀ divisor sign.
4. DIVS: Remainder sign = dividend sign, unless zero.
5. MULS: Product sign = multiplicand sign ∀ multiplier sign.
6. DIVS.W, DIVU.W, MULS.W and MULU.W are the 68020 equivalent of DIVS, DIVU, MULS and MULU on earlier 68xxx processors – all other forms are not implemented on the 68000, 68008 and 68010.

Table E7.8. Arithmetic (4)

DIVS, DIVSL, DIVU, DIVUL, MULS, MULU

Code Word 1				Code Word 2				Code Word 3				Extension		Condition					Time
1	2	3	4	1	2	3	4	1	2	3	4	src	dst	X	N	Z	V	C	
8	d1	11ms		–	–	–	–	–	–	–	–	0-5	0	–	n	z	v	0	56+
4	C	01ms		0q	8	0	0q	–	–	–	–	0-5	0	–	n	z	v	0	90*
4	C	01ms		0q	C	0	0r	–	–	–	–	0-5	0	–	n	z	v	0	90*
4	C	01ms		0q	8	0	0r	–	–	–	–	0-5	0	–	n	z	v	0	90*
8	d0	11ms		–	–	–	–	–	–	–	–	0-5	0	–	n	z	v	0	44+
4	C	01ms		0q	0	0	0q	–	–	–	–	0-5	0	–	n	z	v	0	78*
4	C	01ms		0q	4	0	0r	–	–	–	–	0-5	0	–	n	z	v	0	78*
4	C	01ms		0q	0	0	0r	–	–	–	–	0-5	0	–	n	z	v	0	78*
C	d1	11ms		–	–	–	–	–	–	–	–	0-5	0	–	N	Z	0	0	28+
4	C	00ms		01	8	0	01	–	–	–	–	0-5	0	–	N	Z	v	0	44*
4	C	00ms		01	C	0	0h	–	–	–	–	0-5	0	–	N	Z	0	0	44*
C	d0	11ms		–	–	–	–	–	–	–	–	0-5	0	–	N	Z	0	0	28+
4	C	00ms		01	0	0	01	–	–	–	–	0-5	0	–	N	Z	v	0	44*
4	C	00ms		01	4	0	0h	–	–	–	–	0-5	0	–	N	Z	0	0	44*

Notes. 7. Flag n: Copies quotient msb, undefined on overflow.
       8. Flag z: Flags quotient zero status, undefined on overflow.
       9. Flag v: Set on product or quotient overflow, else reset.
      10. Time: + Add fetch EA calculation time.
      11. Time: * Add fetch #L,EA calculation time.

Table E7.8. (contd)

ABCD, SBCD, NBCD, PACK, UNPK

Mnemonic	Operands source, destination	Action
ABCD	Dn,Dn -(An),-(An)	Dd $\leftarrow$ Dd [+] Ds [+] X As $\leftarrow$ As $-$ 1, Ad $\leftarrow$ Ad $-$ 1 (Ad) $\leftarrow$ (Ad) [+] (As) [+] X
SBCD	Dn,Dn -(An),-(An)	Dd $\leftarrow$ Dd [-] Ds [-] X As $\leftarrow$ As $-$ 1, Ad $\leftarrow$ Ad $-$ 1 (Ad) $\leftarrow$ (Ad) [-] (As) [-] X
NBCD	wdEA	Ed $\leftarrow$ 0 [-] Ed [-] X
PACK	Dn,Dn,#word	UPR $\leftarrow$ Ds.W + #word Dd.B $\leftarrow$ UPR$_{11\sim8}$ (+) UPR$_{3\sim0}$
	-(An),-(An),#word	As $\leftarrow$ As-2, Ad $\leftarrow$ Ad-1 UPR $\leftarrow$ (As).W + #word (Ad).B $\leftarrow$ UPR$_{11\sim8}$ (+) UPR$_{3\sim0}$
UNPK	Dn,Dn,#word	UPR $\leftarrow$ %0000 (+) Ds$_{7\sim4}$ UPR $\leftarrow$ UPR (+) %0000 (+) Ds$_{3\sim0}$ Dd.W $\leftarrow$ UPR + #word
	-(An),-(An),#word	As $\leftarrow$ As-1, Ad $\leftarrow$ Ad-2 UPR $\leftarrow$ %0000 (+) (As).B$_{7\sim4}$ UPR $\leftarrow$ UPR (+) %0000 (+) (As).B$_{3\sim0}$ (Ad).W $\leftarrow$ UPR + #word

Notes. 1. [+], [-]: packed BCD add, subtract on byte operands.
2. (+): Concatenation.
3. UPR: Unpacked BCD Partial Result.
4. -(An),-(An) if either An is A7 then decrement is by 2 to keep A7 (the Stack Pointer) on a word boundary.
5. PACK & UNPK are not implemented on the 68000, 68008 or 68010.

Table E7.9. Binary Coded Decimal

ABCD, SBCD, NBCD, PACK, UNPK

Code Word 1				Code Word 2				Code Word 3				Extension		Condition					Time
1	2	3	4	1	2	3	4	1	2	3	4	src	dst	X	N	Z	V	C	
C	d1	0	0s	–	–	–	–	–	–	–	–	0	0	X	?	E	?	C	5
C	d1	0	1s	–	–	–	–	–	–	–	–	0	0	X	?	E	?	C	17
8	d1	0	0s	–	–	–	–	–	–	–	–	0	0	X	?	E	?	B	5
8	d1	0	1s	–	–	–	–	–	–	–	–	0	0	X	?	E	?	B	17
4	8	00md		–	–	–	–	–	–	–	–	–	0-5	X	?	E	?	B	6
8	d1	4	0s	#worddata				–	–	–	–	0	0	–	–	–	–	–	7
8	d1	4	1s	#worddata				–	–	–	–	0	0	–	–	–	–	–	13
8	d1	8	0s	#worddata				–	–	–	–	0	0	–	–	–	–	–	9
8	d1	8	1s	#worddata				–	–	–	–	0	0	–	–	–	–	–	13

Notes. 6. Z flag: E Cleared for a non-zero result, else unchanged.

Table E7.9. (contd)

AND, ANDI, EOR, EORI, OR, ORI, NOT

Mnemonic	Operands source, destination	Action
AND.B	rdEA,Dn	Dd ← Dd ∧ Es
	Dn,wmEA	Ed ← Ed ∧ Ds
AND.W	raEA,Dn	Dd ← Dd ∧ Es
	Dn,wmEA	Ed ← Ed ∧ Ds
AND.L	raEA,Dn	Dd ← Dd ∧ Es
	Dn,wmEA	Ed ← Ed ∧ Ds
ANDI.B	#data.B,Dn	Dd ← Dd ∧ #byte
	#data.B,wmEA	Ed ← Ed ∧ #byte
ANDI.W	#data.W,Dn	Dd ← Dd ∧ #word
	#data.W,wmEA	Ed ← Ed ∧ #word
ANDI.L	#data.L,Dn	Dd ← Dd ∧ #long
	#data.L,wmEA	Ed ← Ed ∧ #long
EOR.B	Dn,Dn	Dd ← Dd ∀ Ds
	Dn,wmEA	Ed ← Ed ∀ Ds
EOR.W	Dn,Dn	Dd ← Dd ∀ Ds
	Dn,wmEA	Ed ← Ed ∀ Ds
EOR.L	Dn,Dn	Dd ← Dd ∀ Ds
	Dn,wmEA	Ed ← Ed ∀ Ds
EORI.B	#data.B,Dn	Dd ← Dd ∀ #byte
	#data.B,wmEA	Ed ← Ed ∀ #byte
EORI.W	#data.W,Dn	Dd ← Dd ∀ #word
	#data.W,wmEA	Ed ← Ed ∀ #word
EORI.L	#data.L,Dn	Dd ← Dd ∀ #long
	#data.L,wmEA	Ed ← Ed ∀ #long
OR.B	rdEA,Dn	Dd ← Dd ∨ Es
	Dn,wmEA	Ed ← Ed ∨ Ds
OR.W	raEA,Dn	Dd ← Dd ∨ Es
	Dn,wmEA	Ed ← Ed ∨ Ds
OR.L	raEA,Dn	Dd ← Dd ∨ Es
	Dn,wmEA	Ed ← Ed ∨ Ds
ORI.B	#data.B,Dn	Dd ← Dd ∨ #byte
	#data.B,wmEA	Ed ← Ed ∨ #byte
ORI.W	#data.W,Dn	Dd ← Dd ∨ #word
	#data.W,wmEA	Ed ← Ed ∨ #word
ORI.L	#data.L,Dn	Dd ← Dd ∨ #long
	#data.L,wmEA	Ed ← Ed ∨ #long
NOT.B	Dn	Dd ← ¬Dd
	wmEA	Ed ← ¬Ed
NOT.W	Dn	Dd ← ¬Dd
	wmEA	Ed ← ¬Ed
NOT.L	Dn	Dd ← ¬Dd
	wmEA	Ed ← ¬Ed

Notes. 1. AND, EOR and OR are bit to bit operations:
A = %0011, B = %0101, A∧B = %0001, A∀B = %0110, A∨B = %0111.
2. NOT is the logical complement: A = %01, ¬A = %10.

Table E7.10. Logic

AND, ANDI, EOR, EORI, OR, ORI, NOT

Code Word 1 1 2 3 4	Code Word 2 1 2 3 4	Code Word 3 1 2 3 4	Extension src	dst	X	N	Z	V	C	Time
C d0 00ms	– – – –	– – – –	0-5	0	–	N	Z	0	0	3+
C s1 00md	– – – –	– – – –	0	0-5	–	N	Z	0	0	6+
C d0 01ms	– – – –	– – – –	0-5	0	–	N	Z	0	0	3+
C s1 01md	– – – –	– – – –	0	0-5	–	N	Z	0	0	6+
C d0 10ms	– – – –	– – – –	0-5	0	–	N	Z	0	0	3+
C s1 10md	– – – –	– – – –	0	0-5	–	N	Z	0	0	6+
0 2 0 0d	0 0 #data	– – – –	0	0	–	N	Z	0	0	3*
0 2 00md	0 0 #data	– – – –	0	0-5	–	N	Z	0	0	6*
0 2 4 0d	#worddata	– – – –	0	0	–	N	Z	0	0	3*
0 2 01md	#worddata	– – – –	0	0-5	–	N	Z	0	0	6*
0 2 8 0d	#data.L-hi	#data.L-lo	0	0	–	N	Z	0	0	3*
0 2 10md	#data.L-hi	#data.L-lo	0	0-5	–	N	Z	0	0	6*
B s1 0 0d	– – – –	– – – –	0	0	–	N	Z	0	0	3+
B s1 00md	– – – –	– – – –	0	0-5	–	N	Z	0	0	6+
B s1 4 0d	– – – –	– – – –	0	0	–	N	Z	0	0	3+
B s1 01md	– – – –	– – – –	0	0-5	–	N	Z	0	0	6+
B s1 8 0d	– – – –	– – – –	0	0	–	N	Z	0	0	3+
B s1 10md	– – – –	– – – –	0	0-5	–	N	Z	0	0	6+
0 A 0 0d	0 0 #data	– – – –	0	0	–	N	Z	0	0	3*
0 A 00md	0 0 #data	– – – –	0	0-5	–	N	Z	0	0	6*
0 A 4 0d	#worddata	– – – –	0	0	–	N	Z	0	0	3*
0 A 01md	#worddata	– – – –	0	0-5	–	N	Z	0	0	6*
0 A 8 0d	#data.L-hi	#data.L-lo	0	0	–	N	Z	0	0	3*
0 A 10md	#data.L-hi	#data.L-lo	0	0-5	–	N	Z	0	0	6*
8 d0 00ms	– – – –	– – – –	0-5	0	–	N	Z	0	0	3+
8 s1 00md	– – – –	– – – –	0	0-5	–	N	Z	0	0	6+
8 d0 01ms	– – – –	– – – –	0-5	0	–	N	Z	0	0	3+
8 s1 01md	– – – –	– – – –	0	0-5	–	N	Z	0	0	6+
8 d0 10ms	– – – –	– – – –	0-5	0	–	N	Z	0	0	3+
8 s1 10md	– – – –	– – – –	0	0-5	–	N	Z	0	0	6+
0 0 0 0d	0 0 #data	– – – –	0	0	–	N	Z	0	0	3*
0 0 00md	0 0 #data	– – – –	0	0-5	–	N	Z	0	0	6*
0 0 4 0d	#worddata	– – – –	0	0	–	N	Z	0	0	3*
0 0 01md	#worddata	– – – –	0	0-5	–	N	Z	0	0	6*
0 0 8 0d	#data.L-hi	#data.L-lo	0	0	–	N	Z	0	0	3*
0 0 10md	#data.L-hi	#data.L-lo	0	0-5	–	N	Z	0	0	6*
4 6 0 0d	– – – –	– – – –	–	0	–	N	Z	0	0	3
4 6 00md	– – – –	– – – –	–	0-5	–	N	Z	0	0	6+
4 6 4 0d	– – – –	– – – –	–	0	–	N	Z	0	0	3
4 6 01md	– – – –	– – – –	–	0-5	–	N	Z	0	0	6+
4 6 8 0d	– – – –	– – – –	–	0	–	N	Z	0	0	3
4 6 10md	– – – –	– – – –	–	0-5	–	N	Z	0	0	6+

Notes. 3. Time: + Add fetch EA calculation time.
4. Time: * Add fetch #W,EA or #L,EA calculation time.

Table E7.10. (contd)

ASL, ASR, LSL, LSR

Mnemonic	Operands source, destination	Action
ASL.B	Dn,Dn	FOR $Ds_{5\sim0}$: X & C $\leftarrow$ Dd_7 $\twoheadleftarrow_0$ $\leftarrow$ 0
	#count,Dn	FOR #count: X & C $\leftarrow$ Dd_7 $\twoheadleftarrow_0$ $\leftarrow$ 0
ASL.W	Dn,Dn	FOR $Ds_{5\sim0}$: X & C $\leftarrow$ Dd_{15} $\twoheadleftarrow_0$ $\leftarrow$ 0
	#count,Dn	FOR #count: X & C $\leftarrow$ Dd_{15} $\twoheadleftarrow_0$ $\leftarrow$ 0
	wmEA	X & C $\leftarrow$ Ed_{15} $\twoheadleftarrow_0$ $\leftarrow$ 0
ASL.L	Dn,Dn	FOR $Ds_{5\sim0}$: X & C $\leftarrow$ Dd_{31} $\twoheadleftarrow_0$ $\leftarrow$ 0
	#count,Dn	FOR #count: X & C $\leftarrow$ Dd_{31} $\twoheadleftarrow_0$ $\leftarrow$ 0
ASR.B	Dn,Dn	FOR $Ds_{5\sim0}$: Dd_7 $\rightarrow$ Dd_7 $\twoheadrightarrow_0$ $\rightarrow$ X & C
	#count,Dn	FOR #count: Dd_7 $\rightarrow$ Dd_7 $\twoheadrightarrow_0$ $\rightarrow$ X & C
ASR.W	Dn,Dn	FOR $Ds_{5\sim0}$: Dd_{15} $\rightarrow$ Dd_{15} $\twoheadrightarrow_0$ $\rightarrow$ X & C
	#count,Dn	FOR #count: Dd_{15} $\rightarrow$ Dd_{15} $\twoheadrightarrow_0$ $\rightarrow$ X & C
	wmEA	Ed_{15} $\rightarrow$ Ed_{15} $\twoheadrightarrow_0$ $\rightarrow$ X & C
ASR.L	Dn,Dn	FOR $Ds_{5\sim0}$: Dd_{31} $\rightarrow$ Dd_{31} $\twoheadrightarrow_0$ $\rightarrow$ X & C
	#count,Dn	FOR #count: Dd_{31} $\rightarrow$ Dd_{31} $\twoheadrightarrow_0$ $\rightarrow$ X & C
LSL.B	Dn,Dn	FOR $Ds_{5\sim0}$: X & C $\leftarrow$ Dd_7 $\twoheadleftarrow_0$ $\leftarrow$ 0
	#count,Dn	FOR #count: X & C $\leftarrow$ Dd_7 $\twoheadleftarrow_0$ $\leftarrow$ 0
LSL.W	Dn,Dn	FOR $Ds_{5\sim0}$: X & C $\leftarrow$ Dd_{15} $\twoheadleftarrow_0$ $\leftarrow$ 0
	#count,Dn	FOR #count: X & C $\leftarrow$ Dd_{15} $\twoheadleftarrow_0$ $\leftarrow$ 0
	wmEA	X & C $\leftarrow$ Ed_{15} $\twoheadleftarrow_0$ $\leftarrow$ 0
LSL.L	Dn,Dn	FOR $Ds_{5\sim0}$: X & C $\leftarrow$ Dd_{31} $\twoheadleftarrow_0$ $\leftarrow$ 0
	#count,Dn	FOR #count: X & C $\leftarrow$ Dd_{31} $\twoheadleftarrow_0$ $\leftarrow$ 0
LSR.B	Dn,Dn	FOR $Ds_{5\sim0}$: 0 $\rightarrow$ Dd_7 $\twoheadrightarrow_0$ $\rightarrow$ X & C
	#count,Dn	FOR #count: 0 $\rightarrow$ Dd_7 $\twoheadrightarrow_0$ $\rightarrow$ X & C
LSR.W	Dn,Dn	FOR $Ds_{5\sim0}$: 0 $\rightarrow$ Dd_{15} $\twoheadrightarrow_0$ $\rightarrow$ X & C
	#count,Dn	FOR #count: 0 $\rightarrow$ Dd_{15} $\twoheadrightarrow_0$ $\rightarrow$ X & C
	wmEA	0 $\rightarrow$ Ed_{15} $\twoheadrightarrow_0$ $\rightarrow$ X & C
LSR.L	Dn,Dn	FOR $Ds_{5\sim0}$: 0 $\rightarrow$ Dd_{31} $\twoheadrightarrow_0$ $\rightarrow$ X & C
	#count,Dn	FOR #count: 0 $\rightarrow$ Dd_{31} $\twoheadrightarrow_0$ $\rightarrow$ X & C

Notes. 1. The actions of ASL and LSL are identical.
2. #count: 3-bit data (0, 1 to 7) with value (8, 1 to 7).
3. $\twoheadleftarrow$: Left shift all operand bits by one bit (low to high).
4. $\twoheadrightarrow$: Right shift all operand bits by one bit (high to low).

Table E7.11. Shift

ASL, ASR, LSL, LSR

Code Word 1 1 2 3 4	Code Word 2 1 2 3 4	Code Word 3 1 2 3 4	Extension src	Extension dst	Condition X N Z V C	Time
E s1 2 0d	− − − −	− − − −	0	0	X N Z M R	8
E s1 0 0d	− − − −	− − − −	0	0	X N Z M R	8
E s1 6 0d	− − − −	− − − −	0	0	X N Z M R	8
E s1 4 0d	− − − −	− − − −	0	0	X N Z M R	8
E 1 11md	− − − −	− − − −	−	0−5	X N Z M R	7+
E s1 A 0d	− − − −	− − − −	0	0	X N Z M R	8
E s1 8 0d	− − − −	− − − −	0	0	X N Z M R	8
E s0 2 0d	− − − −	− − − −	0	0	X N Z M R	6
E s0 0 0d	− − − −	− − − −	0	0	X N Z M R	6
E s0 6 0d	− − − −	− − − −	0	0	X N Z M R	6
E s0 4 0d	− − − −	− − − −	0	0	X N Z M R	6
E 0 11md	− − − −	− − − −	−	0−5	X N Z M R	6+
E s0 A 0d	− − − −	− − − −	0	0	X N Z M R	6
E s0 8 0d	− − − −	− − − −	0	0	X N Z M R	6
E s1 2 1d	− − − −	− − − −	0	0	X N Z 0 R	6
E s1 0 1d	− − − −	− − − −	0	0	X N Z 0 R	4
E s1 6 1d	− − − −	− − − −	0	0	X N Z 0 R	6
E s1 4 1d	− − − −	− − − −	0	0	X N Z 0 R	4
E 3 11md	− − − −	− − − −	−	0−5	X N Z 0 R	6+
E s1 A 1d	− − − −	− − − −	0	0	X N Z 0 R	6
E s1 8 1d	− − − −	− − − −	0	0	X N Z 0 R	4
E s0 2 1d	− − − −	− − − −	0	0	X N Z 0 R	6
E s0 0 1d	− − − −	− − − −	0	0	X N Z 0 R	4
E s0 6 1d	− − − −	− − − −	0	0	X N Z 0 R	6
E s0 4 1d	− − − −	− − − −	0	0	X N Z 0 R	4
E 2 11md	− − − −	− − − −	−	0−5	X N Z 0 R	6+
E s0 A 1d	− − − −	− − − −	0	0	X N Z 0 R	6
E s0 8 1d	− − − −	− − − −	0	0	X N Z 0 R	4

Notes. 5. Flag M: Set if operand msb changed during shift, else reset.
6. Flag R: Carry is reset if zero shift count (Ds mod 64 = 0).
7. Time: + Add fetch EA calculation time.
8. Time: Shift size does not affect time.

Table E7.11. (contd)

ROL, ROR, ROXL, ROXR

Mnemonic	Operands source, destination	Action
ROL.B	Dn,Dn	FOR $Ds_{5\sim0}$: C ← Dd_7 ←← $_0$ ← Dd_7
	#count,Dn	FOR #count: C ← Dd_7 ←← $_0$ ← Dd_7
ROL.W	Dn,Dn	FOR $Ds_{5\sim0}$: C ← Dd_{15} ←← $_0$ ← Dd_{15}
	#count,Dn	FOR #count: C ← Dd_{15} ←← $_0$ ← Dd_{15}
	wmEA	C ← Ed_{15} ←← $_0$ ← Ed_{15}
ROL.L	Dn,Dn	FOR $Ds_{5\sim0}$: C ← Dd_{31} ←← $_0$ ← Dd_{31}
	#count,Dn	FOR #count: C ← Dd_{31} ←← $_0$ ← Dd_{31}
ROR.B	Dn,Dn	FOR $Ds_{5\sim0}$: Dd_0 → Dd_7 →→ $_0$ → C
	#count,Dn	FOR #count: Dd_0 → Dd_7 →→ $_0$ → C
ROR.W	Dn,Dn	FOR $Ds_{5\sim0}$: Dd_0 → Dd_{15} →→ $_0$ → C
	#count,Dn	FOR #count: Dd_0 → Dd_{15} →→ $_0$ → C
	wmEA	Ed_0 → Ed_{15} →→ $_0$ → C
ROR.L	Dn,Dn	FOR $Ds_{5\sim0}$: Dd_0 → Dd_{31} →→ $_0$ → C
	#count,Dn	FOR #count: Dd_0 → Dd_{31} →→ $_0$ → C
ROXL.B	Dn,Dn	FOR $Ds_{5\sim0}$: X & C ← Dd_7 ←← $_0$ ← X
	#count,Dn	FOR #count: X & C ← Dd_7 ←← $_0$ ← X
ROXL.W	Dn,Dn	FOR $Ds_{5\sim0}$: X & C ← Dd_{15} ←← $_0$ ← X
	#count,Dn	FOR #count: X & C ← Dd_{15} ←← $_0$ ← X
	wmEA	X & C ← Ed_{15} ←← $_0$ ← X
ROXL.L	Dn,Dn	FOR $Ds_{5\sim0}$: X & C ← Dd_{31} ←← $_0$ ← X
	#count,Dn	FOR #count: X & C ← Dd_{31} ←← $_0$ ← X
ROXR.B	Dn,Dn	FOR $Ds_{5\sim0}$: X → Dd_7 →→ $_0$ → X & C
	#count,Dn	FOR #count: X → Dd_7 →→ $_0$ → X & C
ROXR.W	Dn,Dn	FOR $Ds_{5\sim0}$: X → Dd_{15} →→ $_0$ → X & C
	#count,Dn	FOR #count: X → Dd_{15} →→ $_0$ → X & C
	wmEA	X → Ed_{15} →→ $_0$ → X & C
ROXR.L	Dn,Dn	FOR $Ds_{5\sim0}$: X → Dd_{31} →→ $_0$ → X & C
	#count,Dn	FOR #count: X → Dd_{31} →→ $_0$ → X & C

Notes. 1. ROL and ROR are 8, 16 or 32 bit rotations,
ROXL and ROXR are 9, 17 or 33 bit rotations.
2. #count: 3-bit data (0, 1 to 7) with value (8, 1 to 7).
3. ←←: Left shift all operand bits by one bit (low to high).
4. →→: Right shift all operand bits by one bit (high to low).

Table E7.12. Rotate

ROL, ROR, ROXL, ROXR

Code Word 1				Code Word 2				Code Word 3				Extension		Condition					Time
1	2	3	4	1	2	3	4	1	2	3	4	src	dst	X	N	Z	V	C	
E	s1	3	1d	–	–	–	–	–	–	–	–	0	0	–	N	Z	0	R	8
E	s1	1	1d	–	–	–	–	–	–	–	–	0	0	–	N	Z	0	R	8
E	s1	7	1d	–	–	–	–	–	–	–	–	0	0	–	N	Z	0	R	8
E	s1	5	1d	–	–	–	–	–	–	–	–	0	0	–	N	Z	0	R	8
E	7	11md		–	–	–	–	–	–	–	–	–	0–5	–	N	Z	0	R	7+
E	s1	B	1d	–	–	–	–	–	–	–	–	0	0	–	N	Z	0	R	8
E	s1	9	1d	–	–	–	–	–	–	–	–	0	0	–	N	Z	0	R	8
E	s0	3	1d	–	–	–	–	–	–	–	–	0	0	–	N	Z	0	R	8
E	s0	1	1d	–	–	–	–	–	–	–	–	0	0	–	N	Z	0	R	8
E	s0	7	1d	–	–	–	–	–	–	–	–	0	0	–	N	Z	0	R	8
E	s0	5	1d	–	–	–	–	–	–	–	–	0	0	–	N	Z	0	R	8
E	6	11md		–	–	–	–	–	–	–	–	–	0–5	–	N	Z	0	R	7+
E	s0	B	1d	–	–	–	–	–	–	–	–	0	0	–	N	Z	0	R	8
E	s0	9	1d	–	–	–	–	–	–	–	–	0	0	–	N	Z	0	R	8
E	s1	3	0d	–	–	–	–	–	–	–	–	0	0	X	N	Z	0	x	12
E	s1	1	0d	–	–	–	–	–	–	–	–	0	0	X	N	Z	0	x	12
E	s1	7	0d	–	–	–	–	–	–	–	–	0	0	X	N	Z	0	x	12
E	s1	5	0d	–	–	–	–	–	–	–	–	0	0	X	N	Z	0	x	12
E	5	11md		–	–	–	–	–	–	–	–	–	0–5	X	N	Z	0	x	6+
E	s1	B	0d	–	–	–	–	–	–	–	–	0	0	X	N	Z	0	x	12
E	s1	9	0d	–	–	–	–	–	–	–	–	0	0	X	N	Z	0	x	12
E	s0	3	0d	–	–	–	–	–	–	–	–	0	0	X	N	Z	0	x	12
E	s0	1	0d	–	–	–	–	–	–	–	–	0	0	X	N	Z	0	x	12
E	s0	7	0d	–	–	–	–	–	–	–	–	0	0	X	N	Z	0	x	12
E	s0	5	0d	–	–	–	–	–	–	–	–	0	0	X	N	Z	0	x	12
E	4	11md		–	–	–	–	–	–	–	–	–	0–5	X	N	Z	0	x	6+
E	s0	B	0d	–	–	–	–	–	–	–	–	0	0	X	N	Z	0	x	12
E	s0	9	0d	–	–	–	–	–	–	–	–	0	0	X	N	Z	0	x	12

Notes. 5. Flag X: Unchanged if zero shift count (Ds mod 64 = 0).
6. Flag R: Carry is reset if zero shift count (Ds mod 64 = 0).
7. Flag x: Carry = Extend if zero shift count (Ds mod 64 = 0).
8. Time: + Add fetch EA calculation time.
9. Time: Rotate size does not affect time.

Table E7.12. (contd)

BCHG, BCLR, BSET, BTST

Mnemonic	Operands source, destination	Action
BCHG	Dn,wmEA	$Z \leftarrow \neg Ed.B_{Ds}$ $Ed.B_{Ds} \leftarrow \neg Ed.B_{Ds}$
	#bitno,wmEA	$Z \leftarrow \neg Ed.B_{\#b}$ $Ed.B_{\#b} \leftarrow \neg Ed.B_{\#b}$
	Dn,Dn	$Z \leftarrow \neg Dd.L_{Ds}$ $Dd.L_{Ds} \leftarrow \neg Dd.L_{Ds}$
	#bitno,Dn	$Z \leftarrow \neg Dd.L_{\#b}$ $Dd.L_{\#b} \leftarrow \neg Dd.L_{\#b}$
BCLR	Dn,wmEA	$Z \leftarrow \neg Ed.B_{Ds}$ $Ed.B_{Ds} \leftarrow 0$
	#bitno,wmEA	$Z \leftarrow \neg Ed.B_{\#b}$ $Ed.B_{\#b} \leftarrow 0$
	Dn,Dn	$Z \leftarrow \neg Dd.L_{Ds}$ $Dd.L_{Ds} \leftarrow 0$
	#bitno,Dn	$Z \leftarrow \neg Dd.L_{\#b}$ $Dd.L_{\#b} \leftarrow 0$
BSET	Dn,wmEA	$Z \leftarrow \neg Ed.B_{Ds}$ $Ed.B_{Ds} \leftarrow 1$
	#bitno,wmEA	$Z \leftarrow \neg Ed.B_{\#b}$ $Ed.B_{\#b} \leftarrow 1$
	Dn,Dn	$Z \leftarrow \neg Dd.L_{Ds}$ $Dd.L_{Ds} \leftarrow 1$
	#bitno,Dn	$Z \leftarrow \neg Dd.L_{\#b}$ $Dd.L_{\#b} \leftarrow 1$
BTST	Dn,rmEA	$Z \leftarrow \neg Ed.B_{Ds}$
	#bitno,rmEA	$Z \leftarrow \neg Ed.B_{\#b}$
	Dn,Dn	$Z \leftarrow \neg Dd.L_{Ds}$
	#bitno,Dn	$Z \leftarrow \neg Dd.L_{\#b}$

Notes. 1. Ds, #bitno: Range 0-31 for Dd and 0-7 for EA operations.
2. BTST #bitno,rmEA: The #byte form of rmEA is not allowed.
3. ¬ (NOT) is the logical complement: A = %01, ¬A = %10.

Table E7.13. Bit manipulation

BCHG, BCLR, BSET, BTST

Code Word 1				Code Word 2				Code Word 3				Extension		Condition					Time
1	2	3	4	1	2	3	4	1	2	3	4	src	dst	X	N	Z	V	C	
0	s1	01md		−	−	−	−	−	−	−	−	0	0-5	−	−	Z	−	−	5+
0	8	01md		0	0	bitno		−	−	−	−	0	0-5	−	−	Z	−	−	5*
0	s1	4	0d	−	−	−	−	−	−	−	−	0	0	−	−	Z	−	−	5
0	8	4	0d	0	0	bitno		−	−	−	−	0	0	−	−	Z	−	−	5
0	s1	10md		−	−	−	−	−	−	−	−	0	0-5	−	−	Z	−	−	5+
0	8	10md		0	0	bitno		−	−	−	−	0	0-5	−	−	Z	−	−	5*
0	s1	8	0d	−	−	−	−	−	−	−	−	0	0	−	−	Z	−	−	5
0	8	8	0d	0	0	bitno		−	−	−	−	0	0	−	−	Z	−	−	5
0	s1	11md		−	−	−	−	−	−	−	−	0	0-5	−	−	Z	−	−	5+
0	8	11md		0	0	bitno		−	−	−	−	0	0-5	−	−	Z	−	−	5*
0	s1	C	0d	−	−	−	−	−	−	−	−	0	0	−	−	Z	−	−	5
0	8	C	0d	0	0	bitno		−	−	−	−	0	0	−	−	Z	−	−	5
0	s1	00md		−	−	−	−	−	−	−	−	0	0-5	−	−	Z	−	−	5+
0	8	00md		0	0	bitno		−	−	−	−	0	0-5	−	−	Z	−	−	5*
0	s1	0	0d	−	−	−	−	−	−	−	−	0	0	−	−	Z	−	−	5
0	8	0	0d	0	0	bitno		−	−	−	−	0	0	−	−	Z	−	−	5

Notes. 4. Time: + Add fetch EA calculation time.
5. Time: * Add fetch #W,EA calculation time.

Table E7.13. (contd)

CALLM, JMP, JSR, NOP, RTD, RTM, RTR, RTS

Mnemonic	Operands source, destination	Action
CALLM	#argcnt,rcEA	Read Module Descriptor at Ed Type $01, stack change: FOR #argcnt: Copy byte from old to new stack. Build Stack Frame, save Module state Read Module Entry Word Stack Frame ← Dn or An, Dn or An ← Data Area Pointer (SP ← Module Stack Pointer) Jump to called Module.
JMP	rcEA	PC ← <Es>
JSR	rcEA	SP ← SP − 4, (SP) ← PC PC ← <Es>
NOP		No Operation
RTD	#disp16	PC ← (SP), SP ← SP + 4 SP ← SP + s.x.#word
RTM	Dn	read module Stack Frame at (SP) restore Module state Dd ← Module Data Area Pointer (restore SP) SP ← SP+#argcnt Return to calling Module.
	An	as RTM Dn but... Ad ← Module Data Area Pointer
RTR		CCR ← (SP), SP ← SP + 2 PC ← (SP), SP ← SP + 4
RTS		PC ← (SP), SP ← SP + 4

Notes. 1. <Es>: Effective Address (not data at EA) is moved to the PC.
2. RTD is not implemented on the 68000 and 68008.
3. CALLM & RTM are not implemented on the 68000, 68008 or 68010.
4. RTR: High order byte of word pulled from stack is ignored.
5. #argcnt: 0-255 bytes of stacked arguments passed to Module.
6. Module Descriptor at EA:

(EA+$00).W	3-bit Option, 5-bit Type, 8-bit Access Level
(EA+$02).W	Reserved ($0000)
(EA+$04).L	Module Entry Word Pointer
(EA+$08).L	Module Data Area Pointer
(EA+$0C).L	Module Stack Pointer
(EA+$10...)	User Information

7. Module Stack Frame at (SP):

(SP+$00).W	3-bit Option, 5-bit Type, 8-bit Access Level
(SP+$02).W	$00 + CCR
(SP+$04).W	$00 + #argcnt
(SP+$06).W	Reserved ($0000)
(SP+$08).L	Called Module Descriptor Pointer
(SP+$0C).L	Calling Module Program Counter
(SP+$10).L	Calling Module Data Area Pointer (Dn or An)
(SP+$14).L	Calling Module Stack Pointer
(SP+$18...)	#argcnt bytes of passed arguments

Table E7.14. Program control (1)

CALLM, JMP, JSR, NOP, RTD, RTM, RTR, RTS

Code Word 1 1 2 3 4	Code Word 2 1 2 3 4	Code Word 3 1 2 3 4	Extension src dst	Condition X N Z V C	Time
Ø 6 11md	Ø Ø argcnt	– – – –	Ø 0-5	– – – – –	TOA+
4 E 11ms	– – – –	– – – –	0-5 –	– – – – –	7*
4 E 10ms	– – – –	– – – –	0-5 –	– – – – –	11*
4 E 7 1	– – – –	– – – –	– –	– – – – –	3
4 E 7 4	dispword	– – – –	– –	– – – – –	12
Ø 6 C Ød	– – – –	– – – –	– Ø	d d d d d	T
Ø 6 C 1d	– – – –	– – – –	– Ø	d d d d d	T
4 E 7 7	– – – –	– – – –	– –	d d d d d	15
4 E 7 5	– – – –	– – – –	– –	– – – – –	12

Notes. 8. Module Entry Word at ([EA+$04]):
%Ønnn000000000000 – Dn used for Module Data Area Pointer,
%1nnn000000000000 – An used for Module Data Area Pointer.
9. Module Execution begins at Module Entry Word Pointer + 2.
10. Module Data Area Pointer: if A7 is used, it will be
overwritten by the new Stack Pointer value.
11. Flag d: Stacked data is moved to CCR.
12. Time: * Add JMP-EA calculation time.
13. Time: TOA – Type $00 time 36 cycles,
Type $01, Option %100 time 64 cycles,
Option %000, no stack copy, time 56 cycles.
stack copy, time 71 + 6 * #argcnt cycles.
14. Time: T – Type $00 time 22 cycles, Type $01 time 35 cycles.
15. Time: + Add #W,EA calculation time.

Table E7.14. (contd)

BRA, BSR, Bcc, DBcc, Scc

Mnemonic	Operands source, destination	Action
BRA.S	label	PC ← PC + pbd
BRA	label	PC ← PC + pwd
BRA.L	label	PC ← PC + pld
BSR.S	label	SP ← SP − 4, (SP) ← PC, PC ← PC + pbd
BSR	label	SP ← SP − 4, (SP) ← PC, PC ← PC + pwd
BSR.L	label	SP ← SP − 4, (SP) ← PC, PC ← PC + pld
Bcc.S	label	IF cc true THEN PC ← PC + pbd ELSE PC ← PC + 0
Bcc	label	IF cc true THEN PC ← PC + pwd ELSE PC ← PC + 2
Bcc.L	label	IF cc true THEN PC ← PC + pld ELSE PC ← PC + 4

DBcc	Dn,label	IF cc false
		THEN Ds.W ← Ds.W − 1
		  IF Ds.W ≠ $FFFF
		  THEN PC ← PC + pwd
		  ELSE PC ← PC + 2
		ELSE PC ← PC + 2

Scc	Dn	IF cc true THEN Dd$_{7\sim0}$ ← $FF ELSE Dd$_{7\sim0}$ ← $00
Scc	wmEA	IF cc true THEN Ed.B ← $FF ELSE Ed.B ← $00

Notes. 1. pbd, pwd, pld: Byte, word or long signed displacement:
[address of 'label'] − [address of instruction + 2].
  2. cc: State of one or more configurations of N Z V C flags:

cc	meaning, true if: N Z V C					cc	meaning, true if: N Z V C				
(a) Unconditional											
T	True (always)	−	−	−	−	F	False (never)	−	−	−	−
(b) Unsigned conditional											
HI	Higher	−	0	−	0	LS	Lower or Same	−	−	−	1
							(or)	−	1	−	−
(c) Simple conditional											
CC	Carry Clear	−	−	−	0	CS	Carry Set	−	−	−	1
NE	Not Equal	−	0	−	−	EQ	Equal	−	1	−	−
VC	Overflow Clear	−	−	0	−	VS	Overflow Set	−	−	1	−
PL	Plus (positive)	0	−	−	−	MI	Minus (negative)	1	−	−	−
(d) Signed conditional											
GE	Greater or Equal	0	−	0	−	LT	Less Than	0	−	1	−
	(or)	1	−	1	−		(or)	1	−	0	−
GT	Greater Than	0	0	0	−	LE	Less or Equal	−	1	−	−
	(or)	1	0	1	−		(or)	0	−	1	−
								(or)	1	−	0	−

  3. BRA replaces BT and BSR replaces BF

Table E7.15. Program control (2)

BRA, BSR, Bcc, DBcc, Scc

Code Word 1 1 2 3 4	Code Word 2 1 2 3 4	Code Word 3 1 2 3 4	Extension src	dst	Condition X N Z V C	Time
6 0 disp8	- - - -	- - - -	-	0	- - - - -	9
6 0 0 0	dispword	- - - -	-	0	- - - - -	9
6 0 F F	disp.L-hi	disp.L-lo	-	0	- - - -	9
6 1 disp8	- - - -	- - - -	-	0	- - - - -	13
6 1 0 0	dispword	- - - -	-	0	- - - - -	13
6 1 F F	disp.L-hi	disp.L-lo	-	0	- - - - -	13
6 cd disp8	- - - -	- - - -	-	0	- - - - -	9 / 5
6 cd 0 0	dispword	- - - -	-	0	- - - - -	9 / 7
6 cd F F	disp.L-hi	disp.L-lo	-	0	- - - - -	9 / 9
5 cd C 1s	dispword	- - - -	0	0	- - - - -	9 / 10 / 7
5 cd C 0d	- - - -	- - - -	-	0	- - - - -	4
5 cd 11md	- - - -	- - - -	-	012	- - - - -	6+

Notes. 4. cd: Digit depending on condition:

```
cc: T  F  HI LS CC CS NE EQ VC VS PL MI GE LT GT LE
cd: 0  1  2  3  4  5  6  7  8  9  A  B  C  D  E  F
```

5. cc time: Timing is given against the action taken.
6. Time: + Add no-fetch EA calculation time.
7. The Long displacement forms of BRA, BSR and Bcc are not implemented on the 68000, 68008 or 68010.

Table E7.15. (contd)

MOVE from CCR, MOVE to CCR, ANDI to CCR, EORI to CCR, ORI to CCR

Mnemonic	Operands source, destination	Action
MOVE	CCR,Dn CCR,wmEA	$Dd_{15\sim0} \leftarrow$ CCR Ed.W $\leftarrow$ CCR
MOVE	Dn,CCR rmEA,CCR	CCR $\leftarrow Ds_{15\sim0}$ CCR $\leftarrow$ Es.W
ANDI	#data.B,CCR	CCR $\leftarrow$ CCR $\wedge$ #byte
EORI	#data.B,CCR	CCR $\leftarrow$ CCR $\veebar$ #byte
ORI	#data.B,CCR	CCR $\leftarrow$ CCR $\vee$ #byte

Notes. 1. MOVE from CCR is not implemented on the 68000 or 68008.
      2. MOVE from CCR: Word operation, destination high byte cleared.
      3. MOVE to CCR: Word operation, destination high byte unaffected.
      4. AND, EOR and OR are bit to bit operations:
         A = %0011, B = %0101, A$\wedge$B = %0001, A$\veebar$B = %0110, A$\vee$B = %0111.

Table E7.16. System control (1)

MOVE from SR, MOVE to SR, ANDI to SR, EORI to SR, ORI to SR, MOVE USP

Mnemonic	Operands source, destination	Action
MOVE	SR,Dn SR,wmEA	IF S=0 THEN TRAP ELSE $Dd_{15\sim0} \leftarrow$ SR IF S=0 THEN TRAP ELSE Ed.W $\leftarrow$ SR
MOVE	Dn,SR rmEA,SR	IF S=0 THEN TRAP ELSE SR $\leftarrow Ds_{15\sim0}$ IF S=0 THEN TRAP ELSE SR $\leftarrow$ Es.W
ANDI	#data.W,SR	IF S=0 THEN TRAP ELSE SR $\leftarrow$ SR $\wedge$ #word
EORI	#data.W,SR	IF S=0 THEN TRAP ELSE SR $\leftarrow$ SR $\veebar$ #word
ORI	#data.W,SR	IF S=0 THEN TRAP ELSE SR $\leftarrow$ SR $\vee$ #word
MOVE	An,USP USP,An	IF S=0 THEN TRAP ELSE USP $\leftarrow$ As IF S=0 THEN TRAP ELSE Ad $\leftarrow$ USP

Notes. 1. All these instructions are Privileged.
      2. See MOVE from CCR for User mode condition code access.
      3. S=0: Not in Supervisor mode of operation.
      4. AND, EOR and OR are bit to bit operations:
         A = %0011, B = %0101, A$\wedge$B = %0001, A$\veebar$B = %0110, A$\vee$B = %0111.

Table E7.17. System control (2)

MOVE from CCR, MOVE to CCR, ANDI to CCR, EORI to CCR, ORI to CCR

Code Word 1 1 2 3 4	Code Word 2 1 2 3 4	Code Word 3 1 2 3 4	Extension src	dst	Condition X N Z V C	Time
4 2 C 0d	– – – –	– – – –	0	0	– – – – –	5
4 2 11md	– – – –	– – – –	0	0-5	– – – – –	7+
4 4 C 0s	– – – –	– – – –	0	0	d d d d d	5
4 4 11ms	– – – –	– – – –	0-5	0	d d d d d	5*
0 2 3 C	0 0 #data	– – – –	0	0	a a a a a	15
0 A 3 C	0 0 #data	– – – –	0	0	e e e e e	15
0 0 3 C	0 0 #data	– – – –	0	0	o o o o o	15

Notes. 5. Flag: d, Always changed to corresponding moved data bit.
6. Flag: a, Reset if corresponding #data bit 0, else unchanged.
7. Flag: e, Changed if corresponding #data bit 1, else unchanged.
8. Flag: o, Set if corresponding #data bit 1, else unchanged.
9. Time: + Add no-fetch EA calculation time.
10. Time: * Add fetch EA calculation time.

Table E7.16. (contd)

MOVE from SR, MOVE to SR, ANDI to SR, EORI to SR, ORI to SR, MOVE USP

Code Word 1 1 2 3 4	Code Word 2 1 2 3 4	Code Word 3 1 2 3 4	Extension src	dst	Condition X N Z V C	Time
4 0 C 0d	– – – –	– – – –	0	0	– – – – –	5
4 0 11md	– – – –	– – – –	0	0-5	– – – – –	7+
4 6 C 0s	– – – –	– – – –	0	0	d d d d d	11
4 6 11ms	– – – –	– – – –	0-5	0	d d d d d	11*
0 2 7 C	#worddata	– – – –	0	0	a a a a a	15
0 A 7 C	#worddata	– – – –	0	0	e e e e e	15
0 0 7 C	#worddata	– – – –	0	0	o o o o o	15
4 E 6 0s	– – – –	– – – –	0	0	– – – – –	3
4 E 6 1d	– – – –	– – – –	0	0	– – – – –	3

Notes. 5. Flags: d, a, e, o, All bits of SR may be affected.
6. Flag: d, Always changed to corresponding moved data bit.
7. Flag: a, Reset if corresponding #data bit 0, else unchanged.
8. Flag: e, Changed if corresponding #data bit 1, else unchanged.
9. Flag: o, Set if corresponding #data bit 1, else unchanged.
10. Time: + Add no-fetch EA calculation time.
11. Time: * Add fetch EA calculation time.

Table E7.17. (contd)

MOVEC, MOVES, RESET, STOP, RTE

Mnemonic	Operands source, destination	Action
MOVEC	Cr,Dn	IF S=0 THEN TRAP ELSE Dd $\leftarrow$ Cs
	Cr,An	IF S=0 THEN TRAP ELSE Ad $\leftarrow$ Cs
	Dn,Cr	IF S=0 THEN TRAP ELSE Cd $\leftarrow$ Ds
	An,Cr	IF S=0 THEN TRAP ELSE Cd $\leftarrow$ As
MOVES.B	Dn,wmEA	IF S=0 THEN TRAP ELSE DFC:Ed $\leftarrow$ Ds$_{7\sim0}$
	An,wmEA	IF S=0 THEN TRAP ELSE DFC:Ed $\leftarrow$ As$_{7\sim0}$
	wmEA,Dn	IF S=0 THEN TRAP ELSE Dd$_{7\sim0}$ $\leftarrow$ SFC:Es
	wmEA,An	IF S=0 THEN TRAP ELSE Ad $\leftarrow$ s.x.SFC:Es
MOVES.W	Dn,wmEA	IF S=0 THEN TRAP ELSE DFC:Ed $\leftarrow$ Ds$_{15\sim0}$
	An,wmEA	IF S=0 THEN TRAP ELSE DFC:Ed $\leftarrow$ As$_{15\sim0}$
	wmEA,Dn	IF S=0 THEN TRAP ELSE Dd$_{15\sim0}$ $\leftarrow$ SFC:Es
	wmEA,An	IF S=0 THEN TRAP ELSE Ad $\leftarrow$ s.x.SFC:Es
MOVES.L	Dn,wmEA	IF S=0 THEN TRAP ELSE DFC:Ed $\leftarrow$ Ds
	An,wmEA	IF S=0 THEN TRAP ELSE DFC:Ed $\leftarrow$ As
	wmEA,Dn	IF S=0 THEN TRAP ELSE Dd $\leftarrow$ SFC:Es
	wmEA,An	IF S=0 THEN TRAP ELSE Ad $\leftarrow$ SFC:Es
RESET		IF S=0 THEN TRAP ELSE External Reset
STOP	#data.W	IF S=0 THEN TRAP ELSE SR $\leftarrow$ #word WAIT UNTIL Trace, Interrupt or Reset.
RTE		IF S=0 THEN TRAP ELSE SR $\leftarrow$ (SP), PC $\leftarrow$ (SP+2) Read stack format code and deallocate stack accordingly.

Notes.
1. All these instructions are Privileged.
2. S=0: Not in Supervisor mode of operation.
3. MOVEC and MOVES are not implemented on the 68000 or 68008.
4. RTE differs in the 68000, 68008 and 68010 implementations.
5. Control registers:

SFC	Source Function Code	USP	User Stack Pointer
DFC	Destination Function Code	VBR	Vector Base Register
CACR	Cache Control Register	CAAR	Cache Address Register
		MSP	Master Stack Pointer
		ISP	Interrupt Stack pointer

6. CACR, CAAR, MSP and ISP are not implemented on the 68010.
7. Function codes (SFC, DFC):

%000	Not used.	%100	Not used.
%001	User Data space.	%101	Supervisor Data space.
%010	User Program space.	%110	Supervisor Program space.
%011	Not used.	%111	CPU space.

Table E7.18. System control (3)

MOVEC, MOVES, RESET, STOP, RTE

Code Word 1 1 2 3 4	Code Word 2 1 2 3 4	Code Word 3 1 2 3 4	Extension src dst	Condition X N Z V C	Time
4 E 7 A	0d control	- - - -	0 0	- - - - -	7
4 E 7 A	1d control	- - - -	0 0	- - - - -	7
4 E 7 B	0s control	- - - -	0 0	- - - - -	13
4 E 7 B	1s control	- - - -	0 0	- - - - -	13
0 E 00md	0s 8 0 0	- - - -	0 0-5	- - - - -	7*
0 E 00md	1s 8 0 0	- - - -	0 0-5	- - - - -	7*
0 E 00ms	0d 0 0 0	- - - -	0-5 0	- - - - -	8*
0 E 00ms	1d 0 0 0	- - - -	0-5 0	- - - - -	8*
0 E 01md	0s 8 0 0	- - - -	0 0-5	- - - - -	7*
0 E 01md	1s 8 0 0	- - - -	0 0-5	- - - - -	7*
0 E 01ms	0d 0 0 0	- - - -	0-5 0	- - - - -	8*
0 E 01ms	1d 0 0 0	- - - -	0-5 0	- - - - -	8*
0 E 10md	0s 8 0 0	- - - -	0 0-5	- - - - -	7*
0 E 10md	1s 8 0 0	- - - -	0 0-5	- - - - -	7*
0 E 10ms	0d 0 0 0	- - - -	0-5 0	- - - - -	8*
0 E 10ms	1d 0 0 0	- - - -	0-5 0	- - - - -	8*
4 E 7 0	- - - -	- - - -	- -	- - - - -	519
4 E 7 2	#worddata	- - - -	0 -	d d d d d	8
4 E 7 3	- - - -	- - - -	- -	d d d d d	RE

Notes. 8. Code Word 2: control, 3-digit control register codes:

SFC	$000	USP	$800
DFC	$001	VBR	$801
CACR	$002	CAAR	$802
		MSP	$803
		ISP	$804

    9. Flag: d All bits of SR are changed to corresponding moved or
           pulled data bit.
  10. Time: * Add no-fetch #W,EA or #L,EA calculation time.
  11. Time: RE See RTE types in table E.6.02.

Table E7.18. (contd)

BKPT, CHK, ILLEGAL, TRAP, TRAPV, CHK2, TRAPcc

Mnemonic	Operands source, destination	Action
BKPT	#number	Run acknowledge bus cycle IF response normal THEN execute response operation word ELSE illegal instruction exception.

CHK	rdEA,Dn	IF Dd < 0:
		THEN: N ← 1, TRAP
		ELSE: IF Dd > Es:
		     THEN: N ← 0, TRAP
		     ELSE: N ← ?

CHK2.B	rcEA,Dn	Z,C ← status(Dd − Es), TRAP IF CS IF Z V C = 0 THEN Z,C ← status(Dd − Es+1), TRAP IF CS
	rcEA,An	Z,C ← status(Ad − s.x.Es), TRAP IF CS IF Z V C = 0 THEN Z,C ← status(Ad − s.x.Es+1), TRAP IF CS
CHK2.W	rcEA,Dn	Z,C ← status(Dd − Es), TRAP IF CS IF Z V C = 0 THEN Z,C ← status(Dd − Es+2), TRAP IF CS
	rcEA,An	Z,C ← status(Ad − s.x.Es), TRAP IF CS IF Z V C = 0 THEN Z,C ← status(Ad − s.x.Es+2), TRAP IF CS
CHK2.L	rcEA,Dn	Z,C ← status(Dd − Es), TRAP IF CS IF Z V C = 0 THEN Z,C ← status(Dd − Es+4), TRAP IF CS
	rcEA,An	Z,C ← status(Ad − Es), TRAP IF CS IF Z V C = 0 THEN Z,C ← status(Ad − Es+1), TRAP IF CS
ILLEGAL		SSP ← SSP − 2, (SSP) ← vector offset SSP ← SSP − 4, (SSP) ← PC SSP ← SSP − 2, (SSP) ← SR PC ← illegal vector address
TRAP	#vector	SSP ← SSP − 2, (SSP) ← vector offset SSP ← SSP − 4, (SSP) ← PC SSP ← SSP − 2, (SSP) ← SR PC ← vector address
TRAPV		IF V = 1 THEN TRAP ELSE continue
TRAPcc		IF cc true THEN TRAP ELSE continue
TRAPcc.W	#def−word	IF cc true THEN TRAP ELSE continue
TRAPcc.L	#def−long	IF cc true THEN TRAP ELSE continue

Table E7.19. System control (4)

BKPT, CHK, ILLEGAL, TRAP, TRAPV, CHK2, TRAPcc

Code Word 1				Code Word 2				Code Word 3				Extension		Condition					Time
1	2	3	4	1	2	3	4	1	2	3	4	src	dst	X	N	Z	V	C	
4	8	4	1s	-	-	-	-	-	-	-	-	-	-	-	-	-	-	-	10~
4	d1	10ms		-	-	-	-	-	-	-	-	0-5	0	-	n	?	?	?	8+
0	0	11ms		0d	8	0	0	-	-	-	-	0-5	0	-	?	H	?	W	18*
0	0	11ms		1d	8	0	0	-	-	-	-	0-5	0	-	?	H	?	W	18*
0	2	11ms		0d	8	0	0	-	-	-	-	0-5	0	-	?	H	?	W	18*
0	2	11ms		1d	8	0	0	-	-	-	-	0-5	0	-	?	H	?	W	18*
0	4	11ms		0d	8	0	0	-	-	-	-	0-5	0	-	?	H	?	W	18*
0	4	11ms		1d	8	0	0	-	-	-	-	0-5	0	-	?	H	?	W	18*
4	A	F	C	-	-	-	-	-	-	-	-	-	-	-	-	-	-	-	27
4	E	4	vv	-	-	-	-	-	-	-	-	0	-	-	-	-	-	-	27
4	E	7	6	-	-	-	-	-	-	-	-	-	-	-	-	-	-	-	32 5
5	cd	F	C	-	-	-	-	-	-	-	-	-	-	-	-	-	-	-	32 5
5	cd	F	A	#def-word				-	-	-	-	-	-	-	-	-	-	-	33 7
5	cd	F	B	#d-long-hi				#d-long-lo				-	-	-	-	-	-	-	33 10

Continued – Notes.

Table E7.19. (contd)

Notes. 1. ILLEGAL code is guaranteed to initiate illegal instruction
exception processing in all future 68xxx implementations.
2. BKPT is not implemented on the 68000 or 68008 and differs in
its implementation on the 68010.
3. CHK2 is a signed operation, the arithmetically smaller value
should be at EA, the larger at EA+1, EA+2 or EA+4.
4. CHK2 & TRAPcc are not implemented on 68000, 68008 or 68010.
5. Exception stack frames differ on the 68000, 68008 and 68010.
6. #vector is a number 0 to 15 and references one of the 16 trap
vectors 32 to 47.
7. TRAPV is a special instruction form of TRAPVS implemented on
all 68000 series processors.
8. #def-word, #def-long: optional word, long-word data available
for passing user defined information to the TRAP handler.

9. cc: State of one or more configurations of N Z V C flags:

cc	meaning, true if:	N	Z	V	C	cc	meaning, true if:	N	Z	V	C
(a)	*Unconditional*										
T	True (always)	–	–	–	–	F	False (never)	–	–	–	–
(b)	*Unsigned conditional*										
HI	Higher	–	0	–	0	LS	Lower or Same	–	–	–	1
							(or)	–	1	–	–
(c)	*Simple conditional*										
CC	Carry Clear	–	–	–	0	CS	Carry Set	–	–	–	1
NE	Not Equal	–	0	–	–	EQ	Equal	–	1	–	–
VC	Overflow Clear	–	–	0	–	VS	Overflow Set	–	–	1	–
PL	Plus (positive)	0	–	–	–	MI	Minus (negative)	1	–	–	–
(d)	*Signed conditional*										
GE	Greater or Equal	0	–	0	–	LT	Less Than	0	–	1	–
	(or)	1	–	1	–		(or)	1	–	0	–
GT	Greater Than	0	0	0	–	LE	Less or Equal	–	1	–	–
	(or)	1	0	1	–		(or)	0	–	1	–
							(or)	1	–	0	–

Table E7.19. (contd)

Notes.
10. $4AFA and $4AFB are Motorola reserved `ILLEGAL` codes.
11. Code digit: vv, 0-F trap vector number.
12. cd: Digit depending on condition:

cc:	T	F	HI	LS	CC	CS	NE	EQ	VC	VS	PL	MI	GE	LT	GT	LE
cd:	0	1	2	3	4	5	6	7	8	9	A	B	C	D	E	F

13. N Flag: n Undefined if operand Dd is within bounds.
14. Z flag: H Set if Dn or An equal either bound, else reset.
15. C flag: W Set if Dn or An out of bounds, else reset.
16. TRAPV & TRAPcc timing is given against the action taken.
17. Time: * Add fetch #W,EA or #L,EA calculation time.
18. Time: + Add fetch EA calculation time.
19. Time: ~ BKPT time does not include operation word or illegal
    instruction exception processing time.

Table E7.19 (contd)

TAS, CAS, CAS2

Mnemonic	Operands source, destination	Action
TAS	Dn wmEA	$\ll$ Dd.B – 0 $\gg$ and Dd$_7$ $\leftarrow$ 1 $\ll$ Ed.B – 0 $\gg$ and Ed.B$_7$ $\leftarrow$ 1
CAS.B	Dr,Dw,wmEA	$\ll$ Ed.B – Dr.B $\gg$ and IF Z = 1 THEN Ed.B $\leftarrow$ Dw.B ELSE Dr.B $\leftarrow$ Ed.B
CAS.W	Dr,Dw,wmEA	$\ll$ Ed.W – Dr.W $\gg$ and IF Z = 1 THEN Ed.W $\leftarrow$ Dw.W ELSE Dr.W $\leftarrow$ Ed.W
CAS.L	Dr,Dw,wmEA	$\ll$ Ed.L – Dr.L $\gg$ and IF Z = 1 THEN Ed.L $\leftarrow$ Dw.L ELSE Dr.L $\leftarrow$ Ed.L
CAS2.B	Dq:Dr,Dv:Dw,(Rm):(Rn)	$\ll$ (Rm).B:(Rn).B – Dq.B:Dr.B $\gg$ and IF Z = 1 THEN (Rm).B:(Rn).B $\leftarrow$ Dv.B:Dw.B ELSE Dq.B:Dr.B $\leftarrow$ (Rm).B:(Rn).B
CAS2.W	Dq:Dr,Dv:Dw,(Rm):(Rn)	$\ll$ (Rm).W:(Rn).W – Dq.W:Dr.W $\gg$ and IF Z = 1 THEN (Rm).W:(Rn).W $\leftarrow$ Dv.W:Dw.W ELSE Dq.W:Dr.W $\leftarrow$ (Rm).W:(Rn).W
CAS2.L	Dq:Dr,Dv:Dw,(Rm):(Rn)	$\ll$ (Rm).L:(Rn).L – Dq.L:Dr.L $\gg$ and IF Z = 1 THEN (Rm).L:(Rn).L $\leftarrow$ Dv.L:Dw.L ELSE Dq.L:Dr.L $\leftarrow$ (Rm).L:(Rn).L

Notes. 1. TAS operations are indivisible for synchronisation purposes in a multiprocessor environment.
2. CAS and CAS2 operations are indivisible to allow updating of common system data structures in a multiprocessor environment to be performed without risk of multiple access data changes between test and transfer or during transfer.
3. $\ll$ ... $\gg$: No results of the enclosed operation are saved, only the condition codes are affected.
4. (Rm):(Rn): Any combination of Data and Address registers is allowed.
5. CAS2: If Dq and Dr represent the same Data register, then Dq is loaded from (Rm) and the value at (Rn) is not returned.
6. CAS & CAS2 are not implemented on the 68000, 68008 or 68010.

Table E7.20. Multiprocessor environment

TAS, CAS, CAS2

Code Word 1				Code Word 2				Code Word 3				Extension		Condition					Time
1	2	3	4	1	2	3	4	1	2	3	4	src	dst	X	N	Z	V	C	
4	A	C	0d	–	–	–	–	–	–	–	–	–	0	–	N	Z	0	0	4
4	A	1	1md	–	–	–	–	–	–	–	–	–	0-5	–	N	Z	0	0	13+
0	A	1	1md	0	Dw/Dr			–	–	–	–	0	0-5	–	N	Z	V	C	
																			16*
																			13*
0	C	1	1md	0	Dw/Dr			–	–	–	–	0	0-5	–	N	Z	V	C	
																			16*
																			13*
0	E	1	1md	0	Dw/Dr			–	–	–	–	0	0-5	–	N	Z	V	C	
																			16*
																			13*
0	A	F	C	Rm	Dv/Dq			Rn	Dw/Dr			0	0	–	N	Z	V	C	
																			28
																			25
0	C	F	C	Rm	Dv/Dq			Rn	Dw/Dr			0	0	–	N	Z	V	C	
																			28
																			25
0	E	F	C	Rm	Dv/Dq			Rn	Dw/Dr			0	0	–	N	Z	V	C	
																			28
																			25

Notes. 7. Code: Rm or Rn – single hexadecimal digit giving Data or Address register number:

Rm or Rn = D0 D1 D2 D3 D4 D5 D6 D7 A0 A1 A2 A3 A4 A5 A6 A7
$digit = $0 $1 $2 $3 $4 $5 $6 $7 $8 $9 $A $B $C $D $E $F

8. Code: Dv/Dq or Dw/Dr – three hexadecimal digits giving Write and Read Data registers:

Dv or Dw	D0	D1	D2	D3	D4	D5	D6	D7
Dq D0	$000	$040	$080	$0C0	$100	$140	$180	$1C0
or D1	$001	$041	$081	$0C1	$101	$141	$181	$1C1
Dr D2	$002	$042	$082	$0C2	$102	$142	$182	$1C2
D3	$003	$043	$083	$0C3	$103	$143	$183	$1C3
D4	$004	$044	$084	$0C4	$104	$144	$184	$1C4
D5	$005	$045	$085	$0C5	$105	$145	$185	$1C5
D6	$006	$046	$086	$0C6	$106	$146	$186	$1C6
D7	$007	$047	$087	$0C7	$107	$147	$187	$1C7

9. Time: + Add no-fetch EA calculation time.
10. Time: * Add no-fetch #W,EA or #L,EA calculation time.
11. CAS and CAS2 timing is given against the action taken.

Table E7.20. (contd)

cpBcc, cpDBcc, cpGEN, cpRESTORE, cpSAVE, cpScc, cpTRAPcc

Mnemonic	Operands source, destination	Action
cpBcc	label	IF coprocessor condition true THEN PC ← PC + pwd ELSE PC ← PC + 2
cpBcc.L	label	IF coprocessor condition true THEN PC ← PC + pld ELSE PC ← PC + 4
cpDBcc	Dn,label	IF coprocessor condition false THEN Ds.W ← Ds.W − 1 IF Ds.W ≠ $FFFF THEN PC ← PC + pwd ELSE PC ← PC + 2 ELSE PC ← PC + 2
cpGEN	\<cp-params\>	Send command to coprocessor
cpRESTORE	(An)+ wcEA	Restore coprocessor condition from external memory
cpSAVE	−(An) wcEA	Save coprocessor condition to external memory
cpScc	wdEA	IF coprocessor condition true THEN Ed.B ← %11111111 ELSE Ed.B ← %00000000
cpTRAPcc		IF coprocessor condition true THEN TRAP ELSE continue
cpTRAPcc	#data.W	IF coprocessor condition true THEN TRAP ELSE continue
cpTRAPcc	#data.L	IF coprocessor condition true THEN TRAP ELSE continue

Notes. 1. Coprocessor instructions are not implemented on the 68000, 68008 or 68010.
2. cp: Coprocessor identifier − up to 8 coprocessors may be designated.
3. pwd, pld: word or long-word signed displacement following any coprocessor defined extension words, assembled as: [address of 'label'] − [address of displacement word].
4. cc: Coprocessor condition − coprocessor dependent.
5. \<cp-params\>: parameters defined by the coprocessor.
6. cpTRAPcc #data: Immediate data passed to the main processor TRAP handling routine.

Table E7.21. Coprocessor

cpBcc, cpDBcc, cpGEN, cpRESTORE, cpSAVE, cpScc, cpTRAPcc

Code Word 1 1 2 3 4	Code Word 2 1 2 3 4	Extension group one	Extension group two	Extension group three	Time
Fcf0 10ccf	– – – –	cdp: 0-127	disp.W: 1	– – – –	
Fcf0 11ccf	– – – –	cdp: 0-127	disp.L: 2	– – – –	
Fcf0 4 1s	0 0 00ccf	cdp: 0-127	disp.W: 1	– – – –	
Fcf0 00md	cp-command	cdp: 0-127	EA: 0-5	cdp: 0-127	
Fcf1 01md	– – – –	EA: 0-5	– – – –	– – – –	
Fcf1 00md	– – – –	EA: 0-5	– – – –	– – – –	
Fcf0 01md	0 0 00ccf	cdp: 0-127	EA: 0-5	– – – –	
Fcf0 7 A	0 0 00ccf	cdp: 0-127	– – – –	– – – –	
Fcf0 7 B	0 0 00ccf	cdp: 0-127	data.W: 1	– – – –	
Fcf0 7 C	0 0 00ccf	cdp: 0-127	data.L: 2	– – – –	

Notes. 7. Coprocessor instruction length is determined by the amount of
information requested by the particular coprocessor.
8. Code Word 1 high order byte format, Fcf0 (%1111xxx0) or
Fcf1 (%1111xxx1): cf (%xxx) specifies the coprocessor
identification number, 0 to 7.
9. Code Word 1 or 2 low order byte format, 00ccf, 01ccf, 10ccf or
11ccf: the first two digits are bits, ccf is a 6-bit field
specifying the coprocessor condition to be tested, this is
entirely coprocessor determined.
10. cdp: coprocessor defined parameter extension words to be
passed to the coprocessor, the Program Counter moving past
them to address any following main processor data or
displacement words.
11. cp-command: coprocessor instruction command word.
12. Condition codes: May be changed by the coprocessor during
the execution of cpGEN, all other coprocessor instructions
do not affect the Status register.
13. Time: depends entirely on the coprocessor and the length and
complexity of the instruction.

Table E7.21. *(contd)*

BFCHG, BFCLR, BFEXTS, BFÉXTU, BFFFO, BFINS, BFSET, BFTST

Mnemonic	Operands source, destination	Action
BFCHG	Dn[bfo:bfw]	<< Dd_bf — 0 >>, Dd_bf ← ¬Dd_bf
	wcEA[bfo:bfw]	<< Ed_bf — 0 >>, Ed_bf ← ¬Ed_bf
BFCLR	Dn[bfo:bfw]	<< Dd_bf — 0 >>, Dd_bf ← 0
	wcEA[bfo:bfw]	<< Ed_bf — 0 >>, Ed_bf ← 0
BFEXTS	Dn[bfo:bfw],Dn	<< Ds_bf — 0 >>, Dd.L ← s.x.Ds_bf
	wcEA[bfo:bfw],Dn	<< Es_bf — 0 >>, Dd.L ← s.x.Es_bf
BFEXTU	Dn[bfo:bfw],Dn	<< Ds_bf — 0 >>, Dd.L ← z.x.Ds_bf
	wcEA[bfo:bfw],Dn	<< Es_bf — 0 >>, Dd.L ← z.x.Es_bf
BFFFO	Dn[bfo:bfw],Dn	<< Ds_bf — 0 >> Dd ← bfo + offset Ds_bf m.s.setbit
	wcEA[bfo:bfw],Dn	<< Es_bf — 0 >> Dd ← bfo + offset Es_bf m.s.setbit
BFINS	Dn,Dn[bfo:bfw]	Dd_bf ← Ds(bfw), << Dd_bf — 0 >>
	Dn,wcEA[bfo:bfw]	Ed_bf ← Ds(bfw), << Ed_bf — 0 >>
BFSET	Dn[bfo:bfw]	<< Dd_bf — 0 >>, Dd_bf ← 1
	wcEA[bfo:bfw]	<< Ed_bf — 0 >>, Ed_bf ← 1
BFTST	Dn[bfo:bfw]	<< Dd_bf — 0 >>
	wcEA[bfo:bfw]	<< Ed_bf — 0 >>

Notes. 1. Bit field operation instructions are not implemented on the 68000, 68008 or 68010.
2. << .... >>: CCR only is affected by the described operation.
3. ¬ (NOT) is the logical complement affecting each bit in the bit field individually: A = %01, ¬A = %10.
4. BFCLR, BFSET: Each bit in the bit field is reset, set.
5. BFFFO: If bit field = 0 then Dd = bfo + bfw.
6. BFINS: Lowest order Ds bits are transferred to the bit field.
7. [bfo:bfw]: Bit field offset and Bit field width, both may be assembled as immediate data or as Data register held values:

	Assembler form	source	value range
Offset,	[Do:...]	Do31e0	-2^{31} to $2^{31} - 1$
	[#bfo:...]	#5-bit	0 to 31
Width,	[...:Dw]	Dw5e0	32 (Dw = 0), 1 to 31
	[...:#bfw]	#5-bit	32 (#bfw = 0), 1 to 31

8. wcEA[bfo:bfw]: The bit field is in memory, bit 7 of the byte addressed by wcEA is the base bit, e.g. an offset of −3 and width of 9 would specify the field:

```
   address:  wcEA − 1              wcEA           wcEA + 1
memory bit:  7 6 5 4 3 2 1 0   7 6 5 4 3 2 1 0   7 6 5 4 3 ....
 bit field:              0 1 2 3 4 5 6 7 8 9
                         [msb ........... lsb]
```

Table E7.22. Bit field addressing

BFCHG, BFCLR, BFEXTS, BFEXTU, BFFFO, BFINS, BFSET, BFTST

Code Word 1 1 2 3 4	Code Word 2 1 2 3 4	Code Word 3 1 2 3 4	Extension src	dst	Condition X N Z V C	Time
E A C 0d	0 bof/bwf	- - - -	-	0	- N Z 0 0	12
E A 11md	0 bof/bwf	- - - -	-	0-5	- N Z 0 0	16d+
E C C 0d	0 bof/bwf	- - - -	-	0	- N Z 0 0	12
E C 11md	0 bof/bwf	- - - -	-	0-5	- N Z 0 0	16d+
E B C 0s	0d bof/bwf	- - - -	0	0	- N Z 0 0	8
E B 11ms	0d bof/bwf	- - - -	0-5	0	- N Z 0 0	13b
E 9 C 0s	0d bof/bwf	- - - -	0	0	- N Z 0 0	8
E 9 11ms	0d bof/bwf	- - - -	0-5	0	- N Z 0 0	13b
E D C 0s	0d bof/bwf	- - - -	0	0	- N Z 0 0	18
E D 11ms	0d bof/bwf	- - - -	0-5	0	- N Z 0 0	24c
E F C 0d	0s bof/bwf	- - - -	0	0	- N Z 0 0	10
E F 11md	0s bof/bwf	- - - -	0	0-5	- N Z 0 0	15c
E E C 0d	0 bof/bwf	- - - -	-	0	- N Z 0 0	12
E E 11md	0 bof/bwf	- - - -	-	0-5	- N Z 0 0	16d+
E 8 C 0d	0 bof/bwf	- - - -	-	0	- N Z 0 0	7
E 8 11md	0 bof/bwf	- - - -	-	0-5	- N Z 0 0	12a+

Notes. 9. Dn[bfo:bfw]: Data register bit field, bit 31 is the base bit,
e.g. an offset of 3 and width of 5 would specify the field:

```
Dn long-word bit no.:  31 30 29 28 27 26 25 24 23 22 21 ....
Dn bit field bit no.:           0  1  2  3  4
                              [msb ..... lsb]
```

Negative offsets are invalid, as are any offset or width
parameters which cause any part of the bit field to exceed
the 32-bit size of the Data register.

10. Code Word 2 bof/bwf: 12-bit (3 hexadecimal digit) code
specifying bit field offset and width sources as Data
register numbers or immediate data:

Code bit no.	11	10	9	8	7	6	5	4	3	2	1	0
[Do,Dw]	1	0	0	Do	Do	Do	1	0	0	Dw	Dw	Dw
[Do,#bfw]	1	0	0	Do	Do	Do	0	#w	#w	#w	#w	#w
[#bfo,Dw]	0	#o	#o	#o	#o	#o	1	0	0	Dw	Dw	Dw
[#bfo,#bfw]	0	#o	#o	#o	#o	#o	0	#w	#w	#w	#w	#w

11. Time a, b, c, d: If bit field extent is greater than 4 bytes
then add 4 (a), 5 (b), 6 (c) or 8 (d) clock cycles.
12. Time +: Add no-fetch #W,EA calculation time.

Table E7.22. (contd)

Appendix F
Effective Address Formation

The twenty-two figures in this Appendix show the composition of each form of Effective Address. The information is in three parts:

1. The small table at the top of each figure gives (a) the processor(s) which support the mode, (b) standard assembler notation for the form, and (c) the Effective Address mode and register number encoding for the form.
2. The middle section shows the cpu registers and format of program memory involved, giving the sources of all EA addends. (The use of the word 'source' in this Appendix should not be confused with its use in the expression 'source operand' – it refers to the origin of values used in forming the EA; whether that is source or destination operand is immaterial.)
3. The lower section is a sort of flow diagram showing the selection, adjustment and combination of the EA addends to form the Effective Address.

The Effective Address, or EA, is the address of the operand – the location where the *effect* of the instruction takes place. The calculation of this final address can involve a long sequence of actions, with many intermediate values, and in some cases indirection through memory – see, for example, the number of operations and partial source values involved in computing the Effective Address in the 68020 post-indexed and preindexed Memory of Program Indirect modes, Figures F19 to F22.

Figures F1 and F2 show Data and Address Register direct addressing. This is the most fundamental mode, since no EA extension words are needed and no external reference is made – other than the instruction word fetch and decode. The source for the Effective Address is the 3-bit EA register number field, bits 2-0 of the instruction word (an alternative 3-bit field may be used for specific register direct forms), and the operand is contained within the specified register.

Figure F3 shows register indirect addressing. The indirection involves two levels of addressing: (a) address the register containing the operand address, and (b) address the operand, using the value obtained from the register. The first level of addressing, which corresponds to the register direct form of Figure F2, is not shown in the diagram but is assumed to have taken place. Indeed, the calculation of all forms of address which utilise the contents of registers must involve the sub-process of first addressing the source register.

Figures F4 and F5 show rather special cases: the Predecrement and Post-increment

Indirect modes are the only two involving a change to the source registers. Their use may replace up to three instructions, for example:

ACTON.L (AØ)+,(A1)+

replaces the sequence:

ACTON.L(AØ),(A1)
ADD.L #4,AØ
ADD.L #4,A1

(The all-purpose ultrapowerful instruction ACTON is not implemented on the 68000-series, unfortunately.)

The remaining forms are constructed by the same or similar processes to those used for register direct and indirect addressing. The only difference which may need clarification is use of the Program Counter as EA addend. It has two effects:

1. The value read from the Program Counter is always the address of the first byte of the operand EA extension. Note that in order to use program relative addressing when writing directly in machine code, it is necessary to work out displacements from the operand extension address, whereas an assembler often allows location counter offsets from the instruction word address (a difference of +2 bytes for source operands and possibly up to +12 bytes for destination operands) or will automatically calculate displacements to a specified label.

2. Use of the Program Counter in forming the Effective Address automatically locates the operand in program space (note the difference between both memory references in Figures F19, post-indexed memory indirect, and F20, post-indexed program indirect). The reason for this is that the 68000-series processors output a 3-bit address space function code for each bus cycle to enable external memory management of separate program and data memory banks. Since the Program Counter is normally used to address the instruction sequence, all PC references cause output of the program space function code.

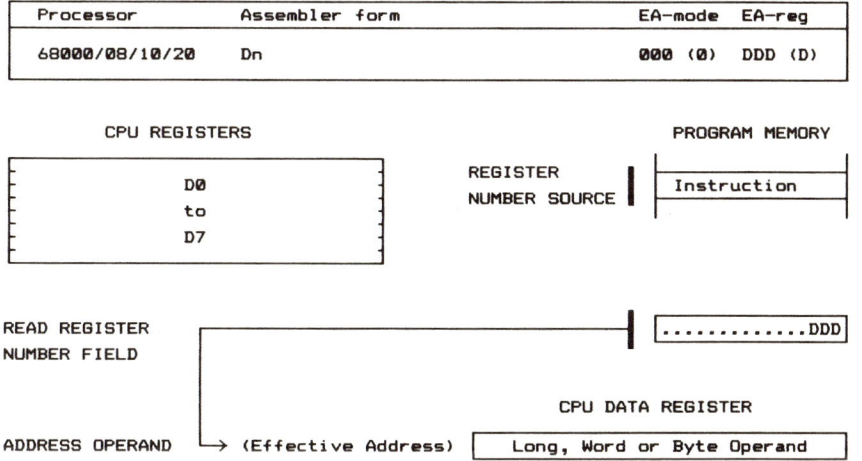

Figure F1. Data Register direct.

Processor	Assembler form	EA-mode	EA-reg
68000/08/10/20	An	001 (1)	AAA (A)

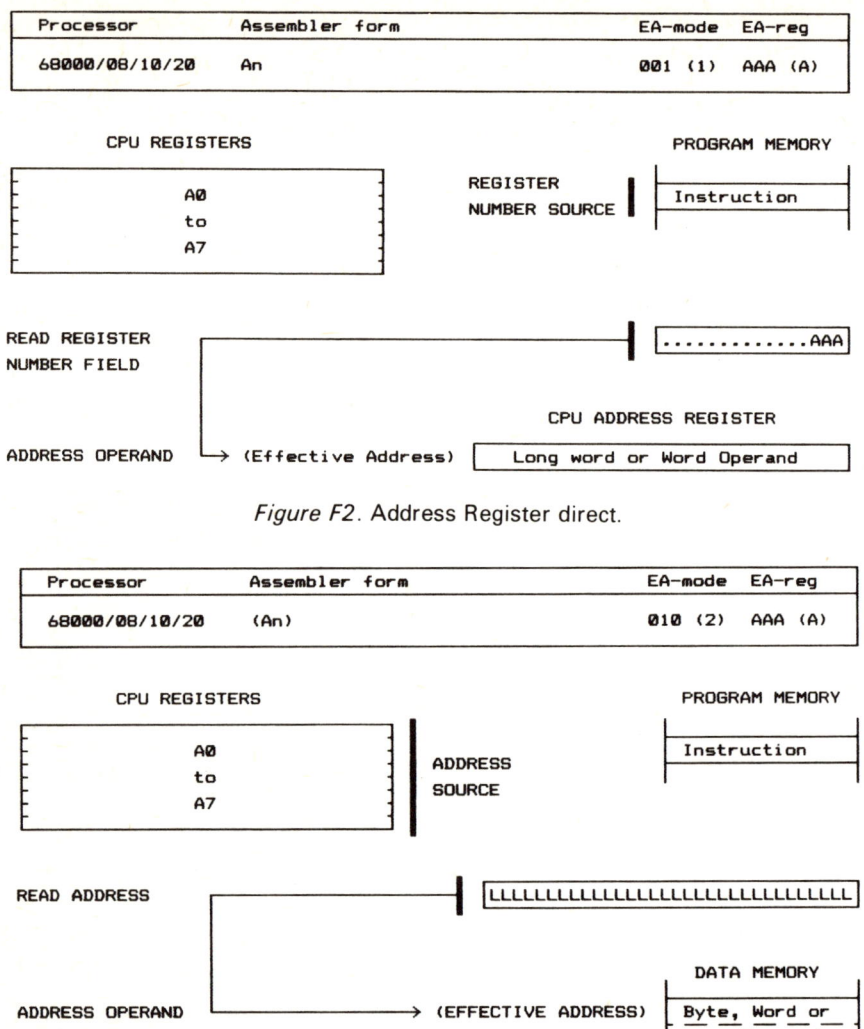

Figure F2. Address Register direct.

Processor	Assembler form	EA-mode	EA-reg
68000/08/10/20	(An)	010 (2)	AAA (A)

Figure F3. Address Register indirect.

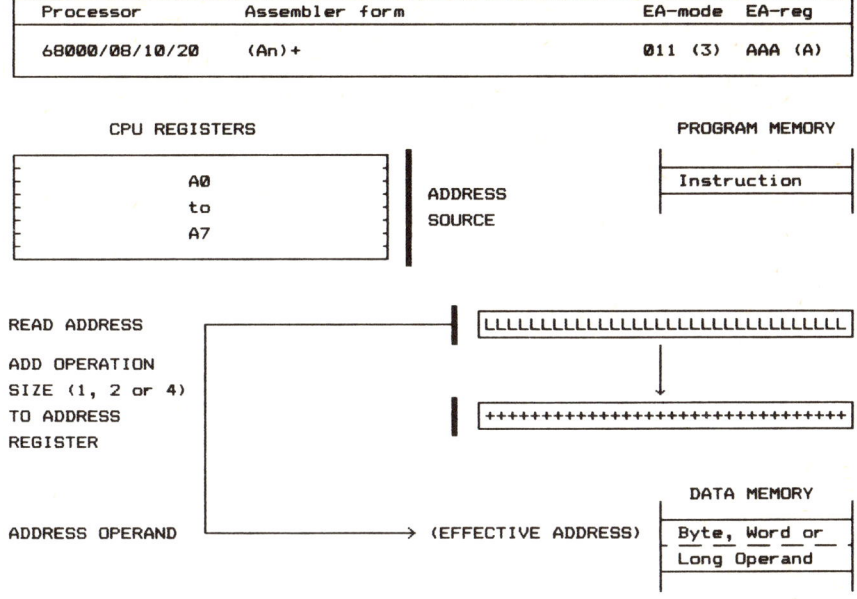

Processor	Assembler form	EA-mode	EA-reg
68000/08/10/20	(An)+	011 (3)	AAA (A)

CPU REGISTERS

PROGRAM MEMORY

A0
to
A7

ADDRESS
SOURCE

Instruction

READ ADDRESS

ADD OPERATION
SIZE (1, 2 or 4)
TO ADDRESS
REGISTER

ADDRESS OPERAND → (EFFECTIVE ADDRESS)

DATA MEMORY

Byte, Word or
Long Operand

Figure F4. Post-incremented Address Register indirect.

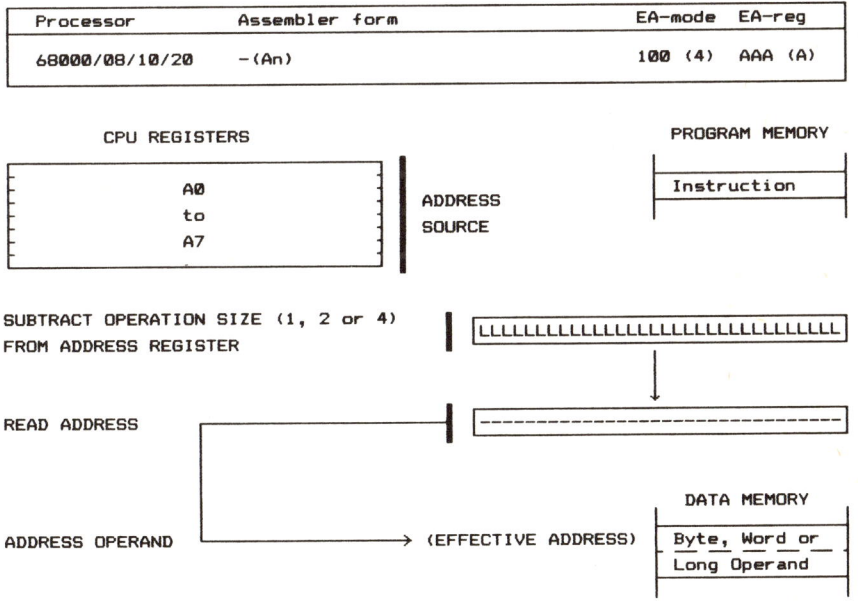

Processor	Assembler form	EA-mode	EA-reg
68000/08/10/20	-(An)	100 (4)	AAA (A)

CPU REGISTERS

PROGRAM MEMORY

A0
to
A7

ADDRESS
SOURCE

Instruction

SUBTRACT OPERATION SIZE (1, 2 or 4)
FROM ADDRESS REGISTER

READ ADDRESS

ADDRESS OPERAND → (EFFECTIVE ADDRESS)

DATA MEMORY

Byte, Word or
Long Operand

Figure F5. Predecremented Address Register indirect.

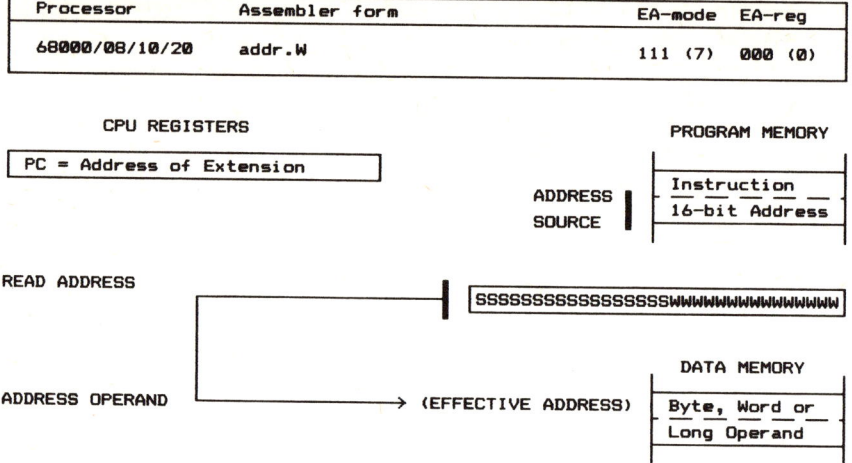

Figure F6. Absolute short memory direct.

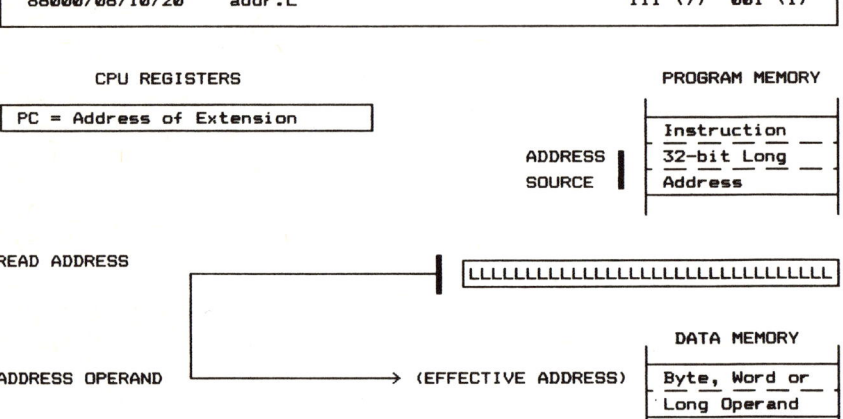

Figure F7. Absolute long memory direct.

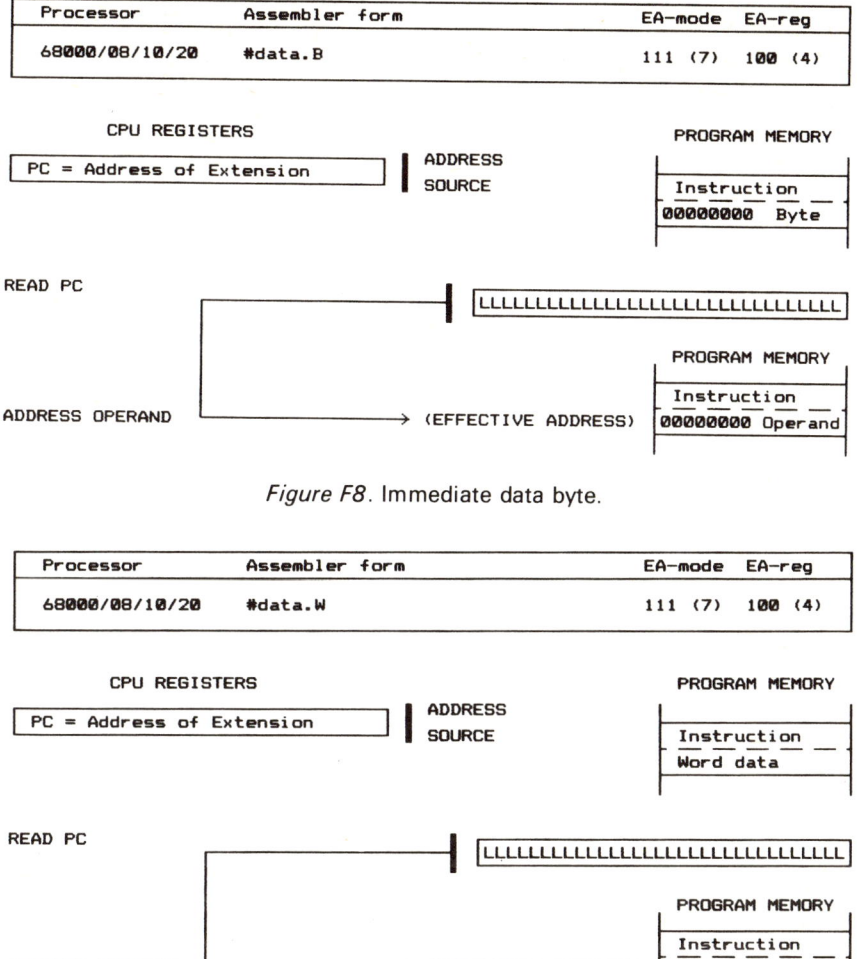

Processor	Assembler form	EA-mode	EA-reg
68000/08/10/20	#data.B	111 (7)	100 (4)

CPU REGISTERS   PROGRAM MEMORY

PC = Address of Extension   ADDRESS SOURCE

Instruction
00000000 Byte

READ PC

LLLLLLLLLLLLLLLLLLLLLLLLLLLLLLLLLLL

PROGRAM MEMORY

Instruction
00000000 Operand

ADDRESS OPERAND   → (EFFECTIVE ADDRESS)

Figure F8. Immediate data byte.

Processor	Assembler form	EA-mode	EA-reg
68000/08/10/20	#data.W	111 (7)	100 (4)

CPU REGISTERS   PROGRAM MEMORY

PC = Address of Extension   ADDRESS SOURCE

Instruction
Word data

READ PC

LLLLLLLLLLLLLLLLLLLLLLLLLLLLLLLLLLL

PROGRAM MEMORY

Instruction
Word Operand

ADDRESS OPERAND   → (EFFECTIVE ADDRESS)

Figure F9. Immediate data word.

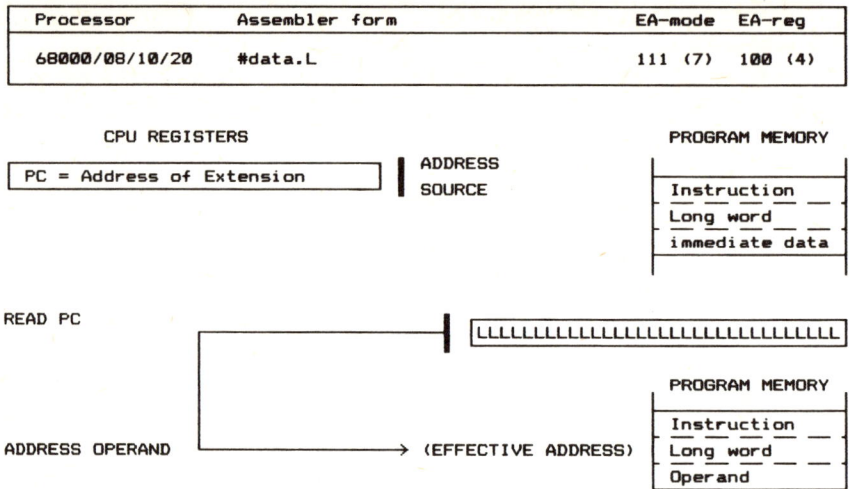

Processor	Assembler form	EA-mode	EA-reg
68000/08/10/20	#data.L	111 (7)	100 (4)

Figure F10. Immediate data long word.

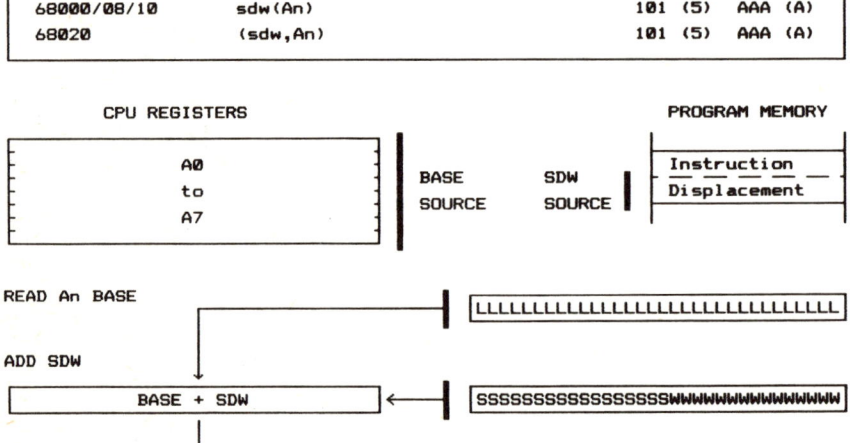

Processor	Assembler form	EA-mode	EA-reg
68000/08/10	sdw(An)	101 (5)	AAA (A)
68020	(sdw,An)	101 (5)	AAA (A)

Figure F11. Displaced Address Register indirect.

Processor	Assembler form	EA—mode	EA—reg
68000/08/10	sdw(PC)	111 (7)	010 (2)
68020	(sdw,PC)	111 (7)	010 (2)

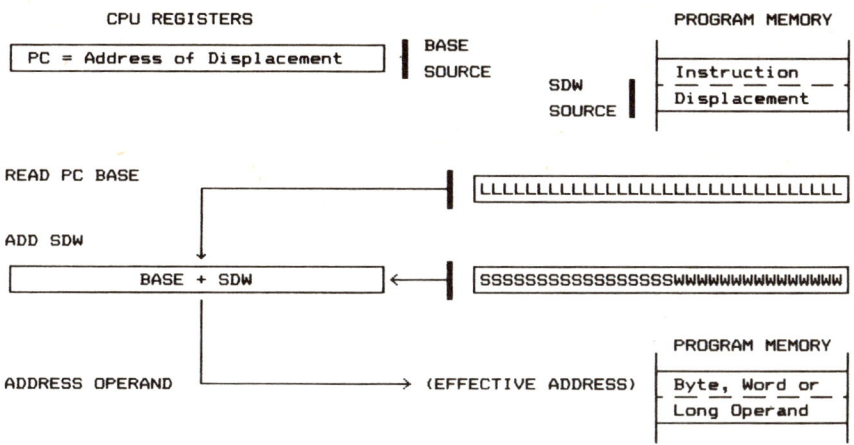

Figure F12. Program relative.

Processor	Assembler form	EA-mode	EA-reg
68000/08/10	sdb(An,Xx.SZ)	110 (6)	AAA (A)

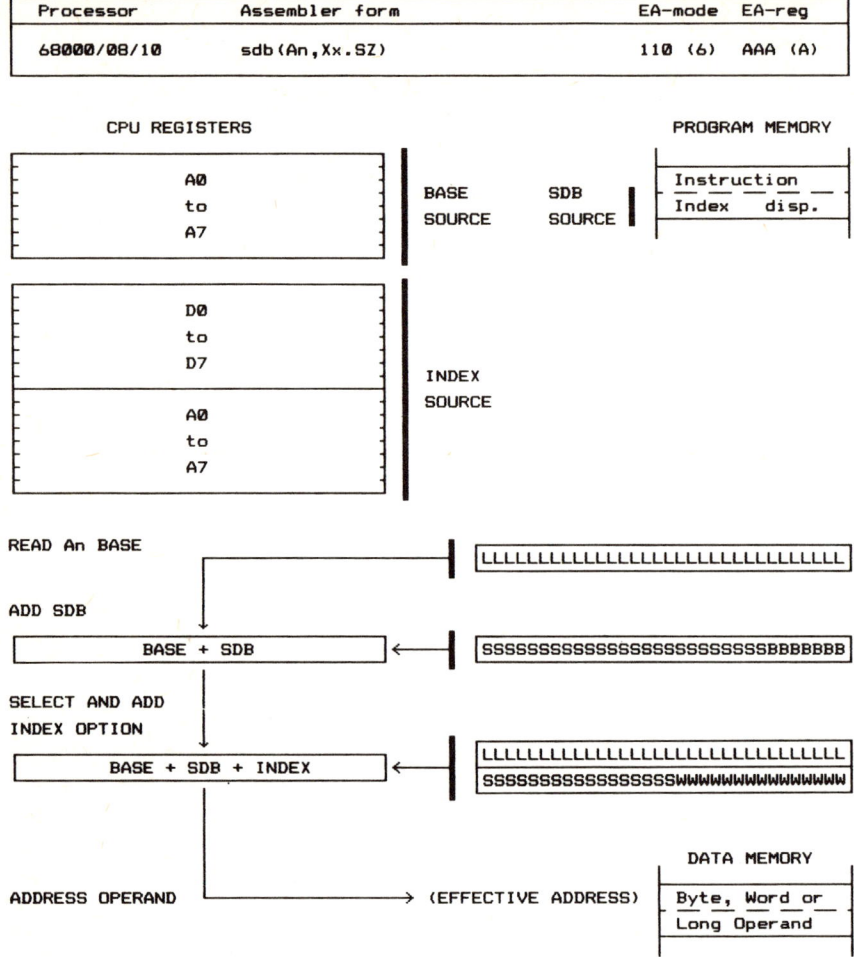

Figure F13. Displaced indexed Address Register indirect.

Processor	Assembler form	EA-mode	EA-reg
68020	(sdb,An,Xx.SZ*SC)	110 (6)	AAA (A)

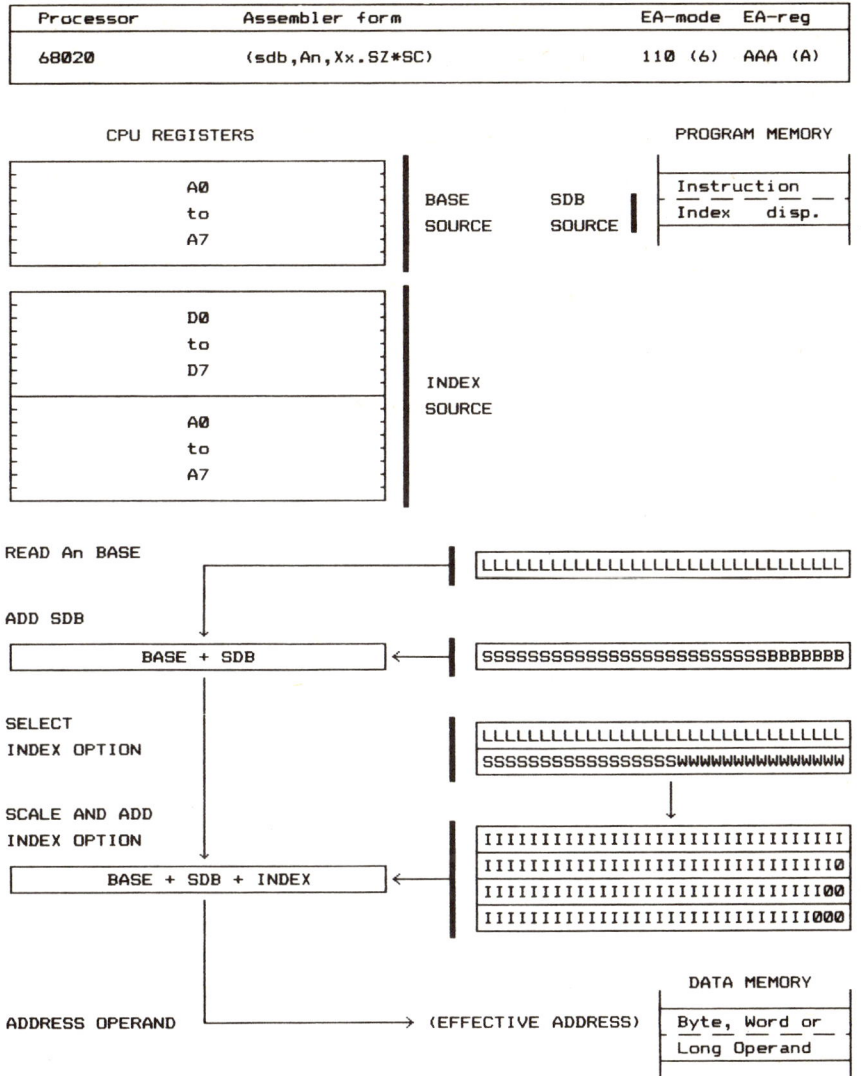

Figure F14. Displaced indexed Address Register indirect.

Processor	Assembler form	EA-mode	EA-reg
68000/08/10	sdb(PC,Xx.SZ)	111 (7)	011 (3)

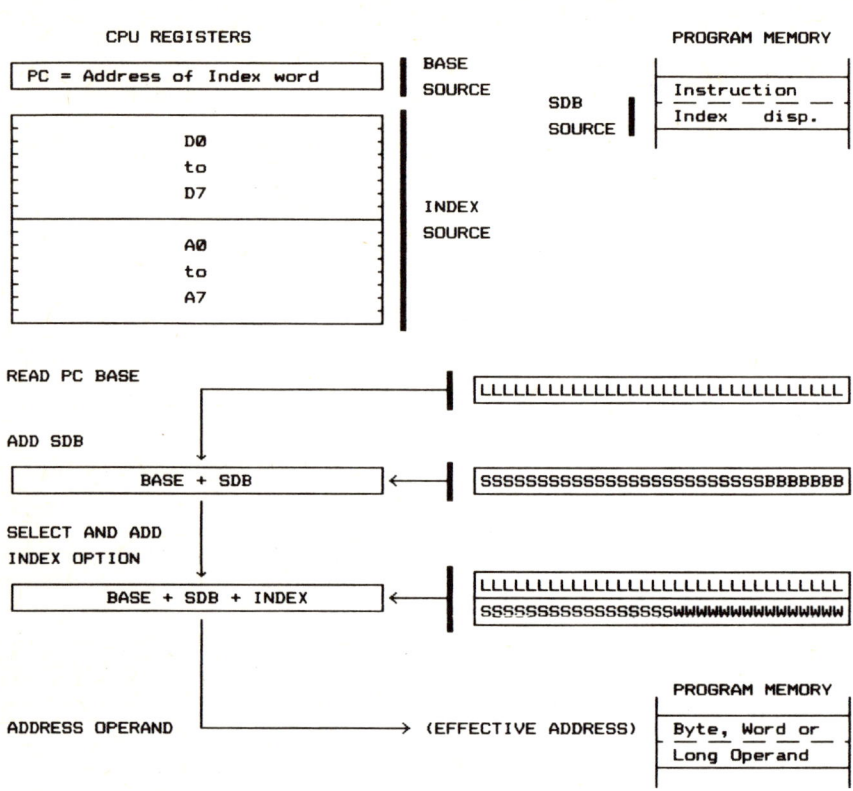

Figure F15. Indexed program relative.

Processor	Assembler form	EA-mode	EA-reg
68020	(sdb,PC,Xx.SZ*SC)	111 (7)	011 (3)

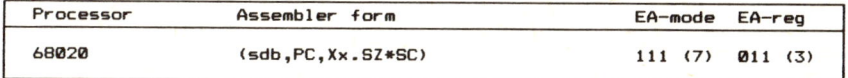

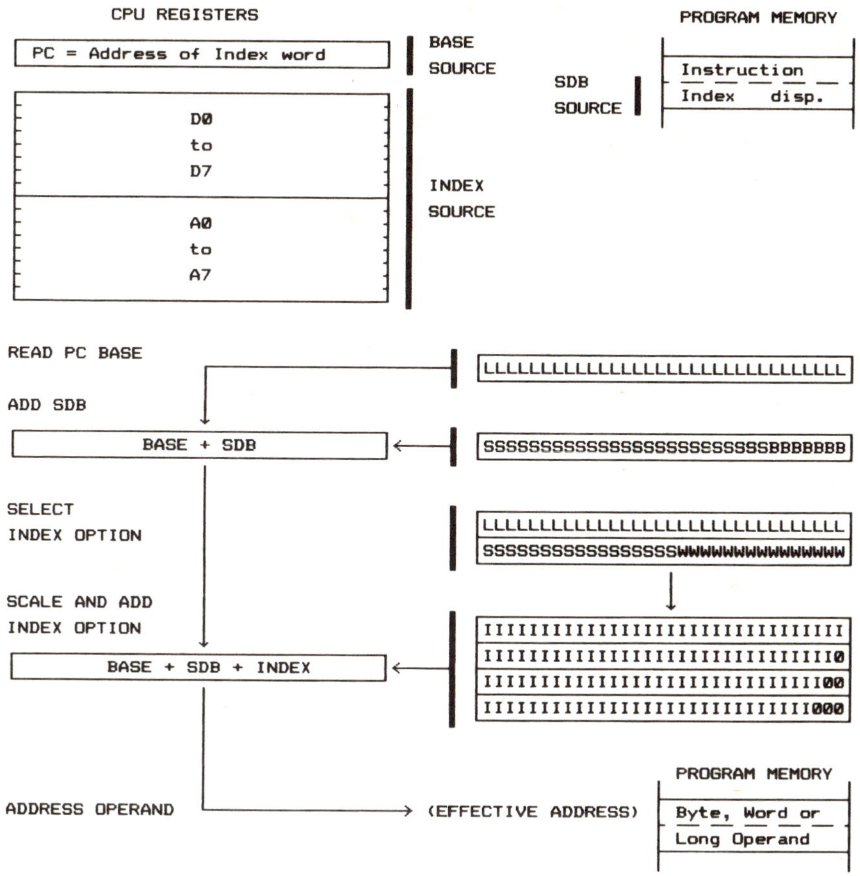

CPU REGISTERS   PROGRAM MEMORY

PC = Address of Index word   BASE
                                SOURCE   SDB   Instruction
                                              SOURCE   Index   disp.
         D0
         to
         D7
                                INDEX
                                SOURCE
         A0
         to
         A7

READ PC BASE   LLLLLLLLLLLLLLLLLLLLLLLLLLLLLLLL

ADD SDB

         BASE + SDB   ◄───   SSSSSSSSSSSSSSSSSSSSSSSSSSSBBBBBBB

SELECT   LLLLLLLLLLLLLLLLLLLLLLLLLLLLLLLLLL
INDEX OPTION   SSSSSSSSSSSSSSSSSWWWWWWWWWWWWWWW

SCALE AND ADD
INDEX OPTION   IIIIIIIIIIIIIIIIIIIIIIIIIIIIIIII
         BASE + SDB + INDEX   ◄───   IIIIIIIIIIIIIIIIIIIIIIIIIIIIIIII0
                                      IIIIIIIIIIIIIIIIIIIIIIIIIIIIII00
                                      IIIIIIIIIIIIIIIIIIIIIIIIIIIII000

                                              PROGRAM MEMORY

ADDRESS OPERAND ───────────► (EFFECTIVE ADDRESS)   Byte, Word or
                                                      Long Operand

Figure F16. Indexed program relative.

Processor	Assembler form	EA-mode	EA-reg
68020	(bsd.SZ,An,Xx.SZ*SC)	110 (6)	AAA (A)

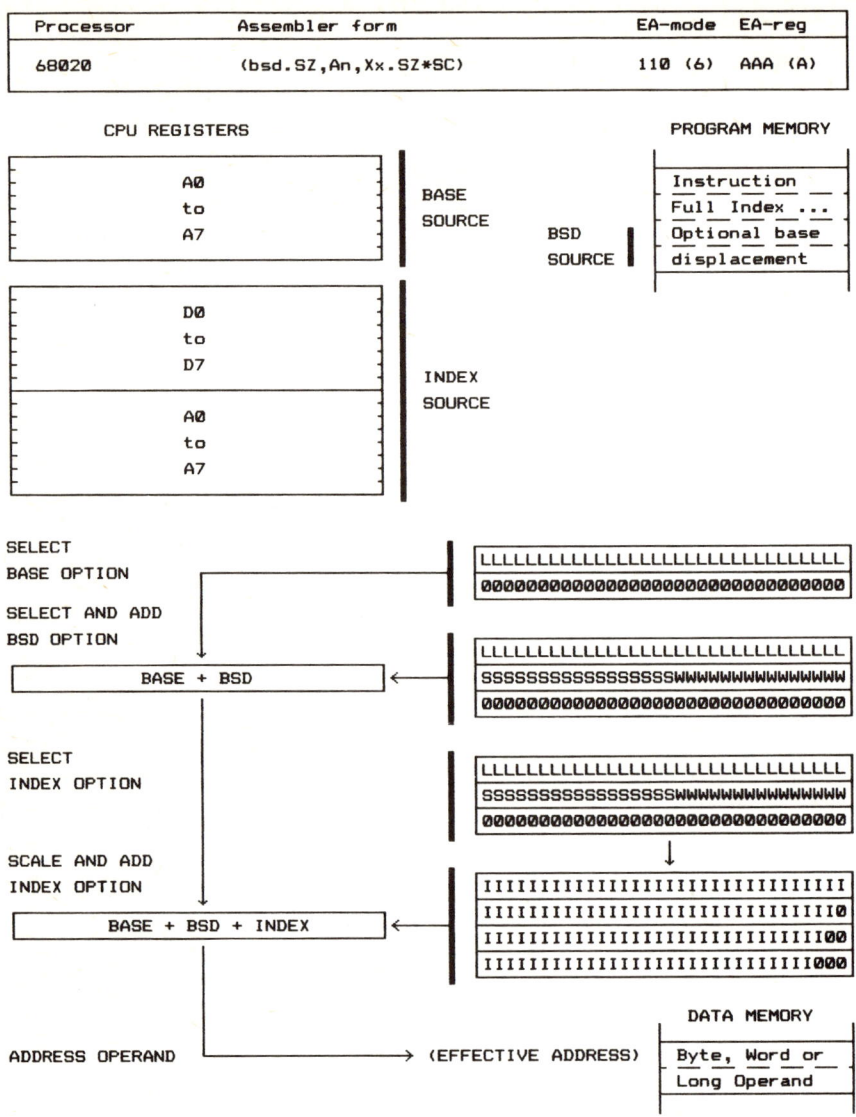

Figure F17. Displaced base indexed Address Register indirect.

Processor	Assembler form	EA-mode	EA-reg
68020	(bsd.SZ,PC,Xx.SZ*SC)	111 (7)	011 (3)

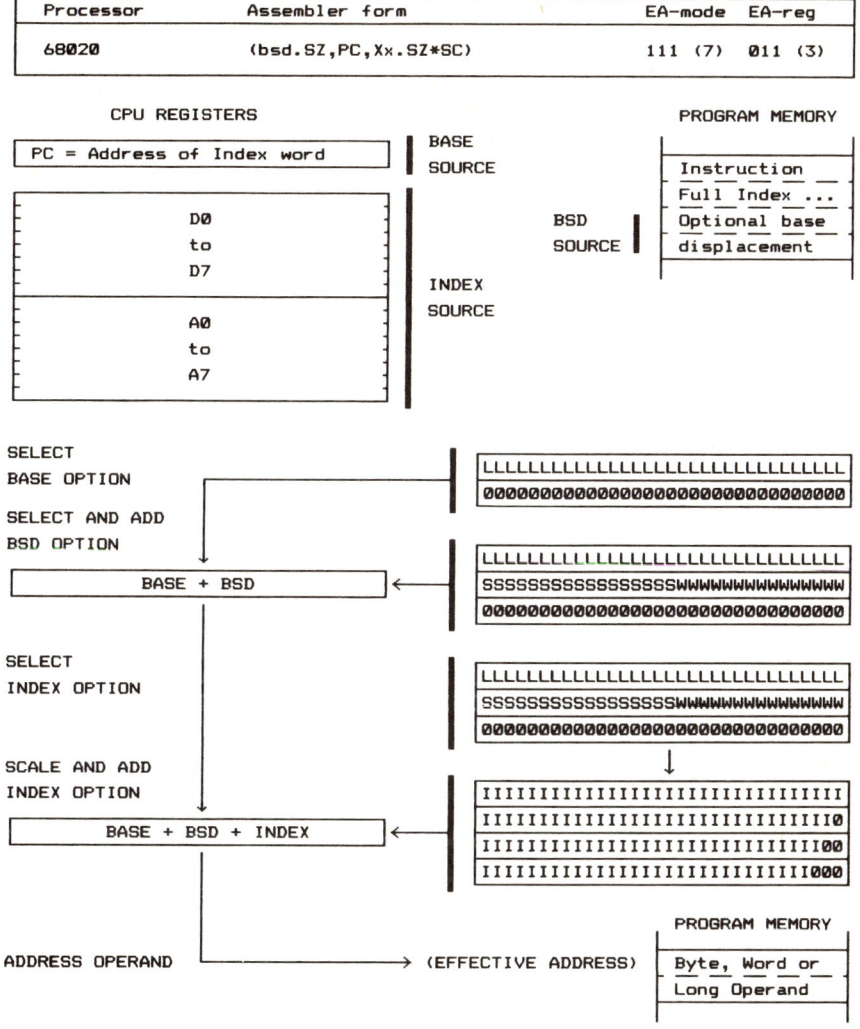

Figure F18. Base indexed program relative.

Processor	Assembler form	EA-mode	EA-reg
68020	([bsd.SZ,An],Xx.SZ*SC,osd.SZ)	110 (6)	AAA (A)

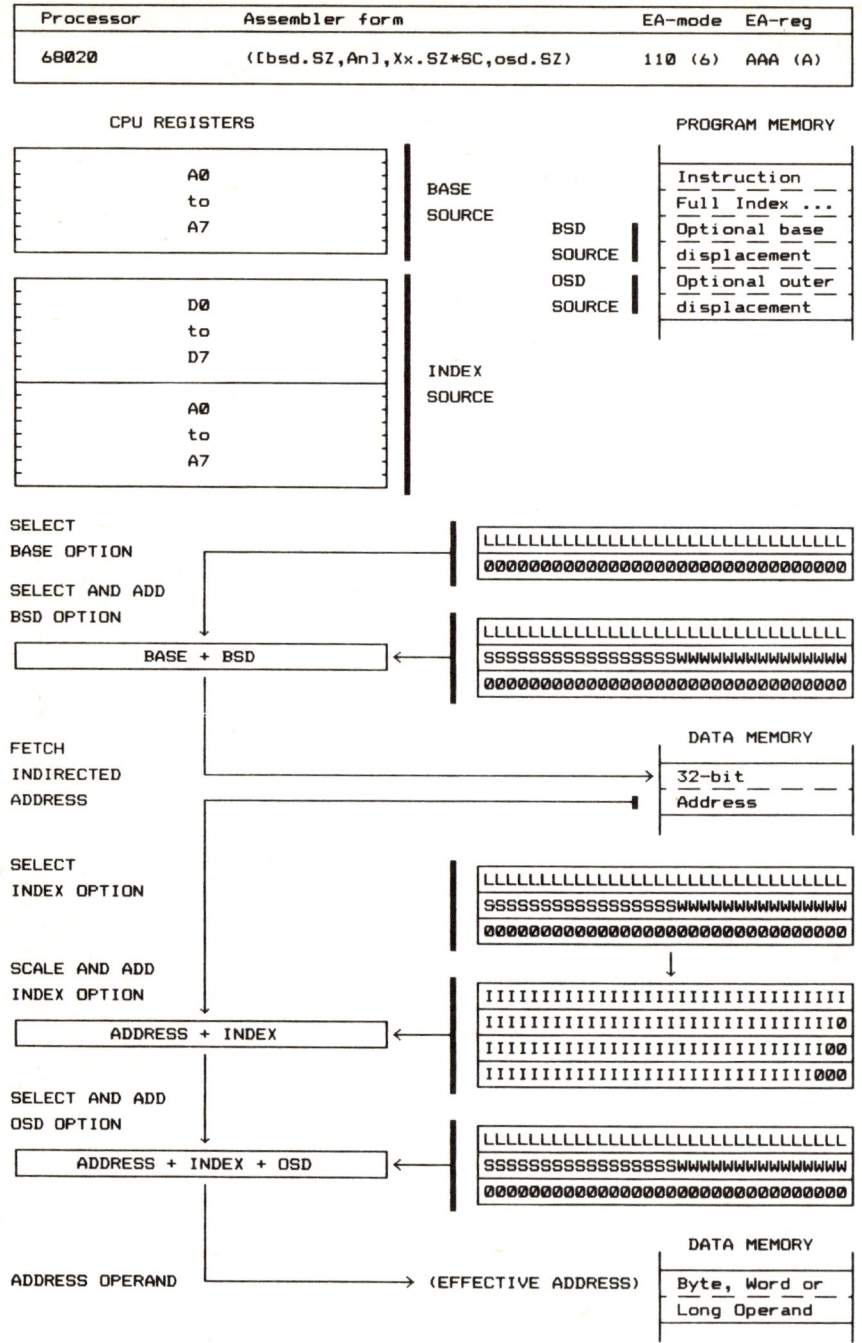

Figure F19. Post-indexed memory indirect.

Processor	Assembler form	EA-mode	EA-reg
68020	([bsd.SZ,PC],Xx.SZ*SC,osd.SZ)	111 (7)	011 (3)

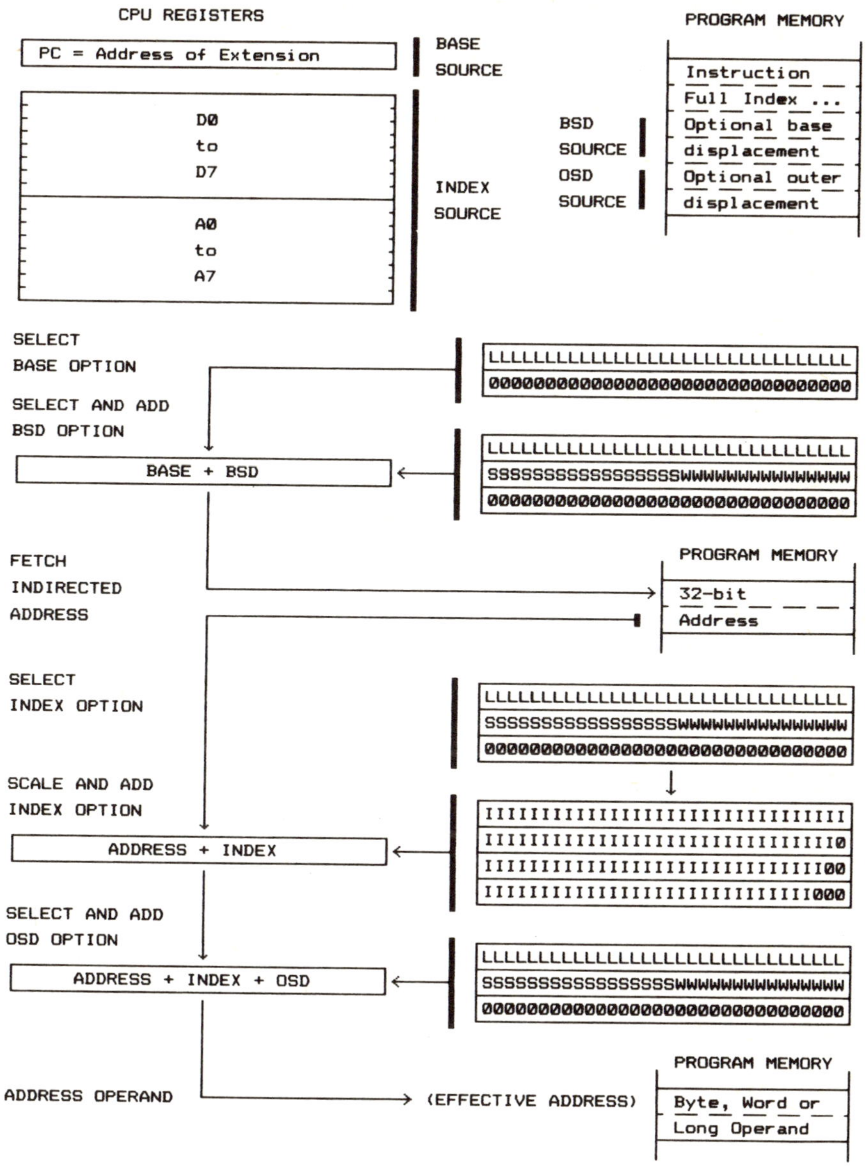

CPU REGISTERS

PC = Address of Extension

BASE SOURCE

D0
to
D7

A0
to
A7

INDEX SOURCE

BSD SOURCE

OSD SOURCE

PROGRAM MEMORY

Instruction
Full Index ...
Optional base displacement
Optional outer displacement

SELECT BASE OPTION

SELECT AND ADD BSD OPTION

BASE + BSD

```
LLLLLLLLLLLLLLLLLLLLLLLLLLLLLLLL
00000000000000000000000000000000
```

```
LLLLLLLLLLLLLLLLLLLLLLLLLLLLLLLL
SSSSSSSSSSSSSSSSSWWWWWWWWWWWWWWW
00000000000000000000000000000000
```

FETCH INDIRECTED ADDRESS

PROGRAM MEMORY

32-bit
Address

SELECT INDEX OPTION

```
LLLLLLLLLLLLLLLLLLLLLLLLLLLLLLLL
SSSSSSSSSSSSSSSSSWWWWWWWWWWWWWWW
00000000000000000000000000000000
```

SCALE AND ADD INDEX OPTION

ADDRESS + INDEX

```
IIIIIIIIIIIIIIIIIIIIIIIIIIIIIIII
IIIIIIIIIIIIIIIIIIIIIIIIIIIIIII0
IIIIIIIIIIIIIIIIIIIIIIIIIIIIII00
IIIIIIIIIIIIIIIIIIIIIIIIIIIII000
```

SELECT AND ADD OSD OPTION

ADDRESS + INDEX + OSD

```
LLLLLLLLLLLLLLLLLLLLLLLLLLLLLLLL
SSSSSSSSSSSSSSSSSWWWWWWWWWWWWWWW
00000000000000000000000000000000
```

ADDRESS OPERAND → (EFFECTIVE ADDRESS)

PROGRAM MEMORY

Byte, Word or
Long Operand

Figure F20. Post-indexed program indirect.

Processor	Assembler form	EA-mode	EA-reg
68020	([bsd.SZ,An,Xx.SZ*SC],osd.SZ)	110 (6)	AAA (A)

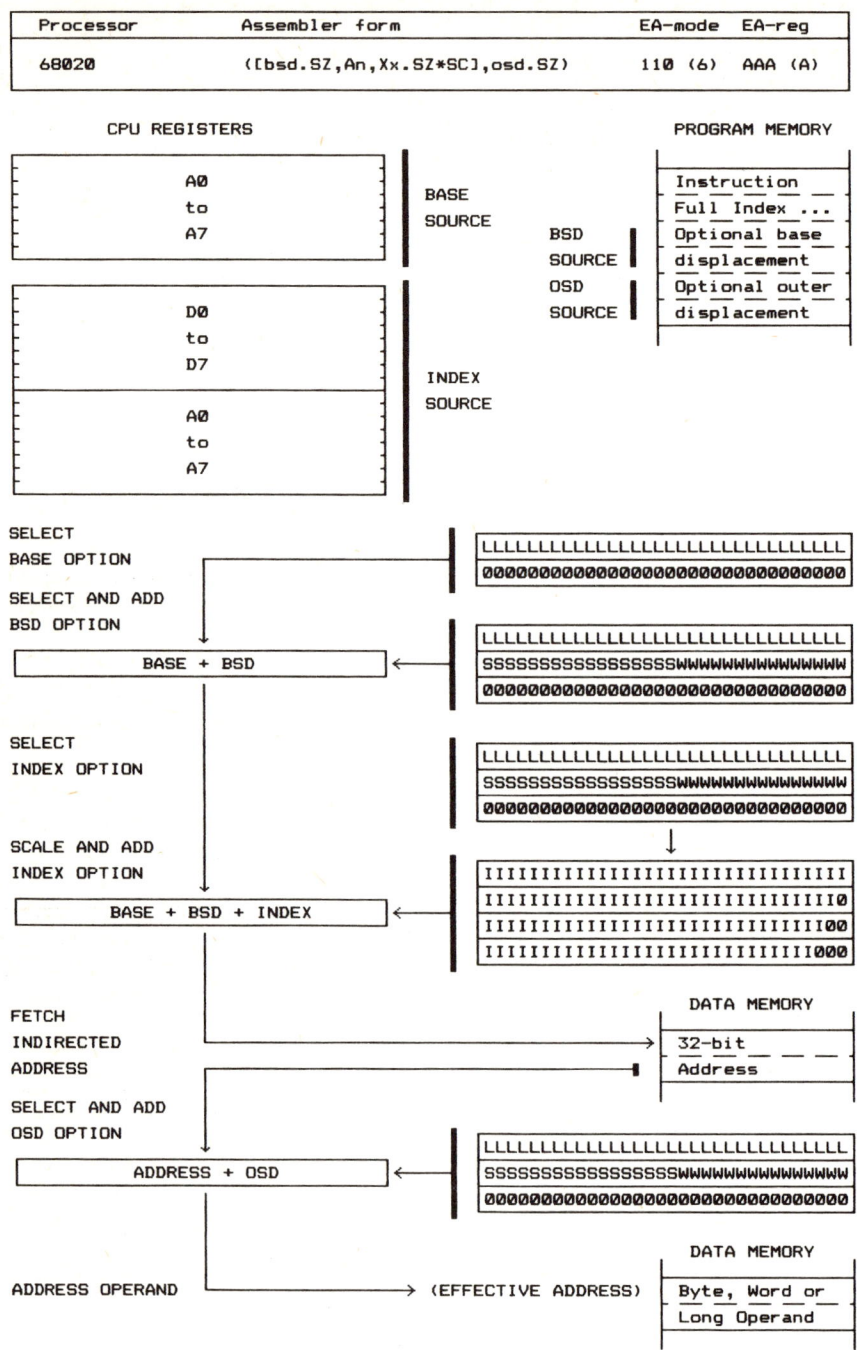

Figure F21. Preindexed memory indirect.

Processor	Assembler form	EA-mode	EA-reg
68020	([bsd.SZ,PC,Xx.SZ*SC],osd.SZ)	111 (7)	011 (3)

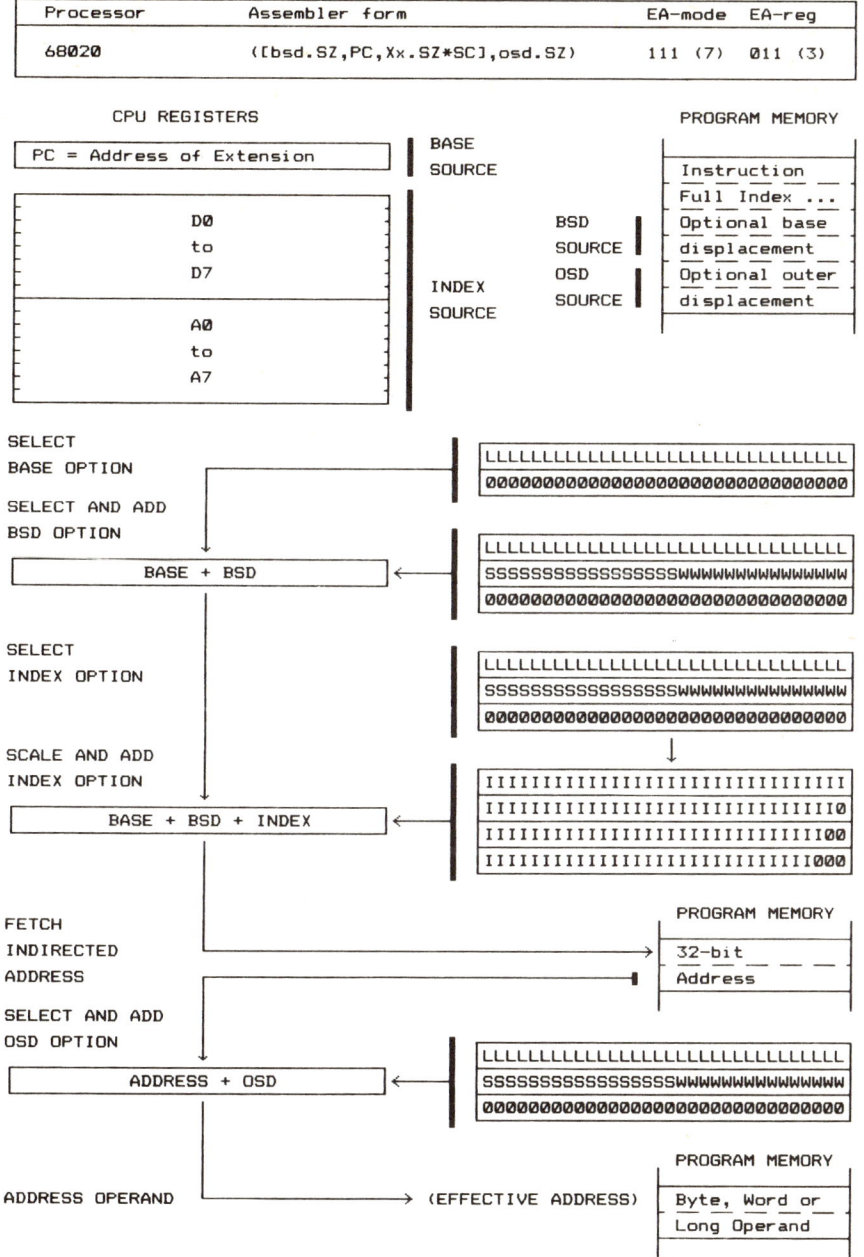

Figure F22. Preindexed program indirect.

Further Reading

Books about the 68000-series

A book like this can only provide a basic introduction to machine code programming on a series of processors as sophisticated as the Motorola 68000 family. More information can be found by reading the manuals specific to the processor and assembler being used.

Motorola produce quite good reference manuals, but they are biased towards the experienced assembly language programmer. Information on the 68000, 68008 and 68010 can be found in:

M68000 16/32-bit Microprocessor Programmer's Reference Manual, published by Prentice-Hall, Inc. 4th ed. 1979 (ISBN: 0-13-566795-X)

Information on the 68020 is given in:

MC68020 32-bit Microprocessor User's Manual, published by Prentice-Hall, Inc., 1984 (ISBN: 0-13-541418-0)

Both of these should be available through any good bookshop or from a Motorola computer systems dealer. They are expensive but worth buying. Motorola also publish informative booklets, known as 'data sheets', about the processors and support devices: these can usually be obtained at no charge from dealers and are indispensable when writing systems software.

For programmers experienced in other codes, *68000 Assembly Language Programming* by Gerry Kane, Doug Hawkins and Lance Leventhal, 1981 (ISBN: 0-931988-62-4) has the advantage of being written to a more or less set formula in the Osborne/McGraw-Hill series. Other codes covered by the series include the 8085, 8086, Z80, Z8000, 6502, 6800 and 6809, so there should be corresponding routines for everyone.

Inexperienced machine coders can find a plethora of books written for specific home computers on the computing shelves of most bookshops. Most are very basic but they do contain a little machine specific information which is necessary when writing for the machine itself. More information about the system can usually be found by a careful search through the system's software.

Books about computing

On computing in general there is no better book than Donald E. Knuth's 3-volume work, *The Art of Computer Programming*, published by Addison-Wesley. Volume 1 can be obtained in paperback and introduces the basic concepts of computer science, going on to describe various data or information structures – stacks, queues, deques, lists, linked lists, circular lists and trees. This is a must. Volumes 2 and 3, available only in hardback at twice the price, offer random numbers, floating point, multi-precision, rational and polynomial arithmetic, a cascade of sorting methods and a bagful of search procedures. The book is written for college level computer scientists, and all the subjects are dealt with in depth and at length, but Knuth provides plenty of exercises to help. The work is a vast fund of ideas that can be picked out without too much study.

Another 3-volume work which is useful as a source of programming concepts, especially in games programming, is *The Handbook of Artificial Intelligence*, edited by Avron Barr and Edward Feigenbaum and published by Pitman. This is occasionally revised to give a fairly up-to-date reference of work in AI. As a follow up to the AI Handbook, try Douglas R. Hofstadters *Godel, Escher, Bach: an Eternal Golden Braid*, published as a Penguin paperback in 1980 (ISBN: 0-14-005579-7).

There exists a work that seems almost a contradiction in terms – a serious book on program design and structure which is not only readable but actually an enjoyable read. This is *Structured Analysis and System Specification* by Tom DeMarco, published by Yourdon Inc., New York, 1978 (ISBN: 0-917072-07-3). It is aimed at the designer of large data-processing systems but much of the content is applicable to all program design.

Magazines

Many computing magazines publish the occasional machine code program or routine. Although most of these are for other codes, they do provide ideas and sometime a sound framework on which to build. Not only are machine code programs useful for ideas: programs written in other languages can easily be converted into machine code – and work much better for it. Magazines also keep you up to date with developments in hardware.

Personal Computer World magazine is a must for serious assembly language programmers, since it regularly publishes fully documented machine code library routines, including many in 68000-series code, in the series Sub Set. The best of Sub Set's routines for the Z80 and 6502 have been published in book form by Century Communications Ltd as *Assembler Routines for the Z80* (ISBN: 0-7126-0506-1) and *Assembler Routines for the 6502* (ISBN: 0-7126-0507-X). These are well worth buying for the clearly expressed programming ideas they contain as well as the 'ready for coding in any language' documentation provided with the routines.

System software

The software provided free, or at a small extra cost, with all computer systems is a veritable goldmine of programming tricks – especially ways to hide the true actions effected by the jumble of hexadecimal digits. If it can be disassembled it does provide software protection methods as well as reasonably structured and efficient machine code routines that carry out all the system control tasks, including screen, keyboard and disk access. Using the code found in any software for commercial gain is an infringement of copyright.

Index